Strategies for Writing

Strategies for Writing

A Basic Approach

Ann E. Healy
University of Wisconsin–Milwaukee

Martha Walusayi
University of Wisconsin–Milwaukee

NTC Publishing Group
Lincolnwood, Illinois USA

Literary and illustration credits can be found in the "Credits" section on page 411, which should be considered an extension of this copyright page.

Sponsoring Editor: Marisa L. L'Heureux
Design Manager: Ophelia Chambliss
Cover and interior design: Ellen Pettengell
Production Manager: Rosemary Dolinski

ISBN: 0-8442-5922-5 (student text)
ISBN: 0-8442-5923-3 (instructor's edition)

Library of Congress Cataloging-in-Publication Data

Healy, Ann E.
    Strategies for writing : a basic approach / Ann E. Healy, Martha Walusayi.
       p.   cm.
    ISBN 0-8442-5922-5 (softbound)
    1. English language—Rhetoric.   2. English language—Grammar.
    I. Walusayi, Martha.   II. Title.
PE1408.H434 1996
808'.042—dc20   96-30726
                                                                            CIP

Published by NTC Publishing Group
© 1997 NTC Publishing Group, 4255 West Touhy Avenue
Lincolnwood (Chicago), Illinois 60646-1975 U.S.A.
All rights reserved. No part of this book may be reproduced,
stored in a retrieval system, or transmitted in any form or by any means,
electronic, mechanical, photocopying, recording, or otherwise,
without prior permission of NTC Publishing Group.
Manufactured in the United States of America.

6 7 8 9 0 ML 9 8 7 6 5 4 3 2 1

Contents

Preface . . . xiii

Part One Writing More Effective Prose . . . 1

Chapter One The Writing Process . . . 2

Accepting Criticism . . . 4
Why Do People Write? . . . 4
Finding Something to Say: Focusing on a Topic . . . 7
Stages in the Writing Process . . . 8
    Stage One: Getting Started, or Prewriting Strategies . . . 10
    Stage Two: Drafting . . . 18
    Stage Three: Revising, Editing, and Proofreading . . . 20

Chapter Two Shaping the Contents . . . 28

Deciding on a Thesis . . . 30
Choosing an Overall Organizational Scheme . . . 33
Writing Introductions and Conclusions . . . 34
    Tips on Introductions . . . 34
    A Word about Conclusions . . . 39
Writing a Title . . . 41

Shaping the Body of the Essay ... 42
    Organization and Coherence: Binding the Parts Together ... 42
    Using Transitional Devices to Cue the Reader ... 45
    Types of Effective Transitions ... 46
    Special Transition Words and Phrases ... 47

Chapter Three   Using Correct Grammar and Usage to Aid Coherence ... 52

Choosing the Right Pronoun ... 52
    Types of Pronouns ... 54
    Choosing the Right Form of Personal Pronouns ... 58
    References Required ... 60
    Making the Pronoun Refer to the Right Word: Common Pronoun Reference Problems ... 61
Using Demonstrative Pronouns Clearly ... 64
    Using Demonstrative Pronouns Correctly ... 64
Avoiding Unnecessary Shifts of Person ... 67
Avoiding the Overuse of Pronouns ... 68
Choosing the Right Form of a Verb ... 69
    Regular Verbs ... 69
    Irregular Verbs ... 71
    Overcorrection of Irregular Verbs ... 73
Monitoring Verb Tense and Tense Consistency ... 74
Understanding Main Verbs and Helping Verbs ... 74
Understanding Action Verbs and Linking Verbs ... 76
Understanding Subject/Verb Agreement ... 77
    Finding the Subject and Verb ... 77
    Detecting Problems of Subject/Verb Agreement ... 78
Avoiding Shifts in Verb Tense ... 81
Spotting Verb Errors: A Review ... 84
    Subject/Verb Agreement ... 84

Chapter Four   Syntax, Diction, and Style ... 86

Diction + Syntax = Style ... 86
    Avoid Slangy Stuff and Clichés ... 87
    Some Words Come in Familiar Packages ... 88

Avoid Sounding Too Precious	89
Help Wipe Out "Formal Speak"	89
Avoiding Padded Prose and Pretentious Language	90
Redundancy	91
Choosing Interesting, Precise Words and Striving for Word Variety	92
Finding Wording Substitutes to Avoid Repetition	94
Using Pronouns and Synonyms to Achieve Word Variety	95
Using Appositives to Avoid Repetition	96
Trying Too Hard	96
Combining Ideas and Cutting Dead Wood	98
Considering the "So What" Factor	99

Chapter Five Fractured and Nonfractured Syntax 100

Experimenting with a Wide Variety of Sentence Types	100
Phrases, Clauses, and Sentences	102
Thinking About Sentences	106
Understanding Kinds of Sentences: How to Tell Whether It's a Sentence	107
Compound Sentences	108
Recognizing the Subjects and Verbs in Compound Sentences	110
Using Subordinators in Complex Sentences	111
A Selection of Subordinators (Joining Devices)	111
Understanding the Basic Sentence Types	113
Classifying Sentences by Their Purpose	114
Avoiding Common Errors in End-Stop Punctuation	114
Run-on Sentences	114
Comma Faults (Comma Splices)	116
Getting Rid of Unintentional Fragments	118
Watch Out for *-ing* Fragments	120
Be on the Lookout for Fragments in Your Drafts	121
Avoiding Fragments	122
Avoiding Faulty Parallelism	125
Parallelism in Lists	126
Deliberate Parallelism	127
Avoiding Dangling and Misplaced Modifiers	129

Avoiding Sexist Language in Your Writing, or
"Excuse me, is my bias showing?"   131

Chapter Six   Demystifying Punctuation   134

Understanding Full-Stop Punctuation   137
- The Period   137
- The Question Mark   139
- The Exclamation Point   139
- The Semicolon   140
- The Colon   143

Using Punctuation with Parenthetical Elements   146
- The Dash   146
- Parentheses   147

Understanding Half-Stop Punctuation   148
- The Comma   148

Understanding Punctuation Marks That Do Not Indicate Pauses   157
- The Hyphen   157
- The Apostrophe   158
- Quotation Marks   163

Understanding Capitalization   168

Part Two   From Others' Writing to Your Writing: Reading Critically   171

Chapter Seven   Critical Reading and Your Writing   172

Understanding What It Means to Read Critically   172
Applying Critical Reading Skills to Writing a Summary   173
- Applying the Four Steps for Writing Summaries to Student Essays   174

Getting the Most from Outside Sources   185
Weighing the Claims of an Argument   209

Chapter Eight Documentation: Incorporating Outside Sources into Your Essays 230

Understanding Documentation 230
Using Quotation Marks in Dialogue 231
   Direct Speech 231
   Indirect Speech 232
Using Ellipses 233
Using Others' Works in Your Writing 234
   Identifying Sources 234
   Using Quotation Marks for Bibliographical Citations 236
   Using Italics 236
   Using Brackets 237
Quoting and Paraphrasing 237
   When to Paraphrase, When to Quote 237
   Paraphrasing 239
   Avoiding Plagiarism 240
Using Sources in a Research Paper 241
Studying a Model Research Paper 242

Part Three Writing Strategies 253

Chapter Nine Narrating 254

Prewriting for a Narrative 256
Writing a Narrative 256
   Involve Your Reader from the Start 258
   Keep Your Audience in Mind at All Times 258
   Concluding a Narrative 259
Selecting a Topic 260
Finding Your Voice 261
Understanding What Makes Writing Effective 262
   The Reviewer's Task: A Guide for Peer-Group Revising 263
   Guidelines for Analysis of a Narrative 264

Exploring Additional Uses of Narratives	279
The Short Narrative as an Introduction	279
Using Narratives to Illustrate General Points	279

Chapter Ten   Describing   280

Understanding the Elements of Effective Description	282
Appealing to the Five Senses	282
Broadening Your Fund of Modifiers	283
Using Specific, Concrete Details	286
Using Modifiers Effectively: Adjectives and Adverbs	287
Using Strong Verbs	289
Using Motion	289
Using Imagery and Figurative Language	290
Using Analogies	293
Making Allusions	293
Avoiding Clichés	294
Remembering People and Places	295
Analyzing Descriptive Essays	296
Student Essays on Remembering People	297
Student Essays on Special Places	313
Exploring and Developing a Topic: The Early Stages	323
Making an Informal Listing	324
Shaping the Contents: Focusing on a Dominant Impression	326
Organizing a Description	327
Avoiding Potential Pitfalls	328

Chapter Eleven   Comparing and Contrasting   330

Writing an Extended Comparison	332
Prewriting for a Comparison and Contrast Paper	334
Deciding on Criteria and an Organizational Scheme	336
Organizational Scheme	336
Considering Invention Strategies for a Comparison Essay	338
Exploring Possible Topics for a Comparison Essay	339
Choosing a Topic for a Comparison	339
Organizing a Comparison	340

Chapter Twelve   Informing and Explaining: The Purpose and Nature of Informative Writing   342

Using Outside Sources: Primary and Secondary Sources   345
Understanding Informative Descriptive Writing   350
Writing to Inform: Citing Outside Authorities   356

Chapter Thirteen   Arguing and Persuading   360

Understanding What Makes an Effective Argument   363
   A Claim Must Be Backed Up with Solid Reasons   364
   Purely Personal Opinions Are Not Convincing   365
Exploring Ways to Support a Claim   367
   Facts   367
   Statistics   367
   Comparisons   368
   Anecdotes and Scenarios   368
Finding a Good, Lively Topic   370
Drafting an Argument   390

Chapter Fourteen   Letters of Application and Résumés: A Special Type of Persuasive Writing   396

Exploring Letters of Application   396
Starting a Letter of Application   398
   Prewriting: The Next Step   400
   Brainstorming about the Potential Employer   401
   Clustering about the Potential Employer   402
Revising Your Letter: Composing the Final Draft   406
Polishing the Final Product   406
Putting Together a Résumé   407
Considering Other Factors about Business Letters   407

Credits   411
Index   415

Preface

A few years ago we asked students for a written evaluation of their composition textbook. One complaint was almost universal: "It doesn't have any illustrations." Almost as frequent were comments that the text was "a little too dry" or that it "didn't have enough examples of student writing." These comments echoed through our heads as we were planning and writing *Strategies for Writing: A Basic Approach.*

We decided from the start that our students were on to something: Why couldn't a composition textbook be illustrated and written in a light, user-friendly tone? We soon discovered that it was fun to find appropriate illustrations, many of which would inject some humor into subjects that are not usually treated in a humorous vein: composition and grammar. We added more illustrations to our course handouts in order to try them out on our students. Many of our students reacted favorably to our more visual, humorous approach to teaching writing, which, in turn, increased our enthusiasm for helping them become more interesting and proficient writers.

One of the major premises of this text is that virtually all composition students have interesting things to say, and, moreover, that many of them are effective writers. Many examples of student writing, from striking similes and moving descriptive passages to complete essays, are therefore included in this text, reflecting our belief that student writing provides more attainable models than the works of professional authors. Furthermore, we hope that seeing a wide range of student writing will encourage you as a writer.

The first two chapters of *Strategies for Writing* are devoted to launching you on your composition voyage. Because the material in these two chapters applies to any writing assignment, you will probably find it beneficial to return to them throughout the term. Chapter One opens with suggestions for finding a topic and getting started on an essay—common roadblocks for many writers. Various prewriting strategies are demonstrated, along with assignments designed to help you experiment with the various strategies to see what works best for you. Remember, however, that what works well for one assignment may not work well for another, so don't be afraid to experiment.

Chapter Two addresses the crucial matters of organizing an essay and improving its coherence. The section on transitions is especially important, because the careful use of transitions is critical for clarity; trying to follow writing that lacks clear transitions is like driving down a highway with no signposts.

Similarly, trying to read an essay that contains incorrect verb forms, numerous misspellings, and garbled syntax is like driving down a bumpy gravel lane instead of a smoothly paved road. Thus, the last four chapters in Part One cover grammar, syntax, and style. By keeping grammar terminology to a minimum, we hope to be exhaustive rather than exhausting. Chapter Six provides a review of punctuation, emphasizing the connection between punctuation and the author's intended meaning.

The topics covered in Chapters Seven and Eight should prove useful to you in many of your courses. We are convinced of the crucial link between reading and writing, and so we have devoted these two chapters to critical reading and procedures for incorporating material from outside sources into your own writing. Once again student models are included to demonstrate crucial skills: picking out major points in what you read; annotating and summarizing; making connections between what you read and your own experiences; and effectively using material from outside authorities in your essays. Chapter Eight concludes with a complete research paper that illustrates using these skills proficiently.

In Chapters Nine through Thirteen we discuss and demonstrate the writing strategies that students are most likely to be asked to use: narration; description; comparison and contrast; explanation; and persuasion. As the model essays in these chapters show, these strategies are rarely mutually exclusive; rather, they are devices you can draw on as needed in any piece of writing. The order in which these strategies are discussed in the text reflect a natural evolution from writing about personal experiences to more idea-based writing.

Finally, Chapter Fourteen, which provides an introduction to writing résumés and cover letters, may prove to be particularly useful to you both in and out of school. Writing a strong letter of application provides excellent practice at persuasive writing—whether you are applying for a job, a scholarship, or something else.

We have included numerous individual and small-group exercises throughout the text. These exercises both reinforce the material covered and provide opportunities for writing practice. The variety of exercises will help you become a more flexible writer.

As any experienced writer will attest, writing can be hard work. Like any skill you acquire, whether it be swimming, saxophone playing, or sewing, writing improves with practice. The rewards of writing well, however, are many: better grades; increased confidence in writing; skills for the job market; and, most important, the personal satisfaction that comes from being able to express yourself clearly in writing. We hope that *Strategies for Writing* will help you achieve these rewards and that you have fun in doing so.

Acknowledgments

Many people have contributed to this book. We would like to thank Marisa L. L'Heureux, a truly model editor, for her always enthusiastic, prompt, and competent assistance. Our colleague Mariann Littell of the Academic Opportunity Center (AOC) at the University of Wisconsin–Milwaukee is responsible for many of the computer graphics and a great deal more. Brenda Jackson, Cindy Le Mieux, and Ellen Lincoln provided considerable help with graphics and typing at an earlier stage. AOC's student employees, Heather Hyland, Luka Gale, and Peter Thomas, provided willing assistance by making copies and performing other tasks, often on short notice. Alan Magayne-Roshak of the University of Wisconsin–Milwaukee Photo Services always came up with exactly the photos we had in mind from his wonderful collection. Sharing ideas over many years with present and former AOC colleagues Mary Helen Halloran, Sara Zimmerman, Julie French, Pat Couillard, Mary Walz-Chojnacki, and Kathy Scullin (now chair of the English department at Mount Mary College in Milwaukee) has been very important. Wallon, Justin, and Nick Walusayi and Dave, Ellen, Jon, and Matt Healy put up with our preoccupation and provided encouragement and/or editorial assistance throughout the entire project.

The biggest stimulus has come, however, from our students of the Academic Opportunity Center, especially, but not only, those who are our coauthors. It is to them that our book is dedicated. We are very grateful to Mary Dunn for tracking down some of these former students so that we could inform them that their work is being published.

Ann E. Healy
Martha Walusayi

Part One

Writing More Effective Prose

Chapter One

The Writing Process

Perhaps somewhere along the line your experiences with writing have been less than positive. Despite considerable effort, some of your writing projects may have not turned out as well as you wished. Comments and corrections on returned assignments may have been discouraging. Rest assured that yours are shared frustrations; many people find writing difficult.

On the other hand, you probably know more about English composition and grammar than a book or instructor can teach you. Almost everything you say or write is understandable because you arrange words and phrases according to recognized patterns, pausing occasionally at logical places in your sentences. Even if your writing contains some spelling errors, a very large percentage of the words is spelled correctly. This textbook will expand on what you already know and help you to build on the strong points of your writing. We hope it also contains information that broadens your knowledge and makes you a better critic and editor of your own writing, as well as others'.

This book deals with writing used in the university, business, and professional worlds. A better command of the language used in these areas can only foster your progress in these worlds. Many of us feel more comfortable in the less formal languages of our families, communities, and peer groups. Preserve that language and use it with pleasure—but not when writing business letters or papers for university courses.

Writing can be frustrating because ideas and emotions must be expressed in a clear, organized fashion to be comprehensible to both the writers and their readers. While this may seem frustrating at first, writing does become easier and more satisfying with practice. You may find yourself working just as hard, perhaps even harder, than before as your writing improves, but you should also find the rewards, both short-term and long-term, worth the additional effort. The process of improving your writing is similar to becoming a better basketball player or drummer. Practice sessions may well be more demanding after joining a varsity team or a jazz quartet, but the rewards are also immeasurably greater.

> ## So you don't like to write.

You may recognize some benefits from your college composition course sooner than you thought: expressing your ideas on paper more clearly and effectively without searching for just the right wording; having a draft turn out as well as, or even better than, you hoped; receiving encouraging input on an essay from fellow students or your instructor. Composition students, particularly those who put considerable effort into their course, often note that they are having less difficulty and getting higher grades on essay exams and papers in other courses.

Being able to write well can have a variety of rewards, some of which can strengthen a résumé. Several of the student essays included in this book were entries in the University of Wisconsin—Milwaukee's annual freshman composition contest; three were winners. Some of our students have become staff writers for a campus student newspaper. Letters of application written for the course have led to interviews, jobs, and internships for several others. These are just a few examples of students who have discovered the power of the written word.

Whether similar and immediate practical results follow your writing efforts, always regard your writing for composition courses as professional writing, as preparation for your future—in the university and in the workplace—and not just as practice writing. In an increasingly competitive workplace, writing well gives you an advantage over other applicants for internships or entry-level jobs and could even play a role in future promotions. Professional schools (nursing, engineering, law, and so on) frequently require applicants to provide evidence of good writing skills.

We challenge you to think and write more professionally. We also encourage you to expect and value criticism that stimulates you to *revise*—to look again at your words and ideas and the honesty with which you expressed them.

Accepting Criticism

If you are like most writers, you dislike exposing your writing to the scrutiny of others—it is rather like asking someone to criticize your child or your best friend to your face. As the author, you have the final decision whether to accept or reject a critic's suggestions. However, without soliciting and carefully considering input from others, painful as that process often is, your writing is less likely to evolve and improve. Accepting advice from thoughtful critics can help you make your writing more interesting, richer in detail, and stronger in conviction, and can also help your writing style to improve and mature. And, like a singer, you can develop your own style by discovering your *voice*. Your readers will appreciate that as well.

Like many of your fellow students, you may be somewhat apprehensive as you embark upon this course in college composition. We hope that this textbook will help you navigate some of the shoals on what can prove to be a productive, even exciting, journey.

Why Do People Write?

On the first day of every semester we ask students: Why do people write? The students seize upon the subject with varying degrees of enthusiasm and humor. The serious types volunteer that they write to express their feelings about ideas or topics. Some say they write to remember (shopping lists, class notes). A few write to keep in touch with absent friends and loved ones, though in this age of almost universal instant communication (telephones, computer networks, fax machines) these last reasons are a decidedly endangered species. Of course, there are always the class wits who are quick to answer that they write because they have to write for English class.

These are all good reasons for people to write, and there are more to add to the list. Some people write to entertain—themselves or others. The well-known author Stephen King, for example, obviously enjoys writing horror stories and millions of readers share this enthusiasm for his drop-dead-from-fright style of novels. It is hard to mention a successful author like Stephen King without noting another good reason to write, which is to earn money. Though not all of us can bank on our writing skills to the extent that people like King or Danielle Steele do, a good command of English style and grammar is an asset in whatever career you choose to pursue. How many general job descriptions have you read that include the stipulation: "Applicant must have good communication skills"? The ability to speak and write well is a requirement in most better-paying jobs.

Perhaps one day, while you are working at just such a job, your boss will ask you to compile a set of instructions for a new employee who needs to learn the office routine. This is still another reason why people write: to instruct and share ideas with other people. If you do this well and clearly, it is a pleasure for the reader of your memo, manual, or report. How often have you complained, "I can't understand these instructions!" or "Why couldn't they make the directions clearer?" This is a failure of communication skills at the most basic level—the failure to express ideas to another person exactly as you want them understood. In its most extreme form, this desire for clarity and precision in writing drives writers to continually struggle over their choice of words and phrasing. It was only half in jest that the British author Oscar Wilde described his day's writing activity to a friend; "This morning I put in a comma; this afternoon I . . . took it out."

This same drive for exactness in writing can cause journalists, reporters, newscasters, and student authors to check and recheck their texts and sources for possible errors before they rush into print with their headlines or articles. They know that when you are writing to *inform*, your data should be both clear and correct. Can your opinions be backed up with facts? Will your reader be convinced that your account is accurate, your viewpoint a reasonable one?

Some of the sections of this book are devoted to informative and argumentative, or persuasive, writing. Having the ability to convince other people of the wisdom and truth of your opinions can be one of the most satisfying reasons for writing.

One of the most compelling reasons people write is to understand themselves and their lives. Students are often asked to write an essay recalling a person, place, or event of significance to them. The papers produced by this assignment are often of such power and beauty that they can stun readers with their depth of feeling. It seems that on their own, these students have discovered the joy of being able to write authentic, literate prose about their own lives. Others have discovered the healing power of words, the therapeutic value of writing about what has been buried in their minds for quite some time.

One such student was freshman Chad Kimerer, whose essay described his anguish at being barred from his high school's Honor Roll because he was a learning disabled student enrolled in special classes. The grades he achieved in those classes, his high school principal told him, could never count toward the Honor Roll, no matter how high they were. Chad's pain on the day the Honor Roll was posted and his firm resolve to turn this setback to his advantage are described in his prize-winning essay "The Light at the End of the Tunnel." Recalling his efforts in composing the story, Chad later advised his readers, his fellow students, to "talk to the paper through a pen," to "let people know what you're going through." "Pull it from your gut," he stressed.

Chad is one of those writers who *needed* to tell their story; another such student author was Amber Brieanna Birts, who wrote essays examining her past for a freshman composition class. Her writings eventually led her to write and self-publish a book about her childhood experience of sexual abuse, the poignantly titled *Mama, Why Didn't You Help Me?* In an interview, Amber said, "One of the reasons that I began to write, after having recovered my past, was because of the therapeutic process that it seemed to take me through . . . . I began to understand the power of the written word." She added, "Now no one can stop me. No one else is going to call the shots. This way I can reach women in Los Angeles. You don't have to be Oprah Winfrey to be listened to."

When the Russian emigre writer Vladimir Nabokov titled his autobiography *Speak, Memory,* he showed an artist's understanding of how effective good prose can be: It "speaks" to the reader across vast physical distances and through centuries of time. By taking a personal experience and sharing it through your writing, you can open a door onto a world the reader can only know through you: your world, your life, your mind and thoughts. It is a powerful feeling to realize that, through the magic of the written word, people living hundreds of years from now will be able to read your writing and know something of you and your world. William Shakespeare knew this when he assured the subject of his famous sonnets:

So long as men can breathe, or eyes can see,
So long lives this, and this gives life to thee.

Exercise

Explore one of the following topic suggestions. Do not be overly concerned with grammar or style, but write a thoughtful, honest—and not too brief—essay on the topic. Include many vivid, concrete examples to make your points clear. Write your response in a journal.

Choose a journal that you would enjoy writing in for a few months, preferably one that can be carried around conveniently. Your journal will then be available when an idea occurs to you, or when you observe something that you want to write about. The most stimulating entries may well be ideas that come to you when least expected. These entries will often develop into your best future writing because they are topics that captured your interest:

1. Write an essay about anything that concerns you.
2. Write an essay about one of your pet peeves, something that irritates you.
3. What's in your name? You may want to interview one or both of your parents or other family members to discover more about how you got your name. Is your name unusual or fairly common? Is that important to you? How do others react to your name? Have you ever wished you had a different name? What do you like or dislike about your name?

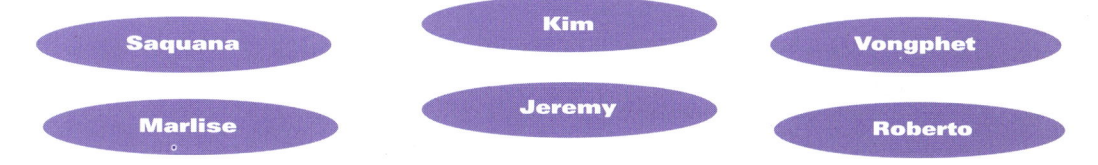

- Saquana
- Kim
- Vongphet
- Marlise
- Jeremy
- Roberto

Other suggestions for topics to write about are scattered throughout this book. Some of these topics may stimulate you, while others may not. We encourage you to try writing about some of them in your journal. Your instructor will undoubtedly have many additional topic suggestions and theme assignments that you can explore in your journal before handing in a final version.

For additional information about keeping a journal, see page 13.

Finding Something to Say: Focusing on a Topic

"I don't have anything to write about." How many times have you said that? Yet you probably have many interesting things to say during conversations with friends, when you find your ideas flowing freely. What are the differences between talking and writing? Why is writing harder than talking for some—though not all—composition students? Why do so many writers panic because they cannot put their ideas down on paper effectively? One answer is that people have more practice talking than writing, but of course there is more to it than that.

Writers who panic due to a lack of confidence often make the mistake of setting their sights too high: They try to sound brilliant or profound for authority figures like their instructors. Confident writers, on the other hand, can envision a more sympathetic audience, such as their peers or other readers who know less about a topic than they do. Drawing frequently on their own experiences, confident writers often go through the world viewing daily occurrences as potential topics that they may enjoy developing in writing.

You may never become as enthusiastic a writer as Jeffrey Schwigel, one of our students who often found himself at his word processor at 2:00 A.M., unable to get back to sleep until he made changes on his latest essay—a state that could be described as "being unable to turn your head off." Try, however, to listen more often and more intently to the ideas that are constantly popping into your brain. Because they are there anyway, you might as well start making better use of these often random and unfocused thoughts. Jot them down in your writer's journal as possible seeds for future essays. Try to be more actively aware of how you are reacting to the world around you, especially to what you are reading.

Another helpful idea is to get into the habit of making marginal notes as you read. Do not simply summarize or highlight main points—*react* to various writers' opinions, style, tone, evidence, arguments, and so on. Imagine yourself in a debate with the author as you read. Becoming a more involved, critical reader will be beneficial in all of your courses, not just composition courses.

Stages in the Writing Process

Good writing does not just happen; it is the result of considerable thought and a careful process. Like any skill worth developing, writing well is achieved only through much effort. The effort involved is very worthwhile because it can result in the satisfaction of doing a good job, in improved writing skills, and in better grades for many of your courses. Writing well can also be fun!

You will rarely have enough time in one sitting to produce an effective paper that you are proud to hand in. Starting early allows time to write more than one or two drafts. Revising a series of drafts is the best way to assure a satisfying final product.

Experiment with different schedules to discover which works best for you. Do you write best in short spurts, or do you need at least two hours in order to concentrate effectively?

It is also helpful to reward yourself with regular short breaks. Some writers find that they work better when they take a break when the writing is going well and they know where they want to go next in an essay. A break can also help if you are stuck about what to say next. Returning after a break that gets your mind completely off an essay often brings a fresh perspective. Mulling over the topic while swimming laps or doing laundry may be beneficial.

Because the best revising often takes place upon returning to a piece of writing, waiting until the last minute to start a theme is not a good idea. Start early enough to work your way through the several stages that make up the writing process:

> Taking a break may give you a fresh perspective.

- Prewriting or invention
- Drafting
- Revising and editing

Only by going through all of these stages will you produce an effective essay that is interesting and contains enough specific material to make your points clear to your readers, your **audience**.

Remember that your audience cannot ask questions as they would during a conversation. Suppose that you assert:

Don't take Mr. Coswell's beginning chemistry class. He is a lousy, unfair teacher.

In a conversation Mr. Coswell's potential future student can keep asking questions until you come up with enough specific examples to make a clear case against Coswell's chemistry class. That kind of interchange is not possible with readers. Your best plan is to anticipate what their questions might be while you are composing your portrait of Mr. Coswell as a teacher. Then answer those questions as clearly as possible in your writing.

In writing, as in conversation, general statements should be backed up with specific evidence, such as descriptive details and appropriate examples and illustrations. Anticipating your readers' questions as you go through the various stages of the writing process is one way to help you choose what material you want in your final draft. You will probably discard some topics or illustrations and add new ones as you revise, as well as elaborating further on those you have decided to keep.

There is no one right way to write, nor is there a right place to compose. You will need to discover the place or places where you are the most comfortable and productive. Likewise, you must determine, preferably through

> People write in all kinds of places and situations.

experimentation with several methods, what writing process works best for you. Only by trying the various techniques that other writers have found effective can you raise your writing skills to the pinnacle you desire—and are capable of achieving.

Experienced writers generally go through several stages while deciding what material to include in their final version of a particular piece of writing and how best to organize that material. They reread what they have written more often than less experienced writers, making frequent changes as they proceed. There is no exact recommended method for writing; however, one thing is certain. Contrary to what less experienced writers may think, few seasoned writers simply sit down at a desk with a clear plan in mind and follow that plan from beginning to end, all in one sitting.

Exercise

How do you usually start to write? Where do you like to do it? Write a thoughtful response to these questions in your writer's journal.

Stage One: Getting Started, or Prewriting Strategies

Even if you have developed a fairly satisfactory method for beginning to write a theme, you might want to try out all of the planning and prewriting devices discussed below. If you suffer from that common ailment, writer's block, experimenting with these devices may prove especially beneficial.

Prewriting, or invention, is that early stage in the writing process when you begin gathering information and ideas for an essay. This is the time to do lots of mulling over and scribbling. Do not be surprised if, like many experienced writers, you find yourself surrounded by wads of discarded paper.

Prewriting serves many useful functions besides helping you overcome writer's block. It is an effective way to explore various options before zeroing in on a final topic. Prewriting enables the writer to narrow down a topic that is too broad. The writer may soon discover that a topic that appeared promising is unsuitable and begin the search for a better alternative. Prewriting helps the writer to gather specific information needed to develop a topic and often shows where the gaps are. However, writers frequently discover that they know more about their topic than they originally thought. This is one reason why some form of prewriting, such as jotting down points you intend to cover, is also an excellent way to begin an essay exam answer, especially if a particular question seems overwhelming at the initial reading. Perhaps most important, prewriting can clarify your insights on a subject, enabling you to think more clearly on paper, which is, after all, what writing well is all about.

> Don't be afraid to plunge right in.

Freewriting. **Freewriting** is an excellent way to explore a potential topic and is, moreover, one of the most highly recommended cures for writer's block. This invention strategy lets you fill up that horrid blank page staring up at you with a minimum of effort. Freewriting is rather like practicing scales on the piano or shooting baskets: The end product is not being judged by anyone else and no one is keeping score.

Writing as quickly as you can, just let the ideas flow from your brain onto your paper. Do not stop to erase or to search for exactly the right phrase. Freewriting lets you discover what you have to say about a subject without worrying about spelling, organization, or syntax. Moreover, freewriting warms you up, loosens and clarifies your ideas, and helps you get into the habit of using writing as a way of thinking.

You can use freewriting as an invention strategy during the initial exploration of a general topic such as: What makes an effective teacher? What effective teachers have I had and what made them so successful? As you see a narrower topic emerging on paper, you can refocus your freewriting on that.

Suppose that you were given the following freewriting assignment.

> *Having had many teachers, both good and bad, students are all experts when it comes to teachers. Draw upon your experiences to do some freewriting for an essay about one of your former teachers.*
>
> *Choose a teacher who made a strong impression on you, a teacher who was effective and inspiring or ineffective and perhaps even destructive. Use as many concrete examples and illustrations of their behavior and methods*

as you can to tell your readers why that person was a good or bad instructor. Include enough vivid details to create a realistic picture of that teacher on paper.

Imagine that your audience is a friend who is considering signing up for a course taught by that teacher. Keeping your audience in mind always helps you to focus during both the invention and writing stages of any piece of writing.

Before you begin your freewriting, look at the following model. Freewriting on the aforementioned "lousy, unfair" chemistry teacher, Mr. Coswell, might sound something like this.

I warned my friend not to sign up for Coswell's class. Besides, Tim hates science and he is a good writer. He is an unfair grader since I got my first "D" ever in Coswell's chemistry which made me furious and my parents even more furious. The obnoxious odor of sulphuric acid assaulted me as I approached his classroom seized with dread. It was the same every day. Science was fun until I met him, the dullest, most dismal teacher in our high school. Terrible speaker. No eye contact. Maybe it's because I had him right after lunch. Always late for class and rushing around. Boy was I thrilled when I got my chemistry set in seventh grade. My mother was less thrilled after I started my bangs on fire. Coswell drones on in a monotone and looks at the ceiling. All the brains take chemistry and they are all in my section. I once planned on being a science teacher, but it is hard for a woman to be in that field anyway. Coswell plays favorites, but not me. Obviously is burned out and bored. The brains never get called on, only the poor students. Always late returning exams. His directions for assignments are never clear and he never allows enough time. If you do not know an answer he humiliates you in public. No one can read the scribblings he sprawls all over the blackboard. Not interested in his subject and not interested in the students. I hear Mrs. Bunson is a great chemistry teacher but I never had her.

Although the above freewriting is often unclear and ungrammatical, and even disorganized and unfocused, it does contain many concrete observations about Mr. Coswell. Hence the writer could mine it for good material that could be incorporated into an interesting, descriptive essay.

Exercise

1. Make a list in your journal of all the specific, concrete details about Mr. Coswell that would contribute to a vivid portrait of him as a teacher.
2. Next, freewrite about a teacher in your journal. Choose a former teacher or coach who made a strong impression—either positive or negative—on you.

Getting the Most out of a Writer's Journal. Here are several tips to help you get the most out of your writer's journal. Instead of using loose sheets of paper, incorporate the above assignments and all of your freewriting into a writer's journal. Write in your journal regularly, experimenting with a variety of entries. Like tennis pros who devote hours to honing their serves, you should discover that writing comes easier and improves with practice, provided you make a consistent effort to write something worth saying.

Students often moan, "Nothing that interesting happens to me." Not true! We have read too many of their papers to believe that claim. If you have that attitude, however, your journal will reflect it. Moreover, you will neither enjoy keeping a journal nor find it beneficial.

For starters, avoid simply writing a chronology of the mundane events of your day. You always owe it to your reader—yourself, in this case—to be as interesting as possible. Otherwise why bother writing?

Many kinds of writing besides freewriting for composition assignments can go into your writer's journal. Experiment with creative writing of all sorts. Spend half an hour in the cafeteria describing the scene around you—the colors, the smells, the noises, the hairdos, the clothing. React to the events of your day. Write about what you are reading, using the opinions expressed by others to stimulate your own analysis of a topic. A journal can be a place to vent your anger, to explore your relationships, to learn about yourself. Look at your journal as letters to yourself.

You also owe it to yourself to become the best writer you can. Experiment with keeping a writer's journal to find out whether it is a helpful technique for you—as it has been for many writers over the centuries.

Clustering. **Clustering**, or clumping, is an invention strategy that is particularly helpful for writers who think visually. On paper, cluster words or phrases around your broad topic to narrow it down. After considering all of your ideas, clump on, or choose, your final topic choice. Do the clumping right in your writer's journal.

There is no correct way to make a cluster diagram, although it is often recommended that the topic appear in an oval in the center of your diagram. The model on the following page shows one method of clustering.

Reprinted with permission.
TM & © 1990 Leigh Rubin

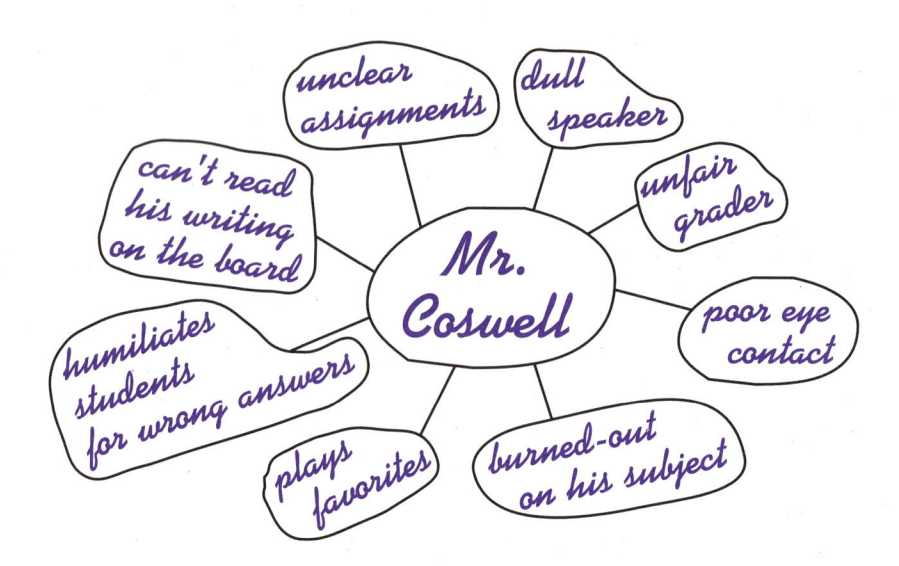

Cluster diagram with "Mr. Coswell" in the center, surrounded by: unclear assignments, dull speaker, unfair grader, poor eye contact, burned-out on his subject, plays favorites, humiliates students for wrong answers, can't read his writing on the board.

Exercise

Pick one of the following topics:

1. an effective or ineffective teacher
2. my best or worst teacher
3. qualities needed to be a good teacher
4. a specific teacher or coach who has most influenced me.

Write your topic in an oval in the middle of a page of your journal. Then cluster your ideas around that subject.

Brainstorming. **Brainstorming** means jotting down all of the short phrases that come to mind about a particular topic. It is another well-known remedy for writer's block because it enables writers to rapidly assemble what they already know about a topic. Jotting down such a list is particularly helpful before writing an impromptu theme or an essay exam. The writer quickly generates a lot of information, which can then be eliminated or used. It is helpful to cross out items on the list that seem unessential; the remainder can then be utilized more effectively, perhaps by preparing a second list that is more logically organized.

It can be very helpful to ask a series of questions about your topic. Questions such as *Who? Where? When? How? Why?* can aid in generating more data for a brainstorming list.

Exercise

Imagine that you are looking for a job. Brainstorm about your experience and qualifications. Before you brainstorm, study the following model:

 junior camp counselor—taught canoeing and swimming
 four years of high school art classes
 familiar with word processing (be specific)
 varsity volleyball—two years
 volunteer at a day care center—one summer
 high school yearbook staff—senior year
 first year student at UWM—intended major, elementary education
 babysat for three neighbor families
 short order cook—Max's Grill—six months
 oldest daughter of six children
 fluent in Spanish
 enthusiastic; like children and relate well to them

Composing this list undoubtedly increased the writer's confidence that she can write a persuasive letter and may have suggested the type of position she might apply for. Her jottings record considerable experience, much of it with children. Because becoming an elementary school teacher is her career goal, a position working with children would be a logical choice for this person to apply for.

Doing a Scratch Outline. Going back to our example, the items in the above brainstorming might be converted into a scratch outline under the following headings. Note that as she organizes her outline, the writer is already beginning to think about expanding on data listed in her brainstorming.

Qualifications for Working with Children:

oldest daughter of six children
babysat for three neighbor families—be specific
volunteer at Happy Child Day Care Center; summer 1995—assisted in the craft room with children ages 3 to 6
junior camp counselor—taught canoeing and swimming to girls ages 8 to 10; summers of 1994 and 1992
enthusiastic; like children and relate well to them (mention supervisors who will attest to this)
first year student at UWM; intended major, elementary education

Additional Skills of Possible Value in Working with Children:
(may not want to use all of these in a letter)

four years of high school art—develop this topic to show the range of art training and experience

yearbook staff—senior year; list responsibilities, etc.

fluent in Spanish—spoken in my home; three years of high school Spanish; member, Spanish Club

varsity volleyball—two years

Additional Experience:
(Better only on résumé?)

short order cook—Max's Grill; gives exact dates and duties

word processing and computer skills; list courses taken, competence, and experience

Exercise

You have already recorded all of your job skills and qualifications. It is time to focus your brainstorming a little more. Using the above as a model for your brainstorming and outlining:

1. Make a list in your journal of all the experiences that you might include in a letter of application.
2. Convert your brainstorming into an informal, or scratch, outline that could function as an organizing device for the body of a letter of application.

What headings or categories, such as coaching or office skills, do the items in your list suggest? Jot down possible categories in your journal, then choose three or four that seem to be the most appropriate and comprehensive. Next, fit the items in your brainstorming under those categories. Cross out items that do not fit under any of the categories. You may, however, want to include some or all of these discarded items on a résumé, because a résumé should present a more comprehensive picture of your qualifications than a letter of application.

Completing the Informal Outline and Composing a First Draft. Once you have organized the items from your brainstorming into appropriate categories, the next step is to arrange those categories in an **informal outline**. This outline is more structured than your scratch outline and can be an organizing device for the **first draft** of your piece of writing. You may change the order of the outline, but you can decide that later. The important thing is to prepare some kind of outline to get started on a draft.

How do you want to organize your qualifications? Having your strongest suit first is probably a good idea for a letter of application, as employers tend to be busy people and you want to get their attention right from the start. In another essay you might prefer to build up an argument gradually and finish with your most persuasive evidence. The order you choose depends on your purpose and on the nature of the topic. Regardless of what order you eventually select, an informal outline provides a kind of map as you embark upon the **drafting stage** in the writing process.

Exercise

Write a draft for a letter of application in your journal. You need not worry about being graded on this draft, so relax. Save it, however, along with your brainstorming and outlines. Even if your instructor does not assign letters of application and résumés later in the semester, you will undoubtedly be writing them sometime in the future.

Discovery Draft. A few students find that they need to write a complete **discovery draft** of a theme before doing any other prewriting. This can be a valuable way to start, provided that first draft is viewed as *only* the initial stage in the writing process, not even close to a final project, and probably not yet worth sharing with your readers. Why not heed the warning of William Safire, well-known political commentator and author of the lively, often pungent, *On Language* column in the *New York Times Magazine:*

> *First, remember that first drafts are usually stupid. If you shoot off your mouth with your first draft—that is, if you say what you think before you've had a chance to think—your stupidity shines forth for all to hear.*

But be encouraged by Safire's subsequent advice:

> *But, if you write your first draft—of a letter, a memo, a description of some transcendental experience that comes to you while jogging—then you fall on your face in absolute privacy. You get the chance to change it all around.*

Through experimentation you will discover which invention or prewriting strategies, or combination of strategies, work best for you. You may also find that the process that resulted in a successful first draft for one essay may not be as effective for another assignment. Time for more trial balloons!

Stage Two: Drafting

The stages in the writing process are not necessarily linear. Halfway into composing a draft, you may opt to go back and insert another category into your informal outline or add some material to your cluster diagram. You might even make an additional cluster diagram on one of the topics included in your initial clustering.

During the drafting stage it is advisable to regularly review all the prewriting you have completed on a topic. Analyze the information and ideas and determine the direction you want your piece of writing to take. What is your purpose? Who are your readers, your audience? What is your **thesis**, that overall main idea that provides unity to your essay? Keep that thesis in mind to give purpose to your draft and determine its direction.

Composing the First Draft. You have now read through your prewriting and are ready, pen or keyboard in hand, to compose a first draft, when it strikes again—writer's block!

Writer's block is a familiar problem that only you can overcome. Do not let it become an excuse for not writing, or you will never get over it. Usually writer's block can be cured by just getting something down on paper, without agonizing over the perfect opening line or the ideal introductory paragraph. Like many experienced writers, you may prefer to compose the **body**, or the middle, of an essay first, then write the **introduction**. Regardless of the order in which you compose them, writing the body and the introduction often suggests ideas about the contents of a good, pithy **conclusion**.

Because you will be making regular changes as you write the sentences and paragraphs that make up a draft, avoid crowding the page. Leave wide margins and write on every other, or even every third, line. Double- or triple-space if you are composing on a typewriter or computer.

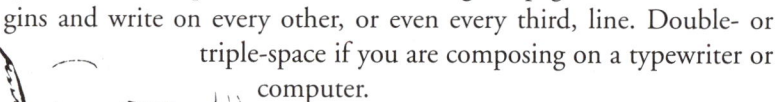

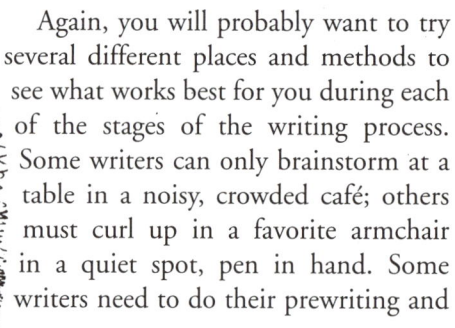

Again, you will probably want to try several different places and methods to see what works best for you during each of the stages of the writing process. Some writers can only brainstorm at a table in a noisy, crowded café; others must curl up in a favorite armchair in a quiet spot, pen in hand. Some writers need to do their prewriting and compose their first draft in longhand. More and more writers, however, are discovering the many advantages of drafting essays—some even do their prewriting—on a computer.

Once you overcome any initial hesitation you may have about using a word-processing program on a computer, you will most likely discover its many advantages. Word processing is faster, quieter, and much easier than using a typewriter. You do not need to be concerned about margins or coming to the end of a page. Using a computer also removes some of the worry about filling up a page, so they can be a great cure for writer's block. Because it is so easy to change what appears on the screen, the fear about "getting it right" the first time is no longer an issue.

If you are not already computer literature, rest assured that you are not alone and that it is never too late to learn word processing.

Making Good Use of Computers. Most student authors will find the computer to be their closest ally and best tool for composing themes, reports, and even lengthy term papers or theses. Some students may own their own computers. For those who do not, some universities have areas where computers can be used free or rented by the hour. Many quick-print stores also rent computer time, as well as other useful equipment such as photocopy machines, fax machines, and manuscript binderies for the finished writing product.

If you have not warmed up to the computer yet, why not start now? Scout out your campus for available machines; ask your professors or friends where they do their word processing. Perhaps a machine is available where you work. Find out where the other students in your classes type their themes. Chances are, they may have already discovered the joys of computer composition.

What is so enjoyable about writing on a computer? A word-processing program on a computer can do many things that a typewriter can't.

For a start, word-processing programs can simplify the writing and editing process. They allow you to move whole sections of your text from place to place in your essay; you can also erase lines by using a single keystroke on the computer. Additional material can be added easily, too, in any place you want in the text. Some programs feature a split screen, which can enable you to review your notes for the text, check on an earlier paragraph, or show you where you are in your outline for a research paper.

When using a computer you can see on the screen what you have written and catch any errors in spelling or grammar *before* you print the text. Some computers have built-in spell-checkers; these alert you to incorrectly spelled words. This useful function is a great boon to poor spellers. If you use this type of mechanical spell-check, remember that a machine cannot tell the difference between two words that are *spelled* correctly in a sentence but *used* incorrectly. For example, a computer cannot tell the difference between the homonyms *herd* and *heard,* as in "I herd him call out my name." Some writing programs for the computer go beyond simple spell-checking and can correct style and usage as well.

A few more functions make the computer user- and writer-friendly. It enables you to print up all or part of your writing with the push of a button. The computer's "save" function records your work on a hard drive or a disk, saving it from day to day or even from year to year.

With all these advantages to composing on the computer, now might be a good time to make the move to computer literacy. After all, the term *user-friendly* developed from the field of computer science. Why not learn how these machines work, then make them work for you? Academically, your writing will probably benefit; personally, you will gain self-confidence from having acquired a new skill. Don't be afraid to try it out!

Stage Three: Revising, Editing, and Proofreading

Deleting, rewording, rearranging—the computer is especially useful during the final stages of the writing process. No piece of writing is ever finished. Nevertheless, at some point, often because of a deadline—or because they are sick of a particular project—writers have to stop drafting and proceed to *revising, editing,* and *proofreading.* These are distinct though equally important processes that like all of the stages in the writing process, are often intermingled.

> Take the time to revise.

Proper **revision** is a complex and time-consuming process. The word *revising* means *reseeing:* effective writers are constantly reseeing what they have written and searching for ways to say it better. Thus a revised paper is much more than a neatly copied version of a rough draft. Revision involves making a variety of real changes in the contents, organization, and wording of a draft: A topic may be further narrowed; terms may be better defined; additional specific examples or more vivid descriptive details may be added; whole sections of the text may be rearranged, expanded, or deleted.

Cutting out material is often the most painful aspect of revision. Because writers—experienced and inexperienced alike—put so much effort into their writing, they are usually reluctant to part with even small scraps of their creations. It is important, however, to delete unnecessary repetition that becomes tedious for your readers. Nor should you leave in more details and examples than readers need to understand your point. In these instances cut you must, sad as it may seem, unless you want to bore your audience.

Cutting excess verbiage is not the only reason to keep your readers in mind during the revision process. Try to imagine what additional information they might need to fully grasp a particular point. Further explanation or examples could be essential, or certain sections might require clarification or elaboration. Revision also involves polishing your writing style by rewording phrases, sentences, and entire paragraphs.

While you have no doubt been doing some revising throughout the composition process, the revising stage takes time. Plan ahead to allow enough time to set aside your completed draft, preferably overnight but at least for a few hours. When you return to it, you can see your piece with a fresh eye that will help you revise effectively. While revising you may conclude that further prewriting on one or another section is necessary, another reminder that the stages in the writing process are always intermingled and that allowing enough time is essential.

Getting Feedback. No matter how hard you try, you will be unable to detect all of the flaws or mistakes in your drafts. Therefore, seeking **feedback** on your drafts is crucial to good revision. For almost all writers—especially for less experienced ones—getting others' opinions is a painful process: No one likes to hear negative comments about something they have worked so hard to create. Frequently imagining—(incorrectly)—that their fellow students write better than they do, student writers worry about others' reactions to their writing style. Understandably, many of them find it difficult to expose their experiences, ideas, and emotions to the scrutiny of others. Try hard to overcome your resistance to having others read your drafts, because everyone's writing benefits from the critical comments of helpful editors.

"We'd do him a big favor if we ate chapter four."

> Revising is a many-faceted process.
>
> Revising means adding, deleting, and rearranging.
> Revise for *ideas* and *examples*.
> Add and sharpen *details*.
> Revise for *organization*.
> Revise for *clarity*.
> Improve the *wording*.
>
> Proofread the final draft for *surface errors*.

Exercise

This is an exercise in peer-group revising. Form small groups of four or five students.

1. All members of each group should quickly read through the *first* draft of the essay below for an overall impression. (Do not read Tamra's revised draft until your group finishes critiquing the first version.)
2. Reread the first version carefully, thinking about ways to strengthen the contents. Then write a short critique of Tamra's first draft in your journal. Mention at least three strong points of her essay, along with several specific suggestions for improving it.
3. Write comments in the margins, indicating places that are especially effective. Mark sections that need further clarification, where you would like additional information, more details and examples, and so on.
4. Imagine that Tamra is a member of your peer revising group. To make her feel at ease, first point out the strengths of the draft. Then share specific suggestions of ways she might improve the contents, drawing from the group's marginal notations as well as the critiques in their journals.
5. First skim, then carefully reread Tamra's revised essay. Note how much it is improved. Could you recommend additional changes? Discuss which of your group's suggestions appear—or do not appear—in her revision.

Working with the Overbearing (First Draft)

I chose the subject of sexual harrassment because this is something that I have to go through at least five days out of every week. For almost two years I have been a cashier at a grocery store and at times it can be pure hell. The store that I work at has a very family like environment within it. The majority of the employees are from the age of 15 to 19. To me this is good because it makes it easier to get along with your fellow employees.

Right now this doesn't sound like a problem but there is one. I have a problem with my employer harrassing me. At times I don't even think that he realizes that he is bothering me. (Because I don't want to use his real name I will call him Ed.) When I first started working there I really didn't pay that much attention to him. I just thought that he was always bothering me because I was new. After awhile I began to realize that something was wrong. Ed didn't harrass me physically, but he did it verbally. Just his making little comments and singling me out from everyone else made me feel uncomfortable. It got to a point where I hated going to work and when I did I dreaded seeing his face. When I told my mother about this she asked if I wanted her to handle it, but I wanted to take care of it by myself. Whenever Ed said something out of the ordinary to me I just went off. The strange thing is that whenever I told him to stop bothering me, he would say that I had an attitude. I didn't have an attitude I just wanted to be left alone. I felt that it was my duty to go to work and do my job as a cashier, not to be bothered.

Sexual harrassment in the work place is rising. For some reason whether it be man or woman some people feel like it is their responsibility to make you feel at home in more ways than one. There is nothing wrong with giving a compliment here and there but to do it continuously just makes the other person feel small. It is your right to be left alone. There are enough problems in this world that people have to worry about besides how are they going to be treated at work. My advice if this is happening to anyone is to take action. If it means going off on the person, quitting, or even taking them to court, do it. Don't just sit around and allow someone to make you feel uncomfortable at your own job place. Don't try to make excuses for the person saying maybe this and maybe that; this is wrong: it dodges the issue, and in the end you are the person that will come up hurt.

Working with the Overbearing (Revised)

I chose the subject of sexual harrassment because this is something that I have had to go through at least five days out of every week. For almost two years I have been a cashier at a grocery store and at times it was pure hell. The store has a family like environment. The majority of the employees are between the ages of 15 and 19. To me this is good because it makes it easier to get along with your fellow employees. Basically these are the reasons why I even stayed at this job. It may sound like I shouldn't have a problem but I do. My problem is with my employer harassing me. At times I don't even think he realized that he was bothering me. (Because I don't want to use his real name I will call him Ed.) Ed is the type of person who feels like everything he says and does is funny no matter how it might make the other person feel.

When I first started working there I really didn't pay that much attention to Ed. I just thought that he was always bothering me because I was new. After awhile I began to realize that something was wrong. Ed didn't harass me physically, but he did so verbally. Just his making little comments and singling me out from everyone else made me feel uncomfortable. I am the very shy type and everybody who knows me is aware of this. It seemed to me that at times Ed used this to his advantage, meaning that he knew he could bother me without getting any kind of reaction.

I remember times when I would be checking out a customer, and he would come by me and say, "I like her the best because she is the prettiest." Of course I would laugh it off in front of my customer, but inside I was really embarrassed. There would be times when he didn't even have to say anything to me, but I could just feel him staring at me from across the room. When I would finally turn around, he would wink at me with this devilish grin on his face. It would just make me feel sick to my stomach. What really pushed me to the edge was his always trying to get me alone with him. I could be packing at a register and he would call me over, but he never wanted anything that dealt with work. All he would say is that he had to take me out to dinner or lunch so that he could wine and dine me. Finally, I couldn't take it anymore. It got to a point where I hated going to work, and when I did, I dreaded seeing his face. When I told my mother about this, she asked if I wanted her to handle it, but I wanted to take care of it myself.

I couldn't understand why Ed just didn't leave me alone. Many questions about what I should do went through my head. Should I let my mother handle it, and feel like a child? Should I find another job, or should I just confront him about it? Well, I chose to confront him about it, not on purpose, but one day I just exploded. I was having problems with my taxes, and when I went to ask Ed what was wrong, he started to flirt with me. He told me that he could take care of the tax problem, and he could take care of me as well. I didn't ask him that because I didn't want him to take care of me; at times, I didn't even want him around me. At that point it seemed like everything he had ever said to me since I started working there just rushed through my head. I remember looking at him with this evil look on my face and saying, "Why are you always bothering me? Why don't you just leave me alone?" Clearly he wasn't expecting my reaction because he got a puzzled look on his face. The strange thing is that after I told him to stop bothering me, he claimed that I had an attitude. I didn't have an attitude, I just wanted to be left alone. Although I didn't say much, my explosion made me feel better and I knew I had gotten my point across. I felt that it was my duty to go to work and do my job as a cashier, and not be bothered.

Things changed a lot after I told Ed that he was bothering me. At first, he didn't even say anything to me, which was fine with me. As time went on he began to drop his former attitude towards me. Ed didn't say anything offensive to me anymore, but every once in a while I could still feel him looking. I guess it is like the old saying, "You can't teach an old dog new tricks." The staring really didn't bother me as much as his making little comments because all I had to do was ignore him and go on with my job.

To me, in such situations, it is better to let the other person know how you are feeling. If you don't, you won't be able to get anything done, because you will remain full of hate and anger against the person who is bothering you.

Sexual harassment in the workplace is an issue of growing concern. For some reason, whether it be man or woman, some people feel it is their responsibility to make others "feel at home." These persons may think that they are helping others by being extra nice to them, when in reality they are making them feel bad about themselves. There is nothing wrong with giving a compliment here and there, but doing so continuously just makes the other person feel small. It is everyone's right to be left alone. There are enough problems in this world that people have to worry about besides how are they going to be treated at work. My advice to anyone experiencing this is to take action. If it means confronting the person, quitting, or even going to court, do it. Don't just sit around and allow someone to make you feel uncomfortable at your workplace. Don't try to make excuses for the person, saying maybe this and maybe that. Doing this is wrong; it dodges the issue, and in the end you are the person who will be hurt.

Minor Repairs May Not Be Enough. When revising, always be guided by what you are trying to tell your readers. Writing involves thinking through your ideas and stating them as clearly as possible. Perhaps your editors or instructor have noted that a sentence, paragraph, or section of an essay is unclear or needs revising for another reason. You may be dissatisfied with a particular section yourself. In such cases, minor cosmetic repairs such as rewording or rearranging a sentence or two are often inadequate and may even make things worse. Frequently, it is best to put aside the whole paragraph or section and begin again. Jot down an informal outline of what you are attempting to say in that place. Making this outline can help you to think through your ideas and organize them more effectively in the revised essay.

Seasoned writers revise more regularly and more thoroughly then less experienced writers. They rarely rely solely on their own editing and revision, often widely circulating their manuscripts to solicit other readers' reactions. Emulating this practice will help you improve your writing. Obtaining feedback on drafts from friends and relatives is an essential part of the revision process, even if exchanging drafts is also a regular part of your composition course format.

Readers do not need to be expert reviewers to detect sections that are unclear and need elaboration or are repetitive and dull. They can also point out sections that are especially effective and thus worthy of more development, as well as discovering many of the careless slips and errors found in virtually every writer's drafts.

Exercise

Imagine that you are talking to the author of this essay. What would you like to know more about? Underline all words and phrases that could be more specific, such as *1995 maroon Ford Escort* instead of *car*. Does your group have other suggestions to help the author make this accident more vivid?

Car Accident

It all started on a sunny morning while I was on my way to school about two years ago. I was driving along a somewhat busy street in my newly purchased car. In the car with me was my four year old brother. Suddenly I saw this station wagon beginning to approach my car and not stopping. The car was headed for the driver's side door; I immediately accelerated to attempt to avoid her from hitting my car. I heard a loud squeal and then felt this impact that I could not believe the force of. The loudness of the impact by far overtook the squealing of the tires attempting to stop. My car did a 180° turn before the car came to a stop. I immediately checked my little brother to make sure that he was all right—thank God he was. After the force of the impact I began to grasp the concept that the car had hit me.

I got out of my car and approached the other driver and the thing she kept saying was that she didn't have any insurance. When I heard this I was really angry because about a year and a half previous to this accident I had another and I knew that I could not claim the damages on my insurance unless I wanted my insurance to go up. After I found this out I figured that the best thing would be to call the police, so I called 911 and it seemed like it took the officers forever. Every time I see an accident now I can understand how the people are feeling and the emotions that are involved. To this day I can still recall the sound and force of the impact and how it made my car spin almost a complete turn. In the back of my head I still have this fear of being involved in an accident that would be of greater severity. I just thank God that nobody was hurt in this one.

Editing Your Writing. **Editing** means checking for errors in usage, grammar, spelling, and punctuation before you write the final draft. Be especially aware of the mistakes you tend to make and look for them in particular as you edit. Many of these mistakes result from lack of knowledge. As you learn more about punctuation and spelling, these errors will decrease.

Proofreading means checking the final draft for typing or handwriting mistakes, for places where you wrote "The Hat in the Cat" instead of "The Cat in the Hat." Proofreading is largely a matter of looking rather than knowing, of spotting *from* where it should read *form*. Train your eyes for a different kind of careful reading. Proofreading cannot be done hastily, so always allow enough time and proofread your essay more than once. Reading essays aloud at least once often helps you catch mistakes you might otherwise have overlooked.

Because we all have the tendency to read right past many of our own small errors, it is also a good idea to find family members, friends, or other students in your class to edit and proofread your final drafts. Keep in mind, however, that you are ultimately responsible for editing your work. It is a good idea, sick as you may be of a paper, to proofread it one last time just before handing it in. You may find that your paper still has a few careless mistakes that you overlooked.

Most teachers are glad to see last-minute, inked-in corrections. Careful editing and proofreading can lead to significant improvements in the overall impression of your writing—and to higher grades.

Chapter Two

Shaping the Contents

The librarian in the picture on the following page has an attentive **audience.** Speakers have an advantage over writers in that they can observe how their audience is reacting to their material. Writers, on the other hand, usually need to visualize an audience and then tailor their material with imaginary, or actual, readers in mind.

Keeping an audience in mind affects many aspects of how you write your essay, including how much explanatory material you need to incorporate to avoid losing your readers. How many times have you given up in despair when trying to figure out a technical manual written in a style way over your head? Many terms and concepts must be defined unless the writer is targeting a specialized audience that does not need that information. For example, you would include less information for a fellow employee reading your proposal for a reform in the workplace than for someone who works elsewhere. Necessary background data should always be included: Never assume that readers know what it is like to go through Marine Corps basic training or to be in college on an athletic scholarship. What you should assume, however, is that some readers may have preconceptions—often incorrect—about your topic, such as, "College athletes are all . . ."

Your audience also affects word choice and tone. **Tone** refers to writers' attitudes toward their material and their readers. The range of tones runs the entire gamut of human emotions and the adjectives that describe them: indignant, sarcastic, playful, serious, concerned, conciliatory, argumentative, or ironic, to name a few. Choice of tone in writing is partly instinctive, just as it is in conversation. Depending on the workplace, you might choose a less formal tone for an interoffice memo than for a research paper or write a different letter to your coworkers than to a supervisor. The choice of words and phrasing of each piece of writing should be changed to suit each varying audience.

Always try to imagine an audience beyond your obvious readers, your instructors. Sometimes, as with a letter of application, your audience will be very specific. Depending on the job you are seeking, your letter would stress those aspects of your employment and educational background that are most likely to persuade a potential employer to interview you. You would write one letter to apply for a position as an assistant soccer coach, a different one for a job as the summer manager of a resort's dining facility. Thus, like a skillful politician, vary the tone and contents of your writing to suit your audience.

However, you need not be a politician to do this. Almost everyone has had some experience in analyzing a potential audience, then making appropriate choices based on that analysis. Audience regularly plays a role in any speaker's or writer's topic selection, diction level, and style of presentation. For example, the contents and tone of a student's letter to the Dean of Students would differ greatly from an angry letter to a younger sibling.

When deciding what points to include in an essay, it is crucial to take your readers' likely background knowledge about a subject into consideration. Most readers have probably not flown a combat mission over Bosnia, worked for the post office, received A.F.D.C. (Aid to Families with Dependent

Keep your audience in mind.

Children), or been a serious collector of insect specimens since the second grade. Take the last topic, for example: It is better to overexplain selected biological terms for those few, unlikely fellow experts among readers than to confuse the majority of them. Similarly, persons not on A.F.D.C. tend to have only a vague knowledge of the complex regulations, requirements, and limitations governing the lives of recipients of that program. Your case for a needed reform of the federal government's child-support system will not be persuasive if the essential background information is missing from your argument.

What do you want to tell your audience, and what is the best way to do it? To answer this question, ask yourself more questions: What is my *purpose* in writing this essay? If you do not know what your purpose is, how do you expect readers to know it? Do you hope to entertain, inform, or persuade your readers? Do you hope to touch them emotionally? Do you want to describe an experience, real or imagined? Do you want your readers to look at a topic from a new perspective? Deciding on a purpose and keeping an audience in mind at all times will greatly help you to structure any piece of writing.

Deciding on a Thesis

Like architects or engineers, writers use the tools of their craft to structure their creation. They go through many stages before they are satisfied with the final product. Generally, they have an overall concept about that final product in mind when they begin a new project. This concept gives an essential, overall sense of direction to their creative efforts. As the blueprints for the project evolve, however, the original concept may change or branch off in unexpected directions before it is completed.

Do not be surprised if the contents of a particular piece of writing do not turn out like you expected. Experienced writers often find that their best ideas emerge *while they are writing.* Thus, even if you draw up a careful plan ahead of time, your final product may look very different from your original idea.

In writing, that overall guiding idea, the point that you are making about a topic, is called a **thesis**. For example, Shirley Walker's essay cautioning her readers against teenage marriage contained this strongly worded thesis:

> Don't get married at an early age. Wait until you experience life and the world on the other side of your parents' front door.

A thesis is not the same as a topic. For example, the topic of David Merriman's essay is hang gliding (page 361). David's thesis is that hang gliding is the "ultimate tension releaser."

A thesis gives direction and unity to a piece of writing. If writing lacks a thesis, readers will not be able to follow what the writer is trying to get across to them. Do not be too concerned if you cannot write down the thesis when you begin your essay. Often the thesis evolves during the prewriting and early drafting stages. Moreover, as you develop an essay, your thesis may change several times. At some point, however, the writer must decide on a thesis to provide the needed focus, or slant on the topic, for the final version of any piece of writing.

Quite by coincidence, as I was writing this paragraph, a former student telephoned me for help getting started on a critical essay about the musical "The King and I" for a class on the visual arts. After a few questions it became apparent that she had no idea of what she wanted to say about the film version of the musical aside from a rather vague, "Well, I like it." It was evident that she needed to watch the video again, take some notes on her reactions, and decide on a tentative thesis for her analysis. I suggested that she imagine that she was telling a friend why he should see the film or was writing a review about it for the campus newspaper. She agreed that once she had an audience and purpose in mind, she would have an easier time deciding on a thesis for her analysis of the famous musical.

All effective writing has a thesis. The thesis may be *explicit*—stated clearly—or *implicit*—not stated, but definitely present—but it must be there. Your composition instructor may strongly urge, or even require, you to include an explicit thesis statement or statements early in an essay.

An explicit thesis is generally stated in the introductory section, usually—though not necessarily—in the first paragraph. Announcing the thesis early in an essay helps readers to anticipate the contents and may give them a sense of control over the subject.

Explicit thesis statements work well for certain kinds of writing. Scientific or technical writing tends to be easier to follow when the thesis is explicit from the start. An explicit thesis statement often provides an ideal opener for a response to an essay exam question.

> Have a plan in mind.

One way to come up with a quick thesis statement during an essay exam is to turn the exam question into a statement. For example:

Question: What are some of the characteristic behavior patterns of a person who suffers from manic depression?

Thesis Statement for the Response: The behavior patterns of a manic-depressive have several characteristic features.

Next, list the points you intend to cover. Making such a list and handing it in with your exam has several advantages. The list helps you to organize your response more effectively and to avoid rambling. You can determine at a glance whether you have left out important points or included nonessential data. The list should also suggest an order for presenting your points. Using this method for organizing your thoughts can help you answer the question more effectively and can improve your grades. Effective organization and clarity play a large role in the way instructors evaluate and grade an essay. If you run out of time, the instructor may take that into consideration, because your list demonstrates that you have a more thorough knowledge of the subject than your essay shows.

Exercise

Write a possible thesis statement for a response to the following question: "What were some of the social welfare policies implemented by the newly elected Labor government of Great Britain after World War II?"

Some kinds of writing, on the other hand, are better with an implicit, or unstated, thesis that does not appear until the conclusion. Narratives, for example, often hold the reader's attention better and are more effective if the outcome is not known from the start. Sometimes writers may choose to build up the evidence for an argument, withholding an explicit, or direct, statement of the overall thesis until the very end.

For more information about framing and locating a thesis, see the section on introductions later in this chapter (pages 34–39).

Choosing an Overall Organizational Scheme

There are three basic methods of organizing an essay:

- **Chronological** (by time sequence)
- **Topical** (by topic)
- **Spatial** (by location)

Chronological organization, or organizing by time sequence, is especially appropriate for a narrative or for explaining a process, such as how to change a tire. In some ways chronological organization is the easiest: The writer simply has to recall the order in which a series of events occurred or be familiar with the step-by-step stages in a process. Jotting down these stages or events in chronological order when prewriting provides a good scratch outline for getting started on a first draft.

Spatial organization, or arranging material by location, is often used for descriptive writing, as in Anne Moody's "The House" (page 137). Moody begins by portraying the overall setting of her childhood home, "up on the hill with Mr. Carter's big white house, overlooking the farms and the other shacks below." She then briefly describes the layout and furnishings inside her family's "rotten wood two room" shack. Finally, to get across her main point, Moody focuses a third of the paragraph on the bulging wallpaper tacked up by her parents with great care: "Momma and daddy did what they could" to make the plantation shack livable.

Topical organization, or ordering by topic, will probably be most appropriate for expository essays, the kind of writing frequently used in college or the workplace. Assigning an order for the topics in an expository essay involves any number of choices. The organization will depend on what kind of writing you are doing, so ask yourself questions about what your reader will look for. Is your potential employer more likely to be impressed with your job experience or with your educational achievements? Do you want to start out with your strongest argument in a persuasive essay or save it for last?

The three kinds of organization are not mutually exclusive. Short narratives can make a point more graphic and liven up a topically organized expository essay. Vivid descriptions of persons or places interrupting the chronology at appropriate junctures can greatly enhance a narrative. Observe how spatial and topical organization are combined in Stella Miranda's description of her initial meeting with her new daughter.

As I looked at my new baby it was as though I were staring at a creature from out of this galaxy. It was slimy and wrinkled. I immediately took the baby into my arms and started wiping the mucous-looking liquid from her face with a towel. She already had hair on the top of her head—I was able to see small curls. Her head was tiny and dented like a prune straight out of a box. I looked into her eyes and saw the most beautifully intense eyes I had ever seen. Her face would squinch as if she were puzzled by the situation. Then she glared at me like she knew who I was—and, naturally, began nursing. As she lay there content, I softly touched her nose, a little button on a wrinkled, olive-colored surface. Her body was as tiny as the dolls I played with as a child. I felt a huge tide of emotions come over me. I knew then that CIERA was the perfect name for this beautiful child—as lovely as the sky on a clear, sunny day.

Stella's narrative is told in the first person, the "I" point of view: We see events through her eyes. If the midwife had written an account of Ciera's birth, it might have been told from the third-person (an observer's) point of view and opened something like the following.

Stella looked at her new baby as if it were a creature from another galaxy. She immediately began wiping the mucous-looking liquid from the baby's wrinkled, olive-colored face.

Deciding on your point of view and your organizational method, or combination of methods, will greatly help you to compose well-organized, cohesive prose.

Writing Introductions and Conclusions

Like a snake, effective writing has a beginning, a middle and an end—in other words, an introduction, a body, and a conclusion. If these three sections flow smoothly into each other, readers may be no more aware of where one finishes and the next begins than they would be when examining a snake. It would be acutely evident, however, if one or another of the sections were missing.

Tips on Introductions

Because the introduction is so important, try very hard not to start out something like this:

It all began when I was ten years old and in the fifth grade.

It was a dark and stormy eve.

It happened on a cold, blustery March day.

This is an essay about the advantages of learning to play a musical instrument.

Instead, aim for something original; be bold and take a chance. The main thing an introduction should do is grab the reader's attention:

> *When heavy metal collided with the eighties, it made a booming, window-rattling racket. Chunks of ceiling plaster fell to the floor, neighbors complained, and the family pet disappeared for days. Nobody was quite ready for it when heavy metal hit the eighties music scene.*
>
> Jason DeVerney

Contrast Jason's introduction with the last one above: "This is an essay about the advantages of learning to play a musical instrument." A typical thesis statement introduction, such openers are as enticing to the reader as cold oatmeal. Like most students, you undoubtedly can compose more effective introductions than a type unfortunately frequenting the pages of textbooks and scholarly journals:

> *The first section of this essay includes a necessary, somewhat detailed, consideration of the significant differences in the symptoms which patients experience during the first twenty-four hours after the initial onslaught of either malaria or cholera.*

Get the reader involved from the start.

In contrast to such an uninspiring statement, an effective introduction arouses readers' interest, as well as setting the scene for the body of the essay. The following powerful opener by Ricky Davis promises personal insights on an issue of growing concern in the United States.

> *"Bang!" We all hit the ground when the gun blasted. We all knew the routine. At the park where I grew up incidents like this happened almost daily and were considered no big deal. Basketball sparked a lot of emotions and often ended in a fight and every once in a while gunfire. Someone looking from the outside would think it was stupid or crazy to play ball in an atmosphere like that. What people don't understand is that when you grow up around stuff like that it's not like you get used to it, you just learn to accept it as a part of life. This particular day when the shooting stopped everyone didn't get back up. My big brother was still lying on the ground.*

Suppose Ricky had opened with, or even included, a thesis statement, such as, "In this essay I will describe the time my older brother got shot at a park and show the influence that event and my brother had on my life." Which of the two options makes the reader eager to read on? Enough said!

An introduction that summarizes the contents of your essay in advance can be dull, as well as involving a certain risk on the part of the writer. You want to tantalize your readers to continue, not give away so much that they will wonder why they should finish reading your piece.

As with everything you write, the contents of an introduction are determined by the purpose and nature of a piece of writing. An introduction should never promise something that the writer does not deliver or be too narrow to cover the contents of what follows. If your topic expands or changes as you write, you may have to broaden or narrow your introduction or change it completely.

Remember that an introduction can always be altered and improved at any stage during the writing process. It is perfectly acceptable to scribble off a rather ordinary introduction, just to get started, rather than staring at a blank piece of paper, trying to compose the perfect introduction. Get *something* written down. Write a tentative introduction or begin with the body of the essay. Many writers compose their introductions after a piece is finished. If you are still unsatisfied with the final product, ask the members of your peer reviewing group or other readers for suggestions for revising your opening section. Ask them how you could make your introduction more enticing, and where it may need clarification. Find what works for you, and do not be surprised if what works best for composing an introduction and getting started on one essay does not work well another time.

Some introductions have a very specific purpose, such as the first paragraph of most business letters. For example, the first paragraph of a letter of application usually states exactly what position the writer is applying for and briefly outlines why the applicant is well qualified for that position. As with any introduction, the purpose is to catch the reader's—in the case the potential employer's—attention so that she or he will want to read the rest of the letter. Letting employers know that you think highly of their enterprise can only put them in a more receptive mood as they continue your letter.

The samples of students' writings below demonstrate some of the characteristics of an effective introduction. Consider the opening paragraph of Lynne Crane's application for a summer job in a resort area of Wisconsin.

Mrs. Penny Scheller, Owner
Tannenbaum
215 Olde Pine Road
Sister Bay, WI 54591

> Dear Mrs. Scheller:
>
> Please consider me for the position of summer manager at your Christmas shop Tannenbaum. I enjoy visiting your shop whenever I am in Door County. Your employees are helpful and kind, your Christmas merchandise is uniquely different. When I saw your ad in the Door County Advocate, I knew I had to apply quickly. I believe that I have the right qualifications for the position you are offering. In my recent jobs I have had considerable experience working with people, taking inventory, handling cash, and advertising retail merchandise.

Sometimes an introduction contains a tightly worded thesis statement right up front, telling the reader what to expect without being dull, wordy, or giving too much away. Sean Vetternick begins his essay "Take It from an Ex-Kid" (page 376) with just such an explicit thesis statement.

> TV commercials which are broadcast during children's shows often take advantage of the gullibility of their audience.

Amy Brinkman's essay, "To Be or Not to Be . . . Thin" (page 378), on the other hand, gets into its thesis more slowly as she sets the scene with observations about her own and others' reactions to the size and shape of their bodies.

> If only it were different—somehow better—then life would also be better. I can't count how many times I have heard someone (including myself) say that is how they felt about their body. Exactly how it would be better is unimportant; it just would be, that's all.
>
> When I take a trip down memory lane and come across photos of myself in a swimsuit, the most vivid memories are those of feeling awkward. There aren't enough curves here and too many there; my waist is too high and too large; my eyes are too small and of course I would like to take off some weight. I'm not fat but I'm never the size I want to be.
>
> Sound familiar? It should. Primarily because of magazines, television advertisements, and certainly the movie industry, more women are striving for the overall perfect body—maybe at the risk of their own health.

Exercise

In what paragraph does Amy Brinkman's thesis first appear? What is that thesis? Restate her thesis in your own words in your journal.

You are probably familiar with the public speaker who opens a speech with a short story, or **anecdote**. Like public speakers, writers frequently begin an essay with an anecdote that catches their readers' attention and is related to the thesis.

Amy Brinkman might have begun her essay on the American obsession with dieting with an introduction like the following.

> *Last summer I was having a reunion lunch with three of my friends from high school, none of whom I had seen for ten years. We were enjoying croissants stuffed with lobster salad and reminiscing about our senior year when Mary Beth suddenly sighed, "Ah, how thin I was then. If only I could still squeeze into a size 6. All this blubber around my . . ."*
>
> *"You," groaned Ruth. "Look at me! I've put on ten pounds in four years, and no matter what diet plan or support group I try, I cannot keep off those extra pounds."*
>
> *Listening to Mary Beth and Ruth, neither of whom were the least bit overweight, provoked some serious thought about the message being endlessly hammered at American women by the media.*

This last sentence would have served as a kind of bridge, a **transition**, from the anecdote, or short narrative, to the body of the essay.

Perhaps the biggest pitfall to avoid is a long, windy, rambling introduction. For instance, if you are writing a narrative, get to the interesting or exciting part *quickly*. Inexperienced writers often include so much extraneous background material that the reader cannot figure out where it is all leading—and often stops trying to find out. If you are writing about a terrifying experience on a trip, it does not really matter how much trouble you had finding a helpful travel agent; who finally sold you the ticket; how it got lost in the mail; what you packed in your bag; what last minute purchases you had to make; who gave you a ride to the airport; how crowded the airport was that day . . . .

Exercise

How to improve a slow-start introduction. Read through this introduction quickly, then jot down at least three adjectives (descriptive words, such as *amusing* or *concise*) that you think best describe it. Then go back and analyze how it might be improved. (Note: the techniques used in this exercise can be employed to cut wordiness in all your writing.)

Chapter Two Shaping the Contents **39**

1. Draw a **line** through sentences that do not really add anything to the story.
2. Put **brackets** around sections that are too repetitive.
3. Look for sentences and ideas that would read more smoothly and be more effective if they were combined.
4. Now **rewrite** the introduction, combining ideas and leaving out sections that are repetitive or do not add anything of importance to the narrative.

The phone rang. I got out of my chair and went into the other room to answer it. It was my mother. From the way her voice sounded I knew something was wrong *and discussed.* [She sounded very tense.] "It's your grandmother. A nurse just called from Grandview Hospital. ~~They took your grandmother there in an ambulance an hour ago.~~ Meet me there in a few minutes." As I was driving to Grandview Hospital I kept imagining the worst. [I kept imagining all kinds of terrible things that could have happened to my grandmother.] When I got to the hospital I parked in the emergency room parking lot. ~~I went into the emergency room lobby~~ and saw my mother. ~~She was sitting in a chair near a reception desk.~~ She looked worried and was talking to a nurse who was standing next to her. The nurse seemed worried. Just then a young doctor walked up to them. ~~He was wearing a wrinkled white gown~~ and had a grave expression on his face. I overheard the doctor say, "Your mother has respiratory failure. You may go in and see her briefly. Follow me." My mother followed the doctor ~~through a door at the end of the hall~~. They had not even noticed me. I felt alone and worried, as well as somewhat miffed for being left out. Hadn't she asked me to meet her there?

A Word about Conclusions

A good writer will not leave the reader hanging, wondering about the final outcome of an essay or feeling mystified about what it all meant. Effective conclusions bring **closure** to a piece of writing. The reader should not have to ponder: How did all this end? What did this mean? What was the writer's purpose?

Conclusions provide the writer with an opportunity to sum up, to put an essay into a long-range perspective, to reflect on the significance of the topic, or to briefly restate an argument. It is important, however, not to confuse the reader by bringing up new information in the conclusion. Just as an introduction should not promise to discuss something that

> The reader does not deserve to be left hanging.

you do not deliver, so a conclusion should not allude to material not included in the body of the essay. If the material is important to the topic, it belongs in the body of an essay where it can be adequately developed; otherwise it is better left out.

The conclusions to the student essays in this text vary considerably, both in purpose and effectiveness. Consider two of the best of them.

Laura Tetzlaff O'Mara's vivid portrayal of her Gammy Grace (page 298) ends with a characteristic quote: "Listen Laura, you are ~~one hell of~~ a girl, I know you are. So get off your duff and get going!" Laura then played off of that quote to sum up her grandmother's importance in her life, thus adding long-range perspective to the essay: "Without her, I'd be on my duff more often than not."

Dan Bartz winds up his "Space Sweepstakes" (page 276) with something rarely achieved—a truly funny conclusion: "I thought to myself, what am I going to do with the bat? I knew exactly what to do: beat my head in with it." (To make any sense out of that conclusion, you will need to read the rest of Dan's amusing essay.)

As is evident from the sample student essays in this text, most conclusions are more prosaic or have a more serious purpose than Dan Bartz's. Some of these conclusions simply restate the thesis and perhaps summarize some of the major arguments of the essay. It is best, however, not to begin a conclusion with one of the stock phrases, such as "to sum up" or "in conclusion," which come readily to mind. Also avoid tedious statements, such as "In this essay I have described the major symptoms of manic-depression and suggested ways for early detection of those symptoms."

Writers who begin an essay with an anecdote or a short narrative may wish to frame the essay by referring to that opening anecdote in the conclusion. In our case we can hark back to the snake at the head of this section, reminding our readers that all three parts—beginning, middle, and end—of a snake, or an essay, are equally essential to the whole.

Richard Marius has a slightly different take on the snake metaphor in his 1995 *A Short Guide to Writing about History:* "An essay is somewhat like a snake biting its tail: The end always comes back to the beginning" (27–28). In other words, the first and last paragraphs, or sections, ought to reflect some of the same ideas and perhaps even the same phraseology.

A reading of those paragraphs alone should give readers a fairly good idea of what comes between them. However, the conclusion ought to be more than a mechanical, dully worded return to the opener. It is as boring to say "I have written about this and that in this essay" as it is to begin with "In this essay I intend to discuss this and that." Grab your readers' attention with more imaginative introductions; leave them with something interesting to ponder.

Writing a Title

Students sometimes ask if they should title their essays, and we almost always answer in the affirmative. Titles can catch the reader's eye—"The Birth of Scarlett"; touch their emotions—"Don't Let Me Die"; or provide information about the contents—"The Writing Process."

As these examples suggest, a good title is short (roughly three to five words) and need not be a complete sentence. It should not be the same as the topic sentence of an essay, because that sentence is almost certain to be too lengthy, making a rather tedious title. Nor should a title be too bland or general, such as "Car Accident," the title given to the first draft of the narrative essay in Chapter One.

If you cannot think of a catchy title, do not be worried about it. A title that simply helps the reader predict the contents of an essay is very appropriate and performs a useful function. If a title comes naturally as you begin an essay, jot it down. You can always change it later anyway. Many titles do not suggest themselves until after an essay is completed. If several title options occur to you, list them. Then let them sit for a day or so before you make a final selection.

While reviewing an essay's contents, watch for that original phrase that might make a great title. Sean Vetternick did exactly that when he came up with "Take It from an Ex-Kid" to entitle his essay criticizing TV commercials aimed at children. Amy Brinkman effectively opted for a play on the opening line of Hamlet's famous soliloquy with her "To Be or Not to Be . . . Thin." If just the right title does not come to mind, ask your peer group reviewers or other readers for title suggestions. If you have a list of several titles, ask your peer reviewers which one they think is the most effective.

However, if you still have not found a catchy title, just give the essay a title that suggests the contents and is not too general or dry. Rather than naming an essay "The Birth of My Child," call it "Rebecca's Arrival." Because few writers can always think up a brilliant title, most of the student essays in this text have titles that simply do the job, such as "My

Gammy Grace"—much more personal and effective than the generic "My Grandmother"—or "France and Euro Disneyland." While not nearly as imaginative as the tongue-twister "The Backpack That Packed a Punch," such titles adequately predict the contents of the essays they head.

Shaping the Body of the Essay

Briefly stated, the *body* is the meat of an essay, the part between the introduction and the conclusion. Most of what follows in this chapter—or is contained in this text, for that matter—is devoted to the body of an essay.

Organization and Coherence: Binding the Parts Together

Effective organization is one of the hardest things to achieve in writing. All of the elements in any piece of writing from the smallest unit, the paragraph, to the entire piece should focus on the topic. That focus gives the piece **unity.** Closely allied to unity is **coherence,** arranging the elements so that the relationships between them are clear.

Connections between ideas that seem apparent to the writer are often lost on the reader. The writer's train of thought may be unclear because clear links between ideas are missing. These gaps or unclear connections can be remedied in part by using a wide range of transitional devices.

Clear, well-organized writing is so easy to follow that the reader is often unaware of all of the devices linking ideas together. Consciously or unconsciously, however, effective writers rely on many kinds of transitional signals, or cues, to link sentences and paragraphs into cohesive prose.

Making Paragraphs Work for You. Look at your draft, then ask yourself some questions:

- Do you realize that your essay is one long paragraph?
- Is this a new topic?
- Should you start a new paragraph here?
- What's the topic of this paragraph?
- Is this material off that topic?
- Could you combine some of these short paragraphs?

Most writers find it fairly simple to divide their writing into a series of paragraphs. However, the above questions point up some of the difficulties that do occur. Many of these are easily remedied once writers become aware of them.

Hints on Paragraphs. Writers place related ideas together to form **paragraphs.** While a shift in topic should be marked by a new paragraph, paragraphs often simply provide a welcome breather, a chance for the reader to pause before reading about another aspect of the same topic. Essays composed solely of one, or a few, very long paragraphs do not give readers enough opportunities to catch their breath. Too many short, one to three sentence paragraphs call for too many pauses. Newspapers, which are deliberately designed with narrow columns and short paragraphs to facilitate quick skimming, should not be a model for your paragraph divisions. On the other hand, used sparingly, the occasional short paragraph can be effective.

There are no exact rules for writing a good paragraph other than the basic requirement that all of its sentences be clearly focused on a topic that gives the paragraph coherence. As in an essay, the topic or thesis of a paragraph may be explicit—stated—or implicit—not stated. But it must be there to give unity to the paragraph and to enable the reader to follow the writer's train of thought. The sentences in a paragraph must be more than a list of poorly linked ideas about a topic. Observe how the sentences in this paragraph flow logically from one to another, thus forming a coherent whole:

> Katmandu is almost too perfect: not too small, not too big, full of cheap hotels, restaurants, bookstores. Hinduism, Buddhism, capitalism, and tourism all meet at the foot of the Himalayas. <u>The town doesn't seem real; but then it is real.</u> Katmandu is dirty and crowded. Lots of people find nothing better to do than hustle tourists. Children have learned to beg. Some poor guy outside my window has a horrible wheezing cough, and a cat which sounds too big to be anybody's pet (a Himalayan mountain lion?) is yowling in the street. Real life keeps poking in around the edges of the postcard.
>
> *Jon Healy*

Exercise

1. What is the topic of the above paragraph? *Katmandu*

2. Does the paragraph have a topic sentence or sentences? Underline them.

3. Are there any sentences that do not fit that topic? If so, put square brackets around those sentences.

4. What is the purpose of the last line of the paragraph? *underlies topic — seems like a postcard, but it's real*

5. What sentence in the paragraph indicates a *transition*, a kind of bridge or cuing device, which leads from one aspect of the topic to another? Mark a "T" (for transition) in the margin next to that sentence.

Effective paragraphs center on one topic and have clear transitions between sentences. Because their sentences flow logically from one to another, they are easy to read aloud. In contrast, poorly organized paragraphs with weak links between ideas result in a choppy, start-stop type of reading with pauses after almost every sentence. Try reading the following paragraph aloud—slowly and with appropriate expression—to hear the difference.

> *I am writing you from Katmandu. Nepal borders India. I have wanted to visit Katmandu ever since I read about it in the* National Geographic. *Katmandu is the largest city in Nepal. Ghurkas are one of the dominant peoples in Nepal. Multi-storied brick-tile dwellings overhang the narrow streets of the capital of Nepal. The city also has an airport. Many tourists spend a brief sojourn there en route to a trek in the Himalayas, but Katmandu itself is worth an extensive stay. My biology teacher showed slides about Katmandu which increased my desire to see the city. It is about 4,000 miles above sea level. Perhaps the world's most skilled mountaineers, Ghurkas frequently lead climbing expeditions into the Himalayas.*

Exercise

Analyze the above paragraph, noting places where it jumps from one idea to another without appropriate transitions. Mark a "T" where a better **connective,** a transitional bridge between ideas, is needed. As you analyze, also keep the questions at the head of this section in mind. Does the paragraph focus on one topic? Mark "Off Topic" for sentences that do not really add anything and might be better left out of this poorly unified, disorganized paragraph. Then rewrite the paragraph in your journal, rearranging the sentences, deleting some of them, and adding the necessary transitions to provide logical connections between the ideas.

Good paragraphs are hard to compose because the writer has to come up with consecutive ideas and arrange them in sentences that "follow each other like elephants holding tails," to quote the wonderful analogy of author Robert Pinckert. However, unless disciplined to write logically, Pinckert stresses, the mind is like a beehive full of good ideas, but it does not naturally organize them into consecutive thoughts. A writer may have dozens of poorly related ideas about a topic, such as the advantages of working abroad for a year, far too many ideas for an essay, much less a paragraph.

Making a cluster diagram or brainstorming to get some of those ideas down on paper is a good initial step. You may prefer to start right off with a discovery draft. At some point, however, those thoughts must be formulated into a series of clear, cohesive paragraphs. One way to organize your buzz of ideas and make them flow logically is to pause regularly, read over what you have written, and ask yourself some questions: What do I want to say next about this topic? What idea does my last sentence suggest? Think of each sentence as something on which to build. For a time you may need to ask questions after almost every sentence to see where your train of thought leads you next. Constructing paragraphs by asking yourself questions may seem like an unnatural, difficult process at first, but it becomes easier with practice. Referring regularly to a cluster diagram or scratch outline composed during the prewriting stage can also help you to write well-organized paragraphs.

Using Transitional Devices to Cue the Reader

Transitions are signposts, signals, or cues inserted along the way that enable readers to follow the writer's train of thought. Sometimes transitions are announcements that in effect provide more subtle phrasing than direct statements like the following:

> This essay will now head in a somewhat new direction, by looking at a different, but closely related, topic.

> In the next section I am going to repeat that last point once again just to be certain that you understand me.

Effective writers use transitional devices to indicate a shift in contents, as well as to add coherence by showing the logical connections between sentences, paragraphs, or longer sections of a piece of writing. A transitional device may be a word, a phrase, a sentence, or one or more paragraphs. Transitional devices are essential components of clear prose; readers are lost without them. Compare the two following introductory paragraphs, which were written by one of our former students.

One of Sherry Klawitter's early versions of an introduction to an essay about Milwaukee's lakefront lacked effective transitions:

> *No other place has warmed so many hearts, been so struck by violence, or been so peaceful at the same time. Milwaukee's lakefront is the place where hundreds first found love. Its secluded areas hide strangers that lurk in the dark, waiting for unsuspecting victims. Its peaceful natural gives many weary thinkers a place to relax and watch the waves.*

Note that in the above paragraph Sherry changed from one topic to another without first cuing the reader about the shifts. By adding transitions, Sherry greatly strengthened her paragraph. Her transitional phrases are in **boldface** in the revised paragraph below:

> *Perhaps no other place has warmed so many hearts, been so struck by violence, or been so peaceful all at the same time. Milwaukee's lakefront is the place where hundreds have first found love.* **Unfortunately,** *its secluded areas* **occasionally** *hide strangers who lurk in the dark, waiting for unsuspecting victims.* **But most of the time** *its peaceful nature gives many weary thinkers a place to relax and watch the waves.*

Types of Effective Transitions

Try to become more aware of the many kinds of transitions used to indicate topic shifts and show connections to help readers follow the train of thought. Then consciously work to improve the transitions in your own writing.

See "Two Jazz Trumpet Players" (page 333) for an example of an essay with clear transitions linking a series of well-organized paragraphs, each of which has a clear thesis or topic. Note how smoothly the ideas in these paragraphs flow from one to another, in part because of the effective transitions.

Write the topic of each of the six paragraphs that make up the body of "Two Jazz Trumpet Players" in the margin next to the appropriate paragraph. Then reread the essay, paying particular attention to the variety and location of its transitions. To serve as models for your writing, some of those transitions are highlighted below.

Announcing the Next Topic. The last sentence of paragraph 2, which discusses Dizzy Gillespie's background, predicts the topic to follow:

> The trip brought Dizzy to the city where there was an abundance of young musicians, *one of whom was a kid from the Midwest named Miles Davis.*

Referring to the Topic Just Covered. The first sentence of paragraph 4 refers to the topic of paragraph 3 (the trumpeters' backgrounds), then announces the next topic (the trumpeters' appearances):

As there are contrasts between Dizzy's and Miles' backgrounds, **so are there contrasts in their appearances.**

Students often ask whether a transition marking a new topic belongs at the end of a paragraph on the old topic or at the beginning of the paragraph about a new topic. As the above examples show, either place may work, depending on the situation.

Repeating Key Words or Phrases and Finding Word Substitutes. Repetition of key words or phrases and using substitute words aids coherence by providing essential links between sentences and paragraphs. Tiresome repetition of the same words can be avoided by using pronouns or synonyms—other words that have the same meaning, such as using "sea" for "ocean." Examples of those kinds of transitions in the following descriptive paragraphs written by student Mequitta Morgan are boldfaced to point out examples of those kinds of transitions:

> *Many people don't realize how precious Lake Michigan is with its different shades of* **blue.** *The closer you are the* **bluer** *the water; the farther you look ahead the lighter the* **shades** *become. The lake looks like it* **never ends.** *My eye searches for a* **stopping point,** *but I don't see one.*
>
> **Lake Michigan** *is my favorite place to visit because it gets my mind to working. The* **lake** *for me is like a child's getaway from life. Going* **there** *is also like visiting an old wise* **man,** *laying every question I have before* **him.** *Sometimes I wish I were a* **bird** *so I could just soar through the sky and* **look down** *upon the lake.* **Birds** *have to be the most grateful creatures to* **view** *the world the way they do. Going to the* **lake** *really makes me appreciate life.*

Special Transition Words and Phrases

While it is preferable to rely on the explicit and implicit relationships between ideas to keep your sentences and paragraphs flowing logically, there are a number of special **transition words and phrases** that can be very useful, provided that they are not overused. Too many such transitions make writing wooden and monotonous, as is evident from the following example.

> *Transition words such as* **moreover, nonetheless, instead,** *or* **but,** *each of which indicates a specific relationship between ideas, provide your reader with useful bridges for following your thought.* **However,** *it is not advisable to insert such a bridge between every*

Meanwhile, back at the ranch . . .

sentence. **On the other hand,** *a paragraph with no transition words may lack coherence.* **Thus** *writers had best arrive at a happy medium,* **neither** *striving to avoid these words at all costs,* nor *prefacing each new example with* **for instance,** *each contrasting idea with* **however. In addition,** *the writer must be aware that many of these transition words denote a very precise logical relationship between the ideas they are connecting.* **In other words,** *they must be chosen carefully and used sparingly.* **Furthermore,** *because these transition words often introduce or interrupt sentences, they usually need to be followed by or set off with commas.* **Conversely,** *when used with care, transition words can enhance writing.* **However,** *too many of them will soon weary your readers.*

If not overdone, a judicious scattering of carefully selected transition words and phrases can greatly improve coherence by pointing up logical relationships and regularly reminding readers where a piece of writing has been or where it is headed. In fact, such signals along the path are so essential to readers that a large array of special *transitional signal words and phrases* has evolved.

The lists that follow contain only a representative sampling; many more transitional words and phrases will probably come to mind as you write. Observe that the categories of lists fit the three basic ways of organizing a piece of writing—chronological, spatial, and topical.

Time Transitions

meanwhile
next
earlier
later; in those days
last summer
two months later
then
afterward
since
previously

Spatial Transitions

one block north
nearby
above
to the left
under
adjacent to

in the distance
far away
in front of
behind
across
three miles farther

Logical Relationships

To indicate an opposing point or a contrast:

but
however
yet
on the other hand
on the contrary
conversely
still
nevertheless

To add more of the same:

furthermore
in addition
besides
as well as
in other words
for example
similarly
likewise
finally

To indicate a causal result or relationship:

hence
because
thus
therefore
consequently

The boldfaced examples in the following paragraphs demonstrate how former students have used various transitions to add coherence to their essays.

To help readers follow his argument Andy Blint included both logic and time transitions.

> *In the last five to seven years the media have increased their coverage of people-related controversies and irrelevant issues.* **One major example of this** *occurred in 1987 with the nomination of Douglas Ginsburg to the Supreme Court.* **After** *the media revealed that Ginsburg had smoked marijuana in college, his chance went from slim to none for getting appointed to the vacant seat. His reputation, life, and dignity were shattered by the repeated coverage of this story.* **Because** *Ginsburg had done what probably three-fourths of the college population did in the '60s, he lost the chance to be on the Supreme Court.* **Hence,** *the media discouraged anyone with a secret in his or her past from running for public office for the fear of losing face at the hands of the media vultures.* **Ever since** *the Ginsburg media lynching of 1987, it has become more acceptable to report on these types of stories.*

Note how time transitions help readers to follow the chronology of Eric Williams' narrative.

> *It* **started when** *I left high school. I was 16 and didn't have any skills that would get me a decent job. So* **when** *the carnival came I saw a chance to get out, a chance to see the country and really be on my own.*
>
> *I took a job on The Screaming Eagle. It was a roller coaster owned by a man named Billy T. I really admired Billy, for he too left home* **when he was 16** *and worked for the carnival. He saved up his money, bought his own ride, and* **by the time** *he was 23 he had made his first million. It wasn't until* **later** *that I found out that he made his money through corruption and deceit.*
>
> **After three months** *of hard work I made my way up to assistant foreman. With the extra money came extra responsibility. I was* **now** *in charge of inspecting the ride* **each morning** *and making sure the proper forms were filled out. On the* **first morning** *of my new duty I found so many things wrong that I didn't think it would be possible to open the ride* **that day.** *I found brakes almost completely rusted through, safety pins and chains that were never installed, seat belts that were so worn and tattered that I could pull them out with my bare hands.*

Exercise

Spatial transitions, such as those italicized in the first part of the paragraph below, orient readers to the objects in a scene. Underline the rest of the spatial transitions in Evelyn Cornelius' description of "The Spider Room" in her grandmother's basement.

We then entered the place where all of our nightmares came from, a huge rectangular room *at the far end* of the basement. It was dimly lit by the bare, low wattage bulb that stuck out of the fixture *in the middle* of the ceiling. The paint had started peeling from the corners near the ceiling. Two good sized windows covered with old, drab flower print curtains hung high on the north and east walls. There were drip mark stains on the walls near the windows, evidence that water often leaked into the damp basement room. Matching the rest of the room, the floor was cold, bare, and concrete; we didn't dare go down into the basement without slippers. Boxes were stacked and staggered all about, leaving many places for an evil creature to hide. But the single thing that scared us more than anything were the countless long stringy floating cobwebs. They were everywhere. Spider webs covered the boxes, blanketed the curtains, and consumed the corners of the room. In each one, to our horror, lay a large child-eating spider. The inhabitant of each web was more gruesome and horrible than the one before it.

Now underline the time transition words that help readers follow the sequence of events in Andy Blint's vivid description of a fateful explosion at a fireworks factory.

Next, as could be expected, within a minute or so after the second blast, the remainder of the 500-600 firework shells still in the building where the explosion had occurred started to go off. It sounded like a continuous drum roll of thunder. I hoped that the other manufacturing buildings, each of which contained large amounts of explosives, would not catch fire. Meanwhile the explosions intensified, and pieces of burning fireworks and fragments of building started to rain down on us. We ran to the employee parking lot which was about 750 feet away from the danger. I turned to watch the remains of the building being thrown effortlessly every which way by the repeated blasts. Finally after about two-and-a-half minutes the blasts subsided. The once strong steel building, said to be state-of-the-art design safety-wise, was totally shredded and melted to the ground. A small but potentially dangerous fire remained. Then it hit me. Two girls had not made it out of the obliterated building.

While transitional devices are great aids to achieving *coherence* in a piece of writing, grammar and wording also play an important role. When the grammar is logical, correct, and consistent, it is much easier for the reader to follow the writer's train of thought.

Chapter Three

Using Correct Grammar and Usage to Aid Coherence

To become a better writer, it will be helpful for you to learn the grammar and syntax—word order—of the written languages of the university, newspapers, and the business and professional worlds. Most of you are studying in the hopes of having a career in one of those worlds; a better command of formal English grammar can only foster your progress toward, and in, that career.

You probably know more about English grammar and syntax than any book or writing course can teach you. This section on grammar reviews much of what you already know and presents material designed to build on that knowledge. Using correct grammar and syntax is not, however, an aim in itself. As the title of this chapter suggests, correct grammar enhances coherence, thus helping writers to communicate more effectively with their readers. Conversely, frequent mistakes, such as choosing the nonstandard form of a pronoun or verb, impede coherence and hinder communication. Furthermore, frequent mistakes put off readers. If the flyer advertising a new magazine contained numerous grammar mistakes and misspelled words, would you be likely to subscribe to that magazine?

Choosing the Right Pronoun

Pronouns—words like *us, they,* or *this* that stand in for nouns or noun phrases—help writers avoid repeating the same nouns over and over. Used correctly, pronouns aid coherence; used incorrectly, pronouns impair coherence and impede understanding. Because a pronoun takes its meaning from the word, or words, it refers to, it must always be clear exactly what that word, or words, is. The following review of pronoun usage, much of which may be familiar, can help you to avoid the most common pronoun errors.

Learn to recognize pronouns readily so that you can check whether you are using them correctly. The pronouns in the following passage are in boldface.

> When **I** first saw **my** Grandma, **I** almost burst into tears. Two big oxygen tanks with tubes that led to **her** nose were keeping **her** alive. **Her** once full head of blond hair was reduced to a few strands. Radiation treatments for lung cancer had made **her** very weak and caused **her** hair to fall out. **She** was very frail looking, due to the disease and a diet of water and IV feedings.
>
> Tim McClone

THE FAR SIDE By GARY LARSON

"So, then . . . Would that be 'us the people' or 'we the people?'"

53

Types of Pronouns

As Tim's paragraph shows, pronouns have several functions.

Personal pronouns, such as *she, he, her, his, they, them,* and so on, stand in for or replace nouns.

She was very frail looking.

Radiation treatments for lung cancer had made *her* very weak.

Possessive pronoun adjectives, such as *my, her, his, their,* and so on, modify, or describe, nouns.

my Grandma
her hair
her family

Exercise

Underline the personal and possessive pronouns in the next part of Tim's description of his dying grandmother.

I sat with her for a long time and she seemed to be sleeping, but every so often she would open her eyes and look at me and ask, "Who are you?" I understood what was happening, but it was hard for me to accept. This person, a former ballet dancer, always full of energy and "on her toes," could not even recognize her own family. I thought of her many years as a heavy smoker and remembered that I had always tried to get her to quit. She would say something like "You are right" or "Who cares?" and go right on smoking. I felt guilty because maybe I should have pressured her more.

Tim's passage would have been boring and repetitious, and even sounded a little silly, without frequent pronouns. Suppose that it had started out like this:

I sat with Grandma for a long time and Grandma appeared to be sleeping, but every so often Grandma would open Grandma's eyes and look at me and ask, "Who are you?"

Tim's passage demonstrates how a writer can use pronouns to refer to the **first, second,** or **third person.**

First person: *I* sat with Grandma. (Tim means himself—I. He is a *participant* in the action.)

Second person: "*You* are right." (His Grandma addresses a second party—*you*.)

Third person: I sat with *her* for a long time and *she* seemed to be sleeping. (Tim writes about a third party—*her* and *she*. He is an observer.)

These pronoun examples—*I, you, her,* and *she*—are all *singular,* meaning that they refer to one person. To write that he and another person had both been sitting with their grandmother, Tim could have used the **first person plural pronouns** *we* and *us.*

subject verb
We sat with our grandmother for a long time.

                subject   verb object
Much of the time she hardly noticed *us.*

Personal pronouns can be classified by person—first, second, or third. Pronouns can also be classified by the way they are used in sentences. For instance, the pronoun *we* in the above example is the first person plural **subject** of the first sentence, while the pronoun *us* is the first person plural **object** of the verb *noticed* in the second sentence.

Tim's version has a first person singular subject:

I sat with her for a long time.

The following is an example of a sentence with a first person singular object:

Much of the time Grandma hardly noticed *me.*

Exercise

Find the pronoun subject of the following sentences and label it first, second or third person, as in the model.

1. *She* was very frail looking.   *third person* (person written about)
2. I almost burst into tears.
3. She seemed to be sleeping.
4. You are right to be worried.

5. We had difficulty accepting her suffering.
6. They all remembered her lively manner.

Tim's passage also contains several uses of **object**, or **nonsubject, pronouns**. The following are two third-person examples.

The radiation treatments had made *her* very weak.

I sat with *her* for a long time.

Exercise

Underline the rest of the object (nonsubject) pronouns in the following passage. The first two are already underlined.

Every so often Grandma spoke to <u>us</u>, but her questions indicated that she did not recognize <u>me</u>. As I looked at her, memories of our many good times together brought her even closer to me. Grandma's energy and love of life had been an inspiration to all of us. But now her lungs had been destroyed by the cigarettes Grandma had smoked so many years. I hated cigarettes that day and I still hate them.

Exercise

Underline the nonsubject personal pronouns in the following sentences and label the person of that pronoun, as in the model.

1. Her suffering was hard for <u>me</u> to accept.   first person; Tim
2. Maybe I should have pressured her more.
3. Once in a while she would look at us.
4. Many family members urged her to stop smoking.
5. Unfortunately she had not listened to them.
6. Grandmother simply ignored you and kept on smoking.

Use the following chart as a guide to pronoun usage:

Person in Pronouns

First person = the writer or speaker
Second person = the person spoken or written to
Third person = the person spoken or written about

  (first) (second)   (third)
Have I told you about them?

Subject Pronouns — Subjective

	Singular	Plural
First person	I	we
Second person	you	you
Third person	he, she, it	they

Today *we* went to the movies, but *I* did not like the film.

He claimed that *you* and Harry do not like most movies.

She and *I* do not rent videos as often as *they* do.

Object (Nonsubject) Pronouns — Objective

	Singular	Plural
First person	me	us
Second person	you	you
Third person	him, her, it	them

Next time invite *me* to go to the play with *you*.

Why didn't Tony ask *us* to go to the play with *him*?

Tony telephoned Antoinette and *her* before ordering tickets.

Please order tickets for mother and *me*.

Possessive Pronouns and Possessive Adjectives

	Singular Pronoun	Singular Adjective	Plural Pronoun	Plural Adjective
First person	mine	my	ours	our
Second person	yours	your	yours	your
Third person	his, hers	his, her, its	theirs	their

Those tickets are not *mine,* so they must be *yours.* (possessive pronouns)

They are not *ours;* maybe those tickets are *his.* (possessive pronouns)

Theirs were the best seats in the theater. (possessive pronoun)

Our math teacher gets angry at *his* students who arrive late. (possessive adjectives)

My friend is usually late for all of *her* lectures. (possessive adjectives)

Their college is slow at getting out *its* grade reports. (possessive adjectives)

Did *your* semester grades arrive yet? (possessive adjective)

Tip: Do not add apostrophes to possessive pronouns that end is *s*, such as *theirs, hers, yours,* and *its*. Those words are already in the possessive form without an apostrophe.

Furthermore, *it's,* a contraction of *it is,* has a different meaning than the possessive pronoun *its*. The following three pronoun/contraction pairs are often confused:

your	you're
their	they're
whose	who's

You're late for *your* appointment.

Choosing the Right Form of Personal Pronouns

Correct Use of Personal Subject Pronouns. The following are some examples to guide you in avoiding problems with pronouns in plural subjects.

Incorrect: Horatio and *me* are going to the movies.
Correct: Horatio and *I* are going to the movies.

Incorrect: *Me* and my brother are going to the movies.
Correct: My brother and *I* are going to the movies.

Incorrect: *Him* and Marina own that video store.
Correct: *He* and Marina own that video store.

Because these pronoun usages are common in today's colloquial speech, they are likely to slip into writing that requires a more formal usage.

One way to avoid such mistakes is to listen to how the sentence sounds without the extra name or pronoun in such plural forms. These mistakes rarely occur if the pronoun subject is singular. Would you ever write or say:

Me is (or am) going to the movies.

Him owns that video store.

This is unlikely because, as the above examples show, the object pronoun sounds funny when the name that accompanies that pronoun is left out.

Exercise

Circle the correct subject pronouns below.

1. (He, Him) and Marina own that video store.
2. Yesterday (she, her) prepared a spaghetti dinner.
3. (She, Her) and Uncle Mario prepared a spaghetti dinner.
4. Last spring (I, me) traveled in New England.
5. Eileen and (I, me) traveled in New England last spring.
6. Now (she, her) and my mother are enthusiastic travelers.
7. Formerly (she, her) was not an enthusiastic traveler.

Correct Use of Object (Nonsubject) Pronouns. Consider the following examples and suggestions regarding the correct use of nonsubject pronouns.

Incorrect: Our boss often gave unclear orders to Sara and *I*.

Correct: Our boss often gave unclear orders to Sara and *me*.

This type of nonsubject pronoun error, which may be the result of overcorrecting, can usually be detected by leaving out the person's name or other noun that accompanies the pronoun. Would you ever say or write:

Our boss often gave unclear orders to *I*.

Often the boss expects our other coworker, Tomas, and *she* to work overtime without extra pay.

Reread the second sentence, leaving out the words, "our other coworkers, Tomas, and."

Exercise

Choose the correct pronoun form. Before choosing, determine how the sentence would sound without the names or other pronouns that are paired with the object (nonsubject) pronouns.

1. Everyone at work gets along well with Tomas and (she, *her*) but none of the employees respect the boss or his father, the company's owner.
2. Because he is the son of an inconsiderate owner, our boss knows that he can treat (we, *us*) unfairly.
3. After an argument with the boss last month, he warned Tomas and (I, *me*) to expect a cut in our hours.
4. Another time, the boss leered at Sara and (I, *me*) in front of a customer.
5. In spite of this unfair treatment, no one dares to complain to his father or (he, *him*).
6. Last year, in retaliation for a complaint filed by Sara and Lissette Riva, a former employee, the boss scheduled Sara and (*she*, her) to work only weekend shifts for three months.

References Required

Perhaps the most frequent pronoun errors occur when the writer knows exactly what noun or noun phrase a pronoun refers to, while the reader has to guess. The noun or noun phrase that a pronoun refers to is called an **antecedent**. Without an exact antecedent, a pronoun lacks specific meaning. Thus, every pronoun should have a clear and correct antecedent, which is close enough to that pronoun to avoid any confusion.

The pronouns and their antecedents are italicized in the following examples.

When *Kemeka* finished her solo, the audience cheered for *her*.

As *Jose* walked towards the microphone, the crowd yelled for *him*.

After the *dolphin* leapt ten feet, the children clapped for *it*.

Before the *gymnasts* had finished their act, the spectators booed *them*.

Each of the pronouns in the above sentences refers to a *specific* noun (antecedent).

Noun	*Pronoun*	*Gender*	*Number*
Kemeka	her	feminine	singular
Jose	him	masculine	singular
dolphin	it	neuter	singular
gymnasts	them	masculine or feminine	plural

The noun being referred to must appear before the pronoun—hence the prefix *ante* (before). A pronoun should appear soon enough after its antecedent to avoid ambiguity. As the above examples show, a pronoun also must agree with its antecedent in number (singular or plural) and gender (feminine, masculine, or neuter).

Exercise

Draw an arrow from the pronoun to its antecedent in each of the following sentences. The first one is done for you.

1. The coach warned the players that they could lose the meet.
2. Children devour ice cream because it tastes so good.
3. Sabena telephoned Lloyd and told him off for forgetting her birthday.
4. The officer spotted the speeding truck as it careened off the slippery highway.
5. To the children's regret, their crabby uncle decided to accompany them on their shopping expedition.
6. If pronouns lack clear antecedents, they are unclear to the reader.

Making the Pronoun Refer to the Right Word: Common Pronoun Reference Problems

Ambiguous Antecedent. It is confusing, and therefore incorrect to have more than one possible antecedent. The following sentences are examples of confusing antecedents.

Confusing: Paula and her mother were in a heated argument until she left the room in tears.

Who left the room? The writer may know, but the reader is unsure. Because the female pronoun *she* could refer to either Paula or her mother, it lacks a clear antecedent. The ambiguity could be corrected as follows.

Clear: Paula and her mother were in a heated argument until the daughter left the room in tears.

Here is another confusing sentence:

Confusing: Rosa planned a surprise party for Susan at her home.

Was the party held at Susan's or Rosa's home? Because both nouns are feminine, the possessive pronoun *her* can refer to either Rosa or Susan.

Clear: Rosa planned a surprise party for Susan at Rosa's home.

If one of those nouns were masculine, the meaning would be clear.

Clear: Rosa planned a surprise party for Robert at her house.

Consider this sentence:

Confusing: Jane told her sister that she needed a new car.

Who needed the new car, Jane or her sister?

Clear: Jane told her sister, "You need a new car."

Clear: Jane told her sister, "I need a new car."

Unexpressed Antecedent.

Confusing: Because Simona has always been interested in medicine, she has decided to be one.

Has Simona decided to become a medicine? The sentence is confusing because it lacks a correct antecedent for *one*.

The following are some possible corrected versions.

Clear: Because Simona has always been interested in medicine, she has decided to be a doctor.

Clear: Because Simona has always been interested in medicine and admired physicians, she has decided to be one.

Here is another confusing sentence:

Confusing: The park commission approved the funding for an outdoor ice rink where they could skate for free.

Who does the pronoun *they* refer to? Is it likely that the park commission funded a free ice rink for itself?

Clear: The park commission approved the funding for an outdoor ice rink where the public could skate for free.

Incorrect Antecedent.

Confusing: That cable TV company warned its customers that they were raising the rates in a month.

In this sentence the only plural noun antecedent for *they* is *customers*. Are the customers likely to raise their own rates?

Clear: That cable TV company warned its customers that it was raising the rates in a month.

Clear: That cable TV company warned its customers that the rates would be raised in a month.

One more confusing example:

Confusing: That district has so many pupils that they need to raise taxes to build a new school.

Who are *they?* The only plural noun that *they* can refer to in the sentence is *pupils*. But do pupils levy taxes to build schools? How could the sentence be reworded to clear up the incorrect pronoun reference? Write a clearer version in your journal.

Exercise

Reword the following sentences so that each pronoun has a clear, appropriate antecedent.

1. Brenda is an avid sports fan, but Ellen is not as interested in them. [sports]
2. Brenda uses the computer efficiently, but she never took a course in it. [computers]
3. Brenda told Ellen that she needed to read the directions again. [Brenda / or "You need to..."]
4. My aunt had a heart attack, but it was as good as ever after two weeks in the hospital. [her heart]
5. His convertible hit a parked car, but it wasn't damaged. [his car]
6. Dennis hurriedly plucked the feathers from the three chickens and popped them into the oven. [the chickens]
7. Because the witness needed police protection, four of them were assigned to her. [policemen]
8. Nick got the keys from Justin before he left for school. [Justin]
9. Victor is a wonderful actor who, like many other actors, cannot make a living doing it. [acting]
10. When Monique told her mother about the broken lamp, she was upset. [her mom]

Using Demonstrative Pronouns Clearly

> Similarly, from a Soviet English-language weekly:
> There will be a Moscow exhibition of Arts by 15,000 Soviet Republic painters and sculptors. These were executed over the past two years.

As worded, what does the plural demonstrative pronoun *these* refer to in the above announcement? Sometimes ambiguous passages like this announcement about a recent exhibit in the former Soviet Union can be fixed by inserting a noun after the demonstrative pronoun.

These works were executed over the past two years.

Using Demonstrative Pronouns Correctly

The chart below shows the two demonstrative pronouns in both their singular and plural forms.

Demonstrative Pronouns (Adjectives)

Singular
this (as in *this* job)
that (as in *that* house)

Plural
these (as in *these* jobs)
those (as in *those* houses)

Demonstrative pronouns point out, or demonstrate, something that the writer is referring to. The following sentences are examples of the use of demonstrative pronouns.

Sam is patient, understanding, and generous; *these* qualities contribute to his success as a social worker.

> My younger brother Leonard never turns out the lights when he goes out. *This* annoys everyone in the family.

Here, *this* refers to something specific—Leonard's habit of leaving the lights on. Compare the next sentence with the one above.

> My younger brother Leonard leaves dirty dishes in the sink and on the kitchen counter, scatters newspapers all over the living room, and never turns off any of the lights before he leaves the house. *This* annoys everyone in the family.

What does Leonard do that annoys everyone in the family? The passage is vague and confusing because there are several possibilities. In this example the demonstrative pronoun *this* lacks a specific antecedent.

Failure to have the pronoun *this* refer to something specific is a recurrent problem. It frequently occurs when the writer knows what is being referred to but fails to make the antecedent clear to the reader.

Demonstrative pronouns that refer to an underlying, rather vague, idea instead of a specific noun or noun clause are also confusing to the reader. Observe the following examples.

> The principal was unsympathetic, mumbled an indefinite response, and hung up abruptly after rejecting the sick boy's mother's request for an extension of the due deadline for her son's research paper. *This* is typical of that school's administrators.

Exactly what was so typical about the principal's response?

> Carlos worked as a technician in a hospital lab for two summers, got A's in all of his science courses, and received much encouragement from his teachers. *That* led to his decision to study medicine.

Which of these factors led to Carlos' decision to study medicine?

Exercise

Reword the following sentences to eliminate faulty or unclear pronoun references. There is no one right answer, and several variants may be correct for each one.

Model: Be wary of the commercials for children's toys that they show on television. (What noun can *they* refer to?)

> Be wary of commercials for children's toys on television.

Because *they* has no correct plural noun antecedent, one way to correct the sentence is to leave out the pronoun *they*.)

1. That town in the midwest is known for their thrifty habits.
2. Evan is working part-time in a computer lab at the university for the summer. This may become his career.
3. Fighting over a will sometimes ruins family relationships. It should not happen like that.
4. Jealousy, unrestrained anger, and indifference to their wants can be very harmful to your children. You should try to get rid of them now.
5. The worried father informed his son that he needed to look for a better-paying job.
6. A group of biology students released two hundred rats in the girls' dormitory, but these were immediately arrested and jailed.
7. The lost pedestrian seemed to be approaching the police officer on the corner, but then he crossed the street.
8. At eighteen I left home and hitchhiked to California. This is not satisfactory because it involves much standing on the highways.
9. She slammed her hand on the table and broke it.
10. Louise constantly complained to the neighbors about their destructive children; yet she let her own children run wild. She neither punished her son nor paid for the damages when he broke Mrs. Frank's window. This did not make her popular.

Exercise

Underline the instances of unclear pronoun references in the following passage, then rewrite it in your journal so that the pronouns all have precise, correct antecedents.

Hugh and Harry's conversation came to an uncomfortable pause after he made a crude remark about women athletes, then laughed as if he were embarrassed and tried to change the subject to his new motorcycle. This especially annoyed his friend, who had become a strong advocate of women's equality. His views on women's rights had changed considerably after they emphasized gender stereotypes in his sociology class. He kept urging his friend to take the class but had not yet persuaded him to sign up for it.

Avoiding Unnecessary Shifts of Person

> Careful writers do not shift your point of view.

Try not to confuse your readers with unneeded **shifts of person** as in the example above: "Writers" is in the *third person* (persons being written about), while "your" is in the *second person* (persons being spoken to). The sentence should be worded as follows:

Careful writers do not shift *their* point of view.

Because "writers" is in the third person, the pronoun should likewise be in the third person plural.

Unnecessary person shifts may occur when writers forget that they have established the person in a sentence, paragraph, or essay—such as the third person—then shift into another person—such as talking directly to the reader using the second person.

Confusing: If a *student* wants good grades, *you* ought to keep up with all of the assignments.

Clear: If a student wants good grades, *he* or *she* ought to keep up with all of the assignments.

Clear: If students want good grades, *they* ought to keep up with all of the assignments.

Clear: Students who want good grades ought to keep up with all of the assignments.

While common in speech, such shifts in person are inappropriate in writing.

Exercise

Avoid person shift by making the pronouns consistent in the following sentences. The first one is done for you.

1. Before lawyers can appear in court, ~~you~~ they have to pass the bar exam.
2. I like visiting my aunt because she makes ~~you~~ me feel special.
3. When we looked through the windows, ~~one~~ we could see the snow-capped peaks in the distance.
4. I enjoy swimming because ~~one~~ I feels so invigorated when ~~you~~ I quit.
5. If ~~you~~ one want to become a good writer, one needs lots of practice.
6. If writers begin a paragraph in the present tense, ~~you~~ they should not shift into the past tense unless ~~you~~ they have a reason.

Avoiding the Overuse of Pronouns

Sometimes it is better to eliminate some of the pronouns to achieve a more crisp style, as in the following:

Wordy: I will save energy if I keep my car tuned.

Crisp: Keeping my car tuned saves energy.

Wordy: If you arrive at the concert early, you are going to get a seat near the stage.

Crisp: Arrive at the concert early to get a seat near the stage.

Exercise

Improve the style of the following sentences by rewording them with fewer pronouns.

1. Swimming is among the best exercises ~~you can do to put you in~~ for getting into shape.
2. If you are a freshman in college, you should not be afraid to ask questions during your first week to avoid ~~your~~ getting lost.
3. Her research paper was excellent; ~~you could tell that~~ obviously she had worked hard on it.
4. He will conserve energy and save money if he takes the bus to work every day. Taking the bus...
5. Your vocabulary should improve rapidly if you read widely. Reading widely...
6. You will find that your writing style will improve if you decide ~~that you are~~ not ~~going~~ to write so many pronouns.

Choosing the Right Form of a Verb

Regular Verbs

Action verbs, such as *shove, stamp,* or *chase,* tell us what a subject is *doing.* Those three verbs are all regular verbs. As the name suggests, **regular verbs** follow a standard pattern: they have an *-ed* ending for the past tense and past participle forms. The following examples show regular verb forms of the verb *chase.*

Present Tense: Wolves often *chase* wounded creatures.

Past Tense: The hungry wolves *chased* the sheep into the barn.

Past Participle: Squirrels and rabbits are often *chased* by cats.

Past Participle: That skinny, tired fellow was *chased* from the park by an angry moose.

Participles can also be used as describing words—**adjectives**—as in "that skinny, *tired* fellow" in the sentence above. *Tired,* used here as an adjective that modifies "fellow," is both the past participle and the past-tense form of the verb *tire.* **Present participles,** or the *-ing* form of verbs, can also be used as describing words: *describing* is the present participle of the verb *describe.*

The following sentences show how the main forms of the verb *tire* can be used.

I do not *tire* easily. (present tense)

My grandmother *tires* easily. (present tense)

The old man is *tiring* rapidly. (present participle)

His is a most *tiring* job. (present participle or adjective)

The waitress soon *tired* of the job. (past tense)

She had been somewhat *tired* all day. (past participle)

By evening she was one *tired* woman. (past participle or adjective)

Those children never seem *to tire.* (infinitive)

Whether used as adjectives or verbs, part participles of regular verbs always have an *-ed* ending. A common mistake is to forget to add that ending.

Incorrect: John is a very *prejudice* person.

Correct: John is a very *prejudiced* person.

THE FAR SIDE By GARY LARSON

"See Dick run. See Jane run. Run run run. See the wolves chase Dick and Jane. Chase chase chase. ..."

THE FAR SIDE © 1987 FARWORKS, INC. Dist. by UNIVERSAL PRESS SYNDICATE. Reprinted with permission. All rights reserved.

Exercise

Correct the following by rewriting the sentences.

1. Joe use to be a poor loser.
2. Mary was embarrass by the teacher's suggestion.
3. Dogs are suppose to be on a leash in the city.

The following chart shows the standard forms and ending changes of regular verbs.

	Present	Past
I, you, we, they	chase	chased
he, she, it, one	chases	chased

As the chart shows, the *-ed* ending is used for all part-tense endings for regular verbs, in *both* plural and singular forms. Thus the *only* ending change for regular verbs is the *-s*—or *-es,* as in *reaches*—that is added to third person singular forms.

The following sentences show the standard ending changes in regular verbs—in this case the verb *chase.*

First- and Second-Person Singular

I do not *chase* daydreams.

Do you *chase* daydreams?

Third-Person Singular

Their dog, Rex, never *chases* our cat, Schwartz.

He never *chases* Schwartz, the toughest tomcat in town.

All Plurals

Can we *chase* your cat outside?

Should Kendra and I *chase* their cat out of the yard?

Will they *chase* our dog from their yard?

Those children always *chase* after the ice cream wagon.

Shanta and Lloyd never *chase* away a stray animal.

It is not important to learn all of this terminology, but it is important to use verbs correctly—as student writers do most of the time. However, because it is so easy to leave out the *-ed* and *-s* endings on regular verb forms, be sure to edit all verbs carefully before turning in the final draft of your papers. It often helps to read your work aloud, as well as to listen for *-s* and *-ed* endings as your teachers, TV announcers, friends, and others speak. Sometimes, the *-ed* is not pronounced distinctly, as in *Last year they never asked me to one of their parties.* If you listen carefully, however, at least a hint of the *-ed* ending can usually be heard.

Irregular Verbs

The English language has thousands of regular verbs that follow the above pattern. On the other hand, like most languages, English also has many **irregular verbs.** These include many of the more commonly used verbs, such as *see* and *run*.

The wolf was *running* fast, but Dick and Jane *ran* faster.

Within minutes they *had run* off from that naughty wolf.

When the wolf *saw* them escape, he could not believe his eyes.

Never before had he *seen* such amazingly fleet children.

The list below shows the major forms of a few of the many irregular English verbs. Even from this small sampling, it is evident that irregular verbs follow several patterns; a few follow no set pattern. It is no wonder they cause confusion!

Base Form	*Past Form*	*Past Participle* (needs helping verb like *was* or *had*)
see	saw	seen (he had seen)
run	ran	run
go	went	gone
read	read	read
lead	led	led
do	did	done
choose	chose	chosen
throw	threw	thrown

The following sentences use the forms of the last verb from the above list of irregular verbs.

Base form: Can I *throw* this old book in the trash?

Past form: Who *threw* out today's *Milwaukee Sentinel?*

Past participle: It was *thrown* out this evening by Matilda.

The "was thrown out" in this last sentence is an example of using the **passive voice** instead of a more **active form** of the verb.

Active voice: Matilda *threw* out today's *Milwaukee Sentinel* this evening.

In the sentence above, the subject, Matilda, is the doer, so the verb is in the active voice: *Matilda threw* . . .

In the passive voice, the subject is acted upon.

Passive voice: The *Milwaukee Sentinel was thrown out* by Matilda.

Compare the active and passive voice in the next examples. Which sentence in each pair is livelier and less wordy?

Passive voice: Last Sunday's Packer game *was seen* on television by many enthusiastic viewers.

Active voice: Many enthusiastic viewers *saw* last Sunday's Packer game on television.

Passive voice: That new TV series on disease control *was written* by a three-person team of experts.

Active voice: A three-person team of experts *wrote* that new TV series on disease control.

While it has legitimate usages, such as in scientific reports, overuse of the passive voice deadens writing and may obscure meaning. Much dull prose today is overladen with the passive voice. Would you rather read the following?

The thirty-yard pass for today's winning touchdown was thrown by Packer quarterback Brett Favre.

Or would you prefer to read this version?

Packer quarterback Brett Favre threw a thirty-yard pass for today's winning touchdown.

To change a sentence from the passive voice to the active voice, ask yourself the following question: Who did what? Then apply that question to this sentence. Look at the following example.

An unfair low grade was given to me by the teaching assistant.

Who did the action? What did the actor do? Reword that sentence in the active voice.

While it is generally best to use the active voice, there are occasions when the passive voice is appropriate. For instance, maybe you want to draw attention to a problem at your workplace without making a direct accusation (and maybe losing your job). Perhaps you do not know who is responsible for something. The following sentence shows the correct use of the passive voice in such circumstances.

A crucial mistake was made in last month's financial report.

Overcorrection of Irregular Verbs

Remembering that regular verbs add *-ed* to the past-tense form, students sometimes overcorrect and add an *-ed* ending to past-tense forms of irregular verbs.

Incorrect: The spoiled toddler *throwed* a temper tantrum.
Correct: The spoiled toddler *threw* a temper tantrum.

Incorrect: He *leaded* me down the path to temptation.
Correct: He *led* me down the path to temptation.

Try to become more aware of the many different ways that irregular verbs form their past tense and past participles. Note that *-ed* is *not* a standard ending for irregular verbs.

Remembering the correct spelling of certain irregular verbs is difficult for many writers. For example, before writing the list of irregular verbs, we checked (for the umpteenth time) the spelling of the past-tense form *led* in the dictionary. We regularly confuse the forms *lead/led/led* with those of *read/read/read*.

Learn the irregular verbs that cause you problems. Get into the habit of regularly checking the forms of those verbs in the dictionary or in a grammar handbook that has a thorough list of irregular verbs. Write the forms of those verbs that continue to confuse you in the back of your dictionary.

Monitoring Verb Tense and Tense Consistency

Be aware that unnecessary **shifts in verb tense** confuse your readers. *Tense* means time, such as the time the action in a sentence or clause is occurring. Below are examples of the major **verb tenses.**

Present: Justin *plays* in the yard every day.

Past: Nick *played* at the park yesterday.

Future: Tomorrow Kelly *will play* with them in the yard.

Note that the future tense is formed here by adding the **auxiliary,** or **helping, verb** *will* to the base form of the verb. Helping verbs are a frequent component of English verb usage. The following sentences show other examples of helping verbs.

Nick *is playing* in the yard. (ongoing present action)

Nick *was looking* for Justin. (ongoing past action)

The tense of such sentences can be shifted by changing the form of the helping verb (without changing the *-ing* form of the verb).

Yesterday Nick *was playing* in the yard. (ongoing past action)

Tomorrow Nick *will be looking* for Justin. (ongoing future action)

Independent clauses describing an ongoing action are often combined with dependent clauses that portray an action occurring at the same time.

      (independent clause)   (dependent clause)
Yesterday Nick was playing in the yard, while Justin was in school.

      (independent clause)   (dependent clause)
Tomorrow Nick will be playing in the yard, while Justin goes to the dentist.

Understanding Main Verbs and Helping Verbs

The **complete verb** in a sentence or clause consists of the **main verb** (MV) and any **helping verbs** (HV). AS the above example shows, a sentence or clause can contain more than one helping verb: Nick *will be* playing. In fact, complete verbs can have more than two helping verbs.

          HV   HV   HV   MV
Nick *may have been playing* with Justin's bike yesterday.

                HV   HV   HV   MV
If so, Justin *would have been annoyed* at Nick last night.

The helping verbs always appear *before* the main verbs. However, other words may appear between helping verbs and main verbs. The sentences below contain some examples:

This restaurant *has* already *raised* its prices.

Maybe we *should* not *have come* to this fancy restaurant.

Have you never *dined* in an expensive restaurant before?

Has the rest of your family ever *eaten* here?

Verbs That Are Always Helping Verbs

could	may	must
should	might	shall
would		

Verbs That Can Be Either Helping Verbs or Main Verbs

Forms of *be*

as	was	be
is	were	being
are	been	

Forms of *do*

do
does
did

Forms of *have*

has
have
had

Examples of Verbs Used Both as Helping Verbs and Main Verbs

      HV MV
am: I *am learning* how to speak French.

    MV
I *am* never late for French class.

                HV MV
did: Sue *did study* very hard for the French exam.

                MV
Sue also *did* all of her French assignments.

           HV MV
has: He *has studied* French for three years.

            MV
He now *has* excellent command of French grammar.

Two Additional Verbs in This Category: **can** *and* **will**

If you *will give* her a ride, Sheila *can go* to the play.

Understanding Action Verbs and Linking Verbs

The previous examples demonstrate how to change the tenses of the two kinds of verbs, action verbs and linking verbs. As the name suggests, an **action verb** tells what the subject of a sentence or clause is *doing*.

Justin *plays* in the park after school.

Nick *chases* after Justin every morning.

Linking verbs link the subject to the predicate. **Predicate** is the term for "what is being said about the subject"—in other words, the rest of a sentence or clause besides the subject. The subject is the noun or pronoun that the predicate is about; the verb, which tells something about that subject, is always part of the predicate. As the following examples demonstrate, however, both subjects and predicates often contain more than one word. The predicates of each of these sentences have a linking verb.

Subjects	Predicates
My uncle's daughter	*was* not at school yesterday.
Active Nick	*is* Justin's younger brother.
My Uncle Spenser	*seems* less tense than his wife.
Inexperienced skiers	*become* exhausted more easily.
Last night's dirty dishes	*remained* in the sink.

Because linking verbs are not as active or specific as action verbs, try not to overuse them in your writing. Which of the next two sentences is more lively and gives more information?

Justin *was* at the Brewers' game last week.

Justin *cheered* at the Brewers' game last week.

Understanding Subject/Verb Agreement

You may also need to check regularly for mistakes in **subject/verb agreement.** Your writing is much easier for your readers to follow when all parts of your sentences agree.

Singular subjects require singular verbs.

A <u>dog</u> <u>barks</u>.

Plural subjects require plural verbs.

Two <u>dogs</u> <u>bark</u>.

Finding the Subject and Verb

The subject is the *something* or *someone* that the sentence is about. The predicate is the part of a sentence that contains the verb; it gives information about the subject. If the sentence contains an action verb, that verb tells what the subject *does*.

<u>Cats</u> <u>yowl</u>.

Cats, the plural subject, is underlined once. (The plural of most nouns is formed by adding an *-s*). *Yowl,* the verb, is underlined twice.

It may help you to think of the subject as the actor, and the verb as the action.

               (actor)   (action)
The frightened <u>elephant</u> <u>stampeded</u> through the jungle.

The <u>hunters</u> <u>followed</u> them with their bows and arrows.

As you already know, however, not all verbs are action verbs. The other kind of verbs, linking verbs, may be a little harder to find in a sentence. Instead of telling what the subject is *doing,* linking verbs tell what the subject *is* or how the subject *felt, looked, smelled, sounded,* and so on. The following sentences show examples of linking verbs.

Babar the elephant *is* the hero of several children's books.

Babar's adventures *remain* popular with many young readers.

A cool bath *feels* great on a hot summer day.

Before him *were* three huge elephants.

(Note that, in a change from the standard order, the verb comes *before* the subject, elephants, in that last sentence.)

These sentences are easy to follow because their subjects and verbs agree. Below are some special cases to consider.

Singular subjects connected by *and* require a plural verb.

That elephant and tiger perform in the circus.

Alphonso and Lenore are siblings.

His cat and dog always follow him.

However, in the case of two subjects joined by *or* or *nor,* if one subject is singular and the other plural, the verb form agrees with the noun that is closest to the verb:

Wine or roses remind me of our vacation.

Roses or wine reminds me of our vacation.

Detecting Problems of Subject/Verb Agreement

Becoming more aware of subject/verb agreement, as well as other verb mistakes, is the first step toward eliminating them from your writing. Edit once just for verb endings, then ask members of your peer revising group or your other editors to go over your verb forms in particular. Check the verbs one last time before handing in a paper. Have you always used singular verbs with singular nouns and plural verbs with plural nouns?

If you tend to make mistakes in subject/verb agreement, it might help you to routinely put one line under the subjects and two lines under the verbs in your drafts. Remember that with a few exceptions, such as the word *children,* most nouns add an *-s* or *-es* to form plurals.

Singular	*Plural*
tourist	tourists
restaurant	restaurants
lunch	lunches

Recall that for regular present-tense verbs, the *only* ending that changes is the *-s* added to the third-person singular.

Third-person Singular   *Third-person Plural*

a tourist finds   tourists find
he/she/it finds   they find

Singular: Finally, that hungry <u>tourist</u> <u>finds</u> a restaurant and <u>pauses</u> for lunch.

Singular: Finally, <u>she</u> <u>finds</u> a restaurant and <u>pauses</u> for lunch.

Plural: Now can those three hungry <u>tourists</u> <u>find</u> a restaurant and <u>buy</u> their lunches?

Plural: Now can <u>they</u> <u>find</u> a restaurant and <u>buy</u> their lunches?

Exercise

Circle the correct forms of the present tense verbs.

Paris (is, **are**) the capital of France and the largest city in Western Europe. Almost two and a half million people (lives, **live**) within its city limits, but metropolitan Paris (has, **have**) more than nine million inhabitants. That figure (includes, **include**) almost one-sixth of the total population of the country. In addition, every month thousands of visitors (swells, **swell**) the population of this magnificent city on the banks of the Seine River. They (climbs, **climb**) the steps or (rides, **ride**) an elevator to the top of the Eiffel Tower, (takes, **take**) a boat trip down the Seine, and (visits, **visit**) Notre Dame cathedral. The Eiffel Tower (dates, **date**) back to the late nineteenth century, while Notre Dame (is, **are**) one of the most famous medieval Gothic cathedrals in Europe. In spite of all of the new construction since World War II, the Eiffel Tower and Notre Dame (remains, **remain**) two of the most familiar landmarks of the city. When finished sightseeing, visitors to Paris (**has**, have) a wide variety of choices for sampling the French capital's famous cuisine, ranging from the smallest neighborhood cafe to the most elegant five star restaurant.

One reason writers make subject/verb agreement mistakes is that certain such usages are common—and more readily forgiven—in speech. Observe the following examples.

Incorrect: Not <u>one</u> of my close friends <u>are</u> here at my wedding.

The subject of this sentence, *one,* is a singular indefinite pronoun, while *are* is a plural verb form. Mistakes such as this occur because the noun that is closest to the verb—in this case, *friends*—is plural, not singular. The sentence should read as follows.

Correct: Not <u>one</u> of my close friends <u>is</u> here at my wedding.

In writing, agreement problems often occur when subject and verb get separated by what Jack Rawlins, author of *The Writer's Way,* aptly calls "distracting business in between" (231). In his 1986 guide to usage, Robert C. Pinckert cautions writers in a similar vein: "Whenever you write a sentence with an inch or more between subject and verb," be sure to check if they agree (92).

The words between the subject and verb are in italics in the examples below.

Incorrect: The rising cost *of tuition, textbooks, and other supplies* force many students to work longer hours.

Because *cost,* the subject, is singular, a singular verb, *forces,* is needed.

Correct: The rising cost of tuition, textbooks, and other supplies *forces* many students to work longer hours.

Incorrect: The long lines *at the bookstore during the first week of the semester* annoys many students.

Because *lines,* the subject, is plural, a plural verb, *annoy,* is needed.

Correct: The long lines at the bookstore during the first week of the semester annoy many students.

Problems in subject/verb agreement also occur when the subject *follows* the verb:

Waiting at the house <u>were</u> all my mother's angry <u>relatives</u>.

The subject *relatives* is plural, so the verb should be plural.

After a few cool greetings, there <u>was</u> little <u>discussion</u>.

Because the subject *discussion* is singular, a singular verb is needed.

Beyond the muddy river <u>stretches</u> the broad <u>flood</u> <u>plain</u>.

The subject *flood plain* is singular, so the verb is also singular.

Exercise

Determine the subject. Then circle the correct verb from the choices in parentheses.

1. Circling the chicken coop (was, *were*) three hungry wolves.
2. Beyond the muddy river (is, *are*) several groves of trees.
3. Along the river (*runs*, run) a four-lane expressway.
4. Lumbering in the bushes (was, *were*) a huge porcupine.
5. There (*was*, were) no places for the frightened creature to hide.

Exercise

Put one line under the subject of the following sentences. Then, before choosing from the verb forms given, lightly cross out the words that come between subject and verb. The first one is done for you.

1. That casual physics *professor* in a sweat shirt and jeans (make, *makes*) students feel comfortable.
2. Diagrams illustrating complex material in an engineering textbook (aid, aids) in comprehension.
3. Studying in a quiet spot without distracting influences like talkative friends (improve, improves) one's concentration.
4. Some members of the dormitory student council (want, wants) to extend the hours reserved for quiet study in Adams Hall.
5. The price of word processors and printers of all types (has, have) fallen rapidly over the last few years.
6. My computer, as well as my printer, (is, are) in need of expensive repairs.
7. Where (was, were) my friends and my dad when I needed them?
8. Does a visit to that city, which many find the most interesting of our region's tourist attractions, (appeals, appeal) to you?
9. That course in European history, along with all the political science classes Estelle had last semester, (give, gives) her an excellent background for law school.
10. Why should Mary and Tom (take, takes) credit for the work that you did?

Avoiding Shifts in Verb Tense

Using action verbs and avoiding unnecessary shifts in verb tense can greatly strengthen your writing. If you begin a paragraph in the past tense, do not confuse your reader by shifting into the present tense without a reason. Here is a paragraph with unnecessary shifts in tense. The verbs are boldfaced.

> *The driver **peers** through the rain-spattered windshield and then **brought** his battered truck to a sudden halt. Seconds later he **hears** the sound of a train whirring past. Simultaneously, he and his companion **heaved** a sigh of relief. "That **is** a close one," the driver **says**. Too stunned to drive on, they **get** out of the truck and **sat** on the grass in a stupor.*

Because of the unnecessary shifts from present to past tense, the above paragraph is hard for readers to follow. Aside from the remark in quotation marks ("That was a close one"), the actions being depicted should be in the present tense because the first verb, *peers,* starts the paragraph off in the present. Make the necessary changes in the verbs in the paragraph so that they are all in the present tense.

Conversely, if you begin a paragraph, or a longer piece of writing such as a narrative, in the past tense, do not confuse your readers by shifting to the present tense without a reason. Observe the unnecessary tense shifts in the following paragraph.

> *Suddenly a neighbor **appeared** on the path leading from the cabin to the lake below. Mr. Toppa **smiles** at the two children in a friendly manner and **held** out his hand for them to examine something. Eight-year-old Rodney **runs** off into the woods, but his little sister **touched** the brilliantly colored creature and **tries** to pick it up. Just as Mr. Toppa **warns** her not to frighten it, the snake **slid** from his palm and **slithers** off into the dense brush. Looking somewhat sheepish, Rodney **rejoins** his sister, and they **continued** their stroll down the path.*

Change the verbs in the above paragraph so that they are all in the past tense.

While fiction writers sometimes effectively use the present tense to achieve a sense of immediacy, overuse of the present tense in narratives can become somewhat tedious—in speaking as well as in writing.

> *I say to him, "Get off my case," and he says to me, "You're the one who always starts nagging at me!" So I hang up, but he calls right back and starts to give me the same old story about how he never criticizes me or accuses me of being unfaithful. Just then my dad stamps into the room and asks what the yelling is about. I glare at him and ask if it is any of his business. He stalks out as usual, I hang up once more, and I leave for work in a terrible mood. So what else is new?*

In general, written narratives about past events, such as a recounting of the above conversation, would be more effective in the past tense. However, writers sometimes *need* to shift tenses within an essay, or even within a paragraph, if the meaning of the material calls for a tense shift. Observe the following examples.

                      past tense
*The summer of 1995 **was** one of the hottest in the history of the upper*
              future tense
*Midwest. People **will tell** stories about that summer for a long time.*
         past tense   past tense
*Temperatures often **reached** the upper nineties and even **surpassed** a*

hundred degrees several times, setting numerous weather records. Hundreds
    past tense
*of people **died** from heat-related causes, especially in Chicago and*
                    present tense
*Milwaukee. Usually those cities **have** much cooler summers, and many*
                          present tense
*dwellings, especially in the central cities, **lack** air conditioning. Government*
      future tense
*officials **will continue** to explore measures to avoid a repeat of this tragedy,*
      future tense
*if the region **faces** another hot, humid summer like the one of 1995.*

Decide if you want your theme in the past or present tense. If you are writing a narrative about events that have already happened, you probably will select the past tense. Once you start a paragraph or theme in one tense, you should *only shift tense for a good reason.*

Exercise

Circle the better form from the verbs given. In some cases either form may be appropriate. Look for cue words, such as *still* and *now,* when choosing verb tense.

    Last year the chairman of the English Department of a small Midwestern liberal arts college (*spends, spent*) the spring semester in Kiev, the capital of Ukraine. To his and his family's surprise, they (*find, found*) that the Ukrainians (*are, were*) exceptionally friendly and hospitable, most anxious to show their American guests everything that Kiev (*had, has*) to offer. Located on a wooded bluff above the Dnieper River, Kiev (*is, was*) a beautiful historic place and (*was, is*) the third largest city in the former Soviet Union. Scholars still (*argue, argued*) about the exact date of the first settlement in the Kiev region, but they (*agree, agreed*) that the present city (*dates, dated*) back more than a thousand years. The twentieth century has (*saw, seen, see*) many changes and much damage to this ancient city. The German Army (*occupied, occupies*) the Ukrainian capital during World War I, and again in late September of 1941, just three months after Hitler's troops (*invade, invaded*) the Soviet Union. The city's main street (*is, was*) virtually (*destroyed, destroy*) during World War II but (*is, was*) now completely rebuilt. Many famous churches and monasteries (*were, are*) also heavily (*damaged, damage*) during the two-year German occupation. Some of them (*are, were*) now restored and (*are, were*) open to tourists as well as to churchgoers.

Spotting Verb Errors: A Review

Forms for the Present Tense of Regular Verbs

	Singular	Plural
First person	I chase	we chase
Second person	you chase	you chase
Third person	he, she, it chases	they chase

Note: Only one ending change occurs, the *-s* added to the third-person singular.

Subject/Verb Agreement

Plural and compound subjects both take the plural form of the verb, while singular subjects take the singular form.

Singular Subject/Verb: Kosika finds a rabbit in her garden.
She chases the rabbit away.

Plural Subject/Verb: Four rabbits dash across the lawn.

Compound Subject/Verb: A mouse and a chipmunk scurry off.

Exercise

Put one line under the subjects in these sentences and circle the correct present tense form of the verb.

1. Suddenly Jutiki (*slams/slam*) the ball and (*runs/run*) to first base.
2. Every season Jutiki and Mario (*scores/score*) the most home runs on the team.
3. Tonya (*makes/make*) more baskets than anyone else on the team.
4. Good players (*knows/know*) when to try to steal a base.
5. Fans usually (*cheers/cheer*) players for stealing a base.

Exercise

Circle the subjects in the following sentences. Then put a wavy line under all of the incorrect verb forms and write the correct form. Some sentences have *more* than one error.

1. Three shrimp and four guppies usually swims in that aquarium.
2. How many frogs is swimming in that pond?
3. My sister Fran and I often argues over the silliest things.
4. Komika and Lavon, the friendly owners of our neighborhood's favorite pizza parlor, is both great cooks.
5. Cynthia never use to get her math assignments done, but Mr. Lopez past her in math anyway.
6. Do teachers like Mr. Lopez realizes that giving unearned grades only harm their students?
7. I haven't never worked harder on an essay in my life.
8. Yesterday my former neighbors phone me from California, the first time they have call me since they move last summer.
9. Unfortunately some employers are prejudice against hiring people who are over fifty years old.
10. Mario and Gwenetta was late for class three times last week.
11. That meeting was reschedule for the following Monday.

Chapter Four

Syntax, Diction, and Style

Diction + Syntax + Style

Syntax refers to word order; **diction** refers to word choice. Proper syntax requires arranging words in sentences that are grammatically correct and clear. Good **style** goes beyond syntax; it means putting well-chosen words together in a fashion that holds the reader's interest, as well as being grammatically correct. Style means the *way* something is written as distinguished from its contents or its meaning.

The same thing may be written in many styles. Observe the following examples:

His car never ran after that accident.

That smash-up totalled his jalopy forever.

Subsequent to that collision his automobile permanently refused to function.

That pile-up transformed his wheels into a heap of junk.

After that crash his auto was as useful as water wings in the desert.

The sentences above have basically the same contents and are all grammatically correct, but each has a different style.

There is no right style, no one way to write something, any more than there is a right way to sing a song. A good style is one that is clear and correct, holds the reader's attention, and is appropriate to the situation.

Avoid Slangy Stuff and Clichés

Most of what you write in college or in the workplace will require a somewhat formal style that is free of slang and not too colloquial, or informal. Colloquial style means the language of ordinary conversation, personal letters, and so on. Colloquial expressions, such as "guys," "kids," or "dazed out," do not usually belong in academic writing. At times writers may use certain colloquial expressions for effect, if they are particularly apt or colorful, but they should do so with care.

Be even more cautious about using slang like "That yucky dessert really grossed me out," or "I finally lost it." The meanings of slang expressions may not be familiar to all of your readers. Furthermore, slang is imprecise and becomes outdated quickly. No doubt the slang of your parents' generation seems very "corny" to you.

Selecting the appropriate style is in part instinctive; the choice of words and sentence structure would of course be more formal in a research paper or a proposal to the dean of students than in a letter to a close friend.

Like singers, writers need to work to develop an effective and appealing style. It is not enough simply to combine words in grammatical fashion. One step towards attaining a better style is becoming more conscious of those aspects of your writing style that you would like to improve, then work on changing them. It helps to read widely and pay close attention to the styles of other writers. Few singers will ever rival Nat King Cole's fluid style, just as most of us will never write as well as Truman Capote. However, all writers can make great strides towards developing a smoother writing style that is unique to them and is not predictable and trite.

Trite writing contains numerous overused expressions, or **clichés**.

It was time to get on with the rest of my life.

He was always there for me.

My heart was in my throat.

That was a different ball of wax.

Famous last words.

Undoubtedly you can complete the following expressions.

flat as a _pancake_

sharp as a _tack_

the bottom _line_

little did I _know_

last but not _least_

interestingly _enough_

shoulder to _shoulder_

better late than _never_

These clichés are so familiar and predictable that the responses to them tend to be uniform. That is exactly why such hackneyed, hand-me-down expressions weaken writing. Fortunately, because they are so familiar, it becomes a fairly easy matter to eliminate most clichés from your writing.

Equally overused are certain adjective/noun pairs such as *icy blast, bitter end, painful duty,* and *babbling brook.* Like many clichés, these phrases once had lots of punch, but they have appeared together so often that they no longer have impact. Weed most of them out of your writing. You can do much better.

Some Words Come in Familiar Packages

four long blocks

by all means

to say the least

all too often

tender young age/ripe old age

Because phrases like these come so readily to mind, most writers use them in early drafts. That is fine: The point is that such **packaged phrases** had best be eliminated from final drafts.

> # Being "Cutesy" is a "No-No"!

Avoid Sounding Too Precious

Writing containing certain clichés and expressions can become a little precious, as in the following:

> When I was a roly-poly young damsel of the tender age of three, I joined three other cute little rascals in a memorable rollicking escapade.

Help Wipe Out "Formal Speak"

A formal style, however, need not mean flowery, wordy, or pretentious. Wordy *formal speak* deadens writing:

> Inasmuch as this is an infraction against a regulation the enforcement of which is essential to the well-being of the entire university community, there is a need for this matter to be brought to the immediate attention of the dean of students.
>
> **Translation:** Because enforcement of that regulation is important to everyone at the university, inform the dean of students about this matter at once.

Formal speak thrives on stock phrases that enable writers to use several words when one or two would suffice.

inasmuch as = because

at this point in time = now

in the not-too-distant future = soon

due to the fact that = because

in reference to = about

aware of the fact that = know

be in a position to
have the ability to } = can

Exercise

Cross out the examples of formal speak and substitute with more concise, clear wording.

~~Due to the fact that~~ [Because] I ~~am in a position to~~ [can] ~~terminate~~ [end] your employment, you would be well advised to alter your work habits and attitude ~~at this point in time~~ [now]. Otherwise, ~~regardless of the fact that~~ [despite] you have many skills that our firm ~~is in need of~~ [needs], in the ~~not-too-distant~~ [soon] future you will find yourself without employment. ~~In the event that~~ [If] you ~~should have the desire~~ [want] to talk with me ~~concerning~~ [about] this matter, ~~kindly make contact with~~ [please call] my secretary as to the most convenient time for an appointment ~~with me~~.

Avoiding Padded Prose and Pretentious Language

"Ladies and gentlemen, we will momentarily be landing in the Atlanta area. We're sorry that, due to operational problems, we'll be experiencing a late arrival. At this time please extinguish all smoking materials. We will be de-planing by the forward exit. . . . blah blah blah . . . Thank you for flying Tin Can Airlines."

Decoded into plain English the above announcement might sound something like this:

Ladies and gentlemen. We are about to land in Atlanta. Sorry we're late, but the plane broke down. Please put out your cigarettes. You will go out the front exit.

Most air travelers have heard this kind of message so often that they do not really listen to the words, but readily translate the gobbledygook into ordinary language. In its December 1990 issue, the *Economist,* a British news weekly famous for its clear, crisp style, aptly labeled such prose "verbal styrofoam."

You could probably collect many similar examples—from textbooks, work manuals, government forms, and so on. Because the purpose of many of those sources is to communicate with a nonspecialized audience, writing in pretentious language that is difficult to follow seems a nonproductive option.

Students sometimes unwisely try to imitate this type of dense writing style because they think that that is how educated people ought to write. (It *is* true that *some* educated people do write that way, but most of their readers wish that they would stop doing so.) These students find themselves trying too hard, choosing too many multisyllable words when shorter ones would do much better, and saying things in an unnecessarily turgid and complicated fashion:

> *Need we bring it to your attention at this point in time that five almost unpronounceable words are frequently employed when one or two shorter, clearer words would suffice nicely for the occasion?*

Try to eliminate words and phrases that are pretentious, wordy, and repetitious from your writing. On occasion, deliberate repetition provides a handy and effective way to provide cohesion or emphasize a point. However, the writer needs to strike a balance and avoid the sort of excessive repetition that can only weaken writing.

Redundancy

Redundancy is useless repetition, writing the same, or almost the same, thing for no good reason. The wording may differ but the meaning does not. The following is an example from the November 23, 1987, sports page of the *Milwaukee Journal*.

> "I think we have a pretty good basketball team. And we're going to get better as we improve."
>
> *Del Harris*

Because speech tends to be full of redundancies, former Milwaukee Bucks' coach Del Harris' statement is understandable. Less understandable was the editor's decision to highlight the coach's redundant remark as a subheadline in a newspaper.

> Free Gift If You
> Open a New Account

Advertising is full of redundancies. If you *open* an account, isn't it *new*? Aren't all gifts *free*? Redundant phrases have become such staples of the language that we write them without thinking.

past memories (Aren't all memories past?)
deliberate lie (Can one tell an "accidental lie?")

The list could go on and on, but here are a few more common examples you should avoid:

few and far between
enclosed inside
each and every
full and complete
personally I think
total capacity
hopes and desires
fuchsia in color
from that moment in time

Choosing Interesting, Precise Words and Striving for Word Variety

Stay away from vague descriptive words, such as *nice* or *pretty,* and from overused superlatives, like *stupendous* or *fabulous.* Do you believe claims about the latest "fantastic thriller?" Does "She's a real nice girl" tell you much?

Find colorful, concrete words that best convey your meaning. There is nothing vague about Amy Schmechel's brief, but graphic, introduction to the scene of an accident.

Squeal, slide, smash, and crash pretty much sums up the horrific sounds echoing from the car that day.

Choose the *specific* rather than the *general: rat,* not *rodent; tricycle,* not *vehicle; poodle,* not *dog.* Selecting concrete words helps your readers understand or visualize what you mean; *glared* or *peered* rather than *looked; silvery grey 1991 Mercedes sedan* for *car; black and white Holstein heifer* instead of *cow.*

Which of these pairs tells the reader more? Choose more concrete words for the last three.

unpleasant noise ➤ shrill whistle
bright creature ➤ crimson starfish
difficult child ➤ stubborn grandson
worn garment ➤ *natty t-shirt*
loud sound ➤ *obnoxious bang*
huge insect ➤ *enormous June bug*

Imprecise general phrases, like those in the first column, have a tendency to appear in early drafts of an essay. Replace them with more colorful, exact words as you revise and edit.

You will also want to eliminate weak **intensifiers,** such as *really* and *very,* from your drafts. Speech is full of such intensifiers, but writing tends to be better without them. Write "boiling water" for "very hot water." If you claim that something is "unique," the word is strong enough by itself: If something could not be "a little unique," could it be "very unique"? Instead of "The hike *really tired* me," use a more precise verb: "The hike exhausted me."

> There's no need to repeat the same tired verbs.

Please do not annoy, torment, pester, plague, molest, worry, badger, harry, harass, heckle, persecute, irk, bullyrag, vex, disquiet, grate, beset, bother, tease, nettle, tantalize, or ruffle the animals.

San Diego Zoo
San Diego Wild Animal Park

Many former students have dipped wisely into the marvelous array of strong verbs available in English.

> *David Hart "heaved and sweated" over many a lawn to earn the money for a bike with a horn that "thundered and bellowed." No wonder he "mumbled" a quick "no" to the insulting purchase price "flapped" at him by school bully, Doug Gilcrest. David's mouth "wouldn't budge" as Doug the Tyrant persisted in his attempt to buy that treasured bike for a measly five dollars. Minutes later Doug "hurled his huge wrecking ball fist" at David's nose.*

Become more aware of how effective writers use verbs. If you find yourself repeating relatively imprecise verbs, like *moved, told,* or *said,* substitute more vivid ones. Write *sauntered* or *darted, stammered* or *screeched,* and your reader will instantly know much more about the situation being described.

When seeking exactly the right verbs, nouns, adjectives, and other words, writers should also be as aware as possible of the **connotations,** the emotional overtones and value judgments, that each choice may convey. Compare the following sentences.

Was the mayor's property tax proposal *criticized by a perceptive opponent* or *attacked by a partisan pit bull?*

Was the vice-president of that company an *overachieving, pushy executive* or an *industrious self-starter who got things done?*

Did those students *patronize a vintage clothing emporium* or *do their shopping at a thrift shop?*

While the meanings of each of the paired phrases is approximately the same, the connotations are quite different.

Keeping your purpose and audience in mind can aid in selecting wording with a connotation that is appropriate to the situation, does the job you want, and will not put off your readers.

Finding Wording Substitutes to Avoid Repetition

Vary your wording, for even the strongest verbs or the most concrete nouns quickly become monotonous. In fact, it would be easier to get by with several repetitions of the relatively colorless "she told the minister" on a single page than to use "she exhorted the dogmatic clergyman" more than once in the same essay.

For better word variety, make a conscious effort to spot and eliminate the kind of repetition that mars the paragraph below.

> Our family's favorite ski area is Arapahoe Basin in Summit County, Colorado. Arapahoe Basin has enough varied and challenging terrain to satisfy every skier from beginner to expert. Compared to many other Colorado ski areas, Arapahoe Basin is small and intimate, because Arapahoe Basin never draws huge crowds like the other three ski areas in Summit County. Because Arapahoe Basin is the highest ski area in North America, Arapahoe Basin has snow after it has melted in other ski areas. That's why so many diehard skiers flock to Arapahoe Basin every spring after the other ski areas have closed for the season.

What name is repeated seven times in that brief five sentence paragraph? What pronoun could have been substituted for that name?

Another option is to use **synonyms**—other names or nouns with about the same meaning—such as "A-Basin," "the Basin," or "the mountain" in place of Arapahoe Basin.

Chapter Four   Syntax, Diction, and Style   95

Exercise

For better word variety, rewrite the paragraph on Arapahoe Basin using a synonym or a pronoun instead of "Arapahoe Basin."

Note how many times the term "ski area" is also repeated in the paragraph. Think of substitutes—pronouns or synonyms—for that term and write them above the words "ski area" in a few instances.

Using Pronouns and Synonyms to Achieve Word Variety

The most common way to avoid monotonous repetition of the same noun is to use a pronoun—a noun substitute: *she* for "the girl" or "Mary"; *it* for "the ship" or "the book"; *they* for a ~~rock group~~ or a football team.

Another option is to find appropriate synonyms—words meaning about the same thing: "the bespectacled elderly gentleman" for "my grandfather"; "Ms. Jackson" (or "Roberta") for "Roberta" Jackson; "grey rodent" or "tiny furry creature" for "mouse."

Exercise

Rewrite the following two paragraphs and underline the repetitive nouns. Then write appropriate substitutes—synonyms or pronouns—for those nouns above them, thus eliminating the repetition. Part of the first one is already done, as a model.

Cosmos High School's Moses Moran won this year's award as the most valuable high school basketball player in Garden City. Moses Moran was Garden City's highest scorer for every one of the four years he played first-string center. Moses Moran also led all Garden City players in the percentage of successful free-throw attempts. But Moses Moran is also a good defensive player who grabbed more rebounds this year than any other player in Garden City. Thus the Garden City sports writers also named Moses Moran the best all-around high school athlete in Garden City in this decade.
  [He] above first "Moses Moran"; [the city's] above "Garden City's"; "He" above second "Moses Moran"; "on his team" above "in Garden City"; "him" above third "Moses Moran"

The dilapidated, but beloved, red brick church that dominated the town's square was in terrible repair. That red brick church had been the town's main attraction for over a century. Last year the county building commission reluctantly decided that the decaying red brick church had to be condemned. Because no one in the town wanted to see the red brick church torn down, the town council authorized a referendum to raise money to repair the red brick church. The old red brick church is already under renovation, as the citizens supported the referendum to save the red brick church by a sizeable majority.
  [The] above "That red brick"; [structure] above second "red brick church"; [it] above third "red brick church"; [old building] above fourth "red brick church"; [since] above "as"; [it] above fifth "red brick church"

Using Appositives to Avoid Repetition

Appositives—noun phrases that name, identify, or give more information about nouns—provide another way of eliminating wordiness and adding variety to your sentences. The appositives are in italics in these examples:

> My friend Francesca's grandmother, *Estelle Jimenez,* hired me for a job last summer. (This appositive *names* the subject.)

> Betty Ford, *the wife of ex-President Gerald Ford,* recounted the story of her recovery from drug and alcohol abuse in a 1987 bestseller. (This appositive *identifies* the subject.)

> Ms. Jimenez, *a staunch proponent of women's rights,* is the owner-manager of a successful travel agency. (This appositive *gives more information* about the subject.)

Because these appositives interrupt the above sentences, they are set off with commas from the nouns that they explain further. Like all modifiers, appositives belong close to the nouns that they modify. The above appositives all appear in the middle of sentences. As the following examples indicate, however, appositives can also be placed at the beginning or end of a sentence.

Note that a sentence can have more than one appositive.

> Pedro Rodrigues, a friend of Estelle's who lives in London, arranged the trip through Shoestring Excursions, an agency for the budget-minded traveler.

Exercise

Identify the appositives in the sentences below.

1. A very hard worker, Estelle Jimenez spends long hours at her agency and brings lots of work home every evening.
2. Her three children, Marc, Roberto, and Ramona, are always urging her to take a long vacation.
3. Last summer Estelle finally took a trip to Seville, a city she had hoped to visit since her childhood.

Trying Too Hard

Trying too hard can produce puffed-up, pretentious writing that sounds overwritten and strained. Do not string too many adjectives together or use too many big words or clichéd expressions, or your prose might read something like this:

> *Before our recent foray into the primeval forests of Alaska where we faced the wrathful anger of a gargantuan, frightened grizzly bear and two bouncing roly-poly cubs, my dauntless traveling companion and I had each been harboring our own private fantasies concerning the joys awaiting us in our upcoming sojourn into the vast open spaces of America's last frontier. Little did we know what frightening adventures awaited two eager and intrepid city slickers almost two hours to the dot after we ventured our first bold steps into the many marvels of the massive, mighty, and mysterious Alaskan forest.*

Among that paragraph's many excesses, consider the **alliteration**—repetition of the same initial sound—in the last sentence: *many marvels of the massive, mighty, and mysterious Alaskan forest.* Does the alliteration seem a bit much?

Although you can have fun playing with words having repetitive initial sounds, words that *shimmer or shout, whisper or wail,* alliteration can be overdone. For example, former President George Bush got carried away during the 1992 campaign when he called Congress a web of "PACs, perks, privileges, partisanship, and paralysis" that "puts politics ahead of principle, and above progress." In contrast, David Hart used alliteration effectively in the title of his narrative: "The Backpack That Packed a Punch."

Exercise

Put brackets around wordy, repetitious phrases, redundancies, unneeded intensifiers, and so on in the following paragraph. The first few sentences are already done for you. Then rewrite the paragraph, eliminating the material between the brackets, combining ideas, and changing the wording as needed.

> Be on the lookout for padded prose in your writing.

Giving birth to a child through a Caesarian section was a more terrifying experience than I had ever imagined. [I was terrified] when the nurses started prepping me for the surgery. [While the nurses were prepping me for the surgery,] an anesthetist came into the room. The anesthetist seated himself at the head of the bed. He placed a mask over my nose and mouth. He kept asking me, "How do you feel?" over and over. The last things I remember were the anesthetist asking how I felt, the surgeon's muttering, and a scraping sound. About an hour later I woke up in the recovery room. I remember that when I awoke I was still not mentally aware of what I had gone through. But I gradually became more aware of what was happening to me. After awhile I remembered that I had just come out of surgery and was on a bed in the recovery room. A few minutes later a cheery smiling nurse wearing a white uniform came up to my bed in the recovery room and told me the good news. She told me that I now had a healthy son who would soon be brought in for me to meet. A few minutes later another nurse in a white uniform brought in my new son for me to see for the first time. The nurse was carrying the most handsome curly-haired baby I had ever seen.

Combining Ideas and Cutting Dead Wood

Overuse of certain expressions, such as "there are" and "there were" can deaden your writing, in part because they become repetitious, in part because often such expressions do not really add anything to a sentence. Compare the following examples.

> From the porch of the cottage *there is* a steep, rocky winding path that leads to the cold, blue lake below.

> A steep, rocky path winds from the porch of the cottage to the cold, blue lake below.

Also cut out wordy expressions, such "at this point in time" (now), "yellow in color" (yellow), and "city of London." Because almost everyone knows that London is a city, just write "London."

Exercise

Put brackets around the "there is's" and the other repetitious phrases in the following paragraph. Then rewrite the paragraph in your journal, leaving out those phrases, combining ideas, and so on. The first sentence has been done for you.

[There is] almost everything the traveler needs in Victoria Station. Victoria Station is in the city of London. There are several restaurants and foodstands. The restaurants include several fast-food establishments. There is a good quality hotel in the station. Having a hotel right there in the train station is a convenience not found in train stations in the United States. There are any number of shops and kiosks located throughout Victoria Station. These kiosks range from the usual tourist trap that sells souvenirs to a drug store and even a shop selling all types of hosiery. There is an instant photo machine where you can get your photo taken. In addition to the usual shoe shine facility there even is a shoe repair stand in Victoria Station. Perhaps most convenient of all, there is a tube station right there at Victoria Station where you can catch the subway—the British call it *the tube*—and go by subway to any part of the city of London.

Considering the "So What" Factor

It is also possible to write too little, to fail to develop your ideas adequately or to include enough examples or explanations. Some students' writings sound like their authors did not put in enough effort. In some cases that may be what happened. What is more likely, however, is that they made the mistake of writing about topics that they did not really care about. Perhaps they unwisely chose to repeat the familiar about subjects that have been widely discussed. In such cases the result is usually a series of dull paragraphs and an uninspired overall product, characterized by what our former colleague Kathy Scullin calls the "so what factor." "So what" essays generally begin something like the following.

A good education is a must in today's competitive world.

A healthy diet means a healthy, longer life.

The essays then proceed to elaborate on the familiar without an original insight on the subject.

To write an effective paper on familiar topics like these, a writer needs to say something *special;* otherwise the essay lacks voice and simply repeats what almost everyone knows and does not care to hear again. Write about drinking and driving only if you have done special research on the topic or if you want to tell the reader what it is like to be the only survivor of a crash when your drunken friend smashed up the family van and killed three people. Then your **voice** will come through loud and clear because you do have something *worth saying.*

As the following example shows, however, good writers can often find unusual ways of describing the usual:

The first thing my mother would do is give me a big hug and kiss. I was given all this affection and all I had done was wake up.

Wade Davis

Chapter Five

Fractured and Nonfractured Syntax

Finding something worth writing about may seem more crucial than writing it clearly and correctly. Both, however, are of equal importance; poor mastery of syntax and grammar can ruin a potentially good essay that has lots of voice. On the other hand, it is also possible to compose an essay that is totally lacking in voice but is written in grammatically flawless, perfectly correct word order, or syntax.

> ### Clinton's Style: Articulate and Direct
>
> . . . The man from Little Rock left not the slightest doubt that the White House will get its syntax tightened when he moves in on Jan. 20.
>
> (*New York Times,* November 12, 1992)

This section includes many suggestions about improving syntax—word order—along with pointing out some of the most common problems of syntax and suggesting numerous ways to avoid these problems. It discusses methods of determining whether what you have written is a sentence, as well as surveying some of the many sentence types available to writers.

Experimenting with a Wide Variety of Sentence Types

Increasing your awareness of the wide range of sentence types can help you to improve your writing style. Effective writers use a variety of sentence patterns and vary the length of their sentences. An essay composed solely of short, three- to five-word sentences is terribly monotonous, but no more so than an essay containing only lengthy, complicated, multiclause sentences of thirty words or more. Keep your reader interested by changing the length of your sentences.

Too many short choppy sentences can result in Dick-and-Jane style prose like you read in the primary grades.

> Mr. Fidget is the worst teacher I ever had. He teaches biology. He is also the football coach. Mr. Fidget teaches at Prairie High School. He is tall. He has too many favorites. He is a dull speaker. I had him sophomore year.

Nor is it effective to string too many independent clauses together into one long sentence.

> I rang the door bell, and I went into the party, and I met some of my friends, and we soon got sick of the loud music, and we left for the movies.

On the other hand, it is occasionally a good tactic to vary word order and abandon conventional syntax. For example, you could write, "A dancer she is not," instead of the more standard "She is not a good dancer."

Phrases, Clauses, and Sentences

Phrases, the most basic groupings of words, consist of two or more related words that act as a unit, and follow recognized patterns, such as *to the reunion, looking terrific,* or *to reminisce.*

Looking terrific, the former class president went to the reunion to reminisce about her high school days.

Because they do not contain both a verb and a subject, phrases usually do not make sense by themselves. They form parts of clauses or sentences where they often act as **modifiers**—adding information about, or modifying, subjects and verbs.

Six striped fish swam in a pond.

The basic, or kernel, sentence in the above example is *fish swam.* The sentence is about fish—the subject—and tells what the fish did: swam—the verb or predicate. Which modifying phrase tells more about the verb *swam?*
Which modifiers tell more about the subject *fish?*
Here is an example of a sentence composed of only a subject and a verb (predicate), with no modifiers:

Monkeys climb.

What is the noun subject? What is the verb?
Now look at that same kernel sentence with modifying phrases added. The modifiers are in italics.

Three skinny monkeys climb *rapidly up the pole.*

"Climb rapidly up the pole," the predicate of this sentence, contains the verb *climb* in the present tense. The action is going on right now.

A **predicate** is composed of a verb, or verbs, and various modifiers, which act as a unit to proclaim something about the subject of the sentence. In the above case the reader hears that monkeys—the subject—climb—the verb.

One useful way to find the predicate—also called the **verb phrase**—is to look for the words that are affected when the time, or tense, of a sentence is changed. The words that change form when the time is changed are the verbs.

Look at the following examples.

Present tense: Three skinny monkeys *climb* rapidly up the pole. (The monkeys are now in the act of climbing.)

Here is how that sentence would read in the past tense.

Yesterday three skinny monkeys *climbed* rapidly up the pole.

Change the sentence to put it into the future tense.

Tomorrow three skinny monkeys _____ rapidly up the pole.

Because the form of the word *climb* changes when the tense, or time, of the sentence is changed, *climb* is the verb of the sentence.

Three skinny monkeys is the subject, or **noun phrase**—the noun plus its modifiers—of that sentence. The noun and its modifiers work as a unit to make up the subject of the sentence.

Exercise

Find the kernel sentence (the subject and verb) and the modifiers in the following sentences. To find the verb, look for the word, or words, that change when you change the time (the tense) of a sentence. Write down the subject and verb, putting one line under the subject and two lines under the verb in each example. The first one is identified for you.

1. Five frivolous <u>frogs</u> <u><u>flip</u></u> foolishly over the dam.

    Yesterday five frivolous frogs flipped foolishly over the dam.

    Next week five frivolous frogs will flip foolishly over the dam.

    What words modify the subject *frogs?* What word and what phrase modify the verb *flipped?*

    Tense forms of the verb flip:

    Flip is the _____ tense.

    Flipped is the _____ tense.

    Will flip is the _____ tense.

2. Three elongated eels edge slowly away from the shore.

    What words modify the subject? What words and what phrase modify the verb?

    The verb is in the _____ tense.

3. Seven slippery snakes will soon slither through the meadow.

    What words modify the subject? What word and what clause modify the verb?

    The verb is in the _____ tense.

Slither, edge, and *flip:* The verbs from the above examples are all *action* verbs. They tell what the subjects are doing.

Not all verbs are action verbs, however. There is another kind of verb, the **linking verb,** which connects subjects to words that identify, describe, or tell something about the subjects.

A frog *is* a tailless amphibian with smooth, moist skin. (present tense linking verb: *is*)

My uncle *was* very weary last evening. (past tense linking verb: *was*)

Next month my coworker Gilberto *will be* my supervisor. (future tense linking verb: *will be*)

Is, was, and *will be* are all forms of the verb *be.*

In addition to the verb *be,* there are several other linking verbs, such as *taste, become, remain, seem,* and so on.

The spaghetti sauce *tastes* flat.

The snake *became* so content that it *remained* on the rock for the rest of the afternoon. Nothing *seemed* to disturb it.

My uncle *will look* weary after his five-set tennis match.

Exercise

Write down the subject and the verb of the following sentences. Put one line under the subject and two lines under the linking verb. The first one is done for you.

1. Normally my Aunt Sue is a placid, well-adjusted woman.
2. She seems unbelievably unflappable at times.
3. Until last month Sue always stayed calm in emergencies, unlike most of her family.
4. Sue remained a placid person until someone broke into her office one night.
5. Will Aunt Sue now become less calm in difficult situations?
6. Will she be as rattled and useless as her timid, nervous husband?

While linking verbs have their appropriate uses, they tend to be overused. In contrast to action verbs, linking verbs are relatively static and less varied and colorful. Compare these two examples:

The women's hockey coach's method of stimulating her team *is* to single out the sluggard and bellow orders in her face.

The women's hockey coach *singles out* the sluggard and *bellows* orders in her face to stimulate the team.

Find the linking verbs in the following sentence.

There is another, more soft-spoken hockey coach in the same conference who has never become demanding enough of her players and therefore her team is never victorious.

Here is how that sentence might read without all the linking verbs.

Another, more soft-spoken coach in the same conference never demands enough of her players, and they never win.

As you read, observe how effective writers rely on strong, active verbs. Avoid too many linking verbs and use a wide variety of concrete action verbs to make your own sentences more clear and expressive.

Exercise

Put brackets around repetitive phrases and excessive linking verbs (phrases such as "there are"). Then rewrite the paragraph. You may need to change the word order to make a revised version read smoothly. The first passage is done as a model for you.

> A surprise greeted us when we drove into our driveway. [There was] a tall gaunt man ringing our doorbell. [He was] wearing a ragged tweed sport coat and tattered tennis shoes. [He is] a distant cousin of my mother. [His name is] Bruce Hutchins. [I remembered how] Bruce used to visit our family every summer, but none of us had seen [my mother's distant cousin Bruce] for several years.

There is no one correct way to reword the passage so that it reads more smoothly, but an improved version might sound something like the following.

> A surprise greeted us when we drove into our driveway. Bruce Hutchins, a tall gaunt man in a ragged tweed sport coat and tattered tennis shoes, was ringing our doorbell. A distant cousin of my mother, Bruce used to visit our family every summer, but none of us had seen him for several years.

When going over drafts, circle repetitious wording and all instances where a more active verb would be preferable to a linking verb. Then change them in subsequent drafts. Practice on the following passage.

The two archers came out into the open meadow, stopped briefly to survey the scene, and excitedly readied their bows. There was a magnificent buck standing on the opposite edge of the clearing, apparently unaware of the intruders. There was a ten-point rack on his head. Nearby there was a doe standing under a small tree who seemed equally oblivious to the danger. There was a stagnant pond in the center of the meadow. Drinking from that stagnant pond there were two spotted fawns who had wandered away from their mother who was standing nearby under a tree. Just as one hunter took aim and was about to fire an arrow, his companion sneezed and broke his friend's concentration. His friend swore at him for sneezing and breaking his concentration, and then took aim again. There was a look of terror in the frightened buck's eyes as he plunged into the brush, followed by the frightened doe and her two frightened fawns. There was nothing for the archers to do but leave the scene in disappointment. Silence covered the meadow once again and nothing could be heard.

Thinking About Sentences

Sentences are composed of parts, or chunks. Draw a line between the first and second parts.

The hungry wolf chased the scared rooster.

He chased the scared rooster away.

The terrified rooster quickly darted under the porch.

How did you divide those sentences? People often divide sentences along the lines of **actor** and **action**.

Actor	*Action*
The hungry wolf	chased the scared rooster.
He	chased the scared rooster away.
The terrified rooster	quickly darted under the porch.

Actor (also called the subject) = **noun** or **pronoun** + **modifiers**.
Action (also called the predicate) = **verb** + **modifiers**.

Modifiers "fine-tune"—that is, give more information—about the words they modify. For example, in the phrase "the hungry wolf," *hungry* modifies the noun, *wolf.*

Actor + modifiers = noun (subject) phrase.

Action + modifiers = predicate (verb) phrase.

Noun Phrase *Predicate Phrase*
(Actor)   (Action)

The hungry wolf   chased the scared rooster away.
The terrified rooster quickly darted under the porch.

Understanding Kinds of Sentences: How to Tell Whether It's a Sentence

It is not always easy to decide whether what you have written is a sentence, in part because it is difficult to define exactly what a sentence is. This may be one reason many college students still have trouble writing complete sentences, as well as separating sentences and clauses with proper punctuation. The fact that there are so many types of sentences in English further complicates the problem. Moreover, most of the standard definitions of a sentence leave something to be desired, because there are exceptions to all of them. For example, the standard definition of a sentence as "a group of words that has a subject and a verb (or predicate)" does not allow for imperative sentences, or commands, such as "Eat your broccoli." Does it really help the puzzled student to say that such commands have the *implied* subject *you?* Even if true?

You may have already noted that the last sentence, a question, also lacks a subject—and a verb, for that matter. You can get away with an implied subject or verb in questions, just as you can in commands, because people do not always use sentences when they issue orders or ask questions. Agreed? (The latter is another example of an exception, the one-word question, such as *Really?*)

Furthermore, sentences can have **compound**—more than one—**subjects** and/or **verbs**:

    (compound subject) (compound verb)
The monkeys and baboons leaped and swung among the trees.

Exercise

Put one line under the compound subjects and two lines under the compound verbs. (*Note:* Not all of the examples have both.) The first one is done for you.

1. He and his father fished and hunted together for more than forty years.
2. Tricia and Bruce gathered nuts and placed them in a barrel.

3. Several boys and girls clambered over the crest of the hill.
4. The scrawny chickens scratched and pecked in the dusty road.
5. She and I whispered and giggled through the entire ceremony.

Compound Sentences

In addition to having compound subjects and predicates, sentences themselves can be compound. A **compound sentence** contains more than one independent clause. An **independent clause** is a group of words that has at least one subject and at least one verb and makes sense by itself. Thus, independent clauses can stand alone as sentences, as well as be combined to form compound sentences. The following is an example of a compound sentence with two independent clauses.

> Ferdinand dreamed about going to Cancún for spring break, but unfortunately he lacked sufficient funds.

The subject of the first clause is *Ferdinand*. The verb of the first clause is *dreamed*. What is the subject of the second clause? What is the verb of the second clause? What word connects these two independent clauses?

That sentence is an example of a compound sentence, which has two independent clauses connected by the coordinating conjunction *but*. **Conjunctions** are words that join clauses, phrases, or words, such as *and, but, since, although,* and *because.*

There are seven coordinating conjunctions (coordinators) that can form compound sentences by joining two independent clauses: *but, and, for, nor, or, so,* and *yet*. To remember them, try memorizing the nonsense word *yabnofs,* formed from the initial letter of the seven coordinators:

The Seven Coordinators

Yet
And
But
Nor
Or
For
So
SPELL **YABNOFS**

If the two independent clauses in the above example were not connected by the coordinating conjunction *but,* they could have been written as two sentences separated by a **period.**

> Ferdinand dreamed about going to Cancún for spring break. Unfortunately, he lacked sufficient funds.

They also could have been joined by a **semicolon,** thus forming another kind of compound sentence—two independent clauses with a semicolon between them.

> Ferdinand dreamed about going to Cancún for spring break; unfortunately, he lacked sufficient funds.

Note that even without the coordinating conjunction *but,* the word *unfortunately* still shows the logical connection between these two independent clauses.

These seven coordinating conjunctions—*but, and, for, nor, or, so, yet*—each have their own uses:

> Many tried out *but* few got a part in the play.

> Shanta is not a good actress, *nor* is she a good singer.

> That village badly needs a new school, *yet* the voters did not approve a tax increase.

The choice of a coordinator is an important part of making your meaning clear for your reader. Does the following sentence make sense?

> The village badly needs a new school, *so* the voters did not approve a tax increase.

Moreover, a sentence lacks unity and sounds silly if the clauses in a compound sentence are not logically related.

> Some tried out for the play but everyone missed the fire drill.

> Shanta is not a good actress, so she is often late for class.

> Note that a comma is not always used in short compound sentences.

> You can add a comma but it is not essential.

When a comma is used, however, it belongs *before* the coordinator and *not after* it.

> Carla added the necessary comma but, she put it in the wrong place in the sentence.

Try reading that sentence aloud. Where do you instinctively want to pause? That is where the comma belongs.

> Carla added the necessary comma, but she put it in the wrong place in the sentence.

Exercise

Underline the coordinators and add commas to the following sentences.

1. Coordinating conjunctions are useful words for combining ideas but you must be careful to choose the appropriate coordinator.
2. The coordinating conjunctions do not have the same meaning so they are not interchangeable.
3. Do not put the punctuation in the wrong place or your readers may be confused by your compound sentence.

Recognizing the Subjects and Verbs in Compound Sentences

Recall that the subject of a sentence or clause—the unit about which something is being said—is usually a noun or a pronoun. (Remember that pronouns are words like *he, she, it,* or *they* that take the place of nouns.) The predicate or verb is the unit that says something about the subject. (Also remember that one way to spot the verb is to look for the words that change if the tense of the sentence is changed.)

Exercise

Unlike simple sentences, compound sentences have more than one independent clause. It follows that they also have more than one subject and predicate. Put one line under the two subjects and two lines under the verbs in the following compound sentences. The first sentence is done for you.

1. The <u>principal</u> <u>mumbled</u> an introduction into the microphone, and then <u>he</u> <u>slouched</u> into a seat in the first row.
2. A tall, sultry vocalist in a silver gown strode on stage proudly, but then she tripped over the cord of the microphone.
3. The surface of the stage was rough, so the singer tripped again and almost fell down.
4. The pianist in black leather trousers rushed to her side; the vocalist smiled in embarrassment at all of the commotion.
5. The pianist returned to his seat at the piano, and the singer soon stood next to him, ready to perform.
6. The impatient audience expected the concert to begin, yet the flustered singer remained silent, unable to recall her opening line.
7. She finally remembered the first words; by then the pianist was too nervous to play his best.
8. The concert was a fiasco, but everyone clapped loudly anyway.

The seven coordinating conjunctions—*but, and, for, nor, or, so,* and *yet*—indicate an equal relationship between clauses. If clauses are joined by coordinating conjunctions, or connectors, they are equals—that is, independent clauses, each of which could stand alone as sentences. The two clauses have the same status, as do you and your coworkers. You are not subordinate to your coworkers as you would be to your boss or another authority figure.

Using Subordinators in Complex Sentences

Clauses can be **dependent,** or subordinate, as well as independent. **Subordinate clauses** do not make sense by themselves, but depend on another clause in a sentence for their meaning. A sentence that has one independent clause and at least one subordinate, or dependent, clause is called a **complex sentence.**

There are several **subordinating conjunctions,** or **connectors,** that may be used to introduce dependent clauses. Examples of such subordinating conjunctions are in italics in the following complex sentences. Identify the clauses, as in the model.

  (dependent clause) (independent clause)
Although many tried out, few got parts in the play.

Selenia would have been very surprised *if* she had not been chosen for the chorus line.

Because she dances well, Selenia enjoys performing.

A Selection of Subordinators (Joining Devices)

Subordinators such as subordinating conjunctions allow us to show logical relationships between ideas, such as cause and effect or purpose.

 Cause and effect: Sam cannot charge our lunch *because* he forgot his credit card.

 Purpose: I assigned the research paper early *so that* students would have enough time to write a good paper.

Joining Devices (Subordinators)	*Relationship Shown*
because	cause/effect
if, whether, unless, until	special condition
so that, in order that	purpose
though, although, even though	limitation or concession
where, wherever	place
after, since, as soon as, when, while, until, before, whenever	time

Dependent, or subordinate, clauses may also be introduced by **relative pronouns,** such as *who, which,* and *that.* Identify the clauses in the following sentences, as in the model.

        (independent clause)   (dependent clause)
Ramona was the only student *who* left the library early that evening.

Boerner Library has one floor, *which* is packed every night.

Ramona had been studying with Henry, *who* had some research to finish.

Unfortunately, the one book *that* he really needed was not on the shelf.

Research is not something *that* should be begun at the last minute.

Hint: If you suspect that you have written a dependent clause and have punctuated it like it is a sentence, cover up the words on either side of the clause. If the clause does not make sense by itself, it is probably a dependent clause.

Exercise

Put brackets around the dependent (subordinate) clauses in the following sentences. The first one is done for you.

1. [If a clause does not make sense by itself,] it is probably a dependent clause.
2. When you punctuate a dependent clause as if it were a sentence, you have written a fragment.
3. A fragment is a phrase or a clause that does not make sense by itself.
4. Often the fragment only needs to be connected to words before or after it that complete the fragment's meaning.
5. Although you may try to avoid them, fragments tend to creep into early drafts of essays.
6. Do your best to eliminate fragments because they may confuse your readers.
7. Because there are so many kinds of sentences, it is not always easy to spot fragments or end-stop punctuation errors.

As the above discussion indicates, there are several kinds of sentences, along with several exceptions to most standard definitions of a sentence. Thus we will have to settle for a somewhat imprecise definition: A sentence is an orderly arrangement of words in phrases that makes sense to the reader. As Scott Rice puts it in his thoughtful and useful *Right Words, Right Places,* a sentence is a sequence of phrases that "accomplishes some kind of business," such as "making a statement for someone to believe" or asking a question.

The examples you have been looking at—simple sentences, complex sentences, and compound sentences—are classified by their structure; that is, by their word arrangement or syntax.

Understanding the Basic Sentence Types

Simple sentences consist of one independent clause.

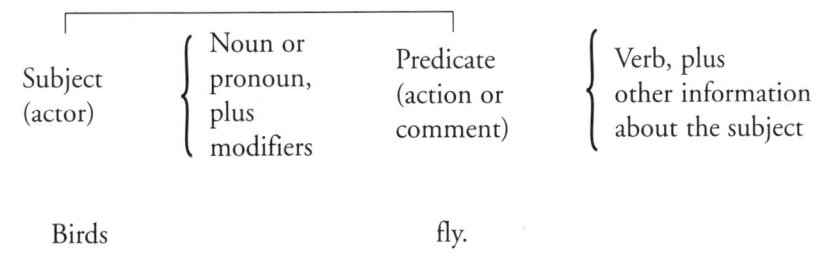

Subject (actor)	Noun or pronoun, plus modifiers	Predicate (action or comment)	Verb, plus other information about the subject
Birds		fly.	

Other examples of common simple sentence patterns:

Most birds can fly in the sky.

Do all birds fly in the sky?

No migrating birds are flying overhead now.

Compound sentences consist of two or more independent clauses. The clauses can be joined by one of the seven coordinating conjunctions—*but, and, for, or, nor, so,* or *yet*—or by a semicolon.

Subject	Predicate		Subject	Predicate
Most birds	fly,	*but*	all fish	swim.
Most birds	fly	;	all fish	swim.

Complex sentences consist of one independent clause, and at least one dependent, or subordinate, clause. The dependent clauses may be joined to the independent clause by a subordinator, such as *when, because, where,* or *so that.*

	Independent Clause			Subordinate Clause	
Subject	Predicate			Subject	Predicate
Birds	can fly	*because*		they	have wings.
Fish	can breathe	*only when*		they	are in water.

Subordinate clauses can also come before the independent clause.

Because they have wings, birds can fly.

Classifying Sentences by Their Purpose

A sentence can be:

A statement: Maria is late.

A question: Is Maria late?

A command: Hurry up, Maria.

An exclamation: Late again, Maria!

Be aware that the type of end-stop punctuation varies with the purpose of a sentence, as in the above diagram. It is the writer's job to punctuate between independent clauses and sentences so that they make sense to the reader. Choosing the right punctuation is not always an easy task, but it becomes much easier with practice. (For more information on end-stop punctuation see the appropriate sections in Chapter 6 on demystifying punctuation.)

Avoiding Common Errors in End-Stop Punctuation

Run-On Sentences

Almost everyone has listened to someone who runs on and on in a monotone, rarely pausing for breath. At best, such speakers are simply hard to follow so listeners tend to tune them out; at worst, they put their audience to sleep. Writers who leave out the necessary punctuation marks between independent clauses or sentences may have the same effect on their readers.

> Avoid run-on sentences they are hard to read.

Run-on, or **fused**, **sentences** join independent clauses without using any punctuation. Independent clauses need to be separated with one of the full-stop punctuation marks: *periods, question marks, exclamation points, semicolons,* and *colons.* Note: Commas are *not* full-stop punctuation marks; they are not strong enough for that purpose.

> Run-on sentences may put your readers to sleep.

Students sometimes think, incorrectly, that a run-on sentence is a sentence that is simply too long. Run-on sentences can be very short. Length is not the issue; the issue is the number of independent clauses—clauses that have a subject and a verb, and make sense by themselves. Keep in mind that either a pronoun or a noun can be a subject.

The bell rang the students left.

What is the first subject? What is the first verb? What is the second subject? What is the second verb?

Here is one corrected version:

The bell rang. The students left.

Find the two subjects in the following short run-on sentence, then rewrite it with the correct punctuation.

The phone rang she answered it.

Exercise

Find the two subjects. Correct the following run-on sentences by adding appropriate conjunctions or full-stop punctuation (and any necessary capital letters) between the independent clauses.

1. Two frogs were sunning on a log suddenly one frog hopped into the pond and disappeared beneath the bridge.
2. A tall chap was dozing on the veranda of a summer cottage his friend sat reading in a nearby rocking chair.
3. The phone rang Keysha answered it.
4. No one responded she hung up in disgust.
5. A few people put cutesy messages on their answering machines I sometimes hang up without leaving a response if the messages are too cutesy.
6. Do you have an answering machine my friends regularly complain because I do not have one.
7. My dad has an answering machine he always forgets to turn it on.

Comma Faults (Comma Splices)

> Commas are not full-stop punctuation marks, commas are placed within independent clauses.
>
> Commas are too weak to separate independent clauses, they belong within them.
>
> Do not join two independent clauses with a comma, you then write a comma fault or comma splice.

The sentences above all contain comma faults. **Comma faults,** or **comma splices,** occur when independent clauses in a compound sentence are joined by a comma instead of a stronger punctuation mark. Commas belong *within* independent clauses, not between them, unless they are used after coordinating conjunctions such as *and* or *but*.

Find the subjects of each of the independent clauses in the sentence above, as shown here:

> *Commas* are not full-stop punctuation marks, *commas* are placed within independent clauses.

In that compound sentence both independent clauses have the same noun subject, *commas*.

Editing Comma Faults. The comma faults above could be edited in more than one way. The following are some of the options.

Put a period between the two independent clauses and add the necessary capital letter to the second sentence.

> Commas are not full-stop punctuation marks. Commas are placed within independent clauses.

Put an appropriate coordinating conjunction between the two clauses.

> Do not join two independent clauses with a comma, *or* you then write a comma fault.

Join the two independent clauses with a semicolon.

> Commas are too weak to separate independent clauses; they belong within them.

Here is a point to remember about semicolons. Because a semicolon acts as a substitute for a period, you should *not* put semicolons *within* independent clauses.

Incorrect: Shanta has passed all the basic requirements; such as math, chemistry, English, and psychology.

Incorrect: Shanta is a dedicated and competent student; who is always in the library and is never late with her assignments.

Remember this rule of thumb: if you would not want a period, then do not use a semicolon. Would you want a period after the words *requirements* or *student* in the above sentences? Read the sentences aloud. Do you instinctively pause after those sounds?

Exercise

Using one of the above options for each sentence, correct the following comma faults, or comma splices.

1. Traditionally, the masculine gender pronouns *he* and *his* were used to refer to people in groups containing both sexes, today many women are actively trying to change that tradition.
2. Each pupil should bring his own lunch to the school picnic, such usage implies that all the pupils in the class are boys.
3. Every doctor should know her patients well, this usage insinuates that all doctors are female.
4. Certain masculine gender words such as *policeman* are no longer appropriate, today's police forces include many female officers.
5. Gender-neutral terms like *police officer* or *mail carrier* are more appropriate, they accurately reflect the changes in today's work force.
6. Yet many popular publications are resisting this trend to get rid of sexist language, unfortunately these publications still use masculine pronouns to refer to people of both genders.

Intentional Comma Faults. You may observe that writers sometimes use commas between independent clauses, generally when the clauses are so closely related that they make a single point. Mark Zukowski used such a deliberate comma fault in an account of a Little League title match.

This isn't just a game, it's the World Series, an event that might not be repeated again.

Gilbert Garcia also used a deliberate comma fault in his recollection of his childhood adventures in a neighborhood woods.

There is more than just trees in there, our childhood is hidden amongst those branches, leaves, and grass.

In general, however, student writers had best avoid such "intentional comma faults" and stick to conventional punctuation between independent clauses.

Exercise

Add appropriate full-stop punctuation marks—periods, question marks, exclamation points, colons, or semicolons—or conjunctions and the necessary capital letters to eliminate any comma faults or run-on sentences in the following. Label each example RO (run-on sentence) or CF (comma fault). Then rewrite the sentences, fixing the errors in them.

1. My mother's car stalled on the freeway, fortunately no one smashed into it before the police arrived
2. Did you detect the terror in his eyes as he opened the door into the cellar maybe he had been watching too many Stephen King movies lately
3. Do not forget to lock the door when you leave, this neighborhood has seen too many burglaries in the past month to take any unnecessary chances
4. One guest was late, the others came right on time
5. The teacher stomped out of the room the students were stunned at his reaction
6. My friend's uncle never has a kind word for anyone why does her family put up with his insults every holiday
7. "You were late, did you get in trouble," mother probed
8. Many are called few are chosen
9. The train pulled away from the platform five minutes early, a few angry passengers were left behind
10. One expects a train to be late one does not expect a train to be early

Getting Rid of Unintentional Fragments

> "Bits and Pieces" of a sentence can frustrate your reader.

Fragments are phrases and clauses that do not make sense by themselves but are punctuated as if they were sentences. For instance, if you open a sentence with a clause which begins with a cue word such as *because,* or *before,* be aware that the clause requires more explanation in the rest of the sentence.

Because I went to the race track, I lost all my money on the horses.

Before that trip to the race track, I had been careful not to spend money foolishly.

Now complete the following fragments.

Until she met Frank, _____.

Although he loved her, _____.

Be on the alert for fragments.

These two fragments, "Until she met Frank" and "Although he loved her" are dependent, or subordinate, clauses. Dependent clauses have a subject and a verb, but they are not sentences; they cannot stand alone because they do not make sense by themselves.

Fragments like these can be corrected in several ways. One way is to connect the dependent clause to an independent clause that completes its meaning.

    (dependent clause)   (independent clause)
While I was at the movies, my husband did the shopping.

Keep in mind that the order of the two clauses can often be reversed.

My husband did the shopping while I was at the movies.

Another way to correct such a fragment is to remove the word or phrases, such as the *while* in the above sentence, that make it a dependent clause.

I was at the movies.

Exercise

Put brackets around the words that make the following fragments dependent on additional unstated information to complete their meaning. Note that they become sentences when those words are removed. The first one is done for you.

1. [Although] Anita is a very good photographer. (fragment)
   Anita is a very good photographer. (sentence)
2. Because Jon and Anita are friends as well as roommates.
3. Until Jon finished writing that last computer manual.
4. While Jon and Anita were unpacking books in their new apartment.

Watch Out for *-ing* Fragments

Beginning a sentence with an *-ing* verb phrase, such as "Dancing through the tulips," also requires something else in the sentence to complete the thought. Otherwise you again end up with a piece of a sentence, a fragment. Fragments are frustrating to the reader. They tantalize, but do not explain, as the following examples demonstrate.

Reaching for his weapon.

Leaping down the chimney.

These *-ing* clauses are fragments because they have *no subject.* The reader does not know who was reaching for a weapon or who is leaping down the chimney. These phrases are dependent on something more to complete their meaning. This kind of fragment can be corrected by adding a subject.

Santa Claus is leaping down the chimney.

You can also connect the phrase to an independent clause that has an appropriate subject.

Leaping down the chimney, Santa Claus landed on the hearth.

Complete the following fragments by adding a subject or connecting them to an independent clause that has an appropriate subject.

Reaching for his weapon.

Ducking behind the door.

Grinning at the photographer.

Sometimes a fragment lacks a *verb.*

A tall skinny man in a grey tweed coat and blue plaid pants.

What was the man doing? Correct the fragment by adding a predicate (verb).
Another way to fix this kind of fragment is to make the man an object, as in the following.

(direct object)
Rondo noticed a tall skinny man in a grey tweed coat and blue plaid pants.

What is the subject of that sentence? What is the verb?

Exercise

Make the following two fragments into sentences by adding a *verb* (predicate).

1. One of the most understanding and demanding teachers in that university.
2. A school known for its academics, not its football team.

Now change the same two above fragments into sentences by making them into direct objects of a verb.

Be on the Lookout for Fragments in Your Drafts

Fragments often occur because less experienced writers put unnecessary full-stop punctuation in the middle of sentences. The result is incomplete thoughts, or fragments, that depend on the words before or after them for their meaning. If you suspect that you have written a fragment, one way to check is to cover up the words on either side of it. Then check if what you have written makes sense by itself.

Do the words between the brackets in the two examples below make sense by themselves? To check, cover up words that are not between the brackets.

[Because I started to worry that I had written too long a sentence.] I went back and added a couple of periods and capital letters. [Thinking that would make the sentence more correct and please my teacher.]

[Whenever I write] I find myself confused by the bewildering array of punctuation marks from which to choose. [Such as exclamation points, semicolons, question marks, dashes, and commas.]

Exercise

The following relatively long sentences have each been mistakenly separated into one sentence (independent clause) and two or three fragments. Copy the sentences, putting brackets around the fragments and a line under the independent clauses, as in the above examples.

1. Having proofread what she viewed as a masterpiece on a major turning point in her life. The proud student turned in her theme on Friday morning. Convinced that even Mr. Nitpicker could not find a single error in it.
2. A genius at spotting every mistake no matter how minor. Mr. Nitpicker was notorious for the many red marks he put on every student's paper. Plus requests that the paper be resubmitted in two days with all of the mistakes corrected.

3. Once that deadline passed. Mr. Nitpicker threw all revised papers that were handed in into the wastebasket. Unnecessarily humiliating the poor student who was late. Right in front of the entire class.

Exercise

Add enough words—either before or after the fragments—to change the following into sentences.

1. Convinced that nothing but good could result from her efforts.
2. Including compact discs, albums, tapes, and sheet music.
3. Having packed all of her supplies for the journey.
4. Because that principal did not attempt to understand the students' viewpoint.
5. As I knew that I could not make the football team because of a back injury.

Exercise

Read each of the following passages aloud, checking for unnecessary full-stop punctuation. Cover sections that you suspect may be fragments to see if they make sense by themselves. Put brackets around all of the fragments. [Like this example in these brackets.] Then change the fragments into sentences by crossing out unneeded punctuation marks, substituting new punctuation where appropriate, and eliminating all unnecessary capital letters.

1. During the last year of my high school athletic career. I suffered a knee injury that still hurts today. And will probably bother me for the rest of my life.
2. While Peter was on the third floor of the library looking for Hermine. She was on the lower floor looking for Peter.
3. Learning to eat low-calorie, balanced meals and saying "no" to rich desserts. Is about the only sure way for many people to lose weight. And not gain it all back again.
4. It was fear of being caught. That caused the thief to lie completely still on the floor of his car for half an hour. Hardly daring to breathe until the police left the alley.
5. Running along the highway with a look of terror in its eyes. The eight-point buck suddenly paused. Then sprang lightly into the dark forest nearby.

Avoiding Fragments

You should be able to find more of your own fragments and punctuate your writing more correctly once you get into the habit of listening for full-stop and half-stop pauses as you read over your drafts. The rhythm of the language, the natural pauses in speech, provide one good guide to placement of many punctuation marks. Reading aloud, or whispering, drafts to yourself or to your fellow students, will often help to eliminate fragments and other common full-stop errors.

You may have observed that professional writers—and some of the students whose writing appears in this book—occasionally use **deliberate fragments** for special effect. These intentional fragments depend on the sentences around them for their meaning, and their writers assume that readers will be able to make the necessary connections to grasp that meaning. For example, in "Don't Let Me Die" Eric Williams used deliberate fragments in the opening paragraph and again toward the end of his essay.

As I stood there with the blood on my hands watching the ambulance lights slowly disappear from sight I wondered how my life had come to this point. This point of such destruction, this point of inhumanity . . . .

When I felt life leave her body, I also felt a part of me go with her. My inhumanity.

(*Note:* The dots, or ellipses, after the first paragraph in this passage indicate that something has been left out from Eric's original.)

Maura John's vivid description of the orphanage in Vietnam where she spent the first few years of her life also contains some effective intentional fragments.

Our orphanage was one of the only buildings left standing . . . . The walls were a bleak white and the floors always stayed cold, but they were covered up with brightly colored area rugs. The rugs had pictures of Vietnam's countryside before the war. It was hard to believe that Vietnam once was so beautiful. The orphanage was located in the middle of nothing. No palm trees. No grass. No pretty flowers, just a dirty junkyard of burnt jeeps, broken guns, empty gun shells and rubble of buildings that once stood so proudly.

Put wavy lines under the deliberate fragments in the above excerpts.

Caution: The meaning of those deliberate fragments is clear and they add to the impact of the passages. Student writers should be warned, however, that employing intentional fragments entails a risk, because your instructors may regard them as mistakes, rather than deliberately chosen stylistic devices. Your instructors may want you to put a note in the margin telling them that you are aware of using a fragment for stylistic effect.

Exercise

Practice combining ideas and embedding, or subordinating, the material in the following groups of short sentences by using coordinating conjunctions, dependent (subordinate) clauses, appositives, and so on. There are *many* good ways—no single correct way—to combine these sentences. You may eliminate or add words as needed, but do not alter the meaning of the original sentences. The first one is done for you.

1. The wall was smooth steel.
   The snake could not climb it.
   The snake could not climb the smooth steel wall.

2. The crocodile stirred suddenly.
   It slowly opened its long, narrow jaws.

3. My ex-husband is a fine father.
   His name is Horace.
   We just couldn't get along.

4. Put the milk in the refrigerator.
   Close the refrigerator door quickly.
   Closing the refrigerator door quickly saves electricity.

5. Snipper is our poodle.
   Snipper has worms.
   She has fleas.
   We are taking Snipper to the vet today.

6. My daughter got an A on her European history exam.
   Her name is Eleanore.
   Usually Eleanore is a mediocre student.

7. Cigarette smoking is bad for your health.
   Cigarette smoking can cause lung cancer.
   It can also cause emphysema and heart disease.

8. Mr. Ramirez found a book in an antique shop.
   The antique shop is in New York.
   The book was mildewed and dusty.
   The book was a first edition of Darwin's *Origin of Species*.

9. We took our vacation in July.
   We camped near Lake Superior.
   We camped in the Bayfield area near Lake Superior.
   The Bayfield area is one of the most beautiful spots in Wisconsin.

10. The professors at Prestige College went on a strike.
    Their assistants also went on a strike.
    The professors and their assistants wanted higher wages.

They also wanted fewer classes to teach.
The strike lasted three months and then it ended.

11. The fire grew greater and greater.
The fire advanced through the town.
It was a wall of flame.
People scattered before it.
They were like frightened beetles.

Apply these same techniques when editing drafts of your own writing.

Exercise

Rewrite the paragraph below, changing the simple, grade school type "primer prose" into smooth, rhythmical, concise sentences. You may eliminate or add words, as well as change the wording, but do not alter the meaning or add new ideas.

> Dridon slipped his supply bag over his shoulder. He started walking in the plain. The plain was dry. Tiny reptilian life forms scurried from his path. They were not like anything Dridon had seen on earth. The sun was purple. It blazed through the atmosphere. The atmosphere was thin and yellow. It was filled with dust. The dust spread itself thinly over Dridon's body. It entered his mouth and nose. It also entered his ears and his eyes. The dust was choking. Dridon sensed the air for water. He could feel none. The ship lay behind him in the plain. It was twisted and burnt. Already the desert reptiles had claimed the ship.

Avoiding Faulty Parallelism

Skiers whose ski tracks are not parallel have frequent accidents and other skiers are frightened.

Read the above sentence aloud. What clause sounds funny and awkward? The last clause in the sentence sounds awkward because it is not of the same grammatical structure, or is **not parallel,** to the previous elements in the sentence. A corrected version might read:

Skiers whose ski tracks are not parallel have frequent accidents and frighten other skiers.

Exercise

Correct the following sentences. First find the awkward sections. Then rewrite the sentences, making all of the elements parallel. They can be reworded several ways. The first one is done for you.

(writing)
1. When Jose entered college he hated geography, history, and <u>to write</u>.
2. Once he learned how to edit and do revising, his grades started to improve significantly.
3. Now Jose likes to read, write, and revising.

Parallelism in Lists

Lists are especially difficult to write correctly because all of the elements that follow the colon or dash must be **parallel;** that is, they must have the same grammatical structure. Leon Bond's sentence is a successful example of a list with parallel elements.

> After the game it doesn't matter to me if we won or lost (even though it's always nice to win), because I do the same thing anyway: shake the coach's hand, turn in my uniform, listen to the coach's speech, and walk home in the cold, windy night.

The following sentence contains another list with correct parallel structure; in this case all of the elements after the colon are noun clauses.

> Students should look for the following factors in a part-time job: flexible hours; cooperative fellow employees; an understanding boss; and a relatively stress-free atmosphere.

In contrast, which elements of the lists below sound awkward, especially when you read them aloud? Determine the awkward sections. Then try to reword the lists so that all of the elements are parallel. You may not always succeed in making all items in a list parallel; if this happens, then the list should be abandoned, perhaps by breaking it up into more than one sentence.

The ideal part-time job for a college student would have several qualities—flexibility; variety; a chance for promotion; relates to the student's career goal.

The junk in the vacant lot was any five-year-old's dream: discarded truck tires to climb on; the old abandoned wagon needed some repairs; there were dozens of discarded antique toy soldiers; a half dozen heavy cardboard boxes were large enough to play in.

Long, complex lists are hard to write. Trying to make all of the elements of a list parallel may prove so difficult that it is better to abandon it. Often, two or three shorter, clearer sentences may be preferable to a long list, even if the items in it are parallel.

Observe the following example.

Wise students look for the following factors in a part-time job: the hours do not interfere with their studies; if it relates to their career goals; it's in a good location; cooperative coworkers are essential.

Because the unparallel elements of the above example are so disparate, the list would be very hard to salvage. Lists like this one may be useful in a draft to get your ideas down on paper. Later they can be scrapped or greatly altered, probably by dividing the list into several sentences.

It is usually unwise to get bogged down in an effort to write an introductory sentence that lists all of the points to be covered in an essay. Because such lists tend to be wordy and dull, and frequently have faulty parallelism, they do not make the most effective introductions.

Deliberate Parallelism

Faulty parallelism weakens writing and frequently confuses the reader. On the other hand, correct, **deliberate parallelism**, which uses repeated structures for emphasis, can greatly strengthen writing as in the following student examples:

Every day at the island was like going to school. I learned how to listen for birds singing, frogs croaking, insects buzzing, woodpeckers pecking, chipmunks foraging, and crickets chirping.

1977 was the year my older brother, my two nephews, and I decided to start a musical group, the Tigers. Having only two real instruments, we borrowed items around the house as substitutes. An old broom stick became a second guitar; the bed was the drums; my mother's worn-out slippers turned into drum sticks; magic markers were microphones.

Use marginal annotations or highlighting to indicate the examples of deliberate parallelism in both of the above examples.

Observe the frequent and effective use of deliberate parallelism and repetition of key phrases in this excerpt from one of the most famous speeches by the great civil rights leader, Dr. Martin Luther King, Jr.

> *I say to you today, my friends, so even though we face the difficulties of today and tomorrow, I still have a dream. It is a dream deeply rooted in the American dream. I have a dream that one day this nation will rise up and live out the true meaning of its creed: "We hold these truths to be self-evident; that all men are created equal." I have a dream that one day, on the red hills of Georgia, sons of farmers and the sons of former slaveowners will be able to sit down together at the table of brotherhood. I have a dream that one day even the state of Mississippi, a state sweltering with the heat of injustice, sweltering with the heat of oppression, will be transformed into an oasis of freedom and justice. I have a dream that my four little children will one day live in a nation where they will not be judged by the color of their skin but by the content of their character. I have a dream today.*

Exercise

Reword the following sentences so that all of the elements are parallel. There is no one correct version, and several variants may be equally effective. The first one is done as a model:

1. The discontented waitress complained about long hours, crabby customers, and that her tips were so low.

   Corrected version: The discontented waitress complained about long hours, crabby customers, and low tips.

2. Writers whose sentences are not parallel make errors of syntax and confusing their readers.
3. Faulty parallel structure is ungrammatical and your readers may be puzzled.
4. Her favorite summer recreational activities were swimming, jogging, boating, and to go on camping trips.
5. That firm expects its employees to look intelligent, work efficiently, and dressing fashionably.
6. I can recommend Francine Harris as a civic leader, a competent supervisor, a dedicated employee, and she is very enterprising.
7. In spite of years of listening to his fussy mother's constant nagging, the bearded young man's appearance remained unkempt: a faded sweater with ripped elbows; his cowboy boots were run-down; he wore ragged jeans with large gaps in the knees.

8. Here is one formula for more success in a writing course: turn in interesting papers that are carefully typed; to attend all classes, especially peer editing sessions; you should carefully make all reasonable designated corrections; never be anything but prompt with assignments.
9. Find an interesting topic; get an early start; a thorough research job must be done; an outline should be composed: these are essential preliminary steps for a good term paper in any course.

Avoiding Dangling and Misplaced Modifiers

> Nibbling at the delicious worm on his line, the fisherman spotted a huge speckled fish.

To keep from confusing your readers, always put modifying phrases and clauses near the words they modify. The opening modifier in the above example, "nibbling at the delicious worm on his line," modifies the first noun in the independent clause that follows it. This happens because otherwise, like the worm, the phrase would be **dangling**. Because it has no subject, the opening phrase attaches itself incorrectly to the nearest noun, the fisherman.

The following example shows another dangling—unattached—or wrongly attached modifier, adapted from the 1949 edition of H. W. Fowler's *A Dictionary of Modern English Usage* (pp. 674–75).

A firm once sent a customer a bill with the following letter:

Dear Sir:
Desirous of clearing our accounts by the end of May, will you kindly pay the $300.00 you owe us immediately?

To which the customer replied:

Sirs:
You have been misinformed. I have no wish to clear your accounts.

Correct the opening phrase in the firm's letter by giving it the proper subject.

> ## Wanted: Man to wash dishes and two women

Exercise

The following sentences have dangling, misplaced, or wrongly attached modifiers. Reword them correctly. Then be on alert for similar examples when editing your own writing.

1. About to give birth to their first child, the frantic husband ran a red light while rushing his wife to the hospital.
2. The next thing the couple noticed was a police car following their speeding vehicle with a flashing red light.
3. Crying in the backseat the police officer sympathized with the man and his nervous wife.
4. Lights flashing and sirens blasting, the couple's car followed the police vehicle the rest of the way to the hospital.
5. Too exhausted even to count her contractions any longer, the emergency room provided a welcome relief to the frantic woman.
6. Within a few minutes a cart was moving her quickly toward the delivery room with four wheels.

Chapter Five   Fractured and Nonfractured Syntax   **131**

> Those two brothers were reunited after five years in a Holiday Inn lobby.

Avoiding Sexist Language in Your Writing, or "Excuse me, is my bias showing?"

At first glance, it is perhaps difficult for some students to see why it is so important to try to avoid showing bias in their language and writing. We sense the question, "What's the big deal?" forming in the minds of some skeptics. Permit us, if you will, a brief digression.

Very few people would deny that our language reflects who we are as people and where we are in our society. Certain groups have certain ways of expressing themselves. For instance, the proliferation of rap style in everything from commercials to public service announcements shows just one interesting example of how the speech patterns of one portion of a group—in this case, African-Americans—can permeate a society on every level, making other forms of expression instantly seem outmoded and old-fashioned. What is more laughable, these days, than the vision of a bell-bottomed, pompadoured John Travolta strutting his stuff in the 1970s film

"In the interests of science, Miss Mellish, I'm going to make a rather strange request of you."

Drawing by Peter Arno; © 1937, 1965 The New Yorker Magazine, Inc.

Saturday Night Fever? Yet Travolta was the height of cool back then, and many people wanted be like him. What is the point of this short pop-culture retrospective? Only to point out that the times change and we must be ready to change with them.

We all know that in the not-too-distant past, racial and sexual epithets, or hate-names, were the common mode of referring to certain groups of people. I grew up with the childhood chant of "Sticks and stones may break my bones, but names will never hurt me!" How wrong that was, and how much more aware of it we are as a society today. The phrase "tongue lashing" is no mere figure of speech; think back on some of the times you have been hurt by someone else's hateful speech and you will see the wisdom of avoiding needlessly wounding others through a careless choice of words.

Former President Jimmy Carter is sometimes remembered for his observation, in response to a reporter's question, that "Life's not fair." Perhaps it is not, Mr. Carter, but you and I can help make it less unfair by using our language carefully.

Fifty years ago there were few female police officers. Today there are many more. So why refer to the people who pursue that career as *policemen?* Is everyone who delivers mail a *mailman?* Is every leader of the Board of Directors of a business a *chairman?* Of course not, and it shows bias in favor of the male gender to call them that. To those who protest that *man* is merely a generic term that includes both sexes equally, I would ask them to consider the phrase often used in history classes, "The great man theory of history." Whose faces come to mind when you picture these movers and shakers down through the ages? Enough said.

A good way to steer clear of the issue of gender exclusive titles (policeman, congressman, stewardess, and so on, is to use gender neutral words: *police officer* instead of *policeman; senator* or *representative* in place of *congressman; flight attendant* to replace *stewardess*. With a little effort the old-fashioned terms can be brought up-to-date for the realities of today's job market.

In recent years people have striven to change to keep up with changing roles in the classroom and the job market. "Every student should have his report done by next week" is needlessly exclusive. Do the women not need to hand in their assignments at the same time? The awkward phraseology "his/her" is inclusive, but also tends to stop the sentence in midbreath. What is usually simpler is to cast the whole sentence in the plural: "Students should all have their assignments done by next week." Instead of "A good doctor knows his patients by name," try, "Good doctors know their patients by name." The switch from singular to plural is a great help in avoiding needless gender bias in your writing. Approach the problem with an open mind; in the global village everyone is our neighbor; avoiding hateful or sexist language is simply putting the "Good Neighbor Policy" into practice. The following exercises will help you practice "gender shifting" in writing.

Exercise

Change the following "gender exclusive" sentences into less sexist, more *inclusive*, language. The first one is done as a model for you.

1. A Congressman's chief responsibility is to the voters who elected him.

    More inclusive: Our representatives' chief responsibility is to the voters who elected them.

2. A shrewd lawyer can get his clients off 80 percent of the time.
3. The policemen were accused of showing bias toward the defendant, who was a homeless vagrant.
4. Every child was told to bring his parents to the school meeting.
5. Mankind has progressed remarkably during the twentieth century; it has all but conquered infectious disease!
6. When the mailman came to the door, she presented me with an envelope marked "Postage due—twenty cents"!

Chapter Six

Demystifying Punctuation

Writers use punctuation marks to help *convey meaning*. Without correct punctuation, writing is at worst almost pure gibberish, at best difficult to follow. Because the purpose of writing is communication with your readers, try to use a variety of appropriate punctuation marks as aids in achieving that goal.

Perhaps you find proper punctuation somewhat mysterious and puzzling. The array of choices may be so bewildering that you avoid some of them, sticking to what seem to be the safer, more familiar options. Even then it may be easy to make mistakes or to leave out some of the punctuation marks that could prove most helpful to your readers.

Although it may sometimes seem to be the case, punctuation was not thought up by composition teachers to torture their students. On the contrary it has evolved gradually, and one of its major useful functions is to aid readers by indicating natural pauses and intonations in speech. We automatically punctuate as we converse; otherwise we would speak in a monotone, causing our listeners either to fall asleep or to stop paying attention to what we are saying.

Thus, you can make great strides toward more effective punctuation by reading drafts of your writing *aloud* and *listening attentively* as you read. Practice reading your own essays as well as the works of others out loud, with feeling, not in a flat, dull voice. Listen to the punctuation marks in others' writings. Some punctuation marks, such as the period or semicolon, represent full stops; others, such as the comma or dash, represent half stops. Try to become more aware of the cadence, or rhythm, of spoken English. Ask yourself, "What do I want this to sound like?" Then attempt to punctuate your writing according to the rhythm of your speech. When you come to a slight natural pause—a half stop, like after the clause you just read—you will probably want to insert a comma. Longer pauses, or full stops, usually call for one of several choices of **end-stop** or sentence-ending punctuation marks: the period, the exclamation point, the question mark, the semicolon, and the colon.

Like a speech delivered in a monotone, writing can be boring and even unintelligible to readers if it lacks proper punctuation. Try to comprehend the following unpunctuated version of Anne Moody's wonderfully graphic description of her childhood home. At first you will probably make no sense out of it at all. Try reading the excerpt aloud, with feeling, either by yourself or with a small group of your classmates. Listen carefully for natural pauses as you read. Add sentence-ending punctuation marks to designate full stops and commas to indicate half stops. Put in necessary capital letters, apostrophes, and so on. Read your completed punctuated version aloud at least once more for any additions or corrections. Finally, compare your final version with the punctuated copy of Anne Moody's description on page 137.

If you were quoting from Moody's excerpt, you would have to punctuate *exactly* like she did. However, when doing this exercise, your punctuated version may differ somewhat from the original without being incorrect.

135

The House

Im still haunted by dreams of the time we lived on mr carters plantation lots of negroes lived on his place like mama and daddy they were all farmers we all lived in rotten wood two room shacks but ours stood out from the others because it was up on the hill with mr carters big white house overlooking the farms and the other shacks below it looked just like the carters barn with a chimney and a porch but mama and daddy did what they could to make it livable since we had only one big room and a kitchen we all slept in the same room it was like three rooms in one mama and the rest of them slept in one corner and i had my little bed in another corner next to one of the big wooden windows around the fireplace a rocking chair and a couple of straight chairs formed a sitting area this big room had a plain dull colored wallpaper tacked loosely to the walls with large thumbtacks under each tack was a piece of cardboard which had been taken from shoeboxes and cut into little squares to hold the paper and keep the tacks from tearing through because there were not enough tacks the paper bulged in places the kitchen didnt have any wallpaper and the only furniture in it was a wood stove an old table and a safe (Adapted from Moody, Anne. Coming of Age in Mississippi. *New York: Dial Press, 1968.)*

Analyzing and punctuating this excerpt from Anne Moody's *Coming of Age in Mississippi* can give you some good ideas for your own descriptive writing. Note how skillfully Moody has varied the length and style of her sentences. Does her description have a focus or purpose? Does it convey a mood or a dominant impression? Does it contain superfluous details that do not add to that impression? Note how she carefully draws her reader from the exterior to the interior of the family's "rotten wood two-room" shack. Then, by including a few deftly chosen details, Moody re-creates the inside of that humble dwelling so vividly that the reader can almost see it. What feature of the room does Moody focus on? Why? What does her description of the wallpaper tell us about Moody's parents?

Exercise

Describe a place that has made a significant impact on you, selecting details to convey a dominant impression as you re-create the place on paper for your reader. For student descriptions of places that are special to them, see pages 314 and 317.

Compare your punctuated version to the copy of Anne Moody's original, which appears below.

The House

I'm still haunted by dreams of the time we lived on Mr. Carter's plantation. Lots of Negroes lived on his place. Like Mama and Daddy they were all farmers. We all lived in rotten wood two-room shacks. But ours stood out from the others because it was up on the hill with Mr. Carter's big white house, overlooking the farms and the other shacks below. It looked just like the Carters' barn with a chimney and a porch, but Mama and Daddy did what they could to make it livable. Since we had only one big room and a kitchen, we all slept in the same room. It was like three rooms in one. Mama and the rest of them slept in one corner and I had my little bed in another corner next to one of the big wooden windows. Around the fireplace a rocking chair and a couple of straight chairs formed a sitting area. This big room had a plain, dull-colored wallpaper tacked loosely to the walls with large thumbtacks. Under each tack was a piece of cardboard which had been taken from shoeboxes and cut into little squares to hold the paper and keep the tacks from tearing through. Because there were not enough tacks, the paper bulged in places. The kitchen didn't have any wallpaper and the only furniture in it was a wood stove, an old table and a safe. (Moody, Anne. Coming of Age in Mississippi. New York: Dial Press, 1968.)

Understanding Full-Stop Punctuation

The Period

A period goes at the end of a declarative sentence. A declarative sentence is one that makes a statement, like this one.

Additional Uses of the Period. Periods are also used after, or within, many abbreviations. Most dictionaries have a list of them, but the following are some examples.

Certain *words* are commonly abbreviated:

Ms.
Mr.
Mrs.
Dr.
St.
Ave.

Some *lowercase-letter* abbreviations:

etc.
a.m.
p.m.
r.s.v.p.
i.e. (that is)

Some *all-capital* abbreviations:

A.M.
P.M. (alternatives to the lowercase-letter form)
M.D.
B.A.
R.N.
U.S.A. (also can be written USA, without periods)

Some abbreviations, such as NBA, CBS, IBM, and mph, do not have periods. Nor do the postal code two-letter abbreviations for the states—for example, TX (for Texas).

Check for the correct form of abbreviations in a grammar handbook. It may also provide guidelines for the use of abbreviations in formal writing. In general, with certain exceptions, such as personal titles (Dr., Mr., Ms.), it is best to avoid abbreviations in formal writing. Another caution is in order: If you suspect that your readers may not know an abbreviation, write out the name for the first usage, followed by the abbreviation in parentheses.

Aid to Families with Dependent Children (A.F.D.C.)

European Community (EC)

The Question Mark

Undoubtedly you know that you should always end a question with a question mark. However, you may be more likely to forget question marks than periods. If so, proofread especially for *question* words at the beginnings of your sentences: *how, who, why, what, when, where, will, would,* and so on. You also may observe that your voice wants to go up at the end of a sentence such as "She did what?" That is an indication that you probably need to insert a question mark. Why make careless mistakes if you can avoid them by more careful proofreading?

The Exclamation Point

Because the exclamation point expresses strong feelings, it should be used sparingly. Otherwise your reader will not believe you.

"What! An exam today!" groaned the doomed student. "I thought it was next Monday. I haven't even opened the book since the last exam."

As we rarely exclaim in complete sentences, exclamations are accepted as legitimate fragments, as are commands. In fact, such a fragment may be both a command and an exclamation as in the following.

Fire! Get moving! Fast!

In the command "Get moving!" the subject *you* is understood and need not be stated.

However, not all commands are exclamations. More often than not, they end with a period.

Put the meat back in the refrigerator.

Exercise

The following sentences should each end in one of the standard marks used for full-stop punctuation: question mark, exclamation point, or period. For some of the sentences either a period or an exclamation point would be appropriate; in these cases it is up to the writer to decide which is preferable, as either is correct. Add the appropriate full-stop punctuation to the following sentences.

1. A declarative sentence, like the one you are reading, usually ends in a period
2. Do you ever leave out the necessary question marks in your essays
3. Yes, and it makes me furious when I make these mistakes
4. Maybe it would help to proofread once just looking for missing question marks

5. It helps to be on the alert for question words, such as *who, have, when, why,* or *will,* at the beginning of sentences
6. Have you ever tried that method
7. Of course, but I still make mistakes
8. The only punctuation mark that I always remember to use is the period
9. Does that surprise you
10. No, it makes me so mad I could spit
11. Punctuation causes most students considerable frustration
12. You said it

The Semicolon

You may be less familiar with the semicolon than with other punctuation, so much so that you either avoid it or use it incorrectly. That is not surprising because semicolons are not used as commonly as periods. Semicolons have several uses.

> A semicolon tells the reader to pause longer than for a comma, but more briefly than for a period.

The Semicolon as a Weak Period. A semicolon acts like a kind of brief period; it does not signal as long a pause to the reader as a period. Because the semicolon substitutes for a period, you must be careful that what is written on either side of it is a complete thought, a sentence. If you would not want a period, then do not use a semicolon. Furthermore, any two independent clauses joined by a semicolon to make one sentence should add up to a single idea.

Latoya rushed to answer the phone; all she heard was a click on the other end as she picked up the receiver.

Never link unrelated ideas with a semicolon, as in the following example.

Latoya rushed to answer the phone; her brother had measles.

Use a semicolon instead of a period only when you want to show your reader that the ideas in two independent clauses are closely related.

My mother's ten siblings are all dead now; most of them died when I was a small child.

Almost all of my friends have uncles and aunts; however, my parents' siblings all died when I was a small child.

Note that in the above examples a *period* instead of a *semicolon* between the independent clauses would also be perfectly correct.

> Think of the semicolon between independent clauses in a compound sentence as a semiperiod.

Exercise

Practice using a semicolon instead of a period between independent clauses—clauses that have a subject and predicate and make sense by themselves. Rewrite the following sentences, separating the following independent clauses with a semicolon. The first one is done for you.

                           (1)   (2)

1. The semicolon can be a substitute for a period, it should not be used instead of a comma.

   subject in independent clause 1 *semicolon*
   predicate (verb) in clause 1 *can be*
   subject in independent clause 2 *it*
   predicate (verb) in clause 2 *should (not) be used*

   Corrected version: The semicolon can be a substitute for a period; it should not be used instead of a comma.

   (In this example a period between the two independent clauses would also be correct, but the semicolon emphasizes how closely the two of them fit together.)

2. In the above example a semicolon shows how closely the two clauses are related a period between them would also be acceptable.

   What is the subject of independent clause 1?
   What is the verb in independent clause 1?

What is the subject of independent clause 2?
What is the verb in independent clause 2?

3. Commas are used *within* sentences semicolons can be used *between* independent clauses that contain ideas that are closely related.
4. Use a semicolon where a period would be appropriate do not use it where you need a comma.
5. Anne Moody's family all slept in the same room it was like three rooms in one.
6. Planning a trip is sometimes half the fun the trip itself may even be a letdown.
7. For her interview Kanika selected a well-tailored gray suit her small red scarf added just the right accent.
8. Semicolons may replace periods they do not replace commas except in some lists.

> **Think of the semicolon between items in a list as a supercomma.**

Semicolons in Lists. Semicolons should also be used instead of commas to separate the items in the list when those items are rather long or have commas within them.

> *Her doting grandmother brought her everything a sick child might enjoy: a bouquet of fresh pansies picked that same morning; a bowl of goldfish to while away the lonely hours; picture books, puzzles, crayons, and construction paper to keep her busy; fruit, candy, and gum to supplement the rather monotonous hospital fare.*

Exercise

Add semicolons to separate the parts of the following lists.

1. We had the usual lousy meal at Aunt Minnie's: greasy fish that was overcooked soggy lettuce soaked in bland vinegar and oil dressing boiled potatoes that were raw in the center.
2. Holiday gatherings at our house meant an amazing array of relatives: crotchety old Uncle Adrian in his maroon sweater talkative Grandpa Burnett with his smelly pipe jovial Aunt Flo and her yappy fox terrier, Henry.

Note how much easier these lists were to understand after you added semicolons.

Observe that a colon was used to introduce the lists in the above examples. That is one of several uses of the colon.

The Colon

> A colon is a tip-off to get ready for what's next.
> — Russell Baker

Punctuating Lists. **Colons** act as a kind of introducer, signaling readers to read on through. Often colons introduce lists, usually to add specific details to a general statement. The details can be single words, phrases, or clauses.

> She packed almost everything necessary for a successful camping trip: insect repellent, tent, lanterns, coolers, cooking gear, and sleeping bags.

> That island is the ideal vacation spot: long, balmy, sunshiny days; white sandy beaches beneath craggy cliffs; warm, sparkling, blue water; numerous handicraft shops, outdoor cafés, and restaurants.

Note that these two lists are punctuated differently. When items in a list, such as duties listed on a résumé, are single words or short phrases, they are separated by *commas*. If the items are longer phrases or clauses, it is easier for the reader to sort them out if they are separated by *semicolons*.

Exercise

Punctuate the following lists. Note that they make almost no sense without punctuation. Try reading them aloud, listening for natural pauses as you decide where to insert punctuation marks.

1. A complete Italian dinner often includes the following a tasty antipasto for an appetizer homemade pasta smothered in spaghetti sauce plenty of garlic bread red Chianti to aid the digestion spumoni and after-dinner mints for dessert
2. A complete Italian dinner often includes the following antipasto spaghetti garlic bread Chianti spumoni and after-dinner mints

Be aware that all the parts of a list, like the elements in a sentence, must have the same—that is, parallel—grammatical structure. Otherwise they sound wrong and are jarring to the ear, as in the following example.

> Anne Moody's childhood home was very poor: sparse furnishings; two crowded rooms; they all slept in the same room; bulging wallpaper.

"They all slept in the same room" jars the ear because it is not the same grammatical structure.

If the parts of a list follow a verb or are introduced by phrases like *such as* or *including,* a colon should *not* be used.

> The group's leaders were Tayotis, Becky, Ed, and Rosa.

> The campers forgot many essentials including bug spray, lighter fluid, firewood, and matches.

> Vaccines can now prevent many contagious diseases, such as measles, diphtheria, smallpox, mumps, and polio.

Without the *such as* the above list would read as follows.

> Today vaccines can prevent many contagious diseases: measles, diphtheria, smallpox, mumps, and polio.

When used in a sentence the colon acts as a kind of opener or introducer. It alerts the reader that a list, an explanation, an example, or perhaps a quotation will follow. If the second part of a sentence explains or elaborates on what has been said, use a colon. The colon follows a complete sentence; it should not follow an incomplete idea (fragment) as in this example.

> Three items on most voters' minds in the 1992 elections were: health care, jobs, and taxes.

Cover up the words "health care, jobs, and taxes" and you have a fragment. Does the first part of the sentence make sense without those words to complete the thought? That sentence could be corrected by leaving out the colon.

> Three items on most voters' minds in the 1992 elections were health care, jobs, and taxes.

It could also be reworded.

> There were three items on most voters' minds in the 1992 elections: health care, jobs, and taxes.

The Colon Between Independent Clauses. The colon can also be used to separate two independent clauses when the second clause explains or gives more information about the first clause.

> Aunt Bertha made a sudden and surprising decision on her sixtieth birthday: she signed up for downhill skiing lessons.

If the second clause brings up a question, begin it with a capital letter:

> All of her children asked themselves the same question: "Who will take care of Uncle Floyd while Aunt Bertha is recuperating from her broken leg?"

Colons can also set off something—not necessarily an independent clause—that makes a point clear, as in the following examples.

> His father lived for only one thing: power.

> During February of 1992, cable TV's ratings suffered in the year-to-year comparison with the networks due to the absence of its most exciting program to date: the war in the Persian Gulf.

> The CBS victory in that season's ratings can be explained by one factor: the winter Olympics of 1992.

The Colon to Introduce Quotations. A colon (or a comma) can be used to introduce a direct quotation when the lead-in is a complete sentence. For example:

> Dr. Martin Luther King, Jr.'s address during the August 1963 March on Washington opened with a refrain that has given the historic speech its name: "I still have a dream. It is a dream deeply rooted in the American dream . . . . I have a dream . . . ."

Additional Uses of the Colon. The colon is used for time expressions.

> 10:15 P.M.

The colon is used after the salutation of a business letter.

> Dear Dr. Rodriguez:
> Dear Ms. Fetter:

To set off material in a less formal manner, *dashes* can be used instead of colons.

My scatterbrained aunt forgot the one thing we asked her to bring—a deck of cards.

Aunt Mary, Uncle Herman, Aunt Flo—all of my relatives are dedicated and skilled card players.

Using Punctuation with Parenthetical Elements

> Use dashes and parentheses.
> Give your sentences and
> your readers a break.

Parenthetical elements are words or groups of words that interrupt the main thought of a sentence. Often they are set off by a comma, as in the sentence you are now reading, but you can also use a dash or parentheses to separate an interrupter from the rest of a sentence.

The Dash

The dash—it looks like an elongated hyphen—tells your reader to pause briefly. The dash can be used in place of the comma to set off material that interrupts the main sentence. Because dashes are more forceful than commas, use them sparingly, only for emphasis. Overuse of the dash—as the name itself suggests—gives a kind of breathless pace to writing. Writing that is overloaded with dashes has an informal quality—sounds dashed off—written much too fast—not thought out enough.

Dashes can signal a break in the thought or set off an interrupter, at the beginning, in the middle, or at the end of a sentence.

An exotic setting, a relaxed schedule, delicious food and wine under the palm trees—that vacation had everything we had hoped for.

All of my relatives—Grandpa Flores, Uncle Mario, and Aunt Rosa—are fanatic and clever Scrabble players.

> I finally pulled an A in that philosophy course—wait until my parents hear that!

Use a dash to set off an interrupter that is internally punctuated.

> Her coworkers—Peter, Paul, and Mary—agree that she deserved a promotion, not a demotion.

Note: Because the dash looks like a stretched-out hyphen, strike the hyphen key twice if your typewriter does not have a dash.

> **To emphasize, use dashes—
> and use them sparingly.
> To de-emphasize, use parentheses.
> (Use them sparingly also.)**

Parentheses

If you do not want to stress an interrupter, use parentheses instead of a dash or a comma. Parentheses often enclose material that adds information that the writer regards as less deserving of emphasis.

> Senator Ted Kennedy (Dem., Mass.) has long supported liberal causes in the United States Senate.

> Dr. Martin Luther King, Jr. (1929–1968) was a prominent American civil rights leader whose eloquent speeches are widely remembered and quoted throughout the world.

> My son is very absent-minded (often he forgets why he went to the grocery store), yet he has the best memory in our family.

Exercise

Rewrite the following sentences, adding the necessary punctuation. In some cases there may be more than one option. For instance, either a dash or a colon could be used to introduce the list in the first sentence.

1. That campsite had every pest one could imagine mosquitoes flies raccoons ticks and wasps
2. Melanie was skilled in all aspects of the sport such as passing rebounding shooting and stealing
3. Melanie was skilled in all aspects of the sport passing rebounding shooting and stealing
4. For his birthday Franco did not receive the one gift he had hoped for a motorcycle
5. Franco was not really surprised that he had not received a motorcycle his mother had often announced that she was violently opposed to his owning one
6. The family had the usual Chinese restaurant meal egg rolls filled with shrimp and chopped vegetables sweet and sour pork that was a bit overcooked crispy lemon chicken dipped in a delicious sauce
7. The meal had everything we could imagine including shrimp chicken tossed salad pasta and anchovies
8. Bryan came up with an appealing idea close the family cafe for opening day at Brewer Stadium
9. All the other employees the cook the dishwasher and the busboy supported Bryan's plan with enthusiasm
10. Bryan's plan had the enthusiastic support of all the employees the cook the dishwasher the waitresses and the busboy
11. Bryan's tightfisted father reluctantly went along with his son's proposal for one reason improved employee morale
12. His father was a sad employer on opening day the game was called during the first inning due to heavy rain

Understanding Half-Stop Punctuation

The Comma

Commas indicate half stops. They are signals to your reader that it is time to take a breath and then read right on. Commas are properly used *within* sentences or independent clauses, not between them.

Commas have many uses that may be very familiar to you, even though you may sometimes forget to insert them. Once again, it is important to proofread your paper thoroughly to avoid careless omissions. Then you will not forget to put a comma between the name of a city and state, as in Cotton Plant, Arkansas, or between the day and year of a date, as in May 3, 1990.

The location of a comma *can* matter. Compare the following sentences.

Woman, without her, man is lost.

Woman without her man is lost.

Where would you add commas to the following sentences to clarify their meanings?

Their comanager quit saying her opinion was always ignored.

The excess of fabric softener is harmful wasteful scientist warns.

The addition, placement, or omission of a comma can change the meaning of a sentence or phrase. It is up to you, the writer, to decide exactly where you want your reader to pause, so you must place commas accordingly.

Compare the following examples:

My third job, at a hockey camp, included some administrative experience.

My third job at a hockey camp included some administrative experience.

Ever since she has been a widow . . . .

Ever since, she has been a widow.

Commas are used *inside* of sentences or independent clauses where a short pause is needed; however, they are not "strong" enough to separate them. You have written a comma fault, or comma splice, if you use a comma between independent clauses—unless they are joined by a coordinator (*and, but, or, nor, for, so,* or *yet*). For more information about coordinating conjunctions, refer to Chapter 5.

               (1)   (2)

Anne Moody's family all slept in the same room, it was like three rooms in one. (comma fault)

What is the subject of the first clause? What is the subject of the second clause? Because both of these clauses have a subject and predicate and make sense by themselves, they are both independent thoughts or sentences. Instead of a comma after *room,* you need a period or a semicolon; the latter can substitute for a period if two independent clauses are closely related.

If you use a period, capitalize the word *it.*

Anne Moody's family all slept in the same room. It was like three rooms in one.

If you use a semicolon, do not capitalize the word *it.*

Anne Moody's family all slept in the same room; it was like three rooms in one.

Exercise

Correct the comma fault in the following sentence.

Anne Moody's girlhood home was a poor two-room shack, her parents made every effort to make it liveable.

What is the subject of the first independent clause? What is the subject of the second independent clause?

Rewrite the sentence, correcting the above comma fault by putting a period between the two independent clauses.

Now correct the same comma fault by putting a semicolon between the two independent clauses.

Commas with Coordinating Conjunctions. When two independent clauses are joined by one of the seven coordinating conjunctions—*and, but, or, nor, for, so,* or *yet*—a comma is sufficient between them.

> Anne Moody's girlhood home was a poor two-room shack, but her parents made every effort to make it liveable.

Exercise

Rewrite each sentence, eliminating the following comma faults by using an appropriate coordinating conjunction.

1. Anne Moody's parents put up wallpaper with great care, it still bulged in some places.
2. The dull-colored wallpaper was tacked loosely to the wall with large thumbtacks, it bulged in places.

> Writers frequently omit the comma before a coordinator when the independent clauses are short or when the sentence is easily understood without a comma.
>
> We go camping and the rain starts to fall.
>
> Add some commas and an unpunctuated list makes sense.
>
> Generally speaking, your readers need more punctuation in long sentences than in short ones. Insert enough commas to keep your reader from getting lost, but resist the temptation to sprinkle unnecessary commas throughout your writing.

Avoid commas, that are unnecessary.

Commas Between Dependent and Independent Clauses. When dependent clauses begin a sentence, they are usually separated from independent clauses by a comma.

> Although Angela was the most aggressive and successful salesperson in the firm, her boss passed her by for a promotion.

When the dependent clause comes *after* the independent clause, however, it is not generally preceded by a comma.

> Angela's boss failed to give her a promotion even though she had the best sales record of the year.

This rule is not as arbitrary as it may sound. Read the two above examples aloud and listen for pauses. Now read the following pair aloud.

> Because her toddler brother was a terror, none of their relatives wanted to babysit for him.

> None of their relatives wanted to babysit for her toddler brother because he was a terror.

Because the second sentence reads better without a pause between *brother* and *because,* do not insert a comma. Otherwise you are giving your reader the wrong signal.

Exercise

Where appropriate, put commas between the dependent and independent clauses in the following sentences. Some of them do not need commas.

1. Tomas went to a movie last night even though our descriptive themes were due today.
2. When Tomas got to class this morning he observed his fellow students making last-minute corrections on some essays.
3. Although the due dates were listed in the syllabus and posted on the blackboard Tomas still insisted he had not known about the deadline.

4. Because Tomas was usually so prompt and diligent about his assignments his teacher extended the deadline for him.
5. Tomas' teacher gave him three more days to complete the theme as he had never missed a deadline before.

Separating Three or More Items in a Series with Commas.

              (1)   (2)   (3)   (4)

Freda made fruit salad, broccoli soup, scalloped potatoes, and chocolate cake for the party.

The gathering storm clouds on the horizon loomed dark, forbidding, and mysterious.

The last comma before *and* may be omitted.

Kanika bought potato chips, soda and napkins.

Nonessential, or Nonrestrictive, Clauses Set Off by Commas. Commas are also used to set off nonessential, or nonrestrictive, phrases or clauses—interrupters. These clauses add information about the words they modify, which is not needed for identifying purposes. Essential or restrictive clauses, on the other hand, are needed to define the word being modified. They are not set off by commas. That may sound pretty complicated, but a few examples can help clear up your confusion.

Essential or Restrictive Clauses Not Set Off by Commas.

A person who witnesses a crime should call the police.

"Who witnesses a crime" is an essential or restrictive clause, which is needed to identify "a person." It would not make much sense to write:

A person should call the police.

Nonessential or Nonrestrictive Clauses Set Off by Commas.

That notorious burglar, who was spotted at the scene of the crime by several witnesses, received a three-year sentence.

It does make sense to write:

That notorious burglar received a three-year sentence.

Therefore, the clause "who had been spotted at the scene of the crime by several witnesses" is set off by commas. That clause adds information about the burglar that is not essential to the meaning of the sentence.

Nonessential or Nonrestrictive Appositives with Commas. The word *appositive* means "next to." **Appositives** are words or phrases placed next to a noun in order to rename or describe it. Appositives can be placed in the beginning, middle, or end of a sentence. The following sentences show some examples.

> That history professor, Dr. Isabel Romero, assigns entirely too much reading.

"Dr. Isabel Romero" is an appositive, naming the history professor.

> The best lecturer in the history department, Dr. Isabel Romero assigns entirely too much reading.

The appositive in the above sentence, "the best lecturer in the history department," describes—that is, gives additional information about—Dr. Romero.

Exercise

Underline the appositives in the following sentences. There may be more than one appositive in each sentence.

1. In 1988 Michael Dukakis, the Democratic candidate for president, was behind his opponent, George Bush, in almost every state.
2. One of Dukakis' rivals for the Democratic nomination, Jesse Jackson, delivered the most compelling speech at the party's convention that year.

Punctuating Nonessential or Restrictive Appositives. Appositives that are nonessential, or nonrestrictive, and thus not needed to clarify a meaning, should be set off by commas.

> Dr. Phyllis Pfleger, a famous local pediatrician, ably chaired the first session of the conference.

The same appositive can also open a sentence.

> A famous local pediatrician, Dr. Phyllis Pfleger, ably chaired the first session of the conference.

Appositives can also come at the end of a sentence. Reword the same sentence, putting the appositive at the *end*.

Exercise

Add commas to set off the appositives in the following sentences.

1. The elderly man a gnarled and humped-over figure passed by the rowdy teenagers in silence.
2. A gnarled and humped-over figure the elderly man passed by the rowdy teenagers in silence.
3. The two Wisconsin senators Herb Kohl and Bob Kasten both came to the groundbreaking ceremony for the new hospital wing.
4. Herb Kohl and Bob Kasten Wisconsin's two senators both came to the groundbreaking ceremony for the new hospital wing.

Punctuating Sentences with Essential or Restrictive Appositives. If the appositive is restrictive—that is, essential to the meaning of the sentence—it is *not* set off by commas. The following sentences show some examples of essential, or restrictive, appositives.

Have you seen the movie *Driving Miss Daisy?*

It would be unclear to ask: Have you seen the movie? Thus the appositive *Driving Miss Daisy* is not set off by a comma.

Here are some other essential or restrictive appositives.

The play *Death of a Salesman* is one of my favorites.

The playwright Tennessee Williams wrote *A Streetcar Named Desire.*

The actor Marlon Brando is famous for his interpretation of the role of Stanley Kowalski in that play.

Appositives for Embedding Ideas. Appositives are very useful devices for embedding the ideas in simple sentences into longer, more complex sentences, as in the following examples:

Virtually everyone in the school knew Michaeleen Streep. She was the class clown. She was tall and lanky.

Those three simple sentences could be combined in several ways by using appositives.

Virtually everyone in the school knew Michaeleen Streep, the tall, lanky class clown.

Michaeleen Streep, the tall, lanky class clown, was known to virtually everyone in the school.

The tall and lanky class clown, Michaeleen Streep was known to virtually everyone in the school.

Commas with Other Elements that Interrupt a Sentence. Commas are also used to set off certain phrases or words, such as conjunctions like *however* or *therefore,* that interrupt or begin a sentence. Following are several examples.

Tisha is a good student. However, grammar has never been one of her favorite subjects. Tisha's brother, on the other hand, is a veritable grammar whiz.

"You, therefore, must answer for that crime. Come now, does that surprise you?"

Her mother, of course, was late for the play. However, the usher led her to her seat with a flashlight.

Exercise

Add commas to the following sentences. Some of them may not need commas. In some instances a comma may be optional.

1. No one in the Yasui family from Dayton Ohio would ever forget July 23 1986.
2. That was the day when their relatives from Iowa arrived unannounced with four small children two large mangy dogs and three scraggly gray cats.
3. Yelling barking and meowing the whole tribe stumbled over each other as they scrambled up the porch steps.
4. The paperboy a skinny redhead on a silver and black bicycle gawked at all the confusion and almost forgot to toss the evening paper on the Yasuis' porch.
5. A stunned Mrs. Yasui never one to hide her true feelings greeted her husband's relatives with a wan smile.
6. Because his wife's lack of enthusiasm was so obvious Mr. Yasui made an extra effort to be cordial.
7. Mr. Yasui a portly jovial man made an extra effort to be cordial because his wife was so curt with the new arrivals.
8. Cold and blunt as always his wife was of course unaware that she was being unusually rude even for her.

9. However the Iowa relatives did not seem to notice or if they did they concealed their reactions amazingly well.
10. Everyone in the Yasui family heaved a sigh of relief when their guests left for Cedar Rapids Iowa on July 30 1986.

Exercise

Add punctuation to the following sentences. Consult the previous sections on the semicolon, dash, and so on as you make your choices. Do not add any words or change the wording. In some cases there are several correct options.

1. The next day Mae's long-time dream would finally come true a trip to London
2. During her sophomore year in high school Mae had begun reading Sherlock Holmes' mysteries those stories whetted a desire to visit the British capital that never diminished
3. When she finished high school Mae took a good paying, dead-end job with one goal in mind to save enough money for a plane ticket to the United Kingdom
4. All of Mae's family her mother father and two younger sisters supported her dream
5. Only one person was not enthusiastic about the plan Mae's boyfriend Horace
6. Mae decided to ignore Horace so in early April she went to a travel agent that a friend had recommended
7. The agent informed her that several airlines including Lufthansa American British Air and United flew regularly from Chicago to London
8. Three airlines United Sabena and British Air even had exactly the same low midweek round trip fare $620
9. After considerable cogitation Mae finally made her choice British Air
10. Mae hardly slept a wink the night before her departure all the necessary details of her preparations kept going through her mind
11. She kept getting up and making a "final" check on the essential items passport air ticket hotel voucher London subway map and a Sherlock Holmes mystery.
12. Outside the airport Mae spotted a familiar figure now white haired Senator Ted Kennedy was getting out of a black airport limo
13. Mae's plane scheduled to depart at 6:00 P.M. took off right on schedule warnings of frequent delayed departures and landings due to London fog had proved not true in this case
14. Much to Mae's surprise dinner on the plane was delicious spinach and bacon salad with sweet-sour dressing noodle-veal casserole flavored with sherry wine sauce breadsticks rye rolls and Italian bread with garlic butter and chocolate cake covered with whipped cream
15. The Tower of London Buckingham Palace Piccadilly Circus and Trafalgar Square all of the sights of London swirled in Mae's head
16. The plane landed right on time Mae's long awaited two weeks in London had begun she decided to check into her hotel and then head for the nearest Tube station

Understanding Punctuation Marks That Do Not Indicate Pauses

Hyphens and apostrophes are punctuation marks that do not indicate pauses. Rather these marks are found *within* certain words, such as re-create (hyphen) or can't (apostrophe). These marks are a part of the spelling of such words, and the words are not correct without them.

Incorrect	Correct
online	on-line
sisterinlaw	sister-in-law
Im	I'm
isnt	isn't

The Hyphen

Which spelling would you use in the following example: coop or co-op?

Save money. Shop at your local _____.

The correct choice of spelling is quite clear in the above example. While the decision about whether to use a hyphen may not always be that clear-cut, a look at some more examples can help to clear up any confusion.

Hyphens are used in many compound words. They help the reader understand what the writer wants to say and sometimes affect the meaning.

Three day-trips are not the same as a three-day trip.

My father often remarked that not all American boys fit the stereotype of the all-American boy.

If my aunt does not recover the money she lost in the slot machines, she cannot afford to re-cover her davenport.

Hyphens also indicate that a word continues on the next line of typing or handwriting. Avoid dividing a word so that only a single letter begins or ends a line, and always divide words between syllables: be-tween, not bet-ween.

To Hyphenate or Not to Hyphenate. If you find hyphens confusing, take comfort that you are not alone. As a major publisher's stylebook put it, "If you take hyphens seriously, you will surely go mad." We hope that the above examples have made hyphenation a bit less confusing. Our best advice, however, is to consult a dictionary when you are uncertain about a word's syllable divisions or need to know whether a word is spelled with a hyphen.

The Apostrophe

The apostrophe is one of the most abused, easily forgotten pieces of punctuation in the English language. Rumors abound as to the demise of the apostrophe, particularly in contractions as they are often understandable without it. Because the apostrophe does convey distinct meaning in many cases, however, we expect it to be around for quite some time. For instance, those two frequently confused words *its* and *it's* have quite different meanings conveyed only by the apostrophe; thus *it's* obvious that *its* use cannot be denied in that case.

The Apostrophe in Possessive Nouns. The location of an apostrophe distinguishes between singular and plural possessives in English.

Singular Possessive Nouns	**Plural Possessive Nouns**
one elephant's trunk	three elephants' trunks
the ship's decks	the ships' decks

Nouns with irregular plurals can be the source of considerable confusion.

Singular Possessive Nouns	**Plural Possessive Nouns**
the man's hats	men's hats
the child's toys	children's toys

The rule for the placement of the apostrophe is fairly simple. If the *s* sound is only needed to indicate possession and is not used in the word's plural form, put the apostrophe *before* the *-s* to show possession.

Many *women* attended that performance.

No *-s* is needed, so it is an irregular plural noun.

Many of those women's husbands were not there.

The apostrophe goes *before* the *-s* because it is *only* needed to indicate possession.

In other words write the word you need, in plural or singular form. If you have a word that already ends in an *-s* or a *-z*, put the apostrophe *after* the *-s*, as in *ladies' hats* or *boss' order*.

The following is another method for writing possessives that we borrowed from Teresa Glazier, author of the very useful *The Least You Should Know about English*. Glazier suggests that you ask yourself: Who (or what) does the noun in question belong to? If your answer ends in *-s*, simply add an apostrophe. If your answer does not end in *-s*, add an apostrophe and an *-s*. For example:

one girls hats	Who do the hats belong to?	girl	add	's	girl's hats
six girls hats	Who do the hats belong to?	girls	add	'	girls' hats
one mans dogs	Who do the dogs belong to?	man	add	's	man's dogs
four mens dogs	Who do the dogs belong to?	men	add	's	men's dogs

> To make a possessive ask, "Who (or what) does it belong to?" If the answer ends in -*s*, just add an apostrophe. If it doesn't end in -*s*, add an apostrophe and an -*s*.

Exercise

Cover the right-hand column. Ask yourself who or what each possessive noun below belongs to. Then write down the answer. Next compare your answers with those in the right-hand column. The first one is done for you.

that boys bikes	that boy—add 's	that boy's bikes
those boys bikes	_____	those boys' bikes
the suns rays	_____	the sun's rays
Janes brother	_____	Jane's brother
James sister	_____	James' sister
todays schedule	_____	today's schedule
that cereals crunch	_____	that cereal's crunch

Note: Never add an apostrophe simply because a noun ends in an -*s*. Only possessive nouns or contractions need apostrophes. If the -*s* is added only to form a plural noun, no apostrophe is needed.

The girls were lost in the huge city.

In the sentence above, *girls* is simply a plural noun subject. No apostrophe is needed because here *girls* is *not* possessive. Nothing belongs to the girls, nor is the word *girls* followed by another noun. Possessive nouns are usually followed by another noun—or adjectives plus another noun as in "three girls' pretty purses." Where should the apostrophe be placed in the following sentence?

Both girls purses were lost in the flood.

Ask yourself, Who do the purses belong to? The girls. The apostrophe thus goes after the *-s:* girls' purses. *Purses,* on the other hand, should not have an apostrophe. Nothing belongs to the purses, nor is the word *purses* followed by another noun.

A Three-Step Method for Forming Possessives.

1. Decide if the word you need in your writing is *possessive*—that is, shows ownership. Let's call that unpunctuated word the "base word." That base word could be singular or plural.

Singular:	girl	child	day
Plural:	girls	children	days

2. Add an apostrophe to that base word.

Singular:	girl'	child'	day'
Plural:	girls'	children'	days'

3. If there is no *-s,* add one.

Singular:	girl's	child's	day's
Plural:		children's	

Exercise

Form possessive nouns by adding apostrophes to the following base words, as in the models.

Base Word	**Add an ' to the Word**	**If There Is no -s, Add One**
house	house'	house's
houses	houses'	
boy		
boys		

hour
women
woman
boss
Joneses
family
families

The Apostrophe in Contractions. Although apostrophes in contractions can be easily forgotten, once you make up your mind not to do that, you'll—you will—find that most contractions give you very little trouble. The rule is simply:

Put the apostrophe exactly where you left out the letter or letters:

you will	you'll
cannot	can't
I am	I'm
does not	doesn't

In general, it is best to avoid contractions in formal writing.

Contractions That Are Homonyms. Now here's where the real confusion arises. There are a few commonly used contractions that are also *homonyms* of possessive pronouns. Homonyms are words like *two* and *too,* or *bear* and *bare,* which are pronounced alike but have different spellings and different meanings.

Remember that possessive pronouns show ownership. The rule is that possessive pronouns—*her, my, his, your, their, ours, yours, its,* and so on—*never* need apostrophes. Because these words already show possession, if you added an apostrophe to them you would be showing possession twice. The fact that a few possessive pronouns sound the same as contractions (which *do* need apostrophes) is no reason to put an apostrophe in the possessive pronoun.

Contractions (need an apostrophe)	**Possessive Pronouns** (no apostrophe)
it's (it is)	its (its tail)
you're (you are)	your (your bike)
they're (they are)	their (their boat)
who's (who is)	whose (whose hat)

Hint: When using contractions, know what your contractions *mean* so that you avoid odd usages like "*it's* tail" or "*they're* bike." You would not want to write, "it is tail" or "they are bike."

Now that you have reviewed possessives, take this self-test. It also covers the use of the apostrophe in contractions.

Contraction	Possessive Pronoun	Possessive Noun
it is = it's	its (possessive of *it*)	dog's collar (singular)
they are = they're	their (possessive of *they*)	children's books (irregular plural)
who is = who's	whose (possessive of *who*)	three dogs' collars (plural)
you are = you're	your (possessive of *you*)	five girls' shoes (plural)

Note: *There*, an adverb of place, is also frequently confused with *their* and *they're*. Variations of *their* and *your* are *theirs* and *yours;* for example, it was *theirs.*

Exercise

Correct the following *as needed*. Some are already correct.

1. a boys car
2. several teachers
3. one familys bills
4. children's dreams
5. their houses
6. There is the picture.
7. Where is you're car?
8. Here's some candy.

two boys' car
the teacher's desk
three families bills
three deers eyes
there hats
Their are the boys.
You're proud of it.
it's tail

Two boys are running.
two teachers offices
Several families came.
mice's cheese
there nice houses
They're practicing.
It's collar was lost.
They're calling you.

Exercise

Circle the correct word from the choices given for each of the choices in the paragraph below.

Because of the apostrophe, *its* and *it's* have quite different meanings. Thus, (*it's, its*) obvious that (*it's, its*) usefulness cannot be denied. Consequently, (*your, you're*) just going to have to face the fact that apostrophes will be around for some time. Unfortunately, (*there, they're, their*) likely to cause you some confusion, but take comfort that (*your, you're*) not alone. Teachers agree that many of (*they're, their*) students find that (*it's, its*) a problem deciding when to use *it's* instead of *its*, or *there* instead of *their.*

Exercise

All of the possessives in the paragraph below use the preposition *of*. Find all of the possessives in the paragraph; note whether they are singular or plural. Then rewrite the paragraph showing possession by using apostrophes. For example, the phrase "party of the Rosenblatts" would be changed to "Rosenblatts' party." The first one is already underlined for you.

> Held outside on the huge lawn <u>of their</u> <u>neighbors</u>, the costume party of the Rosenblatts was a tremendous success. The costume of the hostess was a white satin wedding dress trimmed with the tails of ermines. The black witch costume of my daughter made a wonderful contrast to the white gown of our friend. The elaborate devil costume of her escort won first prize by unanimous vote of the guests. The crimson cocktail dresses of the waitresses, the fuchsia tuxedoes of the bartenders, and the brightly colored costumes of the guests turned the lawn of the Venturas into a Renoir scene from another era. In fact, many of the gowns of the artists at the party found their inspiration from the dress of women during the nineteenth century.

Quotation Marks

Used appropriately, dialogue can liven up your writing. The best way to learn how to use quotation marks is to observe how professional writers use them. Experiment with writing your own dialogue to discover what you know about punctuating conversation. The following rules may be helpful.

Use quotation marks to enclose words spoken or thought, if they are in the form of direct speech:

"How did I get into this mess?" wondered the burglar.

"Hands up! Now!" ordered the officer. "We know you're in there."

However, quotation marks are not needed for indirect speech, or paraphrases of what a speaker said. Here is an example:

The officer shouted that the suspect should put up his hands at once.

When words such as *that* precede the words of a speaker, as in the above example, they indicate that the speaker's words are paraphrased—written in the writer's words—and do not need quotation marks around them.

To indicate a pause, an additional punctuation mark is used inside the quotation marks to separate the words spoken from those that identify and describe the speaker. The choice of that mark varies with the situation. The first example above needs a question mark; other instances call for a comma or an exclamation point. Observe how this is done in this example from Lewis Carroll's *Alice's Adventures in Wonderland*.

"Come, there's no use in crying like that!" said Alice to herself, rather sharply. "I advise you to leave off this minute!" She generally gave herself very good advice (though she very seldom followed it) . . . .

The first word written within the quotation marks generally begins with a capital letter, even when it appears after an introduction. The example below demonstrates this.

So she began: "O Mouse, do you know the way out of this pool? I am very tired of swimming about here, O Mouse!" (Alice thought this must be the right way of speaking to a mouse . . . .)

When the speaker says more than one sentence in a row, quotation marks are used only before and after the entire piece of dialogue.

Oscar insisted, "I will pick you up. It's no bother. I'll be there at six. Please be ready."

Begin the quotation with a capital letter. If the quotation is interrupted, however, do not begin the second part of the quotation with a capital letter unless it is a new sentence.

"A little learning," wrote Alexander Pope, "is a dangerous thing."

"I object," Zelda emphasized. "We have all worked so hard. It's us, not the boss, who deserves a fat raise."

Begin a new paragraph with each change of speaker.

"May I have the car?"

"What for?" Dad asked.

"To go see Myron."

"O.K., but be home by midnight."

Exercise

The quotation marks have been removed from the following conversation from Lewis Carroll's *Alice's Adventures in Wonderland*. Decide where quotation marks should be added and add them.

The Caterpillar and Alice looked at each other for some time in silence: at last the Caterpillar took the hookah out of its mouth, and addressed her in a languid, sleepy voice.

Who are *You?* said the Caterpillar.

This was not an encouraging opening for a conversation. Alice replied, rather shyly, I—I hardly know, Sir, just at present—at least I know who I *was* when I got up this morning, but I think I must have been changed several times since then.

What do you mean by that? said the Caterpillar, sternly. Explain yourself!

I can't explain *myself*, I'm afraid, Sir said Alice because I'm not myself, you see.

I don't see said the Caterpillar.

I'm afraid I can't put it more clearly Alice replied very politely for I can't understand it myself, to begin with; and being so many different sizes in a day is very confusing.

It isn't said the Caterpillar.

Exercise

Now add quotation marks to these stanzas from one of Lewis Carroll's wonderful nonsense poems from the same work. The first and last stanzas are already done for you.

"You are old, father William," the young man said,
    "And your hair has become very white;
And yet you incessantly stand on your head—
    Do you think, at your age, it is right?"

In my youth, father William replied to his son,
    I feared it might injure the brain;
But, now that I'm perfectly sure I have none,
    Why, I do it again and again. . . .

You are old said the youth and your jaws are too weak
    For anything tougher than suet;
Yet you finished the goose, with the bones and the beak—
    Pray, how did you manage to do it?

"In my youth," said his father, "I took to the law,
    And argued each case with my wife;
And the muscular strength, which it gave to my jaw,
    Has lasted the rest of my life."

Note the three dots . . . , plus the period, that appeared between the second and third stanzas of this poem. Those three dots are called **ellipses;** they signify that something from the original version has been left out at that place.

Using Quotation Marks for Direct and Indirect Quoting. Put quotation marks around the exact words of a speaker, but not around indirect speech. The following examples show the difference:

Direct Speech: General Douglas MacArthur said, "I shall return."

These were the general's exact words upon his army's leaving the Philippine Islands during World War II.

Indirect Speech: General Douglas MacArthur said that he would return.

General Douglas MacArthur said he would return.

Because neither of these two sentences quote MacArthur's exact words, they are *indirect,* or reported, *speech.*

If words such as *that* precede the speaker's words, they indicate that the words that follow are not a direct quotation and therefore should not have quotation marks around them. However, as the second example shows, the word *that* is often left out in indirect speech. Here is another example:

Maria said she would not attend the next family reunion.

Written in direct speech, the sentence would read like this:

Maria said, "I will not attend the next family reunion."

Observe that *direct discourse* repeats the actual words said, in the actual order they were said, and therefore needs quotation marks. *Indirect discourse* uses somewhat different words and word order than a direct quotation, and thus does not need quotation marks.

No quotation marks are needed for *reported speech*—also called indirect discourse or indirect quoting—because the *exact* words of a speaker are not repeated. Rather the speaker's words are **paraphrased**—that is, written in the writer's words—as in the following example.

Tayotis asked if the exam would cover the whole novel.

A *direct quote* would read like this:

Tayotis asked, "Will the exam cover the whole novel?"

Observe further that the words that tell who is speaking are set off with a comma, unless, of course, a question mark or exclamation point are indicated. Look at these examples:

"I hate to go to the laundromat," he announced.

"Do I have to go to the laundromat?" he whined.

Glowering at his mother, Fred whined, "Do I really have to go to the laundromat right now?"

"You sure do!" his mother shouted.

His mother glared at him and shouted, "You sure do!"

Note that each of these quotations—the material between the quotation marks—begins with a *capital letter,* whether the quotation is at the beginning or end of the sentence. When a quotation is broken, however, the second part does not begin with a capital letter unless it is a new sentence.

Compare the two examples below.

"One more dumb mistake," the manager warned, "will mean the end of your job."

"Don't bother to report for work next week," his boss concluded. "You can pick up your last paycheck at the end of the month."

Exercise

Punctuate the following, adding capital letters where necessary. The first one is done for you.

1. Patricia asked if Charles wrote long papers. (indirect quote)
   Patricia asked, "Does Charles write long papers?" (direct quote)

2. Betty told John that as she had never skated before she would probably fall down
   Betty told John I have never skated before I'll probably fall down

3. Emily whispered that she would not be able to attend the meeting because she was sick
   I won't be able to attend the meeting whispered Emily because I'm sick

4. Janet sobbed that she would never have made it through the crisis without him because her family could not help her
   without you sobbed Janet I would never have made it through this crisis no one in my family could help me

5. the history professor informed David that his grades were improving
   David the professor beamed your grades are improving keep up the good work

6. Ann asked her mother if she needed any assistance from her
   do you need any assistance Ann inquired if you do call me at work I can stop at your house on the way home from McDonald's

Introducing Quotations into Your Own Writing. Reread the sentences in the previous exercise. Find the verb in each one that introduces the indirect and direct quotations as in the following example:

Patricia *asked* if Charles wrote long papers.

Patricia *asked,* "Does Charles write long papers?"

Next, count the number of different ways of saying *asked* or *said* that were used in the sentences. As you are reading, observe the variety of ways that writers introduce quotations.

Exercise

To add interest to your own writing, when introducing quotations of your own or from outside sources, use as many variations of *said* and *asked* as possible. Look at the following lists and come up with more variations on *said* and *asked*.

said	**asked**	**add some of your own**
gasped	questioned	*claimed*
reported	wondered	
stated	inquired	
yelled	requested	
insisted		
demanded		
whispered		

For additional information about quoting, using quotation marks, and citing outside sources, see Chapter Eight.

Understanding Capitalization

Capital letters give emphasis and make letters or words stand out. Using capital letters where they are unnecessary is as much an error as omitting them where they are needed. Unnecessary capital letters may even change a meaning.

> Four Butt Heads in City Council Race.
> Fred Pryor seminar

Some words, such as the names of cities or brand names, are always capitalized. In other cases, correct usage may vary with the situation. If you are working for an organization, find out its standards about which terms are regularly capitalized. Consult a grammar handbook or a dictionary when you are in doubt. If the word that puzzles you is not listed, you may need to make a somewhat arbitrary decision about whether to use a capital letter. Once you make a decision, consistency is essential. Inconsistent use of capital letters for the same term throughout a text makes a particularly sloppy impression. Careful proofreading should help you catch words that should be capitalized or find those unnecessary capital letters that can pop up in any writer's text. If your eye tends to pass over such errors, however, it is especially important to find someone else to read over your papers.

The following chart (adapted from a workbook used in a Fred Pryor seminar) provides some reminders of the standard uses of capital letters.

Capitalize	Examples	Not Applicable
Languages, religions, races, and peoples	French, Asian, Jewish, Latin	french fries
States, cities, streets, and bodies of water	Ohio, Phoenix, Main Street, Rhine River	"a tourist city on a river"
Months, days, and holidays	June, Monday, Thanksgiving	summer, fall, winter, spring
Buildings, organizations, and institutions	Bijou Theater, Newport Public Library, Greendale Women's Club	movie theater, student union, men's club, a feminist group
Brand names	an old Macintosh computer, Walgreen's	macintosh apple, corner drug store
Names and professional titles	Judge Olga Levin, Dr. Sanchez, Professor Zimmerman	a judge's order, professor's book
Specific academic courses	Biology 101, Urban Sociology, Math II	a business course, science or math major
Historical events, periods, movements, and concepts	the Renaissance, the Civil War, New Deal, Cold War	bitter civil war, the space age, peace march

Also capitalize the major words in the titles of books, chapters of books, TV shows or series, plays, films, and poems.

Gone with the Wind
To Kill a Mockingbird
Days of Our Lives
Mister Roger's Neighborhood
An Affair to Remember
Laverne and Shirley

As these examples demonstrate, articles (*a, an, the*), conjunctions (*but, and,* and so on), and short prepositions (*on, of, with,* and so on) are *not* capitalized unless they are the first word of the title.

Exercise

When appropriate, change the lowercase letters to capital letters in the following letter of request (one of the most common kinds of business letters). Note how hard the letter is to read as it is.

3467 main street
lake mills, mn 01234
february 5, 1993

professor maxine irwin
school of architecture
421 hoover hall
riverside university
lake mills, mn 01234

dear professor irwin:
i have applied for a summer internship with hagge design associates and would greatly appreciate your writing them a letter of recommendation for me.

    i was your student for two very stimulating courses during the academic year 1990–1991: introduction to architecture and architectural fundamentals I. in fact, it was your courses that confirmed my desire to become an architecture major. you gave me an a both semesters, as well as on my research paper, "frank lloyd wright's first usonian house." i still recall our class' field trip to see that house and meet its present owner, professor james dennis of the university of wisconsin-madison, as one of the high points of my college career.

    the form for the recommendation letter, which is due before april 1, 1993, is enclosed, along with my résumé and a transcript. as you can see, i will begin my junior year next august, and have accumulated a 3.6 average as of last semester. if you feel unable to recommend me, could you please return the form to me at the above address? a self-addressed, stamped envelope for that purpose is enclosed. thank you very much for doing this favor for me.

sincerely,
Marianne Doss
marianne doss

Part Two

From Others' Writing to Your Writing: Reading Critically

Chapter Seven

Critical Reading and Your Writing

Understanding What It Means to Read Critically

Critical readers bring a skeptical, jaundiced eye to most of what they read. They look for clues as to whether the writer is adequately informed about a topic. They try to "psych out" the writer's intentions and possible biases, constantly testing an author's presentation against their own knowledge and experience. Critical readers pay regular attention to the writer's sources: When and in what context did former President Jimmy Carter, the Chief Executive Officer of a major corporation, or the owner of the Cleveland Browns make such and such an assertion? Does the writer supply adequate in-text information or bibliographical citations to enable readers to check out those sources? Do some of the claims and information seem to come out of thin air, thus arousing doubts on the part of careful readers?

You have most likely applied your best critical reading skills in numerous instances: carefully reviewing a chapter likely to be on an exam; highlighting text and writing annotations in the margins of a driver's manual after flunking the written test for a learner's permit; skimming the ingredients of a frozen dinner for items containing unsaturated fat; or poring over the directions for installing a stereo system. Observe that the critical reading techniques—skimming, highlighting, annotating, reviewing, and so on—used in each of those instances varied with the situation. All of these techniques, as well as some others, have their own uses; like all readers, you probably find yourself switching from one such technique to another without giving it much thought.

In this chapter, however, we are asking you to devote some effort to becoming more aware of and developing techniques to enhance your critical reading skills. Becoming a more critical reader will benefit you in many ways. You can learn more about the material covered and be more successful in your courses. You will be able to plan your study schedule more effectively, allowing more time to go over more difficult material. Studying for exams will probably become easier and more productive. Perhaps most important, reading should become a more pleasurable activity.

Your writing skills can also be enhanced as you become a more effective critic and editor of both your own and others' writing. You will soon discover that critical reading and good writing go hand in hand. Many assignments in the university and on the job require research and incorporating data from outside sources into your writing. Reading critically enables researchers to better analyze sources and use them more effectively in a variety of assignments: research papers, book reviews, essay exams, science reports, and abstracts or summaries of articles.

Applying Critical Reading Skills to Writing a Summary

The ability to write an effective summary is a very useful skill in many situations. Basically, a **summary** is a restatement, or a paraphrase, of the main ideas of a text in your own words, leaving out most of the examples and supporting details. Always assume that your readers have not read the text of the original. In other words, the summary should be able to stand on its own and make sense by itself, thus giving readers a clear idea about the contents of the material being summarized.

Four Steps for Writing a Clear and Accurate Summary

Step 1: Skimming and prereading
Step 2: Careful reading and annotating
Step 3: Preparing a scratch outline
Step 4: Writing the summary

Applying the Four Steps for Writing Summaries to Student Essays

The following two essays, Ricky Davis's "Making It Out" and Jerome Mason's "Stone City," fit into the genre of **reflective writing.** Both are first-person narratives drawn from the writers' own experiences. Note that the marginal annotations next to Ricky's essay summarize his main points, but leave out most of the details. Those annotations provided the basis for the scratch outline that follows his essay. That scratch outline was in turn the basis for a fairly detailed summary of the main points of Ricky's narrative.

park basketball game ends in a fight, then gunfire, an accepted "part of life," but not something "you get used to."

Making It Out
Ricky Davis

"Bang!" We all hit the ground when the gun blasted. We all knew the routine. At the park where I grew up incidents like this happened almost daily and were considered no big deal. Basketball sparked a lot of emotions and often ended with a fight and every once in awhile gun fire. Someone looking from the outside would think it was crazy or stupid to play ball in an atmosphere like that. What people don't understand is that when you grow up around stuff like that it's not that you get used to it, you just learn to accept it as a part of life. This particular day when the shooting stopped everyone didn't get back up. My big brother was still lying on the ground.

When I saw all that blood I just knew he was going to die. I started crying when it happened and didn't stop until we got to the hospital and the doctor said his wound wasn't as bad as it looked. He had lost so much blood because he caught the bullet in his stomach. He still teases me about crying so much that day. I was only ten at the time. For my brother and I to be six years apart we were very close. I wasn't like most little brothers, telling on my brother and things like that. He wasn't like most big brothers because he didn't mind taking me wherever he went. Since my mother worked a lot it was mostly us two. Neither of us ever knew our fathers. He taught himself the things he needed to know, and also taught me. Since he taught me the things that fathers teach their kids, it made us closer than the average brothers.

Greg was a very street wise sixteen year old and was beginning to teach me the ways of the street at the young age of ten. He took me with him when he stole from stores and stole cars. By the time I turned eleven I could do both by myself, except I didn't know how to drive too well yet, so I stuck mostly to stealing pocket size items. My brother was thinking about selling drugs so he started saving up his money so he could buy a nice amount to get started with. I was soon the only eleven year old in my neighborhood who could roll a joint. I helped him bag the marijuana he was going to sell. It was funny because of all the stuff my brother was teaching me, about half of it was bad. At one point the only thing he was into that was positive was basketball, which he also taught me how to play.

During my brother's junior year in high school things began to change. My mother got a much better job and no longer had to work two jobs. My brother decided to go out for the basketball team and even started doing pretty well in school. All of a sudden my brother always seemed to be on my case about something. My dismal grades were usually the issue. When we took those placement tests to see what reading, writing, and math level we were at I always did well—which showed I had potential but wasn't putting it to use. With my mother around more now, she got on me often about my grades, and about the trouble I was getting into. I expected my mother to yell and get upset about those things, but now my brother was doing it, too.

My brother had started to get close to his basketball coach. His coach knew what kind of situation my brother came from and could relate to it. He was starting to convince my brother that he had the potential to succeed in school and in anything else he wanted to do. My brother and I were always arguing, and for the first time I could remember we weren't getting along at all. I couldn't understand how Greg could change so much so fast. I got to the point where I wouldn't even listen to him. To me it seemed like my mother and brother against me. My mother put me on punishment after punishment and it still didn't help. My mother knew that Greg was the

---

fears about his brother lying bleeding on the ground proved not true—bullet wound in stomach not fatal

unusually close relationship with his brother Greg: mother worked a lot

sixteen-year-old Greg teaches him the "ways of the street": stealing; bagging marijuana and selling joints by age eleven

basketball—the only positive thing Greg taught him

turning points during Greg's junior year in high school— on basketball team and getting better grades

—mother got better job and no longer had to work 2 jobs

Both "on my case" about low grades and not using potential (high test scores)

coach convinces Greg he has the potential to succeed

brother and mother seem pitted against him, but he refuses to change.

Greg blames himself for my getting into "so much trouble"

so many guns on the streets

Greg cried over his and their mother's fears for him

resolved to do better; other turning points
—at Boys and Girls Club had to do homework to play basektball
—move out of old neighborhood

brother teaches him things he "really needed to know"

shedding the "ghetto mind-set" is not just changing address but about "changing your way of thinking"

Greg: 3 years college; good job and 2 kids

Ricky: first of his age group from the old neighborhood in college

only person who could get me to listen.

Now Greg felt guilty because he thought it was his fault that I was getting in so much trouble. I didn't listen until I saw my brother cry. That was the first and only time I ever saw him cry. I had seen him get shot and not shed a tear. He was talking to me, telling me what I was putting my mother through and how it wasn't the same on the streets anymore. The streets were getting to the point where almost everyone was carrying guns. He said if something happened to me my mother would go crazy. As he spoke I saw a single tear drop from his eye and I knew he really meant he would go crazy if something happened to me. I never said what I would stop doing, but we both knew after that night I was going to try to do better.

Since Greg was playing basketball for Hamilton High School we didn't spend too much time together except on weekends. My mother got me in the Boys and Girls Club which was good because they made me do my homework before I could play basketball. The next year we moved out of the old neighborhood which was the last step in turning things around for my brother and me. My brother continued to teach and tell me a lot. The difference was that he began telling me things that I really needed to know.

Over the years we have often talked about how things used to be. How the ghetto mind-set is so hard to break, growing up doing so many bad things and glorifying them like we were doing good things. I think it's a cycle, growing up with one parent, struggling to make ends meet and finally giving up hope. What I mean by the ghetto mind-set is you get to the point where you think there is nothing you can do to better your situation and become content with it. Some people think because they move to a better neighborhood that they're out of the ghetto. To better your situation isn't changing addresses, it's about changing your way of thinking.

After finishing high school on time Greg went to college for three years. He now has a good job and two kids. I remember being proud that I was the first one in my neighborhood my age to be able to roll a joint. Now I'm proud that I'm the first one my age from the old neighborhood to go to college.

Scratch Outline.

- park basketball game ended in a fight, then gunfire, an accepted part of life in that park (but not something "you get used to")

- fears about his brother lying bleeding on the ground proved unwarranted: bullet wound in his stomach not fatal
- unusually close relationship with his older brother, Greg: their mother worked a lot, so "it was mostly us two"
- sixteen-year-old Greg taught him the "ways of the street": stealing, bagging marijuana, and selling joints by age eleven
- basketball: the one positive thing Greg taught him
- turning points during Greg's junior year in high school
    - Greg on basketball team and getting better grades; coach convinced him he had potential to succeed in life
    - mother got better job; no longer had to work two jobs
- both "on his case" about low grades and not using his potential (high test scores): they seem pitted against him, but he refused to change
- Greg blamed himself for Ricky's getting into "so much trouble"
- so many guns on the streets: Greg cried over his and their mother's fears for him
- other turning points and a resolve to do better
    - at Boys and Girls Club had to do homework before playing basketball
    - moved out of old neighborhood
    - brother started teaching him things he "really needed to know"
- shedding the "ghetto mind-set": not just changing addresses but "changing your way of thinking"
- Greg: 3 years college, good job, and 2 kids
- Ricky: the first of his age group from the old neighborhood in college

Summary.

"Bang!" Ricky Davis grabs the reader's attention with an anecdote about a fight at a basketball game that ended in gunfire, an accepted part of life in that park, although not something "you get used to." Ricky's fears that his older brother, lying bleeding on the ground, had received a fatal wound in the stomach, proved to be unfounded.

Ricky and his brother Greg had an unusually close relationship. Their mother worked a lot and "it was mostly us two." Sixteen-year-old Greg taught him the "ways of the street": Ricky was stealing, bagging marijuana, and selling joints by age eleven. The one positive thing Greg taught him was basketball.

The first of several important turning points in their lives occurred during Greg's junior year in high school. Greg got on the high school basketball *team and began getting better grades, and his coach convinced him that he had the potential to succeed in life. Their mother got a better job, so she no longer had to work two jobs. She was around more then, and they both started getting on Ricky's case about his dismal grades and for not living up to the potential indicated by his high achievement test scores.*

Greg also started blaming himself for Ricky's "getting in so much trouble." The streets had changed to the point where "almost everyone was carrying guns." However, Ricky did not listen until, for the first time, he saw his brother cry—over his and their mother's fears for Ricky. He resolved to do better. Fortunately, his mother got him into the Boys and Girls Club where he had to do his homework before he could play basketball.

The next year the family moved out of the old neighborhood. Greg began teaching Ricky things he "really needed to know." Since then they have regularly discussed shedding the "ghetto mind-set," a change necessitating not simply changing addresses, but "changing your way of thinking."

Greg has completed three years of college and has a good job and two kids. Ricky is proud that he is the first one in his age group from the old neighborhood to be in college.

Note that this summary is flatter and much less interesting than the original essay. Why is that? What is missing?

Jerome Mason, a sophomore majoring in social welfare, won a first-place award in the 1994 Virginia Burke Writing Contest at the University of Wisconsin–Milwaukee for this essay.

Stone City
Jerome Mason

Being successful can mean different things to different people. To some people it could mean getting a great job, or accumulating a large sum of money, or achieving some other goal that a person feels is important. In my life, I have had as many successes as failures, some big, and some small. The most important things that I have accomplished are very personal things that give meaning to my life, like being admitted to the University of Wisconsin—Milwaukee. It meant more to me than just being able to further my educational horizons; it was a fulfillment of a childhood dream. Not just a dream to go to college, but a dream to attend this particular school.

Most of my childhood was spent living in a house on the east side of Milwaukee, a little over a mile away from the university in a section of town now called Riverwest. The area has lots of parks and trails along side the Milwaukee River. When I was about nine, I used to go to those nearby parks with my older brother and his friends when they would let me come with them. We would hike up and down the trails as if we were on an expedition into the wilds of some far off country. Mostly we would end up down by the river catching frogs or turtles, or whatever we could find. We would always stay on the west side of the Locust Street bridge because our mother would not allow us to go on the other side by ourselves. Of course, I often crossed the bridge in the family car, but I had never gone over there on foot.

Then one morning on the way to school, my buddy suggested that we go to the other side of the bridge. I had never skipped school, but the idea of going on an adventure sounded much more exciting than school. We took an alternate route to school, so that none of the other kids would see us as we set out to see just what lay ahead on the other side of that bridge.

We forged across the long bridge which, at the time, seemed like the link to another world. It felt as if we were exploring strange new territories, discovering a new land unknown to the rest of the world. In a childlike way we were doing just that. Just on the other side of the bridge was a long concrete trail close to the river. We wandered down the trail for a while, and then decided to climb up the river bank to see what was at the top.

When we reached the peak, not too far off in the distance, we spotted three huge stone buildings towering over the tops of the neighboring houses. There was no question that this was the direction that we wanted to head. To keep a low profile, we stuck to the back streets and alleys as much as possible. When we reached the street where the huge buildings stood, we came across an awesome sight: a large isolated community, which seemed to us to be a stone city. We had to investigate, and find out more about this mysterious place. We explored a couple of the buildings and saw the people in large class rooms that looked to us like movie theaters. The doors to all the buildings were open, so we just roamed around, going from building to building.

One of the buildings was more like a shopping mall without the department stores; it had lots of restaurants and offices, and there was even a recreation room and a bowling alley in the basement. This is the building where we found lots of people "hanging out." They seemed to be coming from every direction. Some were studying big books, and others were eating and talking. The motion of the people appeared almost chaotic, yet synchronized. Everything they were doing seemed to be important, exciting; they just seemed to be enjoying themselves as if they were at a carnival or something. This was living! I was feeding on the intensity of it all. I felt like there was an electric current flowing through my veins. It was as if I was in the place where the people ran the world.

No one said anything to us, and we figured that we were so far away from anybody who would recognize us that we felt pretty safe. We were wrong though. Someone had recognized us. A student teacher who had recently done his field placement in our classroom came over and asked us why we were not in school. We were caught! The adventure was over. We told him the truth in hopes that he wouldn't take us back to school to be punished.

He didn't take us back to the school, but he told us that he was going to telephone later to see if we had made it without him. On the way back, I was worried about facing the consequences, but I was also glad we had found out what a university was like. I had become enlightened. I had discovered a whole other world on the far side of that bridge that I never even knew existed.

This experience had a big impact on me as a young boy. I became fascinated with the university. Every chance I could get to go over there, I took. I found out that the university offered summer youth programs, which I attended every year after that while I was in grade school. Being involved in these activities was important to me, because it made me feel connected to the university. In my mind U.W.M. was the place to be if you wanted to be more than just average; it was the place to be if you wanted to be great.

In the community where I grew up, there wasn't a strong emphasis on education at the college level. I didn't know of any professional people in my neighborhood outside of my teachers at school, who had careers that required a college degree. Sadly, as time passed, I began to feel that it was unrealistic for me to think that I would ever be able to have a chance to do something like go to college. I started to feel as though college, careers, and things like that were only for privileged, well-to-do white people. They were not for a fairly average, everyday young black male like myself. I started losing interest in school completely by the time I was midway through high school. I stopped thinking about ever going to college all together; it seemed way beyond my reach.

When I think back to the days I spent roaming the hallways of my old high school, I must admit they bring out a feeling of emptiness. I find myself replaying the events that took place in my head, trying to untangle the webs that were spun out of youthful ambivalence. I can recall so vividly the melodramatic—and not so melodramatic—scenes of those days when we were hanging out on the school grounds, always in search of something, in need of some kind of stimulation. Most of what we got out of our quest for excitement were some bad habits.

It was soon made very clear to me that my presence at this school was not wanted. I remember one teacher telling me to my face in a very intimidating manner how much he really didn't like me at all. He wasn't even my teacher. He simply stopped me in the hallway as I was passing by and said, "Hey you, why aren't you in class?" I just looked at him without any words to explain my not being in class. He grimaced his face in a way someone does when they despise or loathe something intensely and said in a very serious tone, "I really don't like you." The rest of what he said didn't really make any difference to me because his sentiments were pretty much the same as many of the other teachers', and I had heard their sorry, tired old speeches a thousand times before.

What bothered me the most about what he had said was the fact that he really didn't even know me. He may have heard things about me, or seen me in the hallways, but he knew nothing about my character or personality, in truth because he had never taken the time out to talk to me and discover what kind of person I really was inside.

The only instructor at this school who ever took the time out to talk to me about my passions and my admirations was the music teacher. He seemed to care about what was going on in my life, and sort of took on the role of my confidant. Most of all I remember the very first day of high school when I went into his classroom and he pointed to a sign he had made that said, "YOUGOTTAWANNA." The sign made so much sense to me then, and was to later be the philosophy that I used to get back on the road to my own success.

Eventually I dropped out of high school and ended up going to an alternative school where I received my G.E.D. By the time I had turned eighteen, all the childhood dreams of going to U.W.M. one day and becoming successful had completely faded away. It was also around this time that things in my life really started going wrong. All the things I had experimented with over the years, the drugs, the alcohol, had become more fixed into my lifestyle. Not only had my childhood dreams dwindled down to the point of non-existence, but I was burdened with an even more challenging twist of fate: what to do with my life now?

When I entered the workforce, I had no direction, nor did I have any idea of what kind of work I wanted to do. I just took whatever jobs were offered to me without any concerns or cares, but no job seemed to satisfy or replace the feeling of being connected to something important, like that feeling I had as a child visiting the great stone city.

At age twenty-one, this lifestyle that I had gotten caught up in had started taking its toll on me. The streets had become the center ring in which I needed to perform, my mecca, the only university that I felt I would ever be accepted to. Burned out, frustrated, desperate, and tired, I showed up at my mother's job one afternoon. I had gone there to tell her what I was planning to do. I knew that she had become very disappointed in me and the things that I had gotten involved in, but I could see in her face the sense of relief that I was starting to show signs of being responsible for my actions.

When I left my mother's office, I headed down to a treatment center that I had passed by a short time earlier, to see if there was anything they could do for me. When I got there, a man came into the waiting room and asked me if he could do something for me. I told him that I wanted to get into a drug treatment program. He then asked me if I needed someone to talk to, and I said yes. The counselor patiently listened to my story, and it felt so good to get everything out into the open. When I finished, he said something to me that made everything seem so clear: "That's why they call them drugs." It was the timing of what he said that was so important to me. I was ready for the truth, and the truth was that the drugs were affecting my reasonability, and my judgement.

He told me that getting into a treatment program meant getting on a very long waiting list that would take about six months. Six months proved to be too long. Three days later I was arrested for a burglary and sentenced to four years in prison. I served thirty-two months, mandatory time on a four year sentence.

I recall with a bitter pride the afternoon when I was talking to my assigned social worker in prison about my chances of serving my last few months in a halfway house back in Milwaukee, so that I could get a job and save some money before I got my release. With his face grimaced in the same manner that I had come to know so well, his exact words still echo in my mind: "You are never going to amount to anything! People like you will get out of here and go back to the streets and commit another crime and end up right back in jail."

I am happy to say that I proved him wrong. Most importantly, though, I proved to myself that I am not going to let anything or anybody keep me from doing what I want to do because of their negative stereotypes.

After several years of going through more of life's ups and downs, I decided that it was time for me to pursue what was important; it was time to fulfill my life's dreams. At twenty-five, I enrolled in the Human Services program at the Milwaukee Area Technical College. After completing my studies there, I transferred to the University of Wisconsin–Milwaukee to the Social Welfare program. When I was accepted at the university, it was like a dream come true. Although I do plan to graduate, get my master's degree and work with troubled youth who may need to hear an experienced voice from someone who's been down some of the same roads that they're on now, I have already become personally successful in life. To me, being successful is achieving your own personal dreams, whatever they may be: "YOUGOTTAWANNA."

Today I live about three blocks away from the house I grew up in, and I walk the same route to U.W.M. as I did that very first day we ventured out to see what was on the other side of the bridge. I still get an awesome feeling when I see those tall buildings towering over the tops of the houses as I approach the school, and I again feel the electricity flowing through my veins. My fascination with the chaotic movement of people within the isolated stone city is just as it was when I was a child. Being a student at U.W.M. means more to me than just being able to further my education. It gives me the feeling of being part of something important. It means being connected to the place where the people run the world.

Exercise

Before making a thorough study of the contents of the summary of "Making It Out" (pages 177–78), practice some of the *critical reading strategies* designed to help you read any text more closely and more effectively.

1. **Previewing.** Read through both essays quickly for an overall impression; then respond to these questions.
   a. Jot down several good and bad points about each essay. Did the authors do an effective job? Why?
   b. How can you relate to the experiences they depicted?
   c. Do the titles suggest anything about the contents?
   d. What information about the overall contents of each essay can be gathered from its introduction and conclusion?
   e. What do the essays reveal about their authors? Jot down at least three adjectives that describe each of them.
   f. Can you think of some reasons why these essays are paired?

2. **Reading Carefully and Annotating.**
   a. Go back and reread each paragraph of "Making It Out" carefully, studying the marginal annotations as you go along. Observe that the annotations are largely *paraphrases* of the text, with an occasional short quote (in quotation marks) of Ricky Davis' exact words.
   b. Now reread "Stone City," and write annotations in the margins that paraphrase the text—in other words, put the main points of the text into your own words. Annotations do not need to be complete sentences. In cases where you think short quotes of Jerome Mason's exact words are preferable, be sure to put them in quotation marks, but use direct quotes sparingly. In general it is better to paraphrase, to use your words.

3. **Preparing a Scratch Outline.**
   a. Note that the points listed in the scratch outline following "Making It Out" have generally the same contents as the annotations. Like annotations, the points listed in a scratch outline need not be complete sentences.
   b. After studying the scratch outline of "Making It Out," write a scratch outline of "Stone City," using your annotations as the basis for your outline.

4. **Writing a Summary.**
   a. Observe that the detailed summary of "Making It Out" has basically the same contents as the scratch outline. However, the summary is written in complete sentences and contains the necessary transitions to make it flow smoothly.
   b. Use your scratch outline as the basis for a detailed summary of "Stone City" written in sentence or paragraph form. Your summary should give readers a shortened version—in your words—of the main points in Jerome Mason's essay, without supporting details.

Because "Stone City" and "Making It Out" are both well organized and straightforward, although very thoughtful, narratives, they are somewhat easier to annotate, outline, and summarize than less well-organized or more complex material. Upon mastering this four-step technique for writing a detailed summary, and depending on the complexity of the material you are summarizing, you may be able to cut out some of the steps. You may choose one of the following options to eliminate one of the steps.

Option One: *Highlight* or *underline* main points right on the text page.

Bear in mind, however, that making marginal annotations gets the reader *more actively engaged* and therefore more likely to digest a text, remember it for exams, and use it effectively as a source.

Annotations provide other advantages. The margins are a good place for questioning a writer's views or use of sources and for marking striking passages or memorable figures of speech. Use annotations to point out concepts requiring clarification through further study or by asking a teacher, a tutor, or another student. You can also mark unfamiliar terms or words in annotations. Sometimes the meaning of a word can be deduced from the context of the passage where it appears, but if you are at all uncertain look it up in a dictionary and jot down the meaning in the margin.

Option Two: Eliminate the scratch outline. Proceed directly from marginal annotations, or even from highlighting or underlining, to writing the summary itself.

Exercise

1. Have you had an important turning point, or a series of turning points, in your life that you might like to write about? Explore a potential topic. Write "turning points" in the center of a sheet of paper and see what ideas you come up with.
2. Is attending college a break with your background and traditions? Did you, or do you, encounter support, resistance, or apathy from your family, friends, coworkers, or teachers for your decision to pursue a college education? Has anyone played a particular role in your career decisions?

Getting the Most from Outside Sources

Writing summaries is only one of many useful outcomes of critical reading. Choosing selected data and concepts from outside sources in order to incorporate them into your own research papers, essays, and other writings is an equally valuable, related skill.

Your composition teacher may assign readings for class discussion or as topics for **impromptus,** or essays written in class. This section contains an article we have used for such an impromptu, along with two student papers about it. Both student writers had a clear idea of what they wanted to say and had obviously become quite engaged by the topic. These models demonstrate much about techniques for incorporating outside sources into an essay.

Note: These students both received excellent grades on these impromptus. However, the models included below were also significantly revised.

What is the answer to this riddle?

A father was killed in an auto accident, and his son, badly injured in the seat next to him, was rushed to the hospital. The surgeon assigned to operate on the boy blanched when seeing him and muttered, "I can't operate on this boy, he's my son."

The answer, as science writer K. C. Cole pointed out in her 1984 study, *Sympathetic Vibrations: Physics as a Way of Life* (65), is that the surgeon is a woman, the boy's mother.

Cole's and others' experiences that this riddle stumps many, men and women alike, has been borne out by our observations. At one gathering, only one of a dozen people guessed the right answer. As he put it, "My daughter is a surgeon." Surprisingly, her mother was unable to solve the riddle.

In part, this type of preconceived thinking demonstrates the results of centuries of using the pronoun *he* to refer to both genders, as in "every student must pay his tuition by the third week of the semester." Such usage both reflects and influences reality, and, as Cole points out, can even skew reality, as evidenced by the common failure to solve this riddle even though most people are aware that female surgeons are common today.

The subtle—and not so subtle—ways by which women are discouraged from entering careers in science are one of K. C. Cole's major interests. She began her writing career as a reporter and has published several works about science, education, and women's issues, including the following article from the December 3, 1981, issue of the *New York Times*.

Why There Are So Few Women in Science
K. C. Cole

—unusual occupation—writes about science, especially physics

I know few other women who do what I do. What I do is write about science, mainly physics. And to do that, I spend a lot of time reading about science, talking to scientists and struggling to understand physics. In fact, most of the women (and men) I know think me quite queer for actually liking physics. "How can you write about that stuff?" they ask, always somewhat askance. "I could never understand that in a million years." Or more simply "I hate science."

—discovers is an "odd creature"

I didn't realize what an odd creature a woman interested in physics was until a few years ago when a science magazine sent me to Johns

Hopkins University in Baltimore for a conference on an electrical phenomenon known as the Hall effect. We sat in a huge lecture hall and listened as physicists talked about things engineers didn't understand, and engineers talked about things physicists didn't understand. What *I* didn't understand was why, out of several hundred young students of physics and engineering in the room, less than a handful were women.

Sometime later, I found myself at the California Institute of Technology reporting on the search for the origins of the universe. I interviewed physicist after physicist, man after man. I asked one young administrator why none of the physicists were women. And he answered: "I don't know, but I suppose it must be something innate. My seven-year-old daughter doesn't seem to be much interested in science."

It was with that experience fresh in my mind that I attended a conference in Cambridge, Mass., on science literacy, or rather the worrisome lack of it in this country today. We three women—a science teacher, a young chemist and myself—sat surrounded by a company of august men. The chemist, I think, first tentatively raised the issue of science illiteracy in women. It seemed like an obvious point. After all, everyone had agreed over and over again that scientific knowledge these days was a key factor in economic power. But as soon as she made the point, it became clear that we women had committed a grievous social error. Our genders were suddenly showing; we had interrupted the serious talk with a subject unforgivably silly.

For the first time, I stopped being puzzled about why there weren't any women in science and began to be angry. Because if science is a search for answers to fundamental questions then it hardly seems frivolous to find out why women are excluded. Never mind the economic consequences.

A lot of the reasons women are excluded are spelled out by the Massachusetts Institute of Technology experimental physicist Vera Kistiakowsky in a recent article in *Physics Today* called "Women in Physics: Unnecessary, Injurious and Out of Place?" The title was taken from a nineteenth-century essay written in opposition to the appointment of a female mathematician to a professorship at the University of Stockholm. "As decidedly as two and two make four," a woman in mathematics is a "monstrosity," concluded the writer of the essay.

Dr. Kistiakowsky went on to discuss the factors that make women in science today, if not monstrosities, at least oddities. Contrary to much

What does "innate" mean?

—*why so few women students of physics and engineering at a science conference at Johns Hopkins U.*

—*administrator's remark about 7 year old daughter: lack of interest in science must be "innate"*

—*few women at conference on science literacy*

popular opinion, one of those is *not* an innate difference in the scientific ability of boys and girls. But early conditioning does play a stubborn and subtle role. A recent *Nova* program, "The Pinks and the Blues," documented how girls and boys are treated differently from birth—the boys always encouraged in more physical kinds of play, more active explorations of their environments. Sheila Tobias, in her book, *Math Anxiety,* showed how the games boys play help them to develop an intuitive understanding of speed, motion and mass.

The main sorting out of the girls from the boys in science seems to happen in junior high school. As a friend who teaches in a science museum said, "By the time we get to electricity, the boys already have had some experience with it. But it's unfamiliar to the girls." Science books draw on boys' experiences. "The examples are all about throwing a baseball at such and such a speed," said my stepdaughter, who barely escaped being a science drop-out.

The most obvious reason there are not many more women in science is that women are discriminated against as a class, in promotions, salaries and hirings, a conclusion reached by a recent analysis by the National Academy of Sciences.

Finally, said Dr. Kistiakowsky, women are simply made to feel out of place in science. Her conclusion was supported by a Ford Foundation study by Lynn H. Fox on the problems of women in mathematics. When students were asked to choose among six reasons accounting for girls' lack of interest in math, the girls rated this statement second: "Men do not want girls in the mathematical occupations."

A friend of mine remembers winning a Bronxwide mathematics competition in the second grade. Her friends—both boys and girls—warned her that she shouldn't be good at math: "You'll never find a boy who likes you." My friend continued nevertheless to excel in math and science, won many awards during her years at Bronx High School of Science, and then earned a full scholarship to Harvard. After one year of Harvard science, she decided to major in English.

When I asked her why, she mentioned what she called the "macho mores" of science. "It would have been O.K. if I'd had someone to talk to," she said. "But the rules of comportment were such that you never admitted you didn't understand. I later realized that even the boys didn't get everything clearly right away. You had to stick with it until it had time to sink in. But for the boys, there was a payoff in suffering through the hard times, and a kind of punishment—a shame—if they didn't. For the girls it was O.K. not to get it, and the only payoff for sticking it out was that you'd be considered a freak."

. . .

Science is undeniably hard. Often, it can seem quite boring. It is unfortunately too often presented as laws to be memorized instead of mysteries to be explored. It is too often kept a secret that science, like art, takes a well-developed esthetic sense. Women aren't the only ones who say, "I hate science."

That's why everyone who goes into science needs a little help from friends. For the past ten years, I have been getting more than a little help from a friend who is a physicist. But my stepdaughter—who earned the highest grades ever recorded in her California high school on the math Scholastic Aptitude Test—flunked calculus in her first year at Harvard. When my friend the physicist heard about it, he said, "Harvard should be ashamed of itself."

What he meant was that she needed that little extra encouragement that makes all the difference. Instead, she got that little extra discouragement that makes all the difference.

"In the first place, all the math teachers are men," she explained. "In the second place, when I met a boy I liked and told him I was taking chemistry, he immediately said, 'Oh, you're one of those science types.' In the third place, it's just a kind of a social thing. The math clubs are full of boys and you don't feel comfortable joining."

In other words, she was made to feel unnecessary, injurious and out of place.

A few months ago, I accompanied a male colleague from the science museum where I sometimes work to a lunch of the history of science faculty at the University of California. I was the only woman there, and my presence for the most part was obviously and rudely ignored. I was so surprised and hurt by this that I made an extra effort to speak knowledgeably and well. At the end of the lunch, one of the professors turned to me in all seriousness and said: "Well, K. C., what do the women think of Carl Sagan?" I replied that I had no idea what "the women" thought about anything. But now I know what I should have said: I should have told him that his comment was unnecessary, injurious and out of place.

Exercise

Consider the following questions in small groups.

1. **Mulling over and Discussing the Topic.**

    Have you ever thought about women in scientific careers? Do you see any relationship between your perceptions (and the perceptions of many around you) and the riddle on page 186?

2. **Skimming the Article.**

    Skim through Cole's entire article for an overall impression, then discuss the following questions. (You may refer to the article to find the necessary information.)
    a. Where and when did Cole publish this article?
    b. What does that choice say about Cole's intended *audience?*
    c. What seems to be Cole's intended *purpose* in publishing this essay?
    d. How does Cole establish herself as an authority? Why is that important in her case?
    e. Does Cole reveal any emotional reaction to her topic, or is her attitude purely objective and detached?

3. **Rereading the Article.**

    Reread the introduction and conclusion, looking for hints about the broader contents and purpose of Cole's article. Then carefully reread the entire essay.

4. **Making Annotations.**
    a. Study the marginal annotations next to the first few paragraphs in Cole's essay. Then divide the remaining paragraphs between the members of your group and write your own annotations.
    b. Along with making annotations about the main points, mark all unfamiliar words and terms.
    c. When everyone is finished, discuss all of the unfamiliar terms to see whether anyone in the group knows their meanings. If no one is sure, look the terms up in a dictionary or ask your instructor about the meanings.
    d. Are the annotations correct and complete? Did anyone miss a main point? Distort the meaning? Include too many details?
    e. Put everyone else's annotations on your text so that you have a completely annotated version of K. C. Cole's essay.

5. **Questions for General Class Discussion.**
    a. Bring up unfamiliar terms and concepts, and raise any questions your group had about the essay.
    b. On the blackboard, list the main reasons why Cole thinks that so few women have careers in science in the United States.
    c. How would you categorize the *sources* of Cole's arguments? List three such categories (e.g., personal experience) and find at least three examples of each of them.

The following two student essays were written in response to this question:

Think about gender and career choice in our society. Are some professions traditionally "male"—or "female"?

Studies substantiate the observation that women and members of many minorities are underrepresented in careers in science and mathematics. In her essay, "Why There Are So Few Women in Science," science writer K. C. Cole speculates about possible causes for this underrepresentation.

What are some of the reasons that Cole thinks may cause fewer women to enter a career in science? If possible, strengthen your answer with examples from your own or others' experiences that support, or differ from, Cole's observations.

Caution: The fact that you had a science teacher who encouraged girls, or know of a similar case, does not *refute* Cole's arguments. Such examples simply document experiences different from the cases Cole discussed. Unlike most of her readers, however, Cole is a qualified professional who has researched this issue and given it a great deal of thought. Her claims deserve your consideration and are too carefully documented to be negated by your, or your friends', experiences alone. While it would be an excellent idea to mention such experiences, noting that they differed from the situations Cole described, do not imply that they prove Cole is wrong in her general arguments.

As you study the student models below, be aware that Becky Manuell chose to relate Cole's claims to her own experiences, while Ken Shanovich relied almost exclusively on the Cole text. Both writers, however, skillfully incorporated data from Cole's article into their own sentences. (For more information on how to use outside sources in your writing, see Chapter 8.)

In his opening paragraph Ken Shanovich rightly introduced the source of his essay and briefly identified K. C. Cole. Ken regularly referred to Cole ("according to Cole," "Cole also demonstrates," and so on) throughout, as he brought up specific examples Cole used to back up her thesis. His essay also demonstrates how effective writers largely paraphrase, using only the occasional quote to spice up their work.

Skim both student essays, then reread them at least once before doing the group activity that follows the second essay.

Women In Science
Ken Shanovich

In the essay "Why There Are So Few Women in Science," K. C. Cole, a science writer by profession, offers her insight on the reasons for this disparity. Cole describes numerous misconceptions about the perceived lack of interest and the innate inabilities of women in the field of science. She cites documented evidence which shows that historically women have been discouraged and even prevented from entering the field of science. She notes how she frequently is one of a very few women at scientific gatherings, and demonstrates clearly how women are often made to feel uncomfortable at such meetings, or in science and math classes. For instance, Cole's stepdaughter, a very talented high school math student, flunked calculus at Harvard. She told Cole that the math teachers were all men, and that she did not feel comfortable joining math clubs which were "full of boys." Also a boy she liked termed her "one of those science types" when she told him she was taking chemistry.

According to Cole, the problems begin in early childhood with parents conditioning and channeling their children into traditional roles: boys into math, science and sports; girls toward clerical and domestic roles. This gender oriented role modeling continues throughout their childhood and academic life. Science teachers are usually men, text books have a male bias, and many times their examples use sports or traditional male activities to demonstrate a scientific principle. These factors all inhibit girls from excelling in science.

Cole also demonstrates how girls who overcome these early barriers face additional problems. In the upper education levels success in this field yields some undesirable fallout in the form of stereotypical labeling. This carries a heavy cost when it comes to socializing and dating. One of Cole's friends who won a grade school math contest recalls being warned by boys and girls alike: Don't be too good at math or you'll "never find a boy who will like you."

To Cole it is important that women are given an equal opportunity throughout their education. The educational system often has lower expectations of women, creating a self fulfilling situation. She cited a study for the Ford Foundation by Lynn H. Fox which found that the resistance and hostility of males toward women entering certain fields is the second most common reason for women deciding not to pursue a career in science or math. Science is a difficult subject for everyone, and requires that encouragement be given to all.

The world will never know what scientific achievements have been postponed or never realized because of all the potential women scientists who were never given a chance. Discrimination and destructive traditions are still pervasive in our society. Until this problem is eliminated humankind will never reach its true potential.

Note that Becky Manuell regularly and skillfully relates Cole's examples and conclusions to her own experiences and observations in the following essay.

K. C. Cole: Women in Science
Becky Manuell

Science writer K. C. Cole begins her 1981 article, "Why There Are So Few Women in Science," by describing when she first became aware of the lack of women in the science field, especially physics. She lets the reader know from her own observations that society, including other women, seems to frown on women entering the science field. She tells of other women's lack of interest in science. At a conference at Johns Hopkins University, K. C. Cole noticed the tiny number of women in a lecture hall full of physicists. A male colleague once commented to Cole about the absence of women in science by saying "It must be something innate," basing that statement on his seven-year-old daughter's lack of interest. That seemed to be quite a general statement because of one child's view. To me, it seems to be a wrong generalization; rather the lack of women in science appears to be something society seems to have thrust upon us. I too notice how other women, including myself, shy away from the topic of science.

Early in her article, Cole's interest seems to change to anger over the gender issue. The subject of science illiteracy for women was brought up with a group of men at another conference she attended, and was automatically taken as a social error. This case seemed to show that men don't want to address the topic, as if the gender difference doesn't seem to exist. As a woman, I believe any gender issue on any subject is important enough to address.

Besides her own personal experiences, K. C. Cole researched several important sources and incorporated them into her own article. In one of her sources, Vera Kistiakowsky, a Massachusetts Institute of Technology experimental physicist, spelled out why women are excluded from physics in her article, "Women in Physics: Unnecessary, Injurious and Out of Place?" This title conveys a strong point, which Cole grasps and uses to emphasize her own valid conclusions.

A main point, backed by research, is that even in childhood conditioning exists which encourages boys' and deters girls' development for possible future careers. This early childhood conditioning includes boys' play—more explorative and curious, as opposed to the quiet, organized play expected of girls. I remember enjoying football and tree climbing as a young girl. I would be reprimanded with the comment, "Act like a girl, behave and play quietly." What is "act like a girl?" It is the different behavior expectations thrust upon us by society. Even the types of games played by boys foster many qualities needed later on to succeed. I always noticed how much more competitive boys' activities were. Girls would be laughed at or criticized if they would attempt to play games with the boys such as football, soccer, baseball, wrestling, and basketball. Cole backs up her thesis about the effects of childhood games and conditioning with pertinent statements from both a *Nova* program, "The Pinks and the Blues," and Sheila Tobias' book, *Math Anxiety*.

K. C. Cole further stresses that "women are discriminated against as a class" in science. Since I can identify personally with both minority and gender discrimination, this point was well understood by me. Cole demonstrated that women are made to feel out of place in both science and mathematics. To prove this, she provided both personal examples and information from outside authorities. An analysis by the National Academy on Science proved discrimination in promotions, salaries, and hiring against women in these fields. Conclusions in Dr. Kistiakowsky's and Cole's other sources were also supported by a Ford Foundation Study by Lynn Fox showing how women are made to feel out of place in the field of mathematics.

Cole also provided examples of personal experiences of such discrimination. A female friend with great potential in science and a full scholarship to Harvard switched her major from science to English after one year. Her treatment in science courses deterred her from continuing. Teachers actually expected the girls not to get the course information. For girls, it was more of a punishment (you were considered a "freak") to succeed in science than drop out. Also, Cole's own stepdaughter, with the highest math aptitude score ever recorded in her California high school, flunked calculus at Harvard because of being discouraged instead of encouraged.

I, too, believe that a male dominated field will deter women from succeeding in it. I had my mind set on playing drums in my high school band. I had had private lessons before high school and been told I had good potential at reading music and succeeding in playing. The drum section was filled with twelve boys and myself. I was snickered at, looked down upon, and was never given an equal chance. Mistakes I made were blamed on my gender, while a male could make the same mistake and it would be

> overlooked. I was always shoved off onto the xylophones and once in a while the bass drum. I think the expectation of my failing by everyone around me pushed that outcome. With a little encouragement or belief from people, I believe I would have succeeded.
>
> K. C. Cole relates an incident where she was made to feel out of place by an ignorant comment from a male colleague at a history of science faculty lunch where Cole was the only female. This colleague asked Cole what "the women think of Carl Sagan," the world famous scientist who often appears in television programs on the cosmos. Why didn't he just ask, as one colleague to another, what her opinion of Sagan was? Gender shouldn't have been brought into the question.
>
> In spite of her achievements, when she wrote this article, Cole, a fully qualified professional was still receiving negative vibes from many men in her field of physics. Cole does a good job of proving her point, based on Dr. Kistiakowsky's article title, that women are still made to feel "unnecessary, injurious and out of place" in science.

Exercise

In small groups, consider the following questions.

1. What do you see as the major strengths of Becky Manuell's essay? List at least three of those strengths.
2. What do you regard as the major strong points of Ken Shanovich's paper? Write down at least three of those strong points.
3. List the major similarities between Ken Shanovich's and Becky Manuell's essays.
4. List the major differences between Ken's and Becky's essays.

Exercise

Are Cole's claims about the differences between boys' and girls' toys still largely correct, or has recent heightened awareness of gender issues had an effect on toy manufacturing and marketing?

Test out Cole's claim that boys' and girls' toys provide different sorts of early conditioning with a visit to a toy store or the toy section of a department store. Do current toys and the ways that they are marketed and advertised still support Cole's assertions? Take notes on color, the types of toys, the activities being featured, and so on. Has heightened awareness of gender issues had an effect? What changes, if any, are evident? Bring your notes, along with recent toy catalogues, or the toy sections of general catalogues, to class.

The following example indicates that, while changes have undoubtedly occurred since K. C. Cole published her article in 1981 about women in science, those changes may not be as great as is frequently believed.

> **Only 4% More Graduate Women Study Science and Engineering Than in 1981**
>
> In 1992, 35% of grad students enrolled in science and engineering fields were women, an increase of only 4% since 1981, reports the National Science Foundation. In all science fields, including traditional women's fields such as allied health, women comprised 43% of all grad students.
>
> In engineering, women represented only 15% of the total graduate enrollment, although they earned 14% of all engineering master's degrees, up from 8% in 1981.
>
> The NSF report also notes that although women have earned more than half of all baccalaureates awarded since 1982, their proportion in science and engineering has not yet reached parity. In 1991, women earned 44% of all science and engineering four-year degrees, including almost three fourths (73%) of those in psychology, half (52%) in the biological sciences, but only 15% in engineering.

> Madame Curie received the Nobel Prize for her work. But despite her dramatic success in the laboratory, she could *not* find a way to tear down the barriers that blocked her admittance to the revered French Academie des Sciences.
>
> Her problem?
> Madame Curie was a woman.

Only after winning a second Nobel Prize—for chemistry, in 1911—was Madame Curie admitted to the all-male Academie. More than seventy years later the French Academie still had only three female members. Madame Curie received another belated honor in the spring of 1995, when her and her husband's ashes (they had shared the 1903 Nobel Prize for physics) were finally transferred to the Pantheon in Paris. A monument to the "great men" of France, the Pantheon has only one other female occupant, Sophie Bertholet, buried alongside her chemist husband.

"What do Madame Curie and the French Academie have to do with *you* . . . as an American woman of the 90s?" asked a 1992 letter from the American Association of University Women (AAUW). Among other responses to that question, the letter included the following information.

> Perhaps you have heard about our Foundation's recently released study, *The AAUW Report: How Schools Shortchange Girls*. In it, we awakened the media and the public with a startling, in-depth report about the subtle yet pervasive gender bias that takes place *today* in our schools. Consider this disgraceful finding:
>
> Though girls and boys enter school roughly equal in measured ability, within 12 years girls have fallen behind their male classmates in such key areas as higher-level mathematics and measures of self-esteem.
>
> Our study also documents that girls receive far less attention from classroom teachers than do boys . . . that sexual harassment of girls by boys in our nation's schools is increasing . . . and that the gender gap in science is not decreasing and may in fact be *increasing.*
>
> In response to our report, schoolgirls throughout the country have come forward with stories of their own—like the high school physics student from Michigan who said, "You get the idea you can't do something because you are a girl, not because you don't have the ability."
>
> Gender bias in the classroom hurts all Americans, women and men alike. Think of it: If there is a little girl among us who could grow up to alleviate world hunger, cure cancer, or be the next Madame Curie, we may not be reaching her. Worse, the system is in fact *discouraging* her.

Despite the evidence found in such studies, one often hears assertions that gender discrimination has greatly diminished—if not disappeared—in the United States. Think about that claim as you read Professor of Botany Jaleh Daie's article from the March/April 1995 issue of *On Wisconsin: The Magazine for UW—Madison Alumni and Friends*. What similarities do you see between Professor Daie's and K. C. Cole's experiences and observations?

Choosing to Give Back
Jaleh Daie

In many ways, doing scientific research is much like raising a child. It takes love, hard work, total dedication—and a bit of luck. Research is full of joys and occasional disappointments. A researcher worries about what the work will mean for humanity, just as a parent worries whether a daughter or son will be a good citizen.

As an established professor with a rewarding academic career (notwithstanding sufficient frustrations to prevent complacency), I know I am blessed. But it concerns me that many talented and committed women have not been as fortunate, and I try to understand why. Is it perhaps because only the diehards survive the uneven playing field? Have I succeeded because my early gender stories had happy endings?

In college, where I majored in agriculture/animal sciences, I was one of six women in a class of four hundred students. I made the best of being treated as a novelty, but to my dismay, I learned that women were expected to take home economics courses instead of math-heavy hydrology. I insisted on taking the same courses as men, but was flatly rejected by the dean. Eventually, I took my case to the president, who—recognizing both my determination and the poor logic behind the policy—decided to end the policy. In retrospect, I had innocently challenged the system—without even knowing it! I proudly take credit for that change.

Today, we have yet to achieve gender equity in science and engineering. Indeed, statistics show that in most scientific and technical fields, women face substantial opportunity gaps. The glass ceiling remains firmly in place. Why so? It is a Catch-22. Seldom are women groomed, mentored, or nominated for key assignments. Consequently, requirements such as past experience preclude them as strong contenders for top positions.

We must change the culture of science that has been shaped by men for men. To do so, we must choose enlightened and brave leaders who understand the issue and are willing to challenge the status quo. As a nation, we must achieve genuine equity at all levels and not just because it is the right thing to do. In the third millennium, it is a matter of national survival in an increasingly competitive global economy that requires a technically skilled and scientifically literate workforce. We cannot afford to squander the significant talent of more than half the population.

How can we bring lasting change to this truly human and societal issue? We must create effective institutional policies and programs that are evaluated on an ongoing basis. We must forge long-term partnerships among government, academia, the private sector, the media, and professional societies. We must provide incentives, require accountability, and continue the discourse to improve understanding of the issue. Individuals also must take up the cause by expressing their concerns to key people, advocating specific actions, joining national/local advocacy groups, becoming a "femtor"/mentor to students or young professionals, and helping to raise funds.

Let me close with the good news. Change—albeit slowly—is occurring. Great strides have been made in the past twenty-five years. The scientific community and society as a whole now realize the urgency of the issue. As for me? Because I am concerned about the larger issues, I have decided it is time to give back, to play with larger pieces of an important puzzle. I welcome the national platform that is helping my quest for a level playing field for all scientists.

Consider also the following article from the November 23, 1995, issue of the *New York Times*.

Panel's Study Cites Job Bias For Minorities And Women
Karen De Witt

WASHINGTON, Nov. 22—A bipartisan Federal commission studying discrimination in the workplace issued its final report on Tuesday, noting that minorities and women still faced barriers to advancement in corporations: the so-called glass ceiling.

The commission's report, "A Solid Investment: Making Full Use of the Nation's Human Capital," comes after a three-year study and offers a counterargument to those who maintain that affirmative action is unnecessary because equal opportunity already exists.

"The 'glass ceiling' is a concept that betrays America's most cherished principles," the report states. "It is the unseen, yet unbreachable barrier that keeps minorities and women from rising to the upper rungs of the corporate ladder, regardless of their qualifications or achievements."

Secretary of Labor Robert B. Reich was chairman of the panel, known as the Glass Ceiling Commission. He warned that if changes were not made, "if we don't take advantage of all the talents around us, we simply won't be able to compete successfully."

But he went on, "It is often easier for white males to simply replicate themselves in deciding who is going to be a partner or a manager of a management team or get a tenure track position."

Minorities and women are still consistently underrepresented at the highest levels of corporate America. For example, 97 percent of the senior managers of Fortune 1000 industrial and Fortune 500 companies are white, and 95 percent to 97 percent are men.

In the Fortune 2000 industrial and service companies, only 5 percent of senior managers are women and almost all of them are white. African-American men with professional degrees earn 21 percent less than their white counterparts holding the same degrees in the same job categories, the commission found.

Only four-tenths of 1 percent of managers are of Hispanic descent, although that group makes up 8 percent of the nation's work force. Americans of Asian and Pacific Island heritage earn less than whites in comparable positions and receive fewer promotions, despite more formal education than other groups.

The commission said the statistics were all the more telling, given that 57 percent of workers were women, members of minorities, or both.

The report offers strategies for both business and government to diversify their work forces.

It calls on chief executives of companies to commit themselves to making their work forces diverse; to include diversity in all strategic business plans; to use affirmative action as a tool to select, promote and retain qualified individuals; to prepare minorities and women for senior positions; to educate the corporate ranks; to adopt high-performance practices in the workplace that encourage all workers to participate in the decision-making process, and to share information about the organization and have policies that support family life.

The report recommends that the Federal Government lead by example by promoting women and minorities to senior management and decision-making positions.

It recommends strengthening antidiscrimination laws, improving data collection on minorities and women and publicizing the diversity data so that the public is aware of the true position of women and minorities in the workplace.

"We're making recommendations that are not pie in the sky," said Rene A. Redwood, executive director of the commission. "They can be a manual for change for corporations to effectively diversify."

Some corporations, like Xerox, have been pioneers in the field, despite downsizing and cutbacks, said Paul Allaire, chairman and chief executive officer.

"For us, it really seems to make good business sense, not only because it's the right thing to do," he said. "We make it a business objective, we give people that as an objective and we measure progress because if you don't keep score, you're only practicing."

Gender stereotyping casts both women and men into restricted roles and has considerable impact on the personality and development of people of both sexes. In the next article Noel Perrin, professor of English at Dartmouth College and the author of several works about life in rural New England, recalls how he wrestled with his inability to live up to the traditional view of what a man ought to be. Urging freedom from such confining gender roles, Perrin depicts the relief he has experienced upon realizing that he did not have to fit that image. This article originally appeared in the "About Men" column of the *New York Times Magazine* on February 4, 1984.

The Androgynous Man
Noel Perrin

The summer I was 16, I took a train from New York to Steamboat Springs, Colo., where I was going to be assistant horse wrangler at a camp. The trip took three days, and since I was much too shy to talk to strangers, I had quite a lot of time for reading. I read all of *Gone With the Wind*. I read all of the interesting articles in a couple of magazines I had, and then I went back and read all the dull stuff. I also took all the quizzes, a thing of which magazines were even fuller then than now.

The one that held my undivided attention was called "How Masculine/Feminine Are You?" It consisted of a large number of inkblots. The reader was supposed to decide which of four objects each blot most resembled. The choices might be a cloud, a steam-engine, a caterpillar and a sofa.

When I finished the test, I was shocked to find that I was barely masculine at all. On a scale of 1 to 10, I was about 1.2. Me, the horse wrangler? (And not just wrangler, either. That summer, I had to skin a couple of horses that died—the camp owner wanted the hides.)

The results of that test were so terrifying to me that for the first time in my life I did a piece of original analysis. Having unlimited time on the train, I looked at the "masculine" answers over and over, trying to find what it was that distinguished real men from people like me—and eventually I discovered two very simple patterns. It was "masculine" to think the blots looked like man-made objects, and "feminine" to think they looked like natural objects. It was masculine to think they looked like things capable of causing harm, and feminine to think of innocent things.

Even at 16, I had the sense to see that the compilers of the test were using rather limited criteria—maleness and femaleness are both more complicated than that—and I breathed a huge sigh of relief. I wasn't necessarily a wimp, after all.

That the test did reveal something other than the superficiality of its makers I realized only many years later. What it revealed was that there is a large class of men and women both, to which I belong, who are essentially androgynous. That doesn't mean we're gay, or low in the appropriate hormones, or uncomfortable performing the jobs traditionally assigned our sexes. (A few years after that summer, I was leading troops in combat and, unfashionable as it now is to admit this, having a very good time. War is exciting. What a pity the 20th century went and spoiled it with high-tech weapons.)

What it does mean to be spiritually androgynous is a kind of freedom. Men who are all-male, or he-man, or 100% red-blooded Americans, have a little biological set that causes them to be attracted to physical power, and probably also to dominance. Maybe even to watching football. I don't say this to criticize them. Completely masculine men are quite often wonderful people: good husbands, good (though sometimes overwhelming) fathers, good members of society. Furthermore, they are often so unself-consciously at ease in the world that other men seek to imitate them. They just aren't as free as androgynes. They pretty nearly have to be what they are; we have a range of choices open.

The sad part is that many of us never discover that. Men who are not 100% red-blooded Americans—say those who are only 75% red-blooded—often fail to notice their freedom. They are too busy trying to copy the he-men ever to realize that men, like women, come in a wide variety of acceptable types. Why this frantic imitation? My answer is mere speculation, but not casual. I have speculated on this for a long time.

Partly they're just envious of the he-man's unconscious ease. Mostly they're terrified of finding that there may be something wrong with them deep down, some weakness at the heart. To avoid discovering that, they spend their lives acting out the role that the he-man naturally lives. Sad.

One thing that men owe to the women's movement is that this kind of failure is less common than it used to be. In releasing themselves from the single ideal of the dependent woman, women have more or less incidentally released a lot of men from the single ideal of the dominant male. The one mistake the feminists have made, I think, is in supposing that all men need this release, or that the world would be a better place if all men achieved it. It wouldn't. It would just be duller.

So far I have been pretty vague about just what the freedom of the androgynous man is. Obviously it varies with the case. In the case I know best, my own, I can be quite specific. It has freed me most as a parent. I am, among other things, a fairly good natural mother. I like the nurturing role. It makes me feel good to see a child eat—and it turns me to mush to see a 4-year-old holding a glass with both small hands, in order to drink. I even enjoyed sewing patches on the knees of my daughter Amy's Dr. Dentons when she was at the crawling stage. All that pleasure I would have lost if I had made myself stick to the notion of the paternal role that I started with.

Or take a smaller and rather ridiculous example. I feel free to kiss cats. Until recently it never occurred to me that I would want to, though my daughters have been doing it all their lives. But my elder daughter is now 22, and in London. Of course, I get to look after her cat while she is gone. He's a big, handsome farm cat named Petrushka, very unsentimental, though used from kittenhood to being kissed on the top of the head by Elizabeth. I've gotten very fond of him (he's the adventurous kind of cat who likes to climb hills with you), and one night I simply felt like kissing him on the top of the head, and did. Why did no one tell me sooner how silky cat fur is?

Then there's my relation to cars. I am completely unembarrassed by my inability to diagnose even minor problems in whatever object I happen to be driving, and don't have to make some insider's remark to mechanics to try to establish that I, too, am a "Man With His Machine."

The same ease extends to household maintenance. I do it, of course. Service people are expensive. But for the last decade my house has functioned better than it used to because I have had the aid of a volume called

"Home Repairs Any Woman Can Do," which is pitched just right for people at my technical level. As a youth, I'd as soon have touched such a book as I would have become a transvestite. Even though common sense says there is really nothing sexual whatsoever about fixing sinks.

Or take public emotion. All my life I have easily been moved by certain kinds of voices. The actress Siobhan McKenna's, to take a notable case. Give her an emotional scene in a play, and within ten words my eyes are full of tears. In boyhood, my great dread was that someone might notice. I struggled manfully, you might say, to suppress this weakness. Now, of course, I don't see it as a weakness at all, but as a kind of fulfillment. I even suspect that the true he-men feel the same way, or one kind of them does, at least, and it's only the poor imitators who have to struggle to repress themselves.

Let me come back to the inkblots, with their assumption that masculine equates with machinery and science, and feminine with art and nature. I have no idea whether the right pronoun for God is He, She, or It. But this I'm pretty sure of. If God could somehow be induced to take that test, God would not come out macho and not feminismo, either, but right in the middle. Fellow androgynes, it's a nice thought.

Exercise

1. Like many writers, Noel Perrin opens his essay with an **anecdote,** or short narrative, which leads into his **thesis.** Briefly summarize or make a scratch outline of that anecdote.
2. Observe that Perrin's conclusion "frames the essay," that is, the conclusion refers to his introductory anecdote.
3. What does Perrin mean by *androgyny?* Write his definition in your words.
4. Briefly restate Perrin's thesis in your own words.
5. Once Perrin decided that he need not be constrained by traditional gender stereotyping, what "nonmasculine" activities became permissible to him?
6. What do you think Perrin's *purpose* was in writing this essay?
7. What *audience* might he have had in mind?
8. What are the *sources* of Perrin's arguments?

Exercise

Think about "gender categorization" and your own observations and experiences. Have they been similar to, or different from, those described in Jaleh Daie's and K. C. Cole's articles on women in science? Did science and math teachers encourage girls and boys equally in the schools you attended?

Recall that Becky Manuell related Cole's discussion to her own experience playing the drums. Have you had similar, or different, experiences in connection with things you tried to accomplish? Were you ever warned not to "be a sissy," "be a tomboy," "act like a girl," or "act like a boy?" Did reading "The Androgynous Man" cause you to look at such familiar tags in another way? Have you ever been treated unfairly because of your gender at a job or on a playground, as a member of a team, at school, or in your family life? Did you ever *not* apply for a job you wanted because of your gender?

Exercise

Have you experienced any type of prejudiced treatment because of your gender or for any other reason? Do some freewriting about prejudice and stereotyping. Consider writing an essay on that subject, including specific examples from your own, or friends', experiences. No one likes to be treated unfairly, so you ought to be able to put lots of *voice* into this essay. Why not broaden and strengthen your essay by incorporating outside sources? Because the above readings on gender stereotyping provided some of the stimulus for your topic choice, those essays may contain material appropriate for your essay. Those readings may also have stimulated you to do additional research about gender stereotyping or a related topic.

In the following essay, Robert Darnton reflects on the special language and environment of an American graduate school.

Looking for Meanings
Robert Darnton

A funny thing happened to me on my way home from the semiotics seminar. As I rounded a corner on C floor of the library, I noticed an advertisement from *The New York Times* pasted on the door of a student's carrel: "Fiji $499." Primed by a discussion of Charles S. Peirce and the theory of signs, I immediately recognized it as—well, a sign. Its message was clear enough: you could fly to Fiji and back for $499. But its meaning was different. It was a joke, aimed at the university public by a student grinding away at a thesis in the middle of winter, and it seemed to say: "I want to get out of this place. Give me some air! Sun! *Mehr Licht!*" You could add many glosses. But to get the joke, you would have to know that carrels are cells where students work on theses, that theses require long spells of hard labor, and that winter in Princeton closes around the students like a damp shroud. In a word, you would have to know your way around the campus culture, no great feat if you live in the midst of it, but something that distinguishes the inmates of carrels from the civilian population gamboling about in sunshine and fresh air. To us, "Fiji $499" is funny. To you, it may seem sophomoric. To me, it raised a classic academic question: How do symbols work?

. . . When I ran into "Fiji $499," I found to my surprise that the Peircean categories fit. The "sign" consisted of the letters printed as an advertisement. The "object" or ostensible message concerned the fare to Fiji. And the "interpretant" or meaning was the joke: "I want to get out of here." In fact, the meanings multiplied at my end of the communication circuit. "This Peirce stuff really works," I concluded and then added afterthoughts: "We make our students spend too much time in carrels." "Students are getting wittier." Were my interpretations valid? Yes, as far as I was concerned, but did they correspond to what the student had intended? Unable to resist the chance to question a native informant, I knocked at the door of carrel C l H9 on the following day. It was opened by Amy Singer, a graduate student in Near Eastern Studies. "I put it up two weeks before generals," she reported. "It was the bleakest moment of the winter, and *The New York Times* offered this piece of solace, a warm place, far away." But Amy seemed to be a sunny, upbeat type. (I'm happy to report that she did very well in her general examinations.) She said that she thought of the sign more as an escape fantasy and a joke than as a lament. "It's like a bumper sticker," she explained. I had not thought of the door as a bumper. My ideas did not coincide perfectly with hers, but they were close enough for me to get the joke and to feel reinforced in my admiration for Peirce.

Exercise

Write down the meanings of the following words, as explained in the text of Darnton's narrative.

carrel

thesis (plural theses)

generals

If you are unsure of the meaning of the following words from the **context**—that is, the way they are used in the anecdote—look them up in a dictionary.

semiotics

gloss

Exercise

In your journal write a short summary of Professor Darnton's anecdote, an anecdote that he used to demonstrate how someone could apply Charles S. Peirce's theory of signs.

Robert Darnton's anecdote exemplifies a current scholarly interest in popular culture and the influential role of signs—symbols such as religious objects, team emblems, or company logos—in human existence. Glance through a newspaper or magazine, flip on the television, or drive down a highway or city street, and you are immediately bombarded by such signs. As in the case of the "Fiji $499" sign on the door of the graduate student's carrel, the meaning viewers infer from signs is frequently based on previous knowledge.

Signs, such as company logos, brand names, and familiar packaging that give products national and even international recognition, are important marketing tools. Read the following article about a corporate decision to change "national icons" such as the red-and-white Campbell Soup can, which was "made immortal" by American artist Andy Warhol in his famous 1962 series of paintings. What does the article suggest?

Campbell Soup Noodles Around
Glenn Collins
New York Times

New York—Campbell Soup knows well that you change national icons at your peril. But these days, the once-lumbering soup giant is feeling frisky enough to tinker with its own legendary image—even daring to vary the look of the soup can made immortal by Andy Warhol.

And that is only the most visible of the transformations. Campbell is changing the recipe of its top-selling chicken noodle soup, increasing its advertising expenditures by 50%, upgrading its inventory system and offering a stream of new products.

> "Many people tell us, 'Don't touch the icon,' but we're taking a calculated risk that we can contemporize our products," said Marty Thrasher, president of the Campbell Soup Co.'s U.S. soup business.
>
> Why take the risk?
>
> "Because we needed to get noticed in a new way, and we needed to break through," Thrasher said.
>
> The new products include not only reduced-fat versions of its mushroom, celery and chicken cream soups but also a reformulation of Campbell's biggest seller: its classic condensed chicken noodle soup has a new label that says "Now! 33% more chicken meat!"
>
> But the boldest decision by Campbell has been to re-engineer its classic "red and white" soup line. In September the company tweaked its time-honored slogan (from "M'm-m'm good" to "M'm-m'm better"). And for more than a year it has been morphing its line of condensed soups, updating the traditional packaging with high-gloss color pictures of what's inside.
>
> Given such disastrous chapters in the history of brand management as New Coke and Elsie the Cow, any revamping of the Campbell persona "is clearly a risk, and a development worth watching," said food analyst Les Pugh.

Exercise

In small groups, consider the following questions.

1. List the steps that the Campbell Soup Company has already taken to alter its image and products.
2. Who is Marty Thrasher, and what reason does he give for Campbell's decision to change the familiar soup can label?
3. Based on your knowledge of recent trends in Americans' eating habits and the concerns behind those trends, can you suggest broader reasons for the company's recent decisions?
4. Do you or any of your group members know about the New Coke and Elsie the Cow brand management disasters alluded to in the final paragraph of the article? What happened?

Exercise

1. Bring labels from current Campbell Soup Company cans to class for a general discussion. Try to find examples of both the new versions and the traditional label that was "made immortal by Andy Warhol."
2. Ask someone in the class to volunteer to find reprints of artist Andy Warhol's famous soup can series to bring to class as well.

Weighing the Claims of an Argument

Ask yourself the following questions when analyzing someone's arguments.

- Are the claims backed by good evidence?
- Do the claims seem reasonable when tested against your own reading, experiences, and observations?
- Does the writer's bias detract from the argument?
- Does the argument stick to the issues at hand?

The last two essays in this chapter take a detailed look at the workplace of two very different corporations in the food industry: McDonald's and Ben and Jerry's Homemade, Inc. Both essays are examples of persuasive writing in that the authors attempt to sway their readers to a particular view of the corporation they are describing.

The author of the first essay, Barbara Garson, has also written several articles and plays, including "The Dinosaur Door," a children's play that won an Obie Award. Her essay about McDonald's was excerpted from *The Electronic Sweatshop: How Computers Are Transforming the Office of the Future into the Factory of the Past,* the author's second book about the changing nature of the American workplace in an increasingly competitive and technological society. Largely by letting McDonald's employees speak for themselves, Garson's account gives the reader a real sense of the hectic, computer-driven workplace pioneered by McDonald's founder, Ray Kroc. Occasional quotations from Kroc's autobiography, *Grinding It Out,* and another study of his vast fast-food chain provide useful supplementary data that enriches the employees' narratives of their experiences with the fast-food empire.

> Weigh the claims of an argument.

McDonald's—We Do It All for You
Barbara Garson

Jason Pratt:

"They called us the Green Machine," says Jason Pratt, recently retired McDonald's griddleman, "'cause the crew had green uniforms then. And that's what it is, a machine. You don't have to know how to cook, you don't have to know how to think. There's a procedure for everything and you just follow the procedures."

"Like?" I asked. I was interviewing Jason in the Pizza Hut across from his old McDonald's.

"Like, uh," the wiry teenager searched for a way to describe the all-encompassing procedures. "O.K., we'll start you off on something simple. You're on the ten-in-one grill, ten patties in a pound. Your basic burger. The guy on the bin calls, 'Six hamburgers.' So you lay your six pieces of meat on the grill and set the timer." Before my eyes Jason conjured up the gleaming, mechanized McDonald's kitchen. "Beep-beep, beep-beep, beep-beep. That's the beeper to sear 'em. It goes off in twenty seconds. Sup, sup, sup, sup, sup, sup." He presses each of the six patties down on the sizzling grill with an imaginary silver disk. "Now you turn off the sear beeper, put the buns in the oven, set the oven timer and then the next beeper is to turn the meat. This one goes beep-beep-beep, beep-beep-beep. So you turn your patties and then you drop your re-cons on the meat, t-con, t-con, t-con." Here Jason takes two imaginary handfuls of reconstituted onions out of water and sets them out, two blops at a time, on top of the six patties he's arranged in two neat rows on our grill. "Now the bun oven buzzes [there are over a half dozen different timers with distinct beeps and buzzes in a McDonald's kitchen]. This one turns itself off when you open the oven door so you just take out your crowns, line 'em up and give 'em each a squirt of mustard and a squirt of ketchup." With mustard in his right hand and ketchup in his left, Jason wields the dispensers like a pair of six-shooters up and down the lines of buns. Each dispenser has two triggers. One fires the premeasured squirt for ten-in-ones—the second is set for quarter-pounders.

"Now," says Jason, slowing down, "now you get to put on the pickles. Two if they're regular, three if they're small. That's the creative part. Then the lettuce, then you ask for a cheese count ('cheese on four please'). Finally the last beep goes off and you lay your burger on the crowns."

"On the *crown* of the buns?" I ask, unable to visualize. "On top?" "Yeah, you dress 'em upside down. Put 'em in the box upside down too. They flip 'em over when they serve 'em."

"Oh, I think I see."

"Then scoop up the heels [the bun bottoms] which are on top of the bun warmer, rake the heels with one hand and push the tray out from underneath and they land (plip) one on each burger, right on top of the re-cons, neat and perfect. [The official time allotted by Hamburger Central, the McDonald's headquarters in Oak Brook, Ill., is ninety seconds to prepare and serve a burger.] It's like I told you. The procedures makes the burgers. You don't have to know a thing."

McDonald's employs 500,000 teenagers at any one time. Most don't stay long. About 8 million Americans—7 percent of our labor force—have worked at McDonald's and moved on.[1] Jason is not a typical ex-employee. In fact, Jason is a legend among the teenagers at the three McDonald's outlets in his suburban area. It seems he was so fast at the griddle (or maybe just fast talking) that he'd been taken back three times by two different managers after quitting.

But Jason became a real legend in his last stint at McDonald's. He'd been sent out the back door with the garbage, but instead of coming back in he got into a car with two friends and just drove away. That's the part the local teenagers love to tell. "No fight with the manager or anything . . . just drove away and never came back . . . . I don't think they'd give him a job again."

"I would never go back to McDonald's," says Jason. "Not even as a manager." Jason is enrolled at the local junior college. "I'd like to run a real restaurant someday, but I'm taking data processing to fall back on." He's had many part-time jobs, the highest-paid at a hospital ($4.00 an hour), but that didn't last, and now dishwashing (at the $3.35 minimum). "Same as McDonald's. But I would never go back there. You're a complete robot."

"It seems like you can improvise a little with the onions," I suggested. "They're not premeasured." Indeed, the reconstituted onion shreds grabbed out of a container by the unscientific-looking wet handful struck me as oddly out of character in the McDonald's kitchen.

"There's supposed to be twelve onion bits per patty," Jason informed me. "They spot check."

"Oh come on."

"You think I'm kiddin'. They lift your heels and they say, 'You got too many onions.' It's portion control."

"Is there any freedom anywhere in the process?" I asked.

"Lettuce. They'll leave you alone as long as it's neat."

"So lettuce is freedom; pickles is judgement?"

"Yeah but you don't have time to play around with your pickles. They're never gonna say just six pickles except on the disk. [Each store has video disks to train the crew for each of about twenty work stations, like fries, register, lobby, quarter-pounder grill.] What you'll hear in real life is 'twelve and six on a turn-lay.' The first number is your hamburgers, the

---

[1] These statistics come from John F. Love, *McDonald's Behind the Golden Arches* (New York: Bantam, 1986). Additional background information in this chapter comes from Ray Kroc and Robert Anderson, *Grinding It Out* (Chicago: Contemporary Books, 1977), and Max Boas and Steve Chain, *Big Mac* (New York: Dutton, 1976).

second is your Big Macs. On a turn-lay means you lay the first twelve, then you put down the second batch after you turn the first. So you got twenty-four burgers on the grill, in shifts. It's what they call a production mode. And remember you also got your fillets, your McNuggets . . . ."

"Wait, slow down." By then I was losing track of the patties on our imaginary grill. "I don't understand this turn-lay thing."

"Don't worry, you don't have to understand. You follow the beepers, you follow the buzzers and you turn your meat as fast as you can. It's like I told you, to work at McDonald's you don't need a face, you don't need a brain. You need to have two hands and two legs and move 'em as fast as you can. That's the whole system. I wouldn't go back there again for anything."

June Sanders:

McDonald's french fries are deservedly the pride of their menu: uniformly golden brown all across America and in thirty-one other countries. However, it's difficult to standardize the number of fries per serving. The McDonald's fry scoop, perhaps their greatest technological innovation, helps to control this variable. The unique flat funnel holds the bag open while it aligns a limited number of fries so that they fall into the package with a paradoxically free, overflowing cornucopia look.

Despite the scoop, there's still a spread. The acceptable fry yield is 400 to 420 servings per 100-lb. bag of potatoes. It's one of the few areas of McDonald's cookery in which such a range is possible. The fry yield is therefore one important measure of a manager's efficiency. "Fluffy, not stuffy," they remind the young workers when the fry yield is running low.

No such variation is possible in the browning of the fries. Early in McDonald's history Louis Martino, the husband of the secretary of McDonald's founder Ray Kroc, designed a computer to be submerged in the fry vats. In his autobiography, *Grinding It Out,* Kroc explained the importance of this innovation. "We had a recipe . . . that called for pulling the potatoes out of the oil when they got a certain color and grease bubbles formed in a certain way. It was amazing that we got them as uniform as we did because each kid working the fry vats would have his own interpretation of the proper color and so forth. [The word "kid" was officially replaced by "person" or "crew person" in McDonald's management vocabulary in 1973 in response to union organizing attempts.] Louis's computer took all the guesswork out of it, modifying the frying to suit the balance of water to solids in a given batch of potatoes. He also engineered the dispenser that allowed us to squirt exactly the right amount of catsup and mustard onto our premeasured hamburger patties...."

The fry vat probe is a complex miniature computer. The fry scoop, on the other hand, is as simple and almost as elegant as the wheel. Both eliminate the need for a human being to make "his own interpretation," as Ray Kroc puts it.

Together, these two innovations mean that a new worker can be trained in fifteen minutes and reach maximum efficiency in a half hour. This makes it economically feasible to use a kid for one day and replace him with another kid the next day.

June Sanders worked at McDonald's for one day.

"I needed money, so I went in and the manager told me my hours would be 4 to 10 P.M." This was fine with June, a well-organized black woman in her early twenties who goes to college full time.

"But when I came in the next day the manager said I could work till 10 for that one day. But from then on my hours would be 4 P.M. to 1 A.M. And I really wouldn't get off at 1 because I'd have to stay to clean up after they closed.... Yes it was the same manager, a Mr. O'Neil.

"I told him I'd have to check first with my family if I could come home that late. But he told me to put on the uniform and fill out the forms. He would start me out on french fries.

"Then he showed me an orientation film on a TV screen all about fries.... No, I still hadn't punched in. This was all in the basement. Then I went upstairs, and *then* I punched in and went to work.... No, I was not paid for the training downstairs. Yes, I'm sure."

I asked June if she had had any difficulty with the fries.

"No, it was just like the film. You put the french fries in the grease and you push a button which doesn't go off till the fries are done. Then you take them out and put them in a bin under a light. Then you scoop them into the bags with this thing, this flat, light metal—I can't really describe it—scoop thing that sits right in the package and makes the fries fall in place."

"Did they watch you for a while?" I asked. "Did you need more instruction?"

"Someone leaned over once and showed me how to make sure the fry scooper was set inside the opening of the bag so the fries would fall in right."

"And then?"

"And then, I stood on my feet from twenty after four till the manager took over my station at 10:35 P.M.

"When I left my legs were aching. I knew it wasn't a job for me. But I probably would have tried to last it out—at least more than a day—if it wasn't for the hours. When I got home I talked it over with my mother and my sister and then I phoned and said I couldn't work there. They weren't angry. They just said to bring back the uniform . . . . The people were nice, even the managers. It's just a rushed system."

"June," I said, "does it make any sense to train you and have you work for one day? Why didn't he tell you the real hours in the first place?"

"They take a chance and see if you're desperate. I have my family to stay with. That's why I didn't go back. But if I really needed the money, like if I had a kid and no family, I'd have to make arrangements to work any hours.

"Anyway, they got a full day's work out of me."

Damita:

Damita, the cashier with the glasses, came up from the crew room (a room in the basement with lockers, a table and a video player for studying the training disks) at 4:45. She looked older and more serious without her striped uniform.

"Sorry, but they got busy and, you know, here you get off when they let you."

The expandable schedule was her first complaint. "You give them your availability when you sign on. Mine I said 9 to 4. But they scheduled me for 7 o'clock two or three days a week. And I needed the money. So I got to get up 5 in the morning to get here from Queens by 7. And I don't get off till whoever's supposed to get here gets here to take my place . . . . It's hard to study with all the pressures."

Damita had come to the city from a small town outside of Detroit. She lives with her sister in Queens and takes extension courses in psychology at New York University. Depending on the schedule posted each Friday, her McDonald's paycheck for a five-day week has varied from $80 to $114.

"How long have you worked at McDonald's?" I asked.

"Well, see I only know six people in this city, so my manager from Michigan . . . yeah, I worked for McDonald's in high school . . . my manager from Michigan called this guy Brian who's the second assistant manager here. So I didn't have to fill out an application. Well, I mean the first thing I needed was a job," she seemed to apologize, "and I knew I could always work at McDonald's. I always say I'm gonna look for something else, but I don't get out till 4 and that could be 5 or whenever."

The flexible scheduling at McDonald's only seems to work one way. One day Damita had arrived a half hour late because the E train was running on the R track.

"The assistant manager told me not to clock in at all, just to go home. So I said O.K. and I left."

"What did you do the rest of the day?" I asked.

"I went home and studied, and I went to sleep."

"But how did it make you feel?"

"It's like a humiliating feeling 'cause I wasn't given any chance to justify myself. But when I spoke to the Puerto Rican manager he said it was nothing personal against me. Just it was raining that day, and they were really slow and someone who got here on time, it wouldn't be right to send them home."

"Weren't you annoyed to spend four hours traveling and then lose a day's pay?" I suggested.

"I was mad at first that they didn't let me explain. But afterwards I understood and I tried to explain to my sister: 'Time waits for no man.'"

"Since you signed on for 9 to 4," I asked Damita, "and you're going to school, why can't you say, 'Look, I have to study at night, I need regular hours'?"

"Don't work that way. They make up your schedule every week and if you can't work it, you're responsible to replace yourself. If you can't stay they can always get someone else."

"But Damita," I tried to argue with her low estimate of her own worth, "anyone can see right away that your line moves fast, yet you're helpful to people. I mean, you're a valuable employee. And this manager seems to like you."

"Valuable! $3.35 an hour. And I can be replaced by any [pointing across the room] kid off the street." I hadn't noticed. At a small table under the staircase a manager in a light beige shirt was taking an application from a lanky black teenager.

"But you know the register. You know the routine."

"How long do you think it takes to learn the six steps? Step 1. Greet the customer, 'Good morning, can I help you?' Step 2. Take his order. Step 3. Repeat the order. They can have someone off the street working my register in five minutes." . . .

"In my other McDonald's . . . I was almost fired for my attitude. Which was helping customers who had arthritis to open the little packets. And another bad attitude of mine is that you're supposed to suggest to the customer, 'Would you like a drink with that?' or 'Do you want a pie?'—whatever they're pushing. I don't like to do it. And they can look on my tape after my shift and see I didn't push the suggested sell item."

McDonald's computerized cash registers allow managers to determine immediately not only the dollar volume for the store but the amount of each item that was sold at each register for any given period. Two experienced managers, interviewed separately, both insisted that the new electronic cash registers were in fact slower than the old mechanical registers. Clerks who knew the combination—hamburger, fries, Coke: $2.45—could ring up the total immediately, take the cash and give change in one operation. On the new register you have to enter each item and may be slowed down by computer response time. The value of the new registers, or at least their main selling point (McDonald's franchisers can choose from several approved registers), is the increasingly sophisticated tracking systems, which monitor all the activity and report with many different statistical breakdowns.

"Look, there," said Damita as the teenage job applicant left and the manager went behind the counter with the application. "If I was to say I can't come in at 7, they'd cut my hours down to one shift a week, and if I never came back they wouldn't call to find out where I was ." . . .

Jon DeAngelo:

Jon DeAngelo, twenty-two, has been a McDonald's manager for three years. He started in the restaurant business at sixteen as a busboy and planned even then to run a restaurant of his own someday . . . .

Jon was hired at $14,000 a year. At the time I spoke with him his annual pay was $21,000—a very good salary at McDonald's. At first he'd been an assistant manager in one of the highest-volume stores in his region. Then he was deliberately transferred to a store with productivity problems.

"I got there and found it was really a great crew. They hated being hassled, but they loved to work. I started them having fun by putting the men on the women's jobs and vice versa. [At most McDonald's the women tend to work on the registers, the men on the grill. But everyone starts at the same pay.] Oh, sure, they hated it at first, the guys that is. But they liked learning all the stations. I also ran a lot of register races."

Since the computer tape in each register indicates sales per hour, per half hour or for any interval requested, the manager can rev the crew up for a real "on your mark, get set, go!" race with a printout ready as they cross the finish line, showing the dollars taken in at each register during the race.

The computer will also print out a breakdown of sales for any particular menu item. The central office can check, therefore, how many Egg McMuffins were sold on Friday from 9 to 9:30 two weeks or two years ago, either in the entire store or at any particular register....

"This crew loved to race as individuals," says Jon of his troubled store, "but even more as a team. They'd love to get on a production mode, like a chicken-pull-drop or a burger-turn-lay and kill themselves for a big rush.

"One Saturday after a rock concert we did a $1,900 hour with ten people on crew. We killed ourselves but when the rush was over everyone said it was the most fun they ever had in a McDonald's."

I asked Jon how managers made up their weekly schedule. How would he decide who and how many to assign?

"It comes out of the computer," Jon explained. "It's a bar graph with the business you're going to do that week already printed in."

"The business you're *going* to do, already printed in?"

"It's based on the last week's sales, like maybe you did a $300 hour on Thursday at 3 P.M. Then it automatically adds a certain percent, say 15 percent, which is the projected annual increase for your particular store.... No, the person scheduling doesn't have to do any of this calculation. I just happen to know how it's arrived at. Really, it's simple, it's just a graph with the numbers already in it. $400 hour, $500 hour. According to Hamburger Central you schedule two crew members per $100 hour. So if you're projected for a $600 hour on Friday between 1 and 2, you know you need twelve crew for that lunch hour and the schedule sheet leaves space for their names."

"You mean you just fill in the blanks on the chart?"

"It's pretty automatic except in the case of a special event like the concert. Then you have to guess the dollar volume. Scheduling under could be a problem, but over would be a disaster to your crew labor productivity."

"Crew labor productivity?"

"Everything at McDonald's is based on the numbers. But crew labor productivity is pretty much *the* number a manager is judged by."

"Crew labor productivity? You have to be an economist."

"It's really simple to calculate. You take the total crew labor dollars paid out, divide that into the total food dollars taken in. That gives you your crew labor productivity. The more food you sell and the less people you use to do it, the better your percentage. It's pretty simple.". . .

"But Jon," I asked, "if the number of crew you need is set in advance and printed by the computer, why do so many managers keep changing hours and putting pressure on kids to work more?"

"They advertise McDonald's as a flexible work schedule for high school and college kids," he said, "but the truth is it's a high-pressure job, and we have so much trouble keeping help, especially in fast stores like my first one (it grossed $1.8 million last year), that 50 percent never make it past two weeks. And a lot walk out within two days."

"Aren't you worried that the most qualified people will quit?"

"The only qualification to be able to do the job is to be able physically to do the job. I believe it says that in almost those words in my regional manual. And being there is the main part of being physically able to do the job."

"But what about your great crew at the second store? Don't you want to keep a team together?"

"Let me qualify that qualification. It takes a special kind of person to be able to move before he can think. We find people like that and use them till they quit."

"But as a manager don't you look bad if too many people are quitting?"

"As a manager I am judged by the statistical reports which come off the computer. Which basically means my crew labor productivity. What else can I really distinguish myself by? I could have a good fry yield, a low M&R [Maintenance and Repair budget]. But these are minor.". . .

"When I first came to McDonald's, I said, 'How mechanical! These kids don't even know how to cook.' But the pace is so fast that if they didn't have all the systems, you couldn't handle it. It takes ninety seconds to cook a hamburger. In those seconds you have to toast the bun, dress it, sear it, turn it, take it off the grill and serve it. Meanwhile you've got maybe twenty-four burgers, plus your chicken, your fish. You haven't got time to pick up a rack of fillet and see if it's done. You have to press the timer, drop the fish and know, without looking, that when it buzzes it's done.

"It's the same thing with management. You have to record the money each night before you close and get it to the bank the next day by 11 A.M. So you have to trust the computer to do a lot of the job. These computers also calculate the payrolls, because they're hooked into the time clocks. My payroll is paid out of a bank in Chicago. The computers also tell you how many people you're going to need each hour. It's so fast that the manager hasn't got time to think about it. He has to follow the procedures like the crew. And if he follows the procedures everything is going to come out more or less as it's supposed to. So basically the computer manages the store."

Listening to Jon made me remember what Ray Kroc had written about his own job (head of the corporation) and computers:

> We have a computer in Oak Brook that is designed to make real estate surveys. But those printouts are of no use to me. After we find a promising location, I drive around it in a car, go into the corner saloon and the neighborhood supermarket. I mingle with the people and observe their comings and goings. That tells me what I need to know about how a McDonald's store would do there.

By combining twentieth-century computer technology with nineteenth-century time-and-motion studies, the McDonald's corporation has broken the jobs of griddleman, waitress, cashier and even manager down into small, simple steps. Historically these have been service jobs involving a lot of flexibility and personal flair. But the corporation has systematically extracted the decision-making elements from filling french fry boxes or scheduling staff. They've siphoned the know-how from the employees into the programs. They relentlessly weed out all variables that might make it necessary to make a decision at the store level, whether on pickles or on cleaning procedures.

It's interesting and understandable that Ray Kroc refused to work that way. The real estate computer may be as reliable as the fry vat probe. But as head of the company Kroc didn't have to surrender to it. He'd let the computer juggle all the demographic variables, but in the end Ray Kroc would decide, intuitively, where to put the next store.

Jon DeAngelo would like to work that way, too. So would Jason, June, and Damita. If they had a chance to use some skill or intuition at their own levels, they'd not only feel more alive, they'd also be treated with more consideration. It's job organization, not malice, that allows (almost requires) McDonald's workers to be handled like paper plates. They feel disposable because they are.

I was beginning to wonder why Jon stayed on at McDonald's. He still yearned to open a restaurant. "The one thing I'd take from McDonald's to a French restaurant of my own is the fry vat computer. It really works." He seemed to have both the diligence and the style to run a personalized restaurant. Of course he may not have had the capital . . . .

"Jon," I said, trying to be tactful, "I don't exactly know why you stay at McDonald's."

"As a matter of fact, I have already turned in my resignation."

"You mean you're not a McDonald's manager any more?" I was dismayed.

"I quit once before and they asked me to stay."

"I have had such a hard time getting a full-fledged manager to talk to me and now I don't know whether you count."

"They haven't actually accepted my resignation yet. You know I heard of this guy in another region who said he was going to leave and they didn't believe him. They just wouldn't accept his resignation. And you know what he did? One day, at noon, he just emptied the store, walked out, and locked the door behind him."

For a second Jon seemed to drift away on that beautiful image. It was like the kids telling me about Jason, the crewman who just walked out the back door.

"You know what that means to close a McDonald's at noon, to do a zero hour at lunch?"

"Jon," I said. "This has been fantastic. You are fantastic. I don't think anyone could explain the computers to me the way you do. But I want to talk to someone who's happy and moving up in the McDonald's system. Do you think you could introduce me to a manager who . . ."

"You won't be able to."

"How come?"

"First of all, there's the media hotline. If any press comes around or anyone is writing a book I'm supposed to call the regional office immediately and they will provide someone to talk to you. So you can't speak to a real corporation person except by arrangement with the corporation.

"Second, you can't talk to a happy McDonald's manager because 98 percent are miserable.

"Third of all, there is no such thing as a McDonald's manager. The computer manages the store."

Exercise

Answer these questions in your journal and bring them to class for discussion.

1. If you have worked or are working for McDonald's or another fast-food restaurant, do you find that Barbara Garson's account rings true? Could you depict your experiences as similar to or different from those in Garson's essay?

2. If you have not worked in the fast-food industry, what do you find most surprising in Garson's essay? Will you view McDonald's differently from now on?
3. Does Garson's attitude toward her topic detract from the persuasiveness of her account? What biases does she show?
4. What do you think about her choice of title?

Exercise

Perhaps you have worked in a fast-food establishment or another environment that puts its employees under pressures similar to those described in Garson's account. Your workplace could provide you with a good essay topic.

Do some freewriting and other prewriting on this topic in your journal. Include all of the specific details and examples you can think of that would make that workplace come to life for your readers. Consider interviewing other employees to get their perspective; you might even want to tape-record the interviews. You may also wish to do some library research into publications about the firm.

Freelance writer Maxine Lipner, who specializes in business issues, contributes articles to magazines such as *Executive Female* and *Entrepreneur.* In this article Lipner relates some of the major developments in the history of Ben and Jerry's Homemade, Inc., from its founding in 1977 until 1991, the year she wrote the article. As you read her account, pay particular attention to the sources from which Lipner obtained her information.

Ben and Jerry's: Sweet Ethics Evince Social Awareness
Maxine Lipner

At Ben and Jerry's Homemade, Inc., an ice cream empire, headquartered in Waterbury, Vermont, the taste of success is sweet but not just for the usual reasons. Co-founders Ben Cohen and Jerry Greenfield have made it their business to give something back to their employees, their community, and the world at large.

Among their most recent ventures is the Peace Pop, an ice cream bar on a stick with a marketing twist—1 percent of profits is used to build awareness and raise funds for peace.

Other social endeavors include purchasing nuts harvested from the all too quickly disappearing rain forests for Rainforest Crunch ice cream, and buying brownies made by homeless people for flavors like Chocolate Fudge Brownie and Brownie Bars.

"We believe that business can be profitable and improve the quality of life for people at the same time," says Cohen, a jovial-looking entrepreneur, whose tousled, thinning hair and unruly beard harken back to the era when he and his partner came of age—the now much-heralded 60s.

Greenfield, who gives a slightly trimmer, more mainstream appearance with his close-cropped cut and clean-shaven look, concurs. "Business has an opportunity and a responsibility to be more than just a money-making machine," he notes.

The company's offbeat philosophy also extends to employees. While other businesses may have a yawning salary gap between top executives and office workers, not so at Ben and Jerry's. Here, there's a 7-to-1 salary ratio limiting top salaries to seven times that earned by the lowest-paid staff members—the idea being that employees will have more of a sense of working together as a team if they're not competing for wages.

Such concern for employees and social conscience must be good for business; last year alone, the company sold a whopping six million gallons of ice cream and topped $70 million in sales.

Not bad for an operation that started out as nothing more than a homemade ice cream parlor operating out of a renovated Burlington, Vermont, gas station. It all began quite simply.

Two close friends from Merrick, Long Island, who first partnered up in junior high school where they were the "slowest, chubbiest kids" in the class, Cohen and Greenfield had always toyed with the idea of going into business together. In 1977, after Cohen had tried his hand at everything from being a short-order cook to a Pinkerton guard and Greenfield had reconciled himself to the fact that a career in medicine was not to be, both decided the time was right to start their own venture.

Since the two enjoyed eating so much, starting a food business seemed only fitting. Selecting what to make was easier than one would think. "It seemed like the two things that were starting to become popular in the bigger cities were bagels and ice cream," recalls Cohen. When the would-be entrepreneurs discovered just how much it would cost to start a bagel shop, the choice was clear.

They happened on their Vermont location in much the same backhanded way. "We wanted to locate in a warm, rural college town, but what we discovered was that all the warm, rural college towns already had homemade ice cream parlors," remembers Greenfield. Undaunted, the partners simply changed their plans. "We decided to throw out the criteria of warm and we picked Burlington, Vermont, because they didn't have any ice cream here at all, because it was so cold," he goes on.

The two took $12,000, garnered from their savings as well as a $4,000 bank loan, and bought themselves some secondhand equipment. Then they put an old five-gallon, rock salt, ice cream maker in the window of an abandoned gas station and, with the help of a $5 correspondence course from Penn State University, began churning out their own brand of rich, all-natural ice cream chock full of sweet, crunchy bits of cookies and candies.

In addition to the ice cream, Cohen and Greenfield also initially served food to help make ends meet, particularly during the cold winter months. From the start, each found his own niche. "Ben would cook, I'd make the ice cream, and we'd both scoop," Greenfield recalls.

They were a hit. Sometimes there would be more people in line for the ice cream than there was ice cream available. But, despite the growing popularity of their product, when the time came to tally up, Cohen and Greenfield found they were having trouble turning a profit. "No matter how much ice cream we sold, we always just broke even and never made any money," Greenfield says. He adds with a laugh, "We couldn't figure it out because our sales kept going up, and it seemed like we ought to start making money, but we weren't."

After pondering the situation for awhile, the two realized what the problem was—they were scooping away their profits with every ultra-packed ice cream cone. "We realized that we had to control the size of the scoops of ice cream we were serving," Greenfield explains.

Another more daunting problem was the seasonal nature of their product. To keep the business alive during the slow winter months, Greenfield held down the fort and Cohen took to the road and began selling their ice cream to some of the local restaurants.

Then one day he came up with a brainstorm: why not put the ice cream in packages and stop at some of the local grocery stores along the way as well? Within three months, over 150 stores in the state were carrying their ice cream.

To help raise local awareness of their product, Cohen and Greenfield sponsored a variety of festivals ranging from Fall Down, an autumn celebration marked by Cohen's appearance as the "noted India mystic" Habeeni Ben Coheeni, to an ice cream eating marathon where Vermont schoolchildren had a chance to enjoy the world's largest sundae, made from a whopping nine tons of ice cream.

Word soon got around about the unconventional duo and they found themselves with a loyal local following and mounting sales. Greenfield attributes much of this success to the ripe Vermont market. "I think Vermont is the only state in the country that still doesn't have a Baskin Robbins; it's not really perceived by big companies to be a good ice cream market, so there was a real need here," he observes.

With such success came some unexpected conflicts. By 1982, Greenfield, whose own belief was that business should never be a drag, found that as the company was growing, it was becoming less personal to him.

"We'd started as this homemade ice cream parlor and evolved into a sort of a manufacturing plant," he says woefully. "Where it used to be that we made every batch of ice cream and scooped every cone, now there were people buying our ice cream who had never met Ben or Jerry." Disillusioned by the business, he opted out for a time.

Meanwhile, Cohen found his 60s' value systems at odds with his growing business status. No longer a humble hippie simply cranking out ice cream, suddenly he had turned into that all too familiar symbol of the establishment: a businessman.

After much soul searching, which brought Cohen to the brink of selling the company, a friend pointed out that he could change the business and make it into whatever he wanted it to be. This inspired Cohen to try something new—something he called "caring capitalism."

This meant that instead of pocketing all profits or channeling them back into the business, a portion would go to worthy causes. It also involved finding creative ways to improve the quality of life for employees and the community in which they worked: the state of Vermont.

Accordingly, in 1984, when Cohen needed to raise some money to build a new manufacturing plant, he held a statewide stock offering, the idea being that if the locals were part owners of the business, as it prospered, the community would automatically prosper as well. By the end of the stock offering, 1 out of every 100 Vermont families owned stock in the company.

Informal social gestures and charitable endeavors were all well and good, but Cohen was not satisfied. In 1985, before he held a national stock offering, he set up the Ben and Jerry's Foundation. This organization is dedicated to facilitating social change and charged with finding worthy causes to which 7.5 percent of Ben and Jerry's yearly pretax profits could be donated.

"We wanted to formalize our charitable giving policy and procedures," Cohen explains. "It was at the same time we had our national public offering and we wanted people to understand that when they invested in the business, 7.5 percent of the profits were leaving the company."

Greenfield gravitated back to the company around this time, and found growth was no longer something to be feared—it was a way to ensure that there would be plenty of money for charitable endeavors.

With the company poised for expansion into other markets, Ben and Jerry's began to run into some difficulties with competitors like Steve's Homemade Ice Cream, which, according to Greenfield, launched a look-alike campaign. "When Steve's decided to go national, it put a lot of pressure on us to expand really rapidly because they were essentially copying the flavors we were making and coming up with a package that was flatteringly similar," he says. "We were concerned that if they got into markets before we did, we would be perceived as the imitators, even though it wasn't true."

While rapid expansion helped quell difficulties with Steve's, it led to a distribution dispute with a large, well-known competitor. Claiming that the competitor was keeping Ben and Jerry's out of certain markets, Cohen and Greenfield mounted a national campaign that brought their plight and their ice cream to national attention.

This innovative grass-roots campaign is the stuff that the Ben and Jerry popular lore is made of and which Ben and Jerry's followers can still quote chapter and verse.

Once the campaign drew to a victorious close and Ben and Jerry's ice cream finally did hit the shelves nationally, the company went through a period of unprecedented growth. "We were growing so fast that one year, we essentially doubled the number of people in the company from 150 to 300," says Greenfield.

This concerned the two mavericks who had always prided themselves on running the company like a big family. Trouble was, not only could the "family" no longer squeeze around the table together, but they were also losing touch with their roots. "We were really concerned about communication and not really having people understand the core values of the company—we were afraid that these would get lost," says Greenfield.

To ensure that this didn't occur, Cohen and Greenfield made a conscious decision to slow company growth. "The idea was that if we spent more energy on developing our people, on developing the company from the inside, that we would be much better able to deal with whatever external situations came up," Greenfield explains.

While it was not easy to turn down business, it was essential, Greenfield notes. The company had to be nimble enough to spring into action in the event of an emergency.

It had to be able to contend with crises like the one that occurred in early 1987 when at Cohen's urging, two new machines were installed in the packing plant: one to product pints with tamper-resistant seals and another to automate the process of filling the containers with ice cream.

While both were supposed to be up and running in time to handle the summer crunch, no one had counted on just how difficult the new machine would be to master. Trying to coordinate both turned out to be too much, and with summer fast approaching, management eventually decided to forgo the tamper-resistant packaging and concentrate on getting the other machine going.

Even so, at the last minute it became apparent that they were going to come up short of their quota. Over one weekend, everyone, including Greenfield and Cohen, had to pitch in and make up the difference the old-fashioned way: by hand.

Even in this crisis, the staff members were not forgotten. Greenfield, the company Joymeister, hired a masseuse to come in and give workers massages during their breaks.

Such is to be expected at Ben and Jerry's. While Cohen has been particularly pumped up about social issues, Greenfield, likewise, has been the push behind employee concerns. From the start, he has tried to make the company a place where employees would enjoy working.

Among some of the perks here: three pints of ice cream a day, free health club memberships, and a partially subsidized company child care center. Greenfield even went so far as to institute an official "Joy Gang" to help ensure that work would be as pleasurable as possible.

To watch the employees cheerfully yuk it up during a public tour of the pastel-colored Waterbury facility or to listen to the gleeful way the personnel all seem to answer their calls, the Joy Gang seems to be doing its job. And no wonder. Nothing appears out of bounds at this offbeat company. Take the message left on one executive's answering machine where, instead of the typical "at a meeting" fare, the executive mentions that he may not be available to take the call because, among other things, he may be "off doing transcendental meditation."

Neither Cohen nor Greenfield seems to have any pretense either. They come across as casual, friendly—not at all as if they have the weight of a multimillion-dollar company on their shoulders. They are plain and simply who they are: two guys who surely would rather wear jeans and T-shirts any day than button up their act in suits and ties.

Perhaps it's to be expected that instead of Madison Avenue-style advertising, they've resorted more to grass-roots marketing. "We devote marketing dollars toward things and events that the community would find of value as opposed to buying advertising in TV, radio, or newspapers," stresses Cohen. He adds, "Our marketing strategy is really not much different from what our company does."

This year [1991], marketing at Ben and Jerry's means sponsoring peace, music and art festivals around the country. It also means continuing to draw attention to the many social causes they undertake.

Hot on the agenda are projects like mounting an opposition to the approval of Bovine Growth Hormone, a substance that increases the amount of milk a cow can produce, and that, Cohen and Greenfield worry, will drive a large number of small dairy farms out of the business.

"Small family-owned farms need to be part of our food chain. The goals pursued by family farms go beyond economics—they seek sufficiency, not just efficiency. They are at the heart of a caring, but rapidly disappearing, rural community life," Greenfield wrote in a *Boston Globe* article on the subject.

Despite extensive research on health and safety issues, Cohen and Greenfield are also concerned that the growth hormone might taint the dairy industry's wholesome image. This could, by association, touch Ben and Jerry's as well, since the milk of more than 8,000 cows went into the company's assorted flavors last year.

Another popular undertaking? The Giraffe Project. No, this is not an attempt to spotlight some other very special creatures; the project recognizes people who are willing to stick their own necks out and stand tall for what they believe.

The project is simple. Customers at participating Ben and Jerry's scoop shops receive free information on how to go about nominating local people for a Giraffe Commendation. Also available are posters, flyers, buttons and T-shirts to inspire others to stick their necks out "to make their world a better place."

It's tough to tell where Ben and Jerry's ideals end and their marketing begins. Often, it's their unusual stances that set them apart from their competitors. The customers who buy their super premium product are not kids after their next ice cream treat. They're serious-minded 25- to 45-year-olds who may very likely feel that in some small way they are doing their bit for society when they buy Ben and Jerry's.

If there is a problem in running a company that has actually made it socially responsible to eat ice cream, according to Greenfield, it's in living up to the standards they've set for themselves. "Because we're so vocal about what we believe, we've set up standards that are difficult to maintain," he admits, quickly adding that he wouldn't have it any other way.

Ben and Jerry's is growing up. It has come a long way since the days when Cohen and Greenfield scooped ice cream out of their garage mecca. The company now boasts two manufacturing plants, and is in the midst of building a third. But there have been sacrifices along the way. With a staff of 375 people, gone are the madcap days when anyone could shout out a suggestion at one of the company's frequent meetings.

"We're much more decentralized now," says Greenfield. "We're starting to see ourselves as more branches to a family, with different departments or different sites having monthly meetings, as opposed to everybody trying to get together all the time."

Some things, however, haven't changed. As always, Cohen and Greenfield have new projects in the works. One that both are particularly hopeful about is opening a new scoop shop unlike any other—this one would be located in the Soviet republic of Karelia.

"The whole idea is not to have it be a profit-making venture, but to use the profits from the scoop shop there to help fund cultural exchanges between people in the United States and in the Soviet Union," explains Greenfield.

How will flavors such as Cherry Garcia, Chunky Monkey, Coffee Heath Bar Crunch, and Dastardly Mash go over if this Soviet project takes off? That, of course, is anybody's guess. But if things work out the way Cohen and Greenfield have planned, with Soviets and Americans freely swapping cultural ideas, the end result once again will be sweet success.

Exercise

1. What is Lipner's thesis? Find that thesis in the text. Does her text stick to and develop that thesis?
2. What developments led to Ben and Jerry's adoption of what cofounder Ben Cohen called "caring capitalism"? Write what Cohen means by that term in your journal, then summarize several examples of company practices reflecting its policy of "caring capitalism."
3. What is Maxine Lipner's attitude toward Ben and Jerry's Homemade, Inc.? Does her bias detract from the article's impact?
4. What appear to be the major sources of Lipner's information? Would her arguments be more persuasive if she had consulted outside sources and used Barbara Garrison's technique of interviewing company employees?
5. Suppose that you are doing research on innovative companies and had decided to use Ben and Jerry's as one example. What other sources might you look for to get a more balanced account of the Vermont ice cream empire? Because Lipner's account was written in 1991, might it be advisable to consult more recent sources to learn of any additional developments in company policy?
6. Would you choose to work for Ben and Jerry's? Why or why not? Give specific reasons for your answers.

Exercise

1. Have you worked for a supervisor or a company whose management techniques you found effective for the enterprise, as well as favorable to the employees? Do some freewriting and other prewriting about that person's, or that establishment's, employee management techniques for a possible essay topic. Include as many specific examples as possible so that the reader has a clear picture of the management style you are analyzing.
2. Suppose that you are in a position to manage subordinates and have considerable latitude to develop your own management style. What would your major aims be when dealing with subordinates? What managerial techniques would you use? Freewrite about these techniques in your journal.

Chapter Eight

Documentation: Incorporating Outside Sources into Your Essays

Understanding Documentation

Documentation is giving credit to outside sources—sources beyond the writer's experiences—that are used or quoted in research papers, articles, books, and other documents. Depending on the topic, suitable sources vary widely. They may include written materials, visuals such as paintings or other objects, personal interviews, television and radio programs, and others.

Why should you carefully document your sources? Perhaps the major reason is *to give yourself the proper credit:* Let your readers know that you have used a range of reliable materials and have worked hard to become well informed about your topic. Documentation allows your readers to see what sources you have used and thus verify the competence of your research. Moreover, using data from competent outside authorities is often more believable and persuasive to readers than relying exclusively on your experience and knowledge. The most lively writing frequently combines personal experience with information from outside sources. Thorough, accurate documentation also enables interested readers to locate and consult sources cited in a piece of research.

What ought to be cited? The sources of all direct quotations or of material that is not common knowledge, such as weather statistics or recollections by a participant in a peace conference, should be documented. In general it is better to paraphrase information gained from outside sources, to put it into your own words. However, selective use of direct quotations can greatly enhance your writing.

Using Quotation Marks in Dialogue

Direct Speech

A good grasp of the correct use of quotation marks in dialogue is essential for adding quoted material to your own writing. Look at the following example of a dialogue in Ira Berkow's article, "Stockton: Unrecognized, Unassuming, Unmatched."

> Like a typical tourist, the dark-haired man with the video camera and wife and their three small children in tow was filming the merry scene along crowded Las Ramblas, the heart of Barcelona, Spain, during the Olympic Games in 1992 when a woman caught his attention. She was a vision in red, white and blue, wearing a flowing scarf in the Stars and Stripes and a skirt of the same ilk and a T-shirt with an imprint of the Dream Team.

"Do you mind if I get you on camera?"
"Certainly not," said the woman.
"Are you a fan of the Dream Team?" asked the man.
"Oh yes," gushed the woman, "and I just saw Charles Barkley down the street! And I've seen Magic Johnson, too!"
"So have I," said the man.

The following are some of the rules correctly observed in the dialogue above.

1. Start a new, indented paragraph when changing speakers.
2. Use punctuation to separate quoted material from the rest of a sentence. Usually such punctuation goes *before* the quotation marks. For example,

    Dream Team?"

    or

    certainly not,"

3. When a quotation includes more than one sentence in a row, place quotation marks only at the beginning and end of the entire quote.
4. Punctuate the quotation appropriately: For instance, end a question with a question mark.
5. Interrupted quotations need quotation marks around *each* quoted section. They should be separated from the rest of the sentence with appropriate punctuation, such as a comma or a question mark.
6. If a quotation is a sentence by itself, it needs to begin with a capital letter. For example,

    Yolanda gasped, "You're over eighty!"

7. For quotes *within quotes,* use single quotation marks. For example,

    "And I'll just say, 'Damn, Stock, how ya doing?'"

Indirect Speech

Indirect speech, which is often introduced by phrases such as "The reporter claimed that," need not be placed in quotation marks. Compare these examples.

Indirect Speech: The man asked if he could get her on camera.
Direct Speech: The man asked, "Do you mind if I get you on camera?"

Now punctuate the following sentences.

Direct Speech: Is that you she asked are you John Stockton
Indirect Speech: She asked him if he were John Stockton

Exercise

Copy the following dialogue from Ira Berkow's article on John Stockton, adding appropriate punctuation.

> Are you American, too the woman asked. And just before the man replied, his son Houston, then 4 years old, pointed to a face on her shirt and said, "Daddy!"
> The woman looked down at the shirt, and across at the man behind the camera.
> Is that you she asked. Are you John Stockton
> Well, yes said John Stockton
> The woman flushed, a bit embarrassed.
> I just saw Charles Barkley down the street she repeated. And Magic Johnson, too
> It was not news to John Stockton, point guard supreme, that he would go unrecognized—even by a basketball fan—for he often gets lost in crowds . . . .
> He's so good, you begin to take him for granted said Karl Malone, the All-Star forward and Stockton's teammate on the Utah Jazz for 10 seasons. I've just come to always expect the perfect pass from him, and I get it. And I was thinking not long ago, even I don't appreciate him as much as I should . . . .
> He has to be the most unselfish athlete in any major sport said Jim Chones, a color analyst for the Cleveland Cavaliers, who played 10 years in the American Basketball Association and the N.B.A. He always looks to pass first—to create—and shooting is second. How he does it, and why he does it, is a lost art. This is deep.

Using Ellipses

Note the use of the *ellipses* (. . .) in the article above. Ellipses are three spaced dots, plus a period if the ellipsis dots appear at the end of a sentence, to indicate that words have been omitted from the original text.

Be sure to quote another person's words exactly; *never alter someone else's meaning.* However, you may leave words out of a quotation to shorten it or to fit it smoothly into your wording, as long as those omissions are denoted with ellipses and do not change the meaning. The following example demonstrates the use of ellipses to indicate that words have been left out in the middle of the quoted material.

> *"The Negro has many pent-up resentments . . . . If his repressed emotions are not released in nonviolent ways, they will seek expression through violence," predicted civil rights leader Martin Luther King, Jr., in his famous "Letter from Birmingham Jail" of April 16, 1963. "And now this approach is being termed extremist" (91–92).*

As the first line in the above passage demonstrates, a fourth dot (a period) is placed after ellipses that appear at the end of a sentence: . . . . (ellipses plus period).

You can also use ellipses to indicate an unfinished remark in a dialogue you are writing.

"Could he possibly have . . . ?" Horace began, looking terrified.

Using Others' Works in Your Writing

Incorporating the words and ideas of others into your writing is a complicated business. The student research paper at the end of this chapter provides many examples of the effective use of outside sources. You will also need to consult a writing handbook for the myriad examples that come up in your own essays and research papers.

When the quoted words begin their own new sentence, capitalize the first word.

> *Star point guard John Stockton's wife Nada told reporters:* "But even at home you can see how competitive John is."

However, do *not* capitalize quoted material when it is part of your sentence.

> *According to Ira Berkow, sports writer for the* New York Times, *at 33 John Stockton remains* "a solid, wise and often witty presence on the court" *who can be* "counted on in some surprising ways."

Those words came from this sentence.

> *But now, at age 33, and showing no signs of slowing up, he remains exceedingly valuable to the team on many levels, as a solid, wise and often witty presence on the court as well as in the locker room, and as one who can be counted on in some surprising ways.*

To add authority and help the reader, the source of a quote should be identified.

> *Ira Berkow,* **s***ports writer for the* New York Times . . . .

Identifying Sources

Clearly identify your authorities—the persons, studies, and so on that you are citing—right in the text to enhance their credibility. Compare these two versions of an excerpt from the Health Section of the November 16, 1992, *Milwaukee Journal:*

> *Sports stars get a lot of media attention when they struggle back from an injury, but elderly people who have suffered a hip fracture face the same heroic struggle, says Edmund H. Duthie Jr.*

> *"After a hip fracture, elderly people are struggling to get back on their feet and integrated into the community," says Duthie, "It's a big challenge."*
>
> *Even though great strides have been made in the treatment of hip fractures, which occur almost exclusively among older people, the injury can pose a real threat to a person's well-being, he says . . . .*

This version might make readers wonder who Edmund Duthie is and why they should believe him, since his credentials are not noted. Consider the identifying data in the revised version:

> *Sports stars get a lot of media attention when they struggle back from an injury, but elderly people who have suffered a hip fracture face the same heroic struggle, says Edmund H. Duthie Jr. a physician and gerontologist.*
>
> *"After a hip fracture, elderly people are struggling to get back on their feet and integrated into the community," says Duthie, a professor of medicine at the Medical College of Wisconsin and the chief of geriatrics and gerontology at the Veterans Administration Medical Center in Milwaukee. "It's a big challenge."*
>
> *Even though great strides have been made in the treatment of hip fractures, which occur almost exclusively among older people, the injury can pose a real threat to a person's well-being, he says . . . .*

Identify sources in the text as they are introduced so that the reader clearly understands why you are quoting or paraphrasing them. A source can be identified before or after a quotation, or the quote can be interrupted for that purpose. The following examples show some different ways this can be done.

Interrupted Quote: "I think that we're all mentally ill," claimed Stephen King, America's best-known author of horror fiction, in a 1982 issue of *Playboy;* "those of us outside the asylums only hide it a little better."

Before the Quote: Speculating in a 1982 issue of *Playboy* about the reasons why so many people throng to horror movies, famous horror fiction writer Stephen King made the following assertion: "The mythic horror movie, like the sick joke, has a dirty job to do."

After the Quote: The horror movie is "morbidity unchained." It deliberately appeals to people's "most base instincts" in a harmless setting, and thereby "keeps them from getting out, man," claimed famous horror fiction writer Stephen King in a 1982 article in *Playboy* magazine.

Using Quotation Marks for Bibliographical Citations

When mentioned in your text, the title of a short work, or a section of a longer work, such as a book chapter, a poem, a short story, an episode in a television series, or an encyclopedia, newspaper, or magazine article, should be enclosed in quotation marks. The title of a whole work, such as a newspaper, encyclopedia, or book, should be in italics or underlined. Here are some examples:

> The class analyzed Robert Frost's poem "The Road Not Taken."

> My grandfather has been reading the *New York Times* with his breakfast every morning for the past forty years.

> Lewis Carroll, the pseudonym of Charles Dodgson, was a lecturer in mathematics at Oxford University from 1855 to 1881. He wrote *Alice's Adventures in Wonderland* and its sequel, *Alice Through the Looking Glass* to entertain Alice Liddell, the daughter of the Dean of Christ Church College. "A Mad Tea-Party" is one of the most well-known of Carroll's chapters, the party's Mad Hatter one of his most famous characters.

Using Italics

Italics are a special type of slanted type. The equivalent in handwritten or typewritten work is underlining. If your word processor or typewriter does not make italics, underline words that should be italicized.

Italicize the name of a whole work, like the *Wall Street Journal* or *Huckleberry Finn*. Use quotation marks to indicate part of a work.

> Last evening I fell asleep while reading "Before the War," the seventh chapter of John Irving's 1985 novel, *The Cider House Rules*.

> The third volume of the 1968 edition of *Collier's Encyclopedia* contains articles ranging from "Art Nouveau" to "Beetles."

Foreign words, unless they have become incorporated into English—such as tango or pizza—should also be italicized.

> *coup d'etat*
> *zeitgeist*

Italics can be used for emphasis, but do so *very* infrequently.

Using Brackets

Use brackets to signal readers that you have altered the material you are quoting. Look at the following example.

> "Oppressed people cannot remain oppressed forever. The yearning for freedom eventually manifests itself, and that is what happened to the American Negro," wrote civil rights leader Martin Luther King, Jr., while jailed in Birmingham, Alabama, in April of 1963. "Consciously or unconsciously, he has been caught up by the Zeitgeist [spirit of the times], and . . . is moving with a sense of great urgency toward the promised land of racial justice."

In addition to demonstrating the use of square brackets, the above quote shows how to incorporate someone else's words into your writing. Include a brief introduction about the person being quoted and, if relevant, give the occasion and date of the quoted material.

Quoting and Paraphrasing

When to Paraphrase, When to Quote

It is an excellent idea to back up the claims in your essays with evidence from appropriate outside sources, provided you give proper credit to the authors of those sources. Generally speaking, you will want to *paraphrase,* to use your own words, when using outside sources. You may also occasionally include quoted phrases—within quotation marks, of course. However, it is a good idea to use direct quotes sparingly.

> **Only quote to add flavor to your writing or when the exact words are important.**

Use direct quotes when the language is memorable or vivid, when the exact words are *very* important, as in a statement of President Richard Nixon's during the Watergate scandal, or when you are discussing a literary writer's style.

Sometimes the exact words *are* very important. For instance, you might find contradictory or divergent opinions on a key issue in two participants' accounts of a historic meeting. Perhaps an author may write, or cite, something that could not be said better or that reveals something important about a person or event *because* of the wording. What words could rival a Czech driver's description of the Nazi occupation, as quoted by Soviet journalist Ilya Ehrenburg: "They spat into your soul" (31). Note that in this instance, the writer's name is right in the text, so only the page number must be in parentheses following the quoted material. Here is the full entry:

Ehrenburg, Ilya. *Post-War Years: 1945–54.* Trans. Tatiana Shebunia and Yvonne Kapp. Cleveland and New York: World, 1967.

Incorporate quotes into your own text as smoothly as possible. Perhaps the best way to learn how to do that is to read carefully to discover how skilled professional writers use quotations from outside sources. Then try to emulate them.

Sometimes direct quotations can be broken in the middle, or partial quotations can be incorporated into your own sentences, as in the following example.

Stalin's only surviving child's decision to return to the Soviet Union after seventeen years in the West stunned some acquaintances, left others less surprised. In a March, 1984 interview in the Observer *(London) Svetlana Alliluyeva described expatriate life as, initially "a kind of ecstasy and euphoria," followed by a reality which was "in many ways a disappointment." Life in England, rather than in one of the superpowers was only a "refuge between poor alternatives," Alliluyeva suggested. She cautioned potential defectors that human nature, not governments and regimes ruled the world, adding that it was sometimes "almost a superhuman effort not to drop everything and run and get a ticket" for Moscow: "Sometimes I don't care what the regime is, I just want to see my grandchildren" (quoted in McFadden 4).*

McFadden, Robert D. "Some Say Stalin's Daughter Grew Unhappy in the West." *New York Times,* 3 November 1984: A4.

The above reference is a typical entry for an article from a periodical, in this case a newspaper. Note that the title of an article or a chapter—part of a work—is in quotation marks, while the title of the periodical—the whole work—is italicized or underlined. Enough information should be included (date, page numbers, and so on) so that a reader could locate the article.

> **Generally it is best to paraphrase, to use your own words.**

The following is our paraphrase, with one short quote, of information cited by University of Glasgow political scientist Stephen White in his 1990 study, *Gorbachev in Power*.

> *Concerned that an increasing proportion of sausage contained various fats or additives, in their January 5, 1989 issue the editors of the Russian weekly* Literaturnaya gazeta *(Literary Gazette) described giving sausage samples to thirty cats who knew "nothing of chemistry, bureaucracy or economies of scale," only to discover that twenty-four cats refused any of the varieties offered, while five more refused most of them. (107)*

Paraphrasing

The following example is *not* really worth quoting. The author's exact words are *not* important, nor would they add flavor.

> France granted Algeria full sovereignty in return for the Algerian promise to respect the French settlers' lives and property, as well as French oil interests in the Sahara and military interests in the port of Mers-el-Kebir. Ninety percent of the French approved this settlement in a referendum. (Thompson 135)

Hardly memorable language, the above quotation would be *better paraphrased* to read something like this:

> In return for their independence from France, the Algerians agreed to respect France's military interests in the port of Mers-el-Kebir and its oil interests in the Sahara Desert, as well as the lives and property of French settlers. By referendum vote, ninety percent of the French approved the agreement.

Because the paraphrase still contains a statistic (90%) and other data that is not common knowledge, it should be documented with the appropriate citation.

> Thompson, Wayne C. *Western Europe: 1984*. Washington, D.C.: Stryker-Post, 1984.

Avoiding Plagiarism

Students are usually amazed how easy it is for their teachers to spot **plagiarism.** Author Stephen King's phrase "morbidity unchained" in an earlier example provides a classic case: Few other writers are likely to write those exact words or any of Stephen King's other phrases included within the quotation marks in that example.

We too would be plagiarizing if we did not give credit to Jack Rawlins, author of *The Writer's Way,* for the best definition of plagiarism that we have ever seen.

> *Plagiarism is scholarly stealing: taking someone else's data or words or thoughts and peddling them as your own. In the academic world, our ideas, words and data are our most prized possessions—they're what we make, the way GM makes cars. Stealing them is taking our life's blood. Most universities expel any student caught plagiarizing, and faculty members caught doing it find that their careers are over. (359–60)*

To avoid plagiarism, carefully document all sources; use your own wording, retaining neither the sentence structure nor phraseology of those sources. Paraphrase with care, to avoid distorting a source's meaning by changing or leaving out a word or two.

We agree with Rawlins that much student plagiarism is innocent, as it is often hard to know exactly what needs documentation. Students are sometimes afraid their work will look like they did not do anything themselves if they document too frequently. They may not understand that scholars are *supposed* to read and use each others' works in their own writing—and then thank each other through proper documentation. Do not worry about using numerous documented sources to back up the points you want to make. Acknowledging outside sources gives your own statements additional authority, adds credence to what you say. If you did a lot of research, that is something to be proud of. On the other hand, if you document everything you write, you are probably just stringing quotes and paraphrases together, not using them to back up your own ideas. That also needs to be avoided (Rawlins 359–60).

The preceding paragraphs are a case in point. Reading Jack Rawlins' textbook gave us a new way of looking at and explaining plagiarism and documentation to students, so his important contribution to this discussion should be acknowledged.

"I plagiarized it because I thought it bears repeating."

In the above examples the sources (author, title, and page numbers) are noted right in the text. In-text citations are probably the easiest method of documentation. However, you may be assigned research papers requiring a more elaborate documentation system with partial citations in the text and a "Works Cited" page or a bibliography at the end. For a model, see the student research paper in the last section of this chapter. Find out which form of documentation each of your instructors prefers and follow it.

Using Sources in a Research Paper

Here are a few pointers for using sources.

1. Date statistics exactly and cite their source. Statistics *change—do not use* the present tense for figures from a 1975 source.

2. Paraphrase most sources and use direct quotes sparingly. Quotes that are over three lines long should be introduced properly and indented, or "blocked." In general, however, it is preferable to break up long quotations by putting the information into your own sentences and quoting only key phrases. Use *very few* long (usually undigested) block quotes. They can be boring. (How often do you skip over long block quotes in a piece of writing?)

3. If you find yourself writing *wrote* or *said* too frequently when quoting, use substitutes such as *stated, explained, claimed, proposed,* or *theorized.* Can you think of others?

    For instance, what could be substituted for *wrote* in the following example?

    > "I cannot sit idly by in Atlanta and not be concerned about what happens in Birmingham," wrote Dr. Martin Luther King, Jr. in his famous "Letter from Birmingham Jail." "Injustice anywhere is a threat to justice everywhere" (1).

4. Do not assume background knowledge on the part of your readers.
    a. The first time you mention a person, include their first and last names and identify them briefly. (See the example in part 5 below.)
    b. Explain terms like *Prague Spring* or *Eurocommunism* the first time you mention them.

Get a jump on your deadline.

5. Make it clear whom you are quoting and why. Quotes should not just be plunked down. Rather, they should be integrated into the writer's own sentences, or introduced with a speech tag, such as "To quote Prime Minister Margaret Thatcher," or by a separate sentence followed by a colon:

> *Vladimir Dedijer, a close associate of Marshall Tito and Yugoslavia's Director of Information at the time of the traumatic break with Stalin in June of 1948, recalled the tense atmosphere at a gathering in Tito's home the following New Year's Eve:* "We were all keenly aware" *of the grave situation. Food and manufactured items were being rationed.* "Scarcity prevailed.... The rubble of war had barely been cleared away when the economic blockade started." *Results after over six months of inquiries about expanded trade and economic cooperation with Western countries were* "virtually nil" *(Dedijer 197–99).*

Citations like the one above (Dedijer 197–99) direct the reader to an entry in a "Works Cited" list at the end of a paper. The following is an example of a "Works Cited" entry.

Dedijer, Vladimir. *The Battle Stalin Lost.* New York: Viking, 1971.

The above is a typical entry for a book using the Modern Language Association (MLA) system of documentation (see page 243 for more about this system). Note that the book title is italicized. If your word processor or typewriter does not have italics, underline the title of a book or a periodical, as in <u>Newsweek</u>.

6. The entries in a bibliography or "Works Cited" page are listed in alphabetical order by the author's last name, or by the first major word of the title if no author is listed. Include all information that the reader would need to locate the source. The entries are not numbered. The first line of each entry is not indented; all subsequent lines of that entry are indented five spaces.

See the last pages of the research paper that follows for a model of the "Works Cited" page using the MLA system.

Studying a Model Research Paper

Lisa Marinello wrote the following research paper on Euro Disneyland for a course in contemporary European history. For many reasons this lively paper is a successful example of the brief research paper. First, Lisa's topic is limited enough in scope to be appropriate for a research paper of this nature. Her research in the university library soon revealed that an adequate number of sources were readily available on the topic of Euro Disneyland. Then Lisa made excellent use of these sources, inserting aptly chosen, pithy quotes that support her generalizations, heighten her readers' interest, and even add humor to her topic. The quotations are always clearly and accurately introduced and skillfully woven into her well-organized text. The essay flows smoothly from one section to another and has a clear sense of purpose.

Lisa's enthusiasm for her topic is clear throughout this well-written paper. She wisely selected a topic that interested her, in this case a topic generally familiar to many of her readers. However, Lisa added much to our knowledge of the topic of Euro Disneyland. Appropriately, she opens her paper with a brief discussion of some of the American investments in France that preceded Euro Disneyland and of French efforts to resist what many French people still see as an undesirable American cultural invasion of their society. The paper contains lots of interesting information and also puts Euro Disneyland into the broader historical-cultural context of French-American relations. Her essay likewise stimulates thought about the crucial need—a need often ignored by American management—to consider the local culture when making business investments in other countries. Lisa briefly restates her opinions on this wider topic in her conclusion, thus putting her essay on Euro Disneyland into a broader perspective.

From the technical standpoint, Lisa's paper uses the documentation form currently recommended by the Modern Language Association (MLA), a professional organization of language instructors. The MLA method endorses a parenthetical method of citing sources: Author/page citations between parentheses in the text of the paper are keyed to a "Works Cited" list at the end of the paper. The works in that list, or bibliography, are arranged alphabetically, by the author's last name or by the first major word of the title for works not listing an author.

The MLA system is similar to the American Psychological Association (APA) documentation system, which is recommended by many social and natural science instructors. The APA system also advocates parenthetical citations within the text and a "Works Cited" list at the end of the paper. There are, however, some differences between the MLA and the APA systems. The *MLA system* uses an author-page citation in parentheses with only a space between the author and the page reference.

> Many French intellectuals don't see the mouse their children love; they only smell a rat and refer to the resort as "Euro Disgrace," "Euro Dismal" and a "cultural Chernobyl" (Corliss 82).

In contrast, the APA system documents material with an author-year-page-citation within parentheses. Unlike the MLA system, the APA system has commas between the author, the year, and the page references, as well as a "p." for page.

> Many French intellectuals don't see the mouse their children love; they only smell a rat and refer to the resort as "Euro Disgrace," "Euro Dismal" and a "cultural Chernobyl" (Corliss, 1992, p. 82).

Observe that both the APA and MLA parenthetical citations come before the final sentence period in in-text quotations. When using a blocked, or indented, quotation, however, the parenthetical reference comes after the final period.

It is very important to find out which documentation system or systems each of your instructors expects you to use, and then follow that system in papers for that instructor. Although there is no universally accepted method of documentation, there is agreement on the need for documentation and the kind of items that need to be documented. Lisa Marinello's paper on Euro Disneyland has examples of many of these items: statistics, direct quotations, information that is not commonly known, and so on. Her carefully documented paper also provides a good model for how to use the MLA system.

You will likely have many questions when you document your own sources. Your instructor may hand out a fairly complete set of documentation guidelines, which you should follow carefully for that particular instructor's course. Another option is to purchase the appropriate documentation handbook, such as the latest edition of the *MLA Handbook for Writers of Research Papers,* at your college bookstore. In addition, many writing handbooks have extensive sections on the various methods of documentation.

Marinello 1

Lisa Marinello
Professor Ann Healy
History 375
22 April 1996

France and Euro Disneyland

The French have fought for a long time to preserve their language and culture. Their biggest fight is against English entering their language. In 1975 a Bas-Lauriol law was passed by parliament that required trade names, advertising material, product instruction and receipts to use only

Marinello 2

the French language. The law also gives French replacements for phrases that are based in the English language. In 1983 the High Committee of the French language banned the use of English words in the audio visual field and Anglo-Saxon terms in schoolbooks, speeches, legal contracts and government publications (Thompson 179).

These laws have not stopped American culture from entering France. By the mid-1970's there were already a dozen McDonald's in Paris. Many French people oppose this American cultural invasion but many more embrace it. One of the opponents was French Minister of Culture Jack Lang who refused to attend an American film festival in Deauville for two years. He claimed that the U.S. wants to impose their culture on everyone, creating a "uniform way of life" for the whole world. But the French still go to see as many American films as they do French films (Thompson 179). It seems France is slowly losing its title of the world's cultural leader.

But there also seems to be less anti-Americanism feeling in France these days. Many French people cheered as American cyclist Greg LeMond won the 1986 Tour de France. The most dramatic signal of the fading anti-Americanism is the contract won by France's Socialist government in 1987 to build a $4 billion Disney theme park outside of Paris (Thompson 179).

Even before the Disneyland contract United States investment in France was already strong. American name brand products already could be seen around France. American clothing companies like Esprit and Ralph Lauren had opened Paris boutiques and some French retail stores were carrying American brands like Oshkosh B'Gosh, Timberland and Levi's. Coca-Cola opened "the world's largest" Coke bottling facility in Dunkerque, France to serve the European Community (EC). Haagen Daaz also built a $360 million plant to distribute its American ice cream to the EC. France has also become a hot market for American franchising. Fast food chains like McDonald's and Burger King exist in France, while other chains such as Athlete's Foot, Toys-R-Us and Best Western are opening franchises throughout the entire country (Lever 42).

The growing investment of United States companies in France is due in part to the American firms trying to get into the unified EC market. A big reason for choosing France to expand their foothold into the European Community is its central location. The two main European axis points, Rome-London and Copenhagen-Madrid, cross right through France (Lever 42). This location is also one of the factors that helped France win over other European countries as the perfect spot for a Euro Disneyland. From 1983 to 1987 the Disney company searched Europe for the perfect place for a second foreign location (the first being Tokyo Disneyland which opened in 1983). They looked at sites in the United Kingdom, Germany, Spain, Italy and France before deciding that France would be the perfect spot (Scimone 17).

Euro Disneyland is located at Marne-la-Vallee, a former beet field, 20 miles east of Paris near Versailles. It is on the A4 expressway between Paris and Strasbourg and two new exits have been constructed for the resort. Of the 350 million people in Western Europe, 17 million of them can reach the Euro Disneyland resort in two hours by car. It is located between two international Paris airports, Orly and Roissy-Charles de Gaulle, with shuttles from both airports that go directly to the resort. A regional train at the Arc de Triomphe in Paris will take visitors to a newly built resort station in 23 minutes. Thus it is very easy to get to the resort and will become even easier in the next few years, especially after the channel tunnel opens, linking France with the United Kingdom. The so-called "Chunnel" will allow people leaving London to reach the Euro Disneyland resort in three-and-a-quarter hours. By 1994, France's high speed T.G.V. trains will carry visitors from all over Europe directly to the resort in a matter of hours (Scimone 17).

The over $4 billion Disney resort area is one of the largest United States corporate investments ever made in Europe. It ranks as the second largest construction project in Europe right behind the Chunnel project. It will create jobs, secure billions of francs in revenue and should bring in millions in foreign currency each year ("Euro Disney Theme Park" 21). In February 1992, Disney stock replaced Source Perrier, a mineral water giant, as one of the 40 stocks making up the French equivalent of the Dow Jones industrial average, two months before operation of the resort even began (Toy 32). Euro Disneyland seemed like a positive and profitable project for France, but many French were angry and opposed the resort.

When Disney executives arrived in Paris to announce France as the future home of the Euro Disneyland in 1987, they were pelted with eggs and tomatoes (Corliss 82). In 1989, when Disney chairman Michael Eisner launched the sale of the stock on the Bourse in Paris, he too was pelted with eggs, tomatoes and flour. He also heard cries of "Disney, go home!"

Marinello 4

from Parisians usually unwilling to speak English (Sturz 20). Yet many French children disagree with their parents on the subject of Disney. French children love Mickey Mouse and buy 10 million copies of *Le Journal de Mickey* a year. Many French intellectuals don't see the mouse their children love; they only smell a rat and refer to the resort as "Euro Disgrace," "Euro Dismal" and a "cultural Chernobyl" (Corliss 82).

An example of this adult dislike can be seen in a *Le Monde* cartoon version of the 19th century French painting "L'Angelus du Soir" by Jean Francois Millet. The original pictures a peasant couple praying in the fields to the sound of a bell ringing in a distant church. The cartoonist's version features the peasant couple, but they are wearing Mickey Mouse ears, and the distant church has been turned into the Euro Disneyland's castle: comic strip mythologies in place of the historic religious traditions of the French (Schmertz 44). Other French intellectuals expressed their views on Euro Disneyland in *Le Figaro* after the magazine solicited comments from readers. Here is a statement from Jean Cau, a French novelist:

> I think Arian Mnouchkine, the theater director, put it best when she referred to Euro Disney as "a cultural Chernobyl"—a horror of cardboard, plastic and appalling colors, a construction of solidified chewing gum and idiotic fairy tales lifted straight from comic strips drawn for obese Americans. What better way to describe it—it will irradiate millions of children (not to mention their parents); it will castrate their imaginations and paw at their dreams with fingers the greenish color of dollar bills. The American dream is now within reach of stupefied Europe—this cancerous growth transplanted into millions of young guinea pigs, is non-memory, consumptive make-believe, a cynically fabricated infantility. After twelve Caesars, here comes the thirteenth: Emperor Mickey. No need to worry if you don't understand his edicts; they'll be subtitled in French. (18)

But the Disney corporation remained optimistic despite these negative comments. The company didn't feel the comments would destroy the park and simply shrugged them off. They seemed to be right, because 65,000 pre-sale tickets were sold for the opening of Euro Disneyland and a million Europeans paid $1.75 each to view a model of the park in the Espace Euro Disney Information Center, double the expected number (Toy 32). The people who ask departing park-goers "Well, was it grotesque?" are not Euro Disneyland customers, according to Disney spokespeople (Corliss 82). They state that this is just an amusement park and rightly argue that attendance is not mandatory. "There are always factions of people who are intellectual snobs who will view this as a terrible thing, an invasion of Americanisms into Europe. There are a lot of other people who are more mainstream . . . They are going to love this," one Disney executive explained in response to the negative press the project was receiving (Sturz 20).

Some French citizens are also defending the resort and feel too much is being made out of the resort being an American invasion. A Parisian architect pointed out:

> Too much is being made of the imposition of American culture on France. Paris needs large hotels with full resort facilities just beyond the city limits. Europeans want leisure, golf, tennis, swimming and a place to bring children just like everyone else. (Schmertz 44)

The resort opened April 12, 1992, and from first year sales it can be seen that perhaps Disney executives were being too optimistic about Disney's American approach being appealing to Europeans. Euro Disneyland has five "lands"—Main Street U.S.A., Frontierland, Adventureland, Fantasyland and Discoveryland with a castle of "La Belle au Bois Dormant" (Sleeping Beauty) in the center. There are 29 rides and attractions, and it is pretty much the familiar all-American Disney theme park where visitors eat, breathe, buy and dream Disney.

Euro Disneyland designers recognized that the park is not in America and they tried to pay homage to its European homeland. European legends and fables are incorporated into some rides and shows. These include Le Carrousel de Lancelot, Le Labryinthe and the Adventures of Pinocchio. A new attraction has also opened at Euro Disneyland which takes visitors from one end of Europe to the other and from one end of time to the other: *From Time to Time*. It is a large theatre, called the Le Visionarium, which is equipped with a 360-degree screen. The "Circle Vision 360" puts Jules Verne into the time machine of H.G. Wells. The characters are played by European actors Michel Piccoli (Verne), Jeremy Irons (Wells) and Gerard Depardieu (a baggage handler) (Scimone 32).

But *From Time to Time* is the only attraction that tries to explain Europe to Europeans. Everything else celebrates America and reinvents it—

Marinello 6

Disney Style. This can especially be seen in the Disney-built hotels that surround the theme park. The Hotel Cheyenne has become its own theme park, recreating the Old West complete with gunfights and covered wagons. The Sequoia Lodge takes visitors to the Rocky Mountains for a woodsy, restful stay, while the Hotel Santa Fe takes them to the Southwest. The Newport Bay club, which has become Europe's largest hotel, suggests American east coast beachside elegance. The Hotel New York transports visitors to New York City and even includes a Rockefeller Center complete with ice rink (Corliss 82, 84).

An area that will perhaps push the most Americanism on visitors is Festival Disney, a shopping, restaurant and entertainment center. Some of the restaurant and store themes include a 1950's diner, a wild west rodeo dinner theater and a surf shop (Diets 43). Only one French restaurant is located on the resort grounds—L'Auberge de Cendrillion; the rest are all American (Corliss 84).

However, Disney executives are finding it hard to impose the American-Disney work style on European, especially French, Euro Disneyland workers. Most of the final construction on the resort was done by British and Irish workers because the French refused to work overtime (Sturz 20). Disney got into disputes with French construction workers who wanted an extra $150 million for additional work that Disney did not want to pay for. For example: Disney had 20 different shades of pink applied to one hotel before it was satisfied. The company (Disney) first refused to pay for the repaints, but has now paid about $3 million to about 40 complainants and has opened negotiations with the rest. These payments occurred only after the builders threatened to picket the grand opening and received the support of the French press (Echikson 18).

Construction workers are not the only unhappy Disney employees. Many French feel Disney is being a little "Fasciste" about dress codes. Employees must wear the proper undergarments and deodorant at all times. Black stockings and eyeliner are not allowed and are grounds for a pink dismissal slip (Sturz 20). In the spring of 1992, the company was awaiting a ruling on its ban of beards, mustaches, long hair, long nails and tattoos on employees. The French were trying to determine if these bans are legal (Echikson 18).

Euro Disneyland's manager, Nicholas de Schonen, defended the employee rules and dress code: "When you are a new company like ours, arriving in Europe you have to give details of what is a good look." Disney chairman Michael Eisner also explained that "this is a representation of American culture at its best, we think: clean, safe, creative, theatrical" (Sturz 20).

Even with these employee disputes, Disney claimed that 65% of the staff members were French, with others coming from Britain, Ireland and the Netherlands. When the park opened, the French must have been placed behind the scenes, perhaps because of their disputes, because the front employees were mostly English speakers (Williams "Mart Trips" 89).

The French are also upset that alcohol and cigarettes are not available for sale in the theme park. Alcohol is prohibited to keep the park a place of wholesome, family entertainment. Many French are also staying away because of reports of crowding and traffic problems. Disney executives are becoming worried because the French "are the bedrock of Euro Disney's all important repeat business" (Williams "French dis" 89) and business wasn't very good by midsummer of 1992.

The first release of Euro Disneyland attendance figures was in June of 1992. This semi-annual report showed that after seven weeks only some 1.5 million visitors had attended the parks, a number lower than hoped for. These numbers caused second phase plans for a movie studio park to be shelved and brought no assurance that Euro Disneyland would achieve profitability during the first fiscal year. Euro Disney stock also dropped by the week ending June 5, 1992, from 120 francs ($22.20) to 108.1 francs ($20.00) (Williams "Euro Disney Stock" 30).

A September 1992 report from the investment bank Morgan Stanley did not give any better news. After four-and-a-half months, attendance figures, hotel bookings and spend-per-head figures were all below expectations. Only 1.6 million of the first 6 million visitors to Euro Disneyland were French, which was not a good sign (Ilott and Williams 35, 69). The park did not reach its first year goal of 11 million visitors because it was not attracting the much needed French visitors (Williams "Euro Disney Stock" 34). The park officials said in November, 1992 that they had lost $35.8 million in the first fiscal year which ended on September 30, 1992 ("Euro Disney Discount" 19).

Euro Disneyland made some changes to deal with the first year's loss. The entrance fees were lowered from $42.45 for adults and $28.30 for children under 12, to $28.30 and $19 respectively ("Euro Disney Discount" 19). The biggest change was stopping the plans for phase two: MGM Studios-Europe, a water park, more hotels and residential developments. Chances for a third park, European Epcot Center, are very slim if Euro Disneyland figures don't improve.

A Euro Disneyland response of appointing more European executives, including 44-year-old Frenchman Philippe Bourguignon as president of Euro Disneyland, helped to brighten the future. The company denied that the hiring of more European executives was a reaction to the operating difficulties, but the appointments did help raise Euro Disneyland stock from 75 francs to 81.9 francs per share by September, 1992 (Ilott 35, 69).

The park's slow business caused the company to lower hotel rates and food prices. It has also softened its approach to the travel industry, making it easier for travel agents to prepare tours to Euro Disneyland and earn profits from those tours (Williams "Euro Disney Predicts" 46).

The most debated topic of Disney management is the matter of alcohol on the theme park grounds. Speculation continues on whether the French, expected to make up about half of the visitors each year, will accept the park as an alcohol-free zone. Some feel this policy may keep visitors away. Disney CEO Michael Eisner is adamant on this decision and stated that it will not change (Williams "No Mickey Mouse" 42). It will be interesting to see if it ever does.

So although France and the United States have embraced each other's cultures in many ways, it is easy to see that they still have many small differences that are hard to adjust to and accept. Adjusting to and accepting these differences is going to play a large role in the success of Euro Disneyland and the possibility of its expansion. Each culture, the American and the French, is going to have to be willing to make changes in lifestyles and expectations if this project is going to work. The French might have to learn to live without wine for a few hours and Disney might have to accept the fact that Europeans have a different dress style than Americans. If anyone can make different cultures coexist peacefully in a 5,000-acre area it would have to be the Disney company. After all, they are in the business of making dreams come true.

Marinello 9

Works Cited

Cau, Jean. "Apres Mickey, le deluge." *Harper's Magazine* July 1992: 18.

Corliss, Richard. "Voila! Disney Invades Europe. Will the French Resist?" *Time* 20 April 1992: 82–84.

Diets, Deborah K. "Mickey Goes to Paris." *Architecture* July 1992: 42–43.

Echikson, Bill. "Disney's Rough Ride in France." *Fortune* 23 March 1992: 14–18.

"Euro Disney Discount." *The New York Times* 9 Jan. 1993: 19.

"Euro Disney Theme Park Near Paris Is Europe's Second Biggest Project, Offers Opportunities for U.S. Business." *Business Week* 2 Dec. 1991: 21.

Ilott, Terry and Michael Williams. "Report Casts Pall as Theme Park Gets Gaul." *Variety* 7 Sept. 1992: 35, 69.

Lever, Robert. "U.S. Companies in Love with France." *Europe* January/February 1992: 41–42.

Reina, Peter. "Disney's First European Venture Is a $4.5-billion Fantasyland." *ENR* 13 Jan. 1992: 31–32.

Schmertz, Mildred F. "The French Reaction." *Architecture* July 1992: 44.

Scimone, Diana. "Mickey Mouse Is Coming to Town." *Europe* May 1991: 17–18.

———. "Monsieur Mickey Arrive en France." *Europe* May 1992: 32–33.

Sturz, James. "Euro Dizzy: Disney Opens a Lavish Theme Park Outside Paris in April." *US* March 1992: 20.

Thompson, Wayne C. and Mark H. Mullin. *Western Europe 1992.* Washington D.C.: Stryker-Post Publications, 1992.

Toy, Stewart. "Mouse Fever Is about to Strike Europe." *Business Week* 30 March 1992: 32.

Williams, Michael. "Euro Disney Stock Falls after Release of Figures." *Variety* 8 June 1992: 30, 34.

———. "Mart Trips Mousetrap as French dis Disney." *Variety* 1 June 1992: 1, 89.

———. "No Mickey Mouse Opening for Star-studded Euro Disney Bow." *Variety* 20 April 1992: 30, 42.

Williams, Michael and Terry Ilott. "Euro Disney Predicts Losses for First Year." *Variety* 27 July 1992: 39, 46.

Addendum: A phone call to the Disney Store in Milwaukee, Wisconsin, revealed that one such change had recently occurred. Beginning in July of 1993 beer and wine were being sold at Euro Disneyland. Vive la France!

Part Three
Writing Strategies

Chapter Nine

Narrating

Narrating, or storytelling, one of the earliest and most popular forms of expression, takes many forms: detective mysteries and adventure tales; many novels and poems; a summary of the plot of a story; biographers' renditions of the lives of people from all walks of life; autobiographies, or records of their own lives, by the famous and the not-so-famous; historians' depictions of past events; crime reports on the police blotter; and journalists' accounts of the latest news.

Long before they could write, people exchanged stories of past events. When you get together with old friends, how often does the conversation naturally shift to "Remember that camping trip when . . ."? People write or tell stories because they like doing so and because they hope others will enjoy hearing them: The better the storyteller, the more exciting or interesting the story, the more receptive the audience. Maybe you grew up with a parent, grandparent, or another relative who could tell wonderful stories of the "olden days." On the other hand, perhaps your circle of relatives and friends includes the bore who recounts tedious stories again and again, apparently oblivious to the effect on his or her listeners.

Narratives are usually organized in chronological order, although the narrator may at times interrupt the chronology with a flashback to prior events or a projection into the future. Think of the many movies you have seen that use such devices to interrupt the plot line. Narrators are also prone to interrupt the chronology with a brief description of a character being inserted into the story, or a new location where it is being played out. In other cases the narrator may interject explanatory material to clarify events occurring in the narrative. In an account of a bank robbery, for instance, it might be useful to inform readers about the working of the bank's security system to explain how the robbers were able to disarm it.

People write narratives to discover something about themselves or others and to share that process of discovery and what they have learned with an audience. Writers tell stories for many reasons: to entertain, shock, or move their readers; to recall significant events or people; to illustrate a point; or to heighten reader interest. Narratives may be essays by themselves, or they can be dispersed throughout various types of writing to serve any of the above purposes, as well as many more.

If you are assigned or choose to write a narrative essay, pick a topic that has special significance to you, a topic that you would enjoy writing about and believe is worth sharing. What is it about that particular event that your readers would need to know to grasp its significance to you? As is always the case with a piece of writing, it helps to keep your readers in mind at all times. Include enough information and details so that the event is always clear to your audience—the readers who did not experience this significant event with you.

> *From the very beginning of school we make books and reading a constant source of possible failure and public humiliation. When children are little we make them read aloud, before the teacher and other children, so that we can be sure they "know" all the words they are reading. This means that when they don't know a word, they are going to make a mistake, right in front of everyone. Instantly they are made to realize that they have done something wrong. Perhaps some of the other children will begin to wave their hands and say, "Ooooh! O-o-o-o!" Perhaps they will just giggle or nudge each other, or make a face. Perhaps the teacher will say, "Are you sure?" or ask someone else what he thinks. Or perhaps, if the teacher is kindly, she will just smile a sweet, sad smile—often one of the most painful punishments a child can suffer in school. In any case, the child who has*

made the mistake knows he has made it, and feels foolish, stupid, and ashamed, just as any of us would in his shoes.

John Holt

Exercise

Choose one of the following options for a narrative essay.

1. Recall an incident in school or any other situation (work, social, athletic, etc.) that was especially painful or embarrassing to you. Perhaps you were treated unfairly or your friends did not understand your point of view. Describe the incident as vividly as possible, so that your audience—the readers who were *not there*—can follow exactly what happened and recapture your feelings at the time. Do not end your narrative too abruptly. You still remember the incident and found it important enough to write about, so it must have some long-range significance to you that would be of interest to your readers. While that significance may not be earthshaking, you should still put the event into some kind of long-range perspective in your conclusion.
2. Write about an event that had considerable significance in your life. It could have been a turning point in your life, such as a divorce, a death, a class, a talk, or an illness. Write about the event so that your audience—again, readers who were *not there*—can understand the event itself, as well as its long-range significance. Put the event into perspective in the conclusion, so that your readers are clear about its importance in your life.

See pages 264 to 278 for several student narratives that were written in response to the above assignments. Reading those narratives may help you choose a topic. They will also show you that an event need not be earth-shattering to be a good choice for a narrative.

Note: Some of the student narratives also include prewriting techniques that writers can use to explore their topics.

Prewriting for a Narrative

The perfect topic choice may have occurred to you immediately after reading the above assignment or browsing through the student essays in this chapter. If you are still uncertain what to write about, try making a list of possible topics in your journal. To help narrow down your choices, do some freewriting about those experiences that seem to have the most potential for an essay.

Select the most promising experience from that freewriting and make a *chronological listing* of what occurred. Making such a listing can help you to remember the event in more detail, as well as provide an organizational scheme to follow in your essay. Remember that narratives are usually arranged by time, in chronological order.

Sometimes it helps to close your eyes and recall your feelings at the time as well as the sequence of events—jot them down too. Describing your feelings (such as your terror as you heard someone trying to pry open the back door, for example) can add much to a narrative and help you to put it into some kind of long-range perspective in your conclusion.

Review your chronological listing to see if the sequence of events needs to be altered or whether you should leave out some of the items: Did you go off on a tangent at some point? Would descriptions of people, places, or things add to the impact of your story by making the events more concrete? Would dialogue be appropriate and effective? Reread some of the student narratives in the text and observe how these writers used dialogue and description to enhance their narratives.

Another useful prewriting technique is making a cluster diagram about your topic. Write your topic choice, such as "my divorce," in a circle in the middle of a page. Then jot down everything you can recall about that experience around the encircled topic. See the example of a cluster diagram on page 272.

Now that you have done some prewriting, it is probably time to write an exploratory draft of your narrative. Be sure to refer regularly to your cluster diagram or chronological listing when you compose this initial draft. Occasionally you may want to do some additional prewriting, such as making a supplementary cluster diagram to clarify or elaborate on a topic. Do not be afraid to discard points that seem unessential or to introduce additional subtopics that would strengthen your narrative. Remember, prewriting is only an overall guide, not a blueprint that must be strictly adhered to.

Some writers prefer to write an exploratory draft as the initial stage of prewriting. This is fine, provided you treat it as exactly that: the first stage, a working version of a narrative that calls for considerable revision. An exploratory draft can even serve as the basis for other prewriting techniques on your topic. Make a scratch outline of the events covered in that draft to see how well it is organized and how it could be improved. Use your draft as the basis for a cluster diagram, then delete or include more subtopics to help you write a more effective next draft and final product.

Hint: After some prewriting, you may decide that the event you are exploring is a bit dull or has virtually no long-range significance for you. Or perhaps you can only come up with a paragraph or two on your tentative topic. This may be an indication that the topic is a poor choice. It may be too narrow, or you may not be getting enough out of a perfectly good topic. Ask other people for ideas on expanding your topic.

Show your exploratory draft and other prewriting to a family member or friend, or share it with other members of your writing class, a tutor, or your instructor. You may be pleasantly surprised to discover that your classmates welcome the opportunity to exchange and discuss their papers outside of class. Forming such informal study groups plays a major role in success in college and can lead to friendships as well. A shy member of your class will probably welcome your taking the initiative. In any case, discuss your topic with someone, telling them just what you want to say and asking for their suggestions.

Writing a Narrative

Involve Your Reader from the Start

Successful narratives focus right in on the dramatic events of a topic. Avoid the pitfall of writing a long, windy introductory section describing mundane or dull events that led up to that dramatic moment. If five of your friends were involved in a serious automobile accident after they left a party, do not open an essay with a long discussion about being invited to the party, telephoning friends about what to wear, losing the football game the night of the party, being picked up by your friend's boyfriend, getting to the party late because he got lost, deciding to leave the party early, and so on. By the time they have finished reading all that, your readers are confused and bored, wondering when you are going to get to the point.

Keep Your Audience in Mind at All Times

Imagine that you are describing the event aloud for a friend. What would you emphasize? Begin with an introduction that hooks the reader at once—perhaps one that has an element of suspense—and leads quickly into the topic. Always be aware that your reader was *not* there. It is your job to include enough information to make everything clear. Make your narrative come to life with *concrete* details and descriptions and with effective dialogue.

Here is an example of a dialogue from Eric Williams' "Don't Let Me Die" (pages 264–66).

> *I went to Billy with the inspection sheet and its many discrepancies and to my disbelief he tore it right up in front of my eyes. "What are you doing?" I asked.*
>
> *"If you turned this in we'd be closed down for two weeks. Take this new one and fill it out right."*
>
> *"What if the state inspector finds out? It's my name on the bottom of that."*
>
> *"Don't worry about it. I have it taken care of." It was then I figured out that Billy had been paying the inspectors to overlook our many equipment failures.*

Eric might have summed up the above exchange something like this.

> *When I brought my boss an inspection sheet denoting many discrepancies in the equipment, he just tore it up and told me to fill a new one out right so that we would not be shut down for two weeks. I then figured out that he had been paying off the state inspectors to overlook our many equipment failures.*

Which version is flatter, Eric's telling dialogue or the summary?

A conversational exchange between two people is not always necessary. Sometimes you can enliven a narrative or a character sketch with a typical statement by one of the characters, as in this excerpt from "My Gammy Grace," by Laura Tetzlaff.

> *When I'm having a really low day I drop in and surprise her and she'll sit me down at the table and say, "Listen Laura, you are one hell of a girl. I know you are. So you get off your duff and get going!" Without her, I'd be on my duff more often than not.*

Concluding a Narrative

Knowing how and when to stop can also be a challenge. Finish your narrative when the main events are laid out in enough detail that your readers have gotten your point and it seems appropriate to close. In other words, stop while you still have your readers' attention.

On the other hand, it is possible to conclude a narrative too abruptly. When I finished reading Mary Nelson's first version of her theme (page 270), I gasped: She had failed to tell us whether her tiny premature baby had survived, how old Rory was at the time she wrote the theme, and whether he was in good health. What a terrible thing to do after getting the reader so involved! Do not leave your reader hanging; always reveal how an event turned out.

Finally, wind up your narrative by putting it into some kind of long-range perspective, showing the reader your point without unduly laboring it. Otherwise you may imply that your narrative is about an event that in retrospect has no real significance to you.

If the event you chose to write about seems to have no long-range perspective, your reader cannot help wondering about your topic choice. Its impact need not be earthshaking, but the fact that you chose to write about it indicates that it still means *something* to you. Otherwise you may need a better topic.

Selecting a Topic

If you cannot decide on a topic, browse through the student essays in this chapter for inspiration. Undoubtedly you will like some of these essays better than others. Read each of them *critically*—in other words, with a careful eye—deciding what makes each one effective and looking for places where you think the essay needs some improvement. A good technique is to read through an essay quickly to get an overview, then reread and analyze it, underlining or making marginal annotations. When reading critically or studying, always write down your comments and reactions. Never assume that you can remember all of them. What changes would you suggest to the author if you had the opportunity? What positive comments would you make? Underline visual images or ideas that strike you.

Several of the student essays in this chapter have effective titles or introductions that set the scene and involve the reader from the start. In some cases the dramatic story itself is almost enough to hold most readers' attention. Other essays illustrate how a skillful writer can make an ordinary human experience come to life on paper. Several essays in the text show how an author can use personal experiences to give a different slant to a familiar topic, thus avoiding the common

> Stuck trying to think of a topic?

trap of repeating hackneyed ideas about that topic. This is where voice, vivid details, and appropriate, clear examples come in.

Despite their many differences, these student narratives share two important qualities: Their authors' voices coming through loud and clear, and it is obvious that all of them have chosen a topic that they care about. These writers do not simply repeat vague generalities about familiar topics, such as "Something needs to be done about the environment," or "Smoking is bad for your health," without bringing an interesting new perspective to the topic. The authors have provided many concrete illustrations or anecdotes, usually from their personal experiences or observations, to support their main points. The essays are also well organized and easy to follow.

Finding Your Voice

You too can find your voice. Take chances. Do not be afraid to make mistakes, to reveal something about yourself, to express your views. Back up your generalizations with clear, concrete illustrations. Use *your* examples, *your* words, *your* phraseology and figures of speech. Avoid clichés and bland generalities that do not add very much. Strive for literate, authentic prose that you are proud to write and others will enjoy reading. Aim high, work hard, and your writing is certain to improve.

Several of the student essays included in this text were entries or winners in the University of Wisconsin—Milwaukee's annual composition contest. The writers spent many hours revising a series of drafts of their essays after getting input on each version from peers, family members, and instructors. They became effective writers through exerting considerable effort. If you are a good basketball player, a computer jock, or an artist, you know exactly what we mean. Now try putting similar concentrated effort into becoming a better reader and writer, using some of the same techniques. The results will be more than worth the effort.

Students often discount their abilities as writers. The author of one of these student essays once said that she was amazed that anyone thought that she would have anything interesting to say. I was the one who was amazed: I had just returned a paper to her that opened as follows.

> I was a drug addict. My best friends are drug addicts. I shudder to say that.

Of course she had something interesting to say: Sherry had personal knowledge of drug abuse, one of the most crucial problems of our times. Not only was her topic compelling, but her direct, punchy opener led readers to expect an honest examination of it. Sherry Klawitter had the makings of a good essay: an interesting topic to which she could bring unique personal insights. Why wouldn't her readers be interested?

All of you lead interesting lives and have a great deal of experience and insight that others would like to read about. The trick is to find the right topic for an essay, then to present it in the most effective manner.

How do writers like Sherry and the other student authors whose works appear in this book get their readers involved in what they have to say? After all, that is a major reason why people write—to get others to pay attention to what they are saying. There is no simple answer to that question. As the student essays demonstrate, there are many ways to hold a reader's attention.

One way to discover answers to that question is to become a more observant reader. You already know a lot about good writing because you have read many samples. You have also read many samples of dull, ineffective writing. When you read, think about and analyze what you read in a somewhat different way, as a *writer,* not just as a reader. Look carefully not only at *what* the writer is saying, but at *how* he or she is saying it.

Understanding What Makes Writing Effective

To begin to understand what makes writing effective, critique the six student narratives that appear starting on page 264 in this chapter. Divide the class into six groups to analyze these essays. Each group should first read all six essays, then choose one to critique in more depth and report on for the class. (Have second and third choices so that all the essays are covered.) Those six critiques can provide the basis for a listing on the blackboard of some of the characteristics of effective writing. At the same time, everyone can begin a list on that topic, preferably in a writer's journal, which can be referred to and expanded throughout the semester.

As your group prepares its critique, consider the suggestions and questions in the two following guides, "The Reviewer's Task" and "Analysis of a Narrative."

The Reviewer's Task: A Guide for Peer-Group Revising

1. Make the writer feel comfortable; he or she will probably be more receptive to the group's suggestions.
   —List and discuss three or more good features of the paper.

2. Emphasize the positive by pointing out specific places where the paper could be *improved*. Write comments like the following in the margins.
   —This is interesting—tell us *more*. (develop)
   —Good—add more details and description. (details)
   —Could you be a little clearer here? (unclear)
   —Mark terms or concepts that need explaining. (define)
   —Are you rambling off the topic? (off topic?)
   —Are you getting repetitive here? (repetition)
   —Help readers by adding a better transition here. (transition)
   —How about a lively dialogue here? (dialogue)

3. It is *not* your job to intervene and change the working. Help the writer with the *contents*, not the syntax (word order) or grammar. (Do you want someone to rewrite your text for you?)
   —Suggest places where the wording could be made more vivid and specific.
   —Point out dull, flat verbs, vague nouns, and so on.

4. Pay attention to the individual parts of the essay.
   —Does the introduction raise interest and set the scene?
   —Does the conclusion bring adequate closure and not leave the reader hanging?
   —Is the title appropriate to the contents? Does it catch the reader's attention?

5. If you think a word is misspelled or note a punctuation slip, just underline those places. The writer can then check out your suggestion during the revising process. Remember the wording and grammar are the writer's jobs, not yours.

Guidelines for Analysis of a Narrative

1. Does the introduction get the reader interested in the topic? Does it hold the reader's interest? How? How could it be improved?

2. What is the single most interesting episode or event in this narrative?

3. Does the narrative include enough information about that episode to make it come to life?

4. Write annotations in the margins of the narrative being analyzed. The following suggestions can guide you in things to look for.
   —Mark places where the reader would like to hear more.
   —Mark sections that should be cut or shortened.
   —Mark places that are unclear or need more information.

5. Does the essay end too abruptly? Does it put the topic into long-range perspective?

6. Does the essay have a good, appropriate title that arouses the reader's interest?

Use the questions from these two guides while drafting and revising your narrative. Show these questions to people who are helping you revise your narrative, and take their responses into consideration as you make further revisions. If your class divides into peer revising groups to critique each others' narrative essays, use the questions during those sessions as well. Keep these questions in mind as you read the following essays.

Don't Let Me Die
Eric Williams

As I stood there with the blood on my hands watching the ambulance lights slowly disappear from sight I wondered how my life had come to this point. This point of such destruction, this point of inhumanity.

It started when I left high school. I was 16 and didn't have any skills that would get me a decent job. So when the carnival came I saw a chance to get out, a chance to see the country and really be on my own.

I took a job on The Screaming Eagle. It was a roller coaster owned by a man named Billy T. I really admired Billy, for he too left home when he was 16 and worked for the carnival. He saved up his money, bought his own ride, and by the time he was 23 he had made his first million. It wasn't until later that I found out that he made his money through corruption and deceit.

After three months of hard work I made my way up to assistant foreman. With the extra money came extra responsibility. I was now in charge of inspecting the ride each morning and making sure the proper forms were filled out. On the first morning of my new duty I found so many things wrong that I didn't think it would be possible to open the ride that day. I found brakes almost completely rusted through, safety pins and chains that were never installed, seat belts that were so worn and tattered that I could pull them out with my bare hands.

I went to Billy with the inspection sheet and its many discrepancies and to my disbelief he tore it up right in front of my eyes. "What are you doing?" I asked.

"If you turned this in we'd be closed down for two weeks. Take this new one and fill it out right."

"What if the state inspector finds out? It's my name on the bottom of that."

"Don't worry about it. I have it taken care of." It was then I figured out that Billy had been paying the inspectors to overlook our many equipment failures.

While I felt guilty about lying, I soon got over it. I faked the inspection reports without remorse. I sat by as things got worse and did nothing to alter the inevitable.

Black Friday started just as the word says: Black. The sky was covered with dark clouds and it felt like it wanted to rain but just couldn't find the strength. If it had rained, the outcome of that day would have saved me from many nightmares.

The ride was extremely busy, as it was on all Fridays. And I was bored. So when a boy, who looked to be about eight, and his big sister whose fear made her hesitate to get on, came up, they put a break in my boredom. I went into my usual spiel about how safe it was, and about how there was no way she could get hurt. I put them into a car and sent them on their way. I watched them until they reached the halfway point and sent out the next car. A loud piercing scream turned me around with lightning speed. The girl, her brother, and three other kids were stopped forty feet up. I saw another car bearing down on them first. I reached up and hit the emergency brake; nothing happened. I pounded on that button until its plastic casing cracked in half. Suddenly the power went off and the emergency brakes fired open, but it was too late. The second car had already slipped by the last brake. The people who were still in line looked on in horror as the girl and her brother attempted to climb out of the car and make

> their way down to solid ground. Another man on the crew yelled to them to stay inside, but he couldn't be heard over their feeling of panic.
>
> The 800-pound car slammed into them at about forty miles an hour. I went into shock as I watched this girl, who had just begun to live life, fall to earth, bouncing like a rag doll off of the steel structure. As she lay there with her head resting on my lap I could feel her warm blood soaking my pants. I wiped the only tear she cried away from her bruised face and heard the words: "Don't let me die."
>
> When I felt life leave her body, I also felt a part of me go with her. My inhumanity.
>
> It's been many years since Black Friday, but I remember it as if it were yesterday. The jacket soaked with her blood still hangs in my closet. I leave it there to remind me of what I never want to become again. If only mankind had a blood stained coat hanging in its closet, there might never be another senseless loss of the precious gift we often take for granted, LIFE.

Beginning with the title and introduction of this powerful narrative, Eric Williams holds the reader's attention. Through carefully selected descriptive details and apt use of dialogue, Eric builds up a sense of foreboding that makes the reader anxious to read on to discover the outcome of his story.

Reread the essay, finding phrases or sentences that are especially effective, either in building up that sense of foreboding or for their descriptive power.

Writers often find it helpful to make an *informal* or *scratch* outline as a guide before drafting a narrative. A scratch outline for Eric's "Don't Let Me Die" might have read something like this:

INTRODUCTION
   Ambulance in distance—bloody hands

BODY
   Background information
   —quit high school at 16—no skills
   —took job on carnival roller coaster
   —admired Billy T. my boss (tell why)
   —promoted to assistance foreman
   —found defects in ride (give details)
   —*dialogue* with Billy about the faulty equipment
   —felt guilty but kept lying on inspection forms

Black Friday—set scene with details on gloomy weather
—boy (8) and older sister (seems frightened) arrive
—persuade her to get on—send off
—their car stopped with another on the way
—emergency brake failed
—crowd watched girl and brother climb out of car
—collision and accident (give details)
—girl speaks, then dies

CONCLUSION
—put the event into a *long*-range perspective
—bloody jacket in my closet
—gift of life

In Search of the Eternal Buzz
Sherry Klawitter

Two of my best friends are drug addicts. I shudder at even writing the words. It took me a long time to admit that and even longer to admit that I was, too. I never thought someone like me could ever become an addict, but I was utterly wrong.

Like many others, my experimenting with drugs started at fifteen with prompting from my friends. Bill, John and I had been friends since the start of junior high. We had met at a party through mutual friends. I was a naive suburbanite looking for a few kicks, so it was no surprise that their care-free life-style and constant partying meant instant attraction. Throughout school I had always been an achiever academically, but as our friendship grew our life-styles became similar. By freshman year they were already using marijuana regularly, so as we became closer I became a user too. We spent many nights together, getting high until sunrise, sleeping the day away and getting up only to get high again. None of us ever thought of experimenting with any other drugs, until, as fate would have it, they became readily available.

Our fate was sealed when Bill's pharmacist dad gave him a job at a pharmaceutical warehouse, where drugs were within easy reach and the temptation soon became too much for him. Bill did the ordering, sorting and the inventory, so no one ever noticed (or at least never wanted to notice) that he was taking bottle after bottle of sleeping pills, tranquilizers, pain killers and anything else he could get his hands on, we later found out.

At first, we sold everything he stole to buy marijuana and LSD, but soon all those little pink and white pills became too tempting for any one of us to resist. After trying dozens of different pills, the thrill wore off. So we starting mixing drugs: LSD, liquid codeine, pain killers, and tranquilizers. The more imaginative the combination, the better the high. We spent the entire summer after my junior year in search of the eternal buzz.

I lived for nothing except my next high. I would have given my life for a buzz. My highs were my only escape from my new life that by then was headed nowhere. I altered every mood with a different drug. Without them I was totally lost in a sea of depression.

By this time I had cut off all contact with my family and the rest of the world. My world was Bill, John and a buzz. No one ever saw that I was in desperate need of help, or ever wanted to see. My family ignored the problem completely, refusing to acknowledge the fact that I was an addict. Meanwhile, Bill's job was on its way up. He now worked third shift on weekends and had no supervisor, so he started to steal drugs that could easily kill if taken in the wrong amounts. However, John and I did not realize this until later.

Bill's moods became highly violent and he seemed distant. John and I realized something was terribly wrong. The drugs we used never had these effects. So, acting on our suspicions, we took a look through Bill's things after he left for work. While I was going through Bill's book bag I found something that made my skin crawl and my stomach turn sour. He had a syringe and tiny bottles of liquid. After the initial shock, we decided to confront Bill. Didn't he realize what he was doing? But after he came from work neither John nor I knew what to say, or how to say it. Besides, Bill was our supply of drugs and upsetting him could mean the end of those long, pleasurable highs. So, as soon as Bill handed out the night's supply, we had our minds made up. Neither was willing to risk losing the thing we cared about the most: drugs.

It took two more long years for me to realize that I was not only abusing drugs, but also myself. My highs had changed from an exhilarating rush to shaking fits and paranoid delusions. I thought I was losing my mind. I had no control over anything in my life. I rarely ate and didn't sleep for days on end. Signs of fatigue showed on my face and my once vibrant appearance diminished until I began looking run down and sickly. However, not until a lethal mixture of drugs brought me near to death did I realize I was about to hit rock bottom. Earlier that day I had taken three hits of acid, because John and I decided we wanted to trip together. While

I was peaking I felt a little edgy, so I took a handful of assorted barbiturates and painkillers. Throughout the day we tried to keep our highs going by smoking pot repeatedly. I started to hallucinate and shake badly early in the evening. At times, Bill and John had to hold me down because they feared I might hurt myself. I turned complete white and my heart started to beat a million miles a minute. They stayed with me all night while I threw up continuously and had shaking fits. I could have died that night, but they never called an ambulance for me. They told me it was just a "bad trip." I knew that was a lie. They were scared of being found out. They were willing to sacrifice a friend to their God: drugs.

To me it was obvious that our drug use had not only put a strain on my health, but also our friendship. Our addiction was tearing our friendship apart. I never trusted them after that night. Once, we had been inseparable friends and now we no longer trusted one another and fought constantly. Bill started to keep more drugs for himself and became withdrawn. John no longer talked and showed little emotion, if any. The bond that was once strong had almost disappeared.

One year after my near fatal accident, with our friendship gone and my own health dissipated, I knew I had to stop. I went back to high school, got myself a job and stayed away from my former friends. Through hard work, determination and a lot of family support I have been clean for almost three years.

Bill has since been arrested for possession twice and is now in a rehabilitation center for cocaine addiction. John still leads the life that I ran away from.

Like many people we thought addiction was a disease that only losers suffer from. That is where we were utterly wrong. Like many teenagers, we never realized the effects drug abuse could have on our lives. Doing drugs makes you a loser and anyone can become an addict. Drugs are a very appealing escape to many teenagers. Recently, these thoughts ran through my mind as I heard a fellow UWM student say, "Yeah, I get high, but I can handle it."

Sherry Klawitter's essay on the compelling topic of drug abuse won third prize in the 1992 Virginia Burke Essay Competition for students of freshmen composition courses at the University of Wisconsin–Milwaukee. She brings a fresh, personal approach to a much-discussed topic, and her writing is uniquely and searingly honest.

On the other hand, like almost any piece of writing, Sherry's essay could be strengthened. Suppose that you had a chance to go over this essay with Sherry. Could you indicate specific places in the text where you would like additional information? Where might she include more vivid details? Would dialogue add to this essay's impact? Where?

The Unknown
Mary Nelson

The day my son was born I realized life wasn't always fair. I had listened to all the doctor's advice and followed his instructions to the letter. Then on the horrifying day of October 10, 1982, I realized all my obedience was for nothing. My son was seven weeks premature and weighed all of three pounds. The pain, confusion, and lack of knowledge were hitting me right in the face.

The learning began when the doctors told his father and me that Rory was a very unhealthy child with severe respiratory problems. We were told we would be lucky if he made it through the night. Our struggle and Rory's had just begun.

Several interconnected machines were attached to his pitiful small body, all of which we were to learn about. Rory had an I.V. connected to a vein in the top of his softball sized head and electrodes that ran from his forehead and lower stomach to the main machine. This machine told us he was still living. Taped to his mouth was a tube with a long spiral cord that connected to a respiratory machine and carried air to Rory's lungs, causing drastic pressure in his tiny chest. His chest was pushed high into the air and then sucked way into the rib cage. It looked disgusting and terribly painful. Side effects from this machine can be mental retardation, loss of sight, and loss of hearing. Fortunately none of them happened to Rory.

The next trick was to become a doctor's aide over night. We got pamphlets on all the machines and asked many questions on how to read the charts. Within the next week we were experts. The days in that hospital room were long and nights even longer. As I sat next to the glass box that enclosed my son, I watched this advanced equipment keep my child alive. I would sit and wonder what was going on in his mind, or if he was even capable of realizing anything. To ease my own pain, I was always hoping that he did not.

I was only twenty years old, barely understanding childbirth and its responsibility, and how here I was trying to understand all this too. My family, especially my mother, were very supportive. They were always coming to the hospital to give me breaks from the many hours sitting by the incubator. His father had to work to keep us from being buried by the bills. I had to sit and handle all this stress alone without him. I realize now that it was just as hard on him to be away at work as it was for me to always be at the hospital.

I was knotted up inside by opposing feelings of pain and happiness. I loved this squirrel sized person, but hated his pain. I wanted Rory to live, yet hoped he would die. As time passed he became stronger and stronger until after three weeks he was four pounds four ounces and breathing on his own. The time had actually arrived when his father and I got to hold our son for the first time. He was as light as a feather and we laughed at how Larry could hold him in one hand. What had been so painful to look at had now become a joy to hold and love. I shook with nerves and thought that finally the nightmare had come to an end. This time I was crying out of happiness and absolute joy.

One week later we brought home our four pound twelve ounce son. He had certainly lived up to his name, for Rory means strength and survival.

The road ahead from that point has not been an easy one. Rory is now five years old and a severe asthmatic and still quite sickly. He needs constant care and medicine. He takes three types of medicine twice a day, everyday. He also uses a Palmeo Aid, a machine which regulates breathing during an asthma attack. When all our efforts at home during an asthma attack fail, we take Rory to the hospital for shots and a two or three day stay. The hospital has become our second home over the years. He's known by name there and he knows the staff. Rory has learned to deal with his condition and at times I believe he handles it better than I do. We both have his home and hospital routines down pat, although Rory could live without all those shots and I.V's.! The doctors don't foresee Rory outgrowing his asthma early in life because of the severity of his case. Meanwhile we pray for him and hope that each day brings an easier breath and one less complication.

Many writers find it useful to prepare a *cluster diagram* before drafting a narrative. A cluster diagram for "The Unknown" might have looked something like this:

Cluster diagram around center "Rory's birth" with branches:
- *describe the nursery for premature babies*
- *his father had to work; bills*
- *other babies in the nursery*
- *tiny ribcage moving*
- *our deep fears*
- *followed all the Drs.' orders*
- *"draw picture" of Rory on machines—tubes, tape, etc.*
- *very mixed emotions*
- *possible side effects from machines*
- *the long-range picture & Rory's health*
- *7 weeks premature*
- *competent nurses, etc.*
- *his problems—chance of survival*
- *condition at 3 weeks; 4 weeks*
- *all we had to learn fast*
- *long hours at hospital; family help*

A cluster diagram can also be used as the basis for an additional type of prewriting, such as an informal outline or an exploratory draft. To help organize the material, look for subtopics that fit well together, such as "picture Rory connected to the machines," "long days and nights at the hospital," "tiny rib cage moving," and "possible side effects from the machines." Also note the crossed-out items that seemed "off topic."

Fortunately, not everyone has such traumatic, shattering experiences to share as the previous writers. Even if you do, you may not wish to write on such a wrenching topic and subject your essay to others' scrutiny. Everyone has had many experiences that have left a deep impression on our memories. The next two student narratives show that an event need not be tragic, or even serious, to be well worth remembering.

Airborne
Tisha Beasley

"Maaaaa!" was the word which sirened from my mouth after my unfortunate crash landing. All scarred up and/or bleeding was a common state for me as a child. I was always trying to be a female Evel Knievel on my skateboard.

It was early afternoon during the summer of seventy-seven. My best friend and stunt buddy Jo-Jo and I were doing jumps off the stairs at the end of the walkway. The stairs had about four or five steps that led down from the end of our courtyard to the street. We raced on our skateboard down the walkway, which was about thirty feet long, and to avoid the steps, dove off at the last minute on to the grass with a side roll. You know how the stunt men jump out of moving cars for the movies? Well that's how we looked. After each jump we had to retrieve our boards from the street. "Boy!" Were we having fun. Well at least we were up until Jo-Jo's mother fussed at him for the grass stains on his knees. "Man!" Jo-Jo's mom used to pop up out of nowhere and it would always be when we were enjoying our life as children. Jo-Jo's mom was a hygiene fanatic; everything and everyone around her had to be clean. I don't know how she saw the grass stains on his black jeans, but she did, and she made Jo-Jo go inside and take a bath. "Dang!" She used to spoil everything. I guess it didn't matter. I was getting kind of bored anyway.

Since Jo-Jo had to go, and everyone else I knew was out of town, or on punishment, I decided to go home myself. I flew up the same courtyard that Jo-Jo and I had been playing at . . . it seemed like sixty m.p.h. Then all of a sudden, I hit a rock. "Tick, skiiiid, aaaah!" I was airborne. Although I was only in the air for approximately five seconds, I thought about my landing. I cried out, "May-day!" Then came the contact. Chin first. As I grazed the surface of the concrete, I felt like a skipping rock on very hard water. After the first contact I bounced because I only weighed the amount of a half dollar. Ooooow, was I in a lot of pain as I began to brake. My whole body was on the ground at this point. Then "Crash!" I hit the concrete porch step.

"My gosh! Was I bruised?" I got up and looked around to see if anyone had seen me. Nope, all was clear. I looked at the palms of my hands, my elbows, my knees. Yes, they all were scarred up and bleeding good. Man this was my worst accident ever. I felt my head because I had hit it so hard on the porch step. It was bleeding as well. The blood banks could have used me that day. Blood was everywhere. I began to think about my father's sarcasm as I walked home. I knew I would be put on punishment for acting like a boy again for sure. I could hear my father's voice, "If you'd act like a little girl and stop acting like a little boy all the d——— time you wouldn't always be bruised up." And he was right, but I've always been hard-headed, and what the boys did was my kind of fun.

> As I approached my house, I whipped up some tears. I entered and I couldn't even find my mother. I went upstairs; she wasn't there. The basement light was on. Yeah, there was my mom. Little miss actress went to work. "Maaaaa!" I cried out. My mother came to the steps, and once she saw my blood she didn't waste any time coming up to doctor me. She asked me what happened. So like any mischievous child would have done . . . I lied. "This . . . (sniff) big boy beat me up . . . (sniff, sniff) and he tried to take my skateboard."
>
> "What?" my mother exclaimed. "How big was he? What did he look like? Have you ever seen him before?" Her questions came out so fast I couldn't answer them all. "Just wait until your father gets home. You all can go look for him and your father can kick his a——for hurting my baby." I was happy now.
>
> By the time my mother got me all cleaned up, my father was walking in the door. I told him the same story that I told my mother. He put on his "hitters," (those were his leather gloves) and we went on a journey around the neighborhood in search of a boy who didn't exist. Of course we never found him, but at least I didn't get put on punishment for acting like a boy and being airborne without a plane.

Tisha Beasley effectively employs dialogue, strong verbs, ("'Maaaa!' . . . sirened from my mouth") and the language of childhood to recapture certain aspects of everyone's youthful adventures: bruises and scrapes, scoldings and tears. The essay also brings up the issue of traditional gender roles, a topic of much current interest.

Incidentally, Tisha must have been a good actress, because it was not until her parents read this paper that they realized that the alleged culprit in this tale never existed.

The Backpack That Packed a Punch
David Hart

Now that I look back on it, I could have thought of at least a million ways to avoid the Doug Gilcrest conflict without any physical harm. But I was a young boy who could tolerate Doug the Tyrant's lunch money pick ups, even the Give to Doug's Kids fund until . . . he wanted my bike.

My bike—that polished blue steel dreamy frame, with proud military brass handlebars, a horn that thundered and bellowed as I rode down the street, and super lightweight graphite pedals that made me go faster than a tiger hunting down its prey—served as a symbol for nearly twenty miles of lawn that I had heaved and sweated over the previous summer. It was the best bike in the whole schoolyard and everybody knew it, including Doug.

Doug, although tall and intimidating, was a very insecure person. He thrived on the misery of others. He loved to see others in pain and grief, especially when he was the cause of it. Doug was the kind of person who would choke his teacher because she looked happy. Everything had to be centered around Doug, or it didn't exist.

One morning I was locking my bike up on the rusty bike rack in front of school when old Doug sauntered over. "Hey, dork! That's a pretty crappy bike you got there. Tell you what, I'll take the piece of junk off your hands for . . . say five bucks."

"Sorry Doug, but this bike is not for sale," I mumbled, half delirious and half offended that he had uttered such a ridiculous offer.

"I don't think you understand the proposition: you give me five dollars and I'll take the bike off your hands," flapped Doug.

By that time I was flabbergasted. Nobody could price my bike so unreasonably, not even Doug. Suddenly, my emotions replaced logical thought and I began saying things that I would later regret. Other students heard the profanity and they swarmed like bees over to the bike rack.

"What did you say, moron?" Doug shouted.

I wanted to say "nothing" but my mouth wouldn't budge. I just stood there, mouth shut and hands deathly cold and clammy, as the crowd cheered the mute underdog on. I tried to say something, anything, but nothing came out. Not the "nothing" that would have changed the fate of my sixth grade year, but instead literally silence.

"Okay, that's it. It's time to pay," said Doug. And he reached back and hurled his huge wrecking ball fist at my nose. It was over and I knew it. I could smell the blood before he hit me. I saw at that instant, my life, or at least my entire sixth grade year, flash before me. Then, without thinking, I picked up my backpack and slung it in the path of his punch, throwing it off course. The crowd became hysterical over my giant accomplishment and for that moment, I too commended myself. But in my victory, I forgot one thing: Doug had another fist, and another and another.

As I laid on the ground next to my bike I realized something important: I was badly injured and I would probably get beat up by Doug again tomorrow, but today I had won. I got to keep my bike.

> I don't remember much else about the Doug Gilcrest conflict. But I do know now that I could have avoided the whole thing if I had not relied on my backpack to do the job, and had just run. But then I wouldn't have had my triumph—or my bike.

Almost all of us have unpleasant recollections of the neighborhood or school bully. David Hart skillfully describes that familiar type in his vivid, dramatic account of his memorable encounter with Doug the Tyrant. Once again a clever title and an introduction that arouses the reader's interest engage the reader at once.

Reread the essay twice. What sections are the most effective? Why? Mark phrases and descriptions that you especially like. Does the conclusion end the essay appropriately? Does it put the episode into a long-range perspective?

Writers regularly switch from one writing strategy to another, even in cases where one strategy, such as comparing, dominates. Some writing strategies are interlocked; for example, it is virtually impossible to compare without describing the items being compared. You probably observed how much descriptive details enhance the student narratives in this chapter. Suppose that David Hart had assured us that he owned "the best bike in the whole schoolyard," and left out his detailed description of that bike and all the lawn he had mowed ("nearly twenty miles" of it) to purchase that bike? Suppose that Mary Nelson had not drawn us a word picture of "squirrel-sized" Rory being kept alive by a respirator? How much those narratives would have lost in their effectiveness! In all cases, the writer's purpose and the audience for which a piece is intended play a major role in the choice of writing strategy, or combination of strategies.

Now pay particular attention to Dan Bartz's skillful weaving of description and narrative in the cleverly titled, imaginative and whimsical analytical essay that follows.

Space Sweepstakes
Dan Bartz

> One day I saw a sweepstakes for a free trip in the supermarket. I am usually wary about the free trips that supermarkets give away, but I said to myself, "Entering the sweepstakes for the trip couldn't hurt; it would be great if I won."
>
> As I left the store, I didn't think about the trip again, that is until I was notified by a guy on the phone. The man said, "Congratulations!

You just won an all expenses paid journey to see the planet Jupiter." When I heard that I won, I ran hysterically through the house. I dashed down the stairs at such a rate of speed, I could have been free falling; I forgot about how low the door frame was. When I hit the frame, for me it was lights out!

When I awoke two days later, I learned that the trip was to last two years. My family and friends knew about me winning the trip. My family was worried about it because they wouldn't see me for two years. My friends, on the other hand, gave me all sorts of ideas on what I was to bring, since space on the ship would be limited.

The people at NASA told me that I could bring only three things. The first thing that I thought of was bringing music with me. The NASA personnel said compact discs and cassettes, along with a boombox, was considered one item.

That only left me with two more items that I could take. I asked the NASA people if there would be any artificial gravity. They said, "No, the space for the gravity generator was converted to hold food." I wasn't going to argue with that. I guess I won't be taking my volleyball with me. Every time I eat when I'm on the trip, I will think about my volleyball.

The second item I would bring would be a photo album. I would have all of my best pictures of earth and its inhabitants. I will want to remember all the beautiful scenery like the bluffs in La Crosse, Wisconsin. The bluffs are incredibly gorgeous. On the top of one of them is a park with a long winding road to the top. Where the road ends is a wooden platform-like extension lying out into the sky. From that point you can see the Mississippi as it winds its way through the land, and see rugged scenery for miles in every direction. These pictures from there will be in the album. The inhabitants in the album would be my family and friends during all the good times we had together. I have pictures of our family reunions, when everyone is in a great mood and they do a lot of horsing around. I also have pictures of my friends and me in Florida. Being there on vacation was the best time in my life. We would wake up in the morning, sneak across a parking lot to the next hotel, run through a corridor, and right into our neighbor's pool. We would end the day by doing the same thing. By the time the sweepstakes trip is over, I know that I will have studied all of them intently.

The third thing that I would bring would be a baseball bat. It sounds stupid, but if you think about it, the bat means power. With this bat, I will

> have that power. I'll be able to get the other passengers' three possessions. I'll also be able to tell them what to do and where to sleep. I will have the best of everything while I'm on the trip. I told NASA it had sentimental value.
>
> On the day to leave, I drove to NASA, said my good byes to everyone and hopped aboard the space craft. When I got on it, they took all of my possessions and put them in a storage locker. Then the NASA crew strapped me into a chair. When I asked them where everyone else was they said "In the back." Great, I have preferred treatment already. The lift off was a blast. It felt better than the best roller coaster at any theme park.
>
> After a couple of hours, the people at NASA said I could get out of the seat. When I went in the back to meet my fellow passengers, there were only boxes of mechanical equipment. I just realized to my stupidity that I was a guinea pig. I thought to myself, what am I going to do with the bat? I knew exactly what to do: beat my head in with it.

"Space Sweepstakes" is by far the most playful of these student essays, and it is evident from his amusing opening narrative to the surprise ending that Dan was having a good time with this topic. Do not be afraid of being playful or of taking chances; *good writing is never dull.* Dan's essay shows how humor and a light touch can be strong points when used effectively under appropriate circumstances. Moreover, along with being well organized and clear, the essay contains considerable analysis and is carefully reasoned: Each time Dan introduces a new possession he makes it clear why he chose it for his journey into space.

Dan seemed a bit surprised to see his highest grade of the semester on this paper: "Gee, but this one came so easily!" No doubt that is because the topic so obviously engaged his imagination, another example of the importance of finding a topic that strongly interests you, the writer.

Exercise

Perhaps you too will have your imagination piqued by the assignment option that led to "Space Sweepstakes."

> Imagine you will be leaving next month on a space capsule voyage that will last for two years. Space on board will be limited, so you can only take along three personal possessions. (All of your needs will be provided for.) What *three objects* would you take along? Think about yourself and what possessions are really important to you. Do some clumping or jotting about possible choices. In your essay, describe the three objects you finally decide on and tell the reader why you have chosen them.

What objects would you choose for such a journey? Explore this theme suggestion in your journal. Perhaps you too will be inspired to write a developed theme on the topic that caught Dan's imagination.

Exploring Additional Uses of Narratives

The Short Narrative as an Introduction

Seasoned public speakers often begin with a short narrative, an anecdote that leads into and usually illustrates the thesis of the following speech. Similarly, writers use short, appropriate anecdotes to open an essay. Narratives are human and concrete; they can add drama to writing and grab the reader's attention at the start. A clear transition should then connect the short opening narrative to the body of an essay.

Note the amusing reminiscence about the chase to get him to take a bath that opens "Momma," Calvin Stewart's loving portrayal of his grandmother (page 300). Having caught our interest, Calvin uses the next paragraph as a transition from his opening anecdote to his initial observations about Momma.

Using Narratives to Illustrate General Points

Narratives can also be used throughout the body of an essay to illustrate, or make more concrete, the general topic under discussion. Narratives can make people or events come to life on paper. If you claim that your mother was always the person your relatives could count on, include anecdotes, or short narratives, to show exactly what you mean. Give an example of a time when relatives came to her and what she did for them.

Exercise

The student essays in this book contain many examples of narratives used to illustrate an author's main points.

1. What narrative did Flo Seefeldt (page 305) include to demonstrate how her teacher gave her a lesson about stealing? Summarize that narrative in your journal.
2. What narrative did the author of "Take It from an Ex-Kid" (page 376) use to illustrate his view of television commercials that advertise entertainment places for children? Summarize the episode in your journal.

Chapter Ten

Describing

Both writers and artists create pictures by arranging appropriate details on paper or another surface. Artists do not tell us what a picture is about, they show us by producing the painting or drawing. Writers ought to do the same thing, but often they do not. Too often they merely tell instead of showing; for example, writing a generalization like "He was an unfair coach," instead of including concrete details to demonstrate exactly how that coach acted unfairly.

Describing is painting a picture with words. Ordinary conversations are peppered with descriptions, often in response to questions: What was Monika wearing the night you proposed to her? What was the stage set for *Cats* like? What does your new dinette set look like? What facilities does that campground have? Concrete descriptions make conversation lively and vivid.

> Describing is painting a picture with words.

Word pictures are also scattered throughout good writing. Composing descriptions that get your readers' attention by evoking images in their minds is indeed a challenge, but it can also be fun. Moreover, it is very exciting to develop a formerly untapped ability to capture a special place or person on paper. The descriptive writing talent of students is amazing.

The student essays in this book contain many fine examples of effective descriptive images: the "softball sized head" of Mary Nelson's "squirrel sized" premature baby (page 270); the "Maaaa!" which "sirened" from Tisha

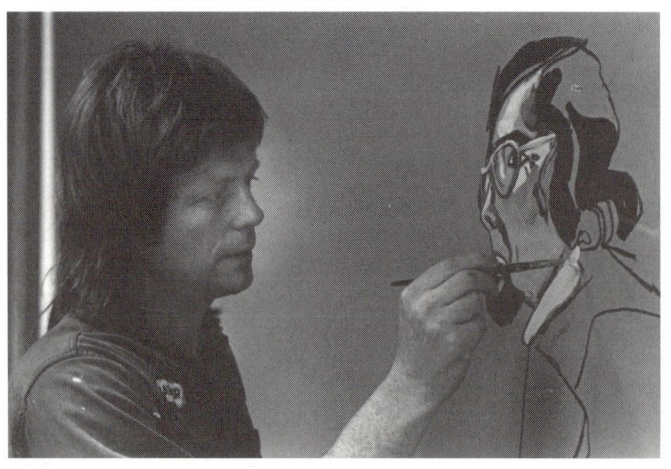

Beasley's mouth after an "unfortunate crash landing" with her skateboard (page 272); James Airoldi's skis, "blurs of motion" as he plunged blindly through a mogul field, "alone in a pocket of exquisite motion" (page 319); the five baby robins that "seemed to sing in harmony, in tones you could almost put words to" in nests built in opposite corners of Jeffrey Schwigel's treehouse (page 314).

In many cases, these descriptive images are what stick in the reader's mind, and for good reason. Descriptive words and phrases make writing vivid, keep it from being vague and boring. Including lively descriptions throughout your writing helps to make it concrete and human, as opposed to abstract and mechanical.

Description is essential to all types of writing. The objects, places, and people in a narrative can be brought to life through effective description, thus adding greatly to the impact of the story. A short description of one of the characters involved might be a good way to begin a narrative. Through description, narrators can share their emotions, the fear and uncertainty, joy or misery, that they experienced during the events being recorded. Mary Nelson wanted her readers to feel the pain and stress she experienced sitting for days and nights at an incubator, most of the time by herself, watching her premature son's "tiny chest . . . pushed high into the air and then sucked way into the rib cage. It looked disgusting and terribly painful" (page 270).

Description can be personal, subjective, and involved, or it can be impersonal, objective, and detached. Objective description is an important element of informing and explaining. Scientists, technical writers, lawyers, and journalists make frequent use of factual, objective descriptions to illustrate what they are saying and make their points clear. As even the most casual reader of the popular press knows however, journalists may also appeal to their readers' emotions, often through unnecessarily lurid and sensational descriptions of the events they cover.

Understanding the Elements of Effective Description

Appealing to the Five Senses

Write about things that your readers can *touch, hear, smell, taste,* or *see* in their minds as they are reading along. Because English has many more words for visual images than for the other four senses, you may need to think a little harder to find words appealing to your readers' tastebuds, for example. Overcome the tendency of less experienced writers to limit themselves to visual descriptions. Make certain that your readers do more than see the ocean. They also ought to hear it, sniff it, feel the cool ocean spray on their hot bodies, and taste the salt in the air.

Certain words, of course, convey meanings that appeal to more than one sense. For instance, a mountain just visible in the distance may have a *sharp* outline, a good knife feels *sharp*, aged cheddar tastes *sharp*, vinegar has a *sharp* odor, the little girl next door has a *sharp* yell, and comedian George Carlin has a *sharp* wit. Most descriptive **adjectives**—words that describe nouns—are not so versatile, although a few are.

To help yourself become a better descriptive writer, look for effective appeals to the five senses in other people's writing. The student essays in this text contain many examples. Train yourself to be more observant of what your senses are telling you as you go about your daily affairs. Writers constantly observe the world around them, storing images in their minds for future writing.

Because descriptive writing has so many uses and can be fun to experiment with, this chapter contains more writing suggestions than the other chapters of this book. Try out these suggestions over the course of the semester, then incorporate the results into all of your essays. It is a rare piece of writing that is not improved by adding concrete description, whether factual or literary.

Listen and watch as you sit alone in a noisy crowd, then spend a few minutes describing all you see, hear, and smell in your journal. Your audience is someone who is not there at the time to share the scene with you. Include more than visual images in your word picture;

> Writers observe the world around them.

and recapture some of the motion in that scene. Make your record as specific as possible by using strong, vivid verbs, concrete nouns, and well-chosen modifiers.

Modifiers are words, phrases, and clauses that give the reader more information about nouns and verbs, thus making them more precise. Remember that adjectives are words like *timid* that modify nouns, as in *timid chipmunk.* Adverbs are a bit more versatile; they sometimes modify verbs, such as the word *rapidly* in the following:

The frog *rapidly* fled from the newly painted barn.

Sometimes adverbs modify adverbs, as in *newly painted* in the example above. Look at the following sentence for more examples. The modifiers are in italics.

(modifying   (modifying adjective   (modifying
adjective)   phrase)   adverb)
A *rusty* tricycle *with dented, once-silver fenders* leaned *crazily* against the

(modifying
adjectives)
dilapidated wooden shed.

Tricycle, fenders, and *shed* are specific nouns with adjective and phrase modifiers that tell more about them. *Leaned* is a concrete verb modified by the adverb *crazily.* In addition, the modifying phrase "against the dilapidated wooden shed" tells more about the verb *leaned.*

Broadening Your Fund of Modifiers

Look at the movie ads in a newspaper for an array of overworked modifiers: sensational, thrilling, dynamic, chilling, sexy, and so on. What impact do these words have? Do you tend to discount them? Why?

Look at the first draft of a piece of your descriptive writing. Do certain overused, somewhat vague modifiers, like *beautiful, attractive, nice,* or *kind,* appear too frequently? "She was a sweet guest." Does that sentence convey a precise meaning? "She was a really sweet guest." Does adding the intensifier *really* make the sentence any more precise?

Becoming aware of overused modifiers (like *special* or *unique*), some of which also lack specific meaning, is the first step toward eliminating them from your prose. It may also be beneficial to work at developing a ready fund of concrete replacements for your active writing vocabulary. Think about concrete appeals to *all five senses* as you put modifiers in the following charts.

Exercise

Fill in the columns with several modifiers, or adjectives and adverbs, that start with the letter at the top of each column. Now fill in the charts. The first row is done for you. Remember to search for appeals to all five senses. Resist using mostly visual image words and concentrate on the other four images.

A sister can be _____.

s	i	s	t	e	r
sullen	icy	sarcastic	timid	early	rich

Places can be _____.

p	l	a	c	e	s
popular	lush	aromatic	craggy	eerie	smelly

Exercise

Now that you are thinking in terms of adding concrete and vivid descriptive words to your writing, try the following suggestions.

1. Write a detailed description of a familiar or a unique object. Try to include enough information and images so that readers not looking at the object can visualize it. What shapes, colors, textures, and smells are crucial aspects of the object's essence?
2. Go alone to one of your favorite outdoor spots. Listen quietly for a few minutes, then imagine that you are writing a letter to a friend unable to share this special spot with you (audience). Include as many concrete details as possible so that your friend gets a clear mental picture of what you are describing. What sights, sounds, smells, and textures can you describe to make the scene vivid and concrete?
3. Write a description of a favorite spot that could make your readers, and possibly even you, look at that scene from a new perspective.

Effective descriptions of nature often cause the reader to view the familiar in a new way. Stunned by the beauty of her first Wisconsin autumn, Californian Laura Weiler's description had just such an impact on fellow students from the Midwest.

> *Red, yellow, and orange leaves were falling softly to the ground like snow flakes spiraling from the heavens above. As we were driving through a cascade of leaves, we came upon a tree. It was a petite tree with a thin reed-like trunk. But it was full of leaves on top, like an oversized wig on the head of an old, frail woman. The tree was a cross between ruby red and deep crimson. Yet some leaves were the color of bright red cherry wine. The red seemed to be iridescent. Every time I looked at it, it seemed different. The color was so unbelievable that I had to get out of my car and feel a leaf to make sure it was real.*

Another possibility is a description of nature on the rampage. Cindy Moran did just that in her narrative about a hike in the Rocky Mountains.

> *The wind started to howl as trees, plants, and any other living thing were stung by its whip. This once mystical place had taken on an evil, dark face where fear could be smelled by both men and beast. An uneasy feeling crept over me as mother nature was teaching me exactly how small and weak I was.*

Which images appeal to which senses in Cindy's account of the sudden onslaught of a mountain storm?

Does the following description by Felicia Sutton make your tastebuds jump? Read it carefully and make annotations in your journal, noting which senses Felicia appeals to.

> *Not only was the pineapple brought back from Hawaii by my sister, but she also picked it out herself. I wanted to cut the pineapple as soon as it came through the door, but she insisted it would taste better chilled. My temptations were aroused at the thought of that delicious fruit sitting in our isolated refrigerator all alone. As I watched the hands on the face of the clock move like the sun across the sky it seemed as though time was at a standstill. Finally, after hours of waiting, the pineapple had chilled to my sister's satisfaction. She removed the long, shiny butcher knife from its place of rest, then proceeded to sit the chilled pineapple on the pullout cutboard. As the tip of the knife punctured this tropical monocotyledonous plant with its stiff, spiny sword-shaped leaves and short flowering stalk, the juices flowed like a happy river. My mouth began to water as if someone*

had turned on a faucet. I stood nearby waiting patiently for her to finish dicing it up into those small bite-size cubes. As she dropped the little tidbits into the green Tupperware bowl, the juice dripped off as if it were moisture from a steamed window. I, trying to speed up the process, moved to the cabinet to get a small dish to pour the sugar into. The sugar crystals hit the dish as if they were looking forward to meeting the cubes of pineapple. I wandered back over to the wet cupboard where my delicious feast was being prepared. As I stood there holding my glittering crystals for my wet cubes, my temptations finally conquered me. I took a chance, and stuck my trembling hand into the green container that was sitting off to the side of the cupboard. I laid the pineapple on its side in the dish of sugar, then flipped it over with caution so as not to knock off some of the crystals. I opened my mouth—I could no longer resist. My taste buds were jumping, and my stomach had prepared for its arrival hours ago. I laid the wet, sugar covered fruit on my tongue, closed my mouth and chewed very slowly, wishing that the flavor would last forever.

Exercise

1. Write a journal entry describing the sensations of eating or drinking something you strongly like or dislike, such as liver or cold beer. Appeal to as many of the five senses as you can.
2. In your journal, describe a person's face using a live person, a photograph, or your own image in the mirror as your model. Read over what you have written to determine whether your description would present a clear impression to a reader who has not seen the person you are writing about. Add, delete, or rearrange details to improve your portrayal.

Using Specific, Concrete Details

Always use the particular instead of the general when describing anything. A particular category is one having fewer, more specific items than a general category. The items in the first column below are arranged from the general to the particular. The items in the second column are arranged randomly. Using the first column as a model, rearrange the items in the second column from general to specific.

soft drink	clothing
cola	shoe
Pepsi	running shoe
Diet Pepsi	athletic shoe

Using the particular instead of the general means writing "brown suede moccasin with a ripped seam" instead of "worn old shoe," "1916 Model-T Ford" instead of "vehicle" or "car."

In his essay about an encounter with the school bully, Doug Hart recalled his prized "polished blue steel dreamy" bike with "military brass handlebars," a symbol of the "nearly twenty miles of lawn that I had heaved and sweated over the previous summer" (pages 274–75). Doug might have written, "I earned my fancy new blue bike by taking care of people's lawns," a bland, less concrete—and therefore less effective—statement. Instead of merely saying that the equipment on the Screaming Eagle roller coaster was in lousy condition, Eric Williams painted us an exact picture: "I found brakes that were completely rusted through, safety pins and chains that were never installed, seat belts that were so worn and tattered that I could pull them out with my bare hands" (page 265).

Because of the need for precise explanations, scientific and technical writing relies particularly heavily on the use of concrete descriptive details. Note the following example.

> Catfish are identifiable by their feelers (barbels), catlike whiskers used to probe murky waters where their weak eyes cannot penetrate. The barbels have tastebuds that help in the constant search for food.

Using Modifiers Effectively: Adjectives and Adverbs

Adjectives tell more about, or modify, nouns: The *creaky* floor. Adverbs tell more about verbs: Clambered *cautiously*. Put adjectives and adverbs to work for you. If they do not add anything to your writing, it is better to skip them. Look at these examples:

    (adjective)   (adverb)
The frustrated coach bellowed loudly into a megaphone.

    (adjective)   (adjective)
The striped tiger let out a loud roar.

Aren't all tigers striped and all roars loud? Can one bellow softly?

What about the next sentence?

    (adjective)   (adverb)   (adjective)
A young toddler stumbles clumsily through the yellow daffodils, trying

        (adjective)(adjective)
to catch a round purple ball.

What words would you cut? What would you leave?

As these examples show, adjectives modify, or tell more about, nouns.

a *purple* ball
a *poor* exam
an *excellent* performance

Adverbs often modify, or tell more about, verbs.

performed *poorly*
worked *harder*
ate *slowly*

Exercise

Rewrite the following sentences, making them more vivid and interesting by adding active verbs, concrete nouns, modifiers, and so on. For instance, write *weeping willow* instead of *tree*. Try *bellowed* instead of *said*. Use *agitated attorney* instead of *she*.

1. A vehicle passed by a building that day.
   (Ask yourself: What kind of vehicle? What building?)

2. The people came upon a surprising sight.

3. A creature moved to another place.

Note how much more you can show the reader by using concrete, specific nouns, verbs, and modifiers.

Try to employ the same techniques to make your essays more concrete and vivid. First and even second drafts tend to be full of generalities, so always go over them carefully, searching for vague words and phrases that you can make more specific and interesting. Ask your reviewers to help you spot such instances, and point them out to others when reviewing their themes.

Using Strong Verbs

Strong specific verbs—*swagger* instead of *move, whimper* instead of *speak*—add vitality and convey much with a single word. Write *whispered* or *stammered* instead of *said,* and the reader instantly knows more about the speaker and the situation being depicted. Susan Krenn's intimidating new teacher "cackled out" where she was to sit (page 304). The horn on Doug Hart's bike "thundered and bellowed" for all to hear and envy; small wonder the school bully coveted it (page 274).

Exercise

List several more precise verbs to replace each of the vague verbs below.

walked	**spoke**	**moved**
ambled	yelled	wiggled

Using Motion

Motion does not have to be spectacular to be worth describing. Even in seemingly tranquil scenes curtains flap, spoons somersault to the floor, and people gesture, knead dough, and stir batter. On the other hand, active motion is central to many scenes, such as the dance studio where Amy Brinkman was about to become a nervous, but excited, student.

> *Five studios with five styles of dance were in session. The smell of hard work was in the air and the constant bellow of counts and directions captured my already disorganized attention. There were dancers everywhere.*

Exercise

Try to capture the wonderful motion in one of the two pictured dance scenes in your journal.

If you are writing about a dance floor, a gymnasium, or an athletic field, describing motion should be an essential part of your essay. James Airoldi's vivid description of skiing down "Mt. Heaven" may give you some ideas (page 319). Observe that he uses both chronological and spatial organization in his essay.

Remember, however, that it is not only athletic events or dances that have lots of motion and that motion is not confined to people. People are fascinated by animals in part because they like to observe their movements.

Describe your favorite pet.

Using Imagery and Figurative Language

A pond coated with a layer of ice
So thin that an insect could crack its silky surface,
Rendering the serene scene wrinkled . . .
        Chris Erickson

The front porch, where the swing once hung, had rotted boards hanging from the ceiling, like dismal skeletal figures . . . . The barn had slumped over to one side, like an old man with a bad back.
        Ronald Ream

Her face began to be a sculpture in my mind.
                                                       Hector Rivera

Figurative images like the ones above are the stuff of descriptive writing. They make writing more concrete, more interesting, and help readers to see the world in a different way. Poets, dramatists, and song lyricists, authors of children's books, people who compose words to be heard, not read, make wide use of figurative language. Listen to their works for ideas.

Dr. Seuss, for example, relied regularly on **alliteration**—using words with the same initial letter—with marvelous results.

"I am the Lorax," he coughed and he whiffed.
He sneezed and he snuffled. He snarggled. He sniffed.

Atypical word arrangement is another important element of many memorable works. "Life is easy in summer" could never replace the unforgettable "Summertime, and the livin' is easy," any more than "I will never forget you" would equal Nat King Cole's "Unforgettable . . . that's what you are."

Deliberate parallellism—repeating the same grammatical structure and phraseology, or wording—is another type of word arrangement that can be effective, if it is used sparingly. Lori L. Long's (her parents may or may not have consciously used alliteration when naming her) recollection of her deceased father contains a good example.

Eventually, my father had to quit smoking because he had emphysema. He started taking oxygen pills and wound up hooked to an oxygen machine. From the medication and the ailment his once sturdy body became weak and fragile. His once sharp mind converted to a confused and tired one. His once sparkling eyes became sad and weary . . . .

Personification, or assigning human characteristics to animals or inanimate objects, is another often-used figure of speech. Indian jewelry gave Kendra Rabideaux "winks through the glass case," and she and her sister soon had shiny new silver rings. Jill Sweeney used personification to describe a special sunrise: "About 5:30 A.M. the sun slowly started to peek out, like a child checking to see if the coast is clear." Amy King depicted a sunset: "Eventually the ocean extinguished this glowing hot ball, making the clouds on the horizon look like steam rising from the water."

Like many writers, Jill and Amy also used **comparisons** to make their descriptions more concrete. Some comparisons are explicit; that is, the meaning is spelled out, often by using *like* or *as*. Such explicit comparisons are called **similes**. Here are some more examples:

A day in the sun turned Sheri Piccolo's skin into a "blistered, burning two-toned layer that looked like early morning, sizzling breakfast bacon."

Cynthia Goodwin recalled "sweating like a pig in a sauna" while writing the exam for a Wisconsin driver's license.

Randy Haasch's mother used a lively simile to tell him to go back to school: "Otherwise the years will roll on by like cars passing a hitchhiker waiting for a ride at the side of the road."

In a **metaphor,** on the other hand, the comparison is implicit, not spelled out. Suppose that Shakespeare had written "The world is *like* a stage," instead of "All the world's a stage . . ." in his famous metaphor. Not only would he have written a simile in place of a metaphor, his figure of speech would have been notably less effective.

The following examples should point out the difference between metaphors and similes a little more graphically.

"Mr. Haley is falling away to a needle," remarked ninety-eight-year old Hazel Erickson about another resident of a Milwaukee nursing home.

My "valium" is sketching brightly colored fish.

Writing "For me, sketching brightly colored fish is like taking a tranquilizer," would have been using a simile instead of a metaphor. Had Sherri Piccolo written, "My skin became a two-toned layer of early morning, sizzling breakfast bacon," she would have been using a metaphor.

Exercise

Respond to the following questions.

1. The "glowing hot ball" in the description on page 291 is obviously a metaphor for what?
2. Which of the literary images that set off the beginning of this section (pages 290–91) is a metaphor?
3. Now reword that metaphor so that it becomes a simile.

The trick about using similes and other figures of speech is to avoid those that are overused; otherwise, you risk sounding like a broken record. We should warn you in no uncertain terms that henceforth, now and forever, such overused expressions ought to be few and far between in each and every essay you send down the pike. Do we make ourselves clear at this point in time?

Using Analogies

An **analogy** is another, somewhat more extensive, form of comparison used by many writers. Instead of simply stating the comparison, the writer spells it out in some detail, giving examples to show how the two things are alike. You probably have noticed the frequent comparisons between writing and painting throughout this book. That analogy might be further developed as follows: Effective writers, like artists, pay special attention to composition, to the way they arrange things on paper. The analogy could then be made even more concrete with explicit examples.

Exercise

Experiment with the literary devices mentioned above as you describe a familiar scene in your journal. It could be a scene on campus, in your neighborhood, at an athletic event, and so on. Use fresh images and strong verbs. Be as precise and concrete as possible as you write for readers who were not at the scene. Review your description, underlining phrases that could be more vivid and concrete, then rewrite it.

Making Allusions

Our students regularly come up with fresh, vivid allusions, such as Daniel Parker's reference to his boxer grandfather's "huge, muscular Popeye-like forearms." Tisha Beasley termed herself a "female Evel Knievel" on the skateboard, and James Adams is still whopping proud of "that Moby Dick of a bass," caught over a dozen years ago and still mounted on his wall.

These three student writers assumed, perhaps unconsciously, that their readers would know what these allusions meant. Expecting their readers to bring past experiences with life and books to what they read, writers often make short references, or **allusions**, to ideas and information outside the text of what they are writing. They allude, or refer, to well-known people, places, or events, assuming that the reader will grasp their intended meaning, just as Dan Parker assumed that his readers would know who Popeye was.

Do not be surprised if you do not catch the meaning of all the allusions you come across. Few readers do. The sources of allusions are many: the Bible; Greek mythology; the words of Shakespeare and other famous writers; important events in history; and popular culture.

What are the sources of the three student allusions mentioned above? Popeye and daredevil stuntman Evel Knievel belong to the latter category, popular culture. Moby Dick is the whale in Herman Melville's famous novel of the same name.

If a reader does not happen to be familiar with what is being referred to, then the writer's intended meaning may be unclear to that reader. Sometimes, but not always, it is possible to guess the meaning of an allusion from the context. Even readers unfamiliar with Popeye or *Moby Dick* are likely to surmise that this ex-boxer's arms were mighty impressive or that James Adams caught a huge fish.

Allusions are sometimes explained in the marginal annotations or footnotes in literature and textbooks. In addition the meaning of many allusions can be found in larger dictionaries, so get into the habit of looking them up. Sometimes doing a more thorough research job or asking questions until you find someone who knows the context of an allusion is necessary to discover the precise connotation.

What allusions need to be clarified to determine the meaning of the following examples? Find those allusions, then bring them up in a class discussion.

Dr. Martin Luther King, Jr., praised the James Merediths of the world for their noble sense of purpose in his 1963 "Letter from Birmingham Jail."

Beware of modern-day Don Juans in Wranglers lest they find your Achilles heel.

A piece of tape at the Watergate led to Richard Nixon's Waterloo.

Avoiding Clichés

How would you complete the following:

Fit as a _____.

Maria is the _____ of his eye.

Quiet as a _____.

Strong as an _____.

More than likely you filled in *fiddle, apple, mouse,* and *ox.* These once-fresh expressions have become **clichés,** sayings that are worn out from overuse and are therefore predictable. No writer is likely to keep clichés from creeping into his or her writing. Undoubtedly you have spotted clichés in the student essays in this text, as well as in our prose. You can, however, work at eliminating the most blatant examples, such as the following: "booming metropolis"; "illustrious age of 21"; "different ball of wax"; "merry quest"; "one in a million"; "she was always there for me." Advertising contains numerous such expressions, but you can do much better.

Brochures for "tourist paradises" abound in "quaint, narrow, winding streets," "sparkling white, sandy beaches," "picturesque Alpine villages," and "intimate, romantic, off-the-beaten-path cafés." This brings up another warning related to the matter of clichéd writing. Because many mountains have snow-covered peaks in the winter, while tropical resorts tend to have white sand, sparkling, clear, blue water, palm trees, and crowded outdoor cafés, find something *different* if you choose to write about such a place. Vacation spots usually have well-equipped motels with verandas and balconies, and potted plants in the lobby. Nearby restaurants may not be look-alikes to Wendy's, but many will have soft music and dim lighting, candles and fresh flowers on tables covered with red-and-white checkered tablecloths. In other words, including lots of concrete details is not always enough. If you cannot write something unique about a restaurant or motel, leave it out of your essay; otherwise, what you describe would be interchangeable with many other essays about similar places. On the other hand, if the shower head was missing and a spring pierced a hole in the center of the mattress and poked you in the hip, those things are worth recording. Tell the reader about *your* particular cottage on a lake, not everyone's cottage.

For an example of the oft-repeated place made special, read Jeffrey Schwigel's wonderfully detailed recollection of his treehouse in the field behind his house (page 314). Maybe Jeffrey's essay (and the clumping that accompanies it) will suggest a special place in your childhood that you would like to recall, if not for an essay, at least for a journal entry.

> Last but not least, avoid clichés like the plague.

Remembering People and Places

The essays below were written in response to the following assignment, which calls upon writers to experiment with largely descriptive writing. As you will see, some of the results are quite wonderful.

Exercise

Write an essay about an important person in your life, someone with whom you have had a significant relationship. Try to present a vivid image of that person so that your readers can see both the person's character and significance to you. Remember that what a person does tells the reader much more than purely physical descriptions can possibly convey. Try to connect physical descriptions with the person's character traits and actions, like some of the writers below. Back up abstractions and generalizations such as "My Aunt Tillie was (or is) the one all of the nephews and nieces could come to" with concrete illustrations of what you mean. How did Aunt Tillie treat her young relatives? What did she do for them? What made her so appealing? Was she fun? Was her appearance a factor in her appeal? Whenever possible, connect descriptions of peoples' appearances to the way they act. Show the reader what that person is (or was) like through concrete illustrations, expressive dialogue, and apt descriptive details. In other words, *don't tell us, show us*. And remember that in spite of what media advertising would seem to have us believe, what people *do* is more important than what they look like.

Show, don't tell. In addition to being rather flat and clichéd, general statements, like "Ricardo has a really great personality" or "Emma was fun to be around," do not really say much. It is better to let particular details speak for themselves. Give the reader some "for instances," the kind of examples someone could elicit in conversation through a series of probing questions: Exactly what is it about Polly that makes you think I would like a blind date with her? What's she like? Does she enjoy sports and the outdoors? How does she move on a dance floor, or a tennis court? What kind of music does she listen to? What do her friends like—and dislike—about her? Is she moody? Sarcastic? Funny? Is she always late? You know how that bugs me. What does she look like? Looks don't really matter, but . . . . Does the way she dresses reflect her personality? What does she value? Is she a good conversationalist? Is she a good listener? What *one* thing about her most sticks in your mind? If you bought a small gift for Polly, what might it be? What objects surround her in her room or apartment? (We have an artist friend whose portraits always contain one object the person treasures as a featured element in the background.)

Try to imagine the kind of questions a reader might ask about the person you decide to write about. Jot them down and then add concrete details that could help answer those questions. Do some freewriting in which you create miniscenes that characterize the person. Be as specific as possible.

What are you trying to recapture about this person? Eventually these telling details should help you arrive at a focus, a dominant impression, which pulls all of the details together into a meaningful essay. Each section of the essay ought to add to that dominant impression.

Analyzing Descriptive Essays

Read through the following descriptive essays for ideas about a topic for your own essay. The essays are preceded by a list of points to consider when analyzing a descriptive essay. Use that list as a guide while drafting and revising your own descriptive essay. The list can also provide guidelines for both general class discussions and small group analysis of descriptive essays.

Exercise

As always, read through the entire essay quickly for an overall impression. Then reread the essay slowly, with the following in mind.

Have your peer revising group members use these guidelines as they analyze your descriptive essay. Then consider their suggestions while preparing your final version.

1. What are the three best things about the essay?
2. Comment on the introduction.
3. Does the essay have a dominant impression, or a focus, about the topic? Summarize that impression.
4. Mark places that have good, concrete details or striking images *right on the essay*. What senses—sight, sound, smell, touch, taste—are appealed to? Mark any clichés or trite expressions.
5. Note places in the essay where you would like more details.
6. Does the essay have enough examples to back up the main points (generalizations)? Are the examples interesting and appropriate? What would you like to hear more about?
7. Never leave the reader hanging. Is the conclusion effective? How might it be improved?

Student Essays on Remembering People

For a look at an essay that moves very effectively from concrete details to an overall thesis, read Laura Tetzlaff O'Mara's lively and humorous portrait of her Gammy Grace. Laura takes us along on a visit to her grandmother's home where we first meet Teddy, the mutt who plays a major role in Laura's grandmother's life. What details does Laura use to show us a sprightly lady (instead of telling us, "My grandmother is . . .)? Single out those details by highlighting them in the text or making marginal notations on the essay. (See the first pages for examples of annotations.) Does the use of dialogue add to the essay? Why?

After meeting Laura's grandmother, we listen to typical conversation (once again enlivened by Gammy Grace's pithy language). Only in the conclusion does Laura bring all these details into a general focus by telling us how important her grandmother is in her life, a conclusion that she had been showing us and leading up to throughout the essay.

All writing needs a thesis, but it does not always have to be stated explicitly toward the beginning of an essay. "My Gammy Grace" demonstrates that it can sometimes be effective to wait until the conclusion.

My Gammy Grace
Laura Tetzlaff O'Mara

Her name is Grace Moungey but all of her grandchildren call her Gammy Grace. The way I heard the story was that my grandma disliked her mother-in-law, who was known as Grandma Moungey, so much that when she became a grandma she refused to be called Grandma Moungey. So she came up with GAM—which years later became Gammy Grace.

dialogue catches how GAM talks

I love going over to my Gammy's house. A feeling of anticipation always grows as I walk into her back hall. It's most fun when I go over unannounced. She can't hear me come in the back door because she hates wearing her hearing aid. "Oh that damn thing," she says. "Excuse my language—it always squeaks when I have it on and everyone sounds like they're yelling!" So we all yell at her and then she hears us all right. Anyway, I walk in the back door and she's usually in the back of the house busy with something or another. The first thing I hear is the radio next to the coffee maker. Gammy likes it up really loud. I think it keeps her from getting lonely and she likes relaxing while listening to WZUU, the station that plays that old music. I laugh because whenever we (the grandchildren) switch the channel to put our music on, she can only listen for about two minutes and then she starts complaining. "What is this that we're listening to—and what are they saying? Oh geez', can't understand a word of that stuff." Then she gets all flustered and walks over to the radio and changes it back to elevator music. Sometimes we'll turn on some Bruce Springsteen or something, just to see how long it takes her to notice. You can always tell when she finally hears it and her brain registers "garbage music." She gets flustered, walks over to turn it off and there we are, giggling in the dining room, a little disappointed because we couldn't hear the end of the song.

loud radio playing old music

quotation catches her reaction to "our music"
she turns off Bruce Springsteen or . . .

good phrase

So . . . I walk through the kitchen, past the blaring radio and I step over Teddy, who's yipping at my feet. Gam loves her little Teddy, her little baby. She talks to him all the time just as if he were a person. He's cute and everything, but he's got one of those mutt dog mouths where the bottom row of teeth comes up and over the top one's like a piranha's. Sometimes

great description of Teddy—good detail

excellent simile: teeth like . . .

I feel like kicking that little yipper right in the chops and fixing those teeth for good, but Gammy would never forgive me if I hurt little Teddy. By this time the yipper alert warns Gammy that someone's here and you can hear her comin' down the hall. "Whooooooose heeeeerre" she chimes. And I yell, "It's me Gammy; It's Laura."

effective dialogue

"Oooohhhhhh! Laura!" she says as she wraps her arms around me and gives me a huge hug. She grabs my face, gives me a kiss and then puts her arm over my shoulder and says, "I'm so glad you stopped by! Come in and sit. Have you eaten? What can I get you?" She leads me into the dining room to the table and makes me recite everything I've eaten all day to make sure that I'm eating right. God forbid that I tell her I had a hot dog or a Big Mac. Then she gets a big frown on her face, gives me the "you're too skinny" speech, tells me that I have to eat more and makes me feel really bad. Then she makes me eat a huge lunch—which is great if I'm hungry but terrible if I've just eaten a burger and fries.

For the next hour or so Gam and I talk about everything. First she asks about classes. She might give me a little pep talk about how smart I am and how I have to do homework and stay on top because I've got lots of brains, she's counting on me and she's right behind me all the way. Then we might talk about boys. She might ask me if I've got anyone special that I like and I'll say no. Then she'll say, "Good, you don't need them anyway because at your age they're out to getcha. Men are like cowboys and all they want is another notch on the belt!" All the granddaughters get this lecture every once in a while until we're married, but I must admit that although her delivery is really funny a lot of the time, we all appreciate the content.

My grandma has a great sense of humor, she's quick with a comeback and sometimes she'll come up with a great joke or two. She treats all of her granddaughters like her daughters. She wants us all to be successful and happy and she gives us support, guidance and great pep talks that none of us could ever do without.

My Gammy Grace is my inspiration and my strength sometimes. When I'm having a really low day I drop in and surprise her and she'll sit me down at the table and say "Listen Laura, you are one hell of a girl, I know you are. So you get off your duff and get going!" Without her, I'd be on my duff more often than not.

Gammy Grace died in August 1995, and this essay was read at her funeral.

Calvin Stewart's marvelously detailed and sensitive recollection of his grandmother won first prize in the Virginia Burke Essay Contest at the University of Wisconsin–Milwaukee. Read it and you will see why.

Momma
Calvin Stewart

Back when I was about four years old, my home was on a farm in Hayti, Missouri. I lived there with my mother and grandmother, who had been a widow for many years. Often, when my mother was off in the city working, my grandmother would try to make me take a bath. We didn't have a bathroom in our house. Most people didn't there. My grandmother would go in the back of the house and get a #3 metal tub, a round metal tub similar to an oversized mop bucket, which people used to wash clothes or take baths in. After filling the tub up with water and soap, she would more times than not have to chase me down and force me into the huge tub. When I gave her a hard time she would often go out to the weeping willow tree on the side of the house, and pick off a nice sized branch. She would then peel off the leaves and use it as a whipping tool. "Wayne I hate to be whipping yo butt all the time," she would say in her simple Mississippi accent, "but you gotta lon how to ack."

Though I don't remember getting a lot of these whippings, I did get my share. With my mother not around a lot, I considered my grandmother to be my real mother. I even called her Momma.

Momma was a strict disciplinarian. Whenever I was bad she let me know right away. The switch (willow branch) was her favorite tool. But sometimes she grabbed whatever was closest to her whether it was a shoe, belt or some other solid object. Anything would do. A great deal of the time she would just snatch me up and we would have a good lectured conversation, with her doing most of the talking.

The piercing stare that usually accompanied one of her lectures felt as though it was going to burn the skin right off my forehead. Her stare alone was usually enough to keep me out of trouble for awhile. These and her other early disciplinary actions, I believe, helped me to become a more disciplined person.

For a woman in her seventies Momma was a very strong woman (she had to be to chase me around) mentally and physically. She stood about five feet six inches in height and weighed about 160 pounds. She had a top heavy figure which was held up by two sticks for legs and man-sized feet to balance it out. Her long gray hair, with streaks of black from past years, surrounded a face of an almost grayish brown complexion. Her brown eyes could be so still that they seemed as though they were staring right through you.

After we moved to Milwaukee, Momma would often walk me the one block I had to go to school. I felt more safe walking with her than I did walking with anyone else because she could handle any situation that could come up.

Unfortunately during the severe winter of our first year in Milwaukee Momma took a fall on the ice and broke her hip. After a long stay in the hospital, she emerged in a wheel chair. With a lot of determination and will power she was able to put the wheel chair in the closet within the month. But physically Momma was not the same as before. Her long, almost military stride had been reduced to a cane assisted shuffle.

After the accident our relationship changed somewhat. She depended on me more to run the errands that she used to run. Such things as going to the store, and getting the newspaper were now my responsibility. I didn't mind running the errands because as a first grader it made me feel as though I was doing something important. I would grab the money out of her hand and run to the store and back as fast as I could. Sometimes she would even let me have the change.

I could tell that Momma missed the country life she had lived for more than seventy years. She would often sit on the porch of the duplex we lived in for hours at a time as though she were trying to absorb what little fresh air there was in the city. Sometimes when Momma was out on the porch I would join her and we would sometimes get into conversations which would range from what was going on in television, to what was going on in school. Through these "porch chats" I felt as though we were getting closer together.

By this time she had long stopped whipping me. It wasn't like she couldn't still do it if she wanted, she just didn't. Of course I was greatly appreciative.

Most of the time when I received my report card from school Momma was the first person to see it. I had known for some time that she could not read, so I would try to explain the report card as best I could, without making her feel insecure. One time when I got my report card, I ran home from school as fast as I could. When I got up to the porch, Momma was out there as usual. I took my report card from out between my book pages and explained what the grades meant. "You see those right there," I said, pointing to the A's and B's. "That means that I am doing good. And those over there," pointing to the C's, "means I could do a little better."

"Well you got more of them goodens than the baddens."

"Yep."

"Give yo Grandma a hug." Then after she would let me go, she would look up at me and say, "Bo you gon be somebody."

I would just smile and bask in the moment. It was nice to have someone who believed in you. I felt that she believed in me more than I believed in myself.

A couple years later when we were outside on the porch just staring at the white house across the street, the topic of the conversation was death. This was a topic that we had never talked about before. "Bo you know Imma getting ole."

"I know, but you still got twenty-five years to go."

"Twenty-five years, where you got that notion from?"

"Don't everybody supposed to live to be a hundred years old?"

"No son, ya ain't guaranteed to live that long. Hell, I could die tomarra."

I cried out, "You can't die yet."

"I ain't saying umma die yet, um just saying that there will be a day when the Lord gon call me home."

At ten years old, and having never experienced death in my own family, I had this idea that everyone was supposed to live to be a hundred years old. But about five years later I would find out that I was wrong.

I clearly remember the day that Momma died. It was a cold wintery day just after Christmas. I was sitting in the living room watching television, when my mother came into the house and asked, "Where's Momma?" I replied, "In her room."

My mother rushed to Momma's bedroom which was in the back of the house. When she came back into the living room, she knelt down beside the chair I was sitting in. I asked her, "What's wrong," my own voice quivering slightly.

She put her hand on top of my head and said, "It's Momma, she's dead."

> The funeral was held about a week later. I didn't want to go because I didn't want to see Momma dead. I wanted to remember her as I did when we sat on the porch talking. But after thinking it over I felt that by going I would be able to say goodbye face to face.
>
> Looking back over the course of our lives together, I believe that Momma's loving discipline in my early years taught me to be a more respectful person. And the determination she showed in walking again after breaking her hip in her seventies showed me that if someone worked hard enough almost anything can be accomplished. I have tried my best to apply both her discipline and her determination to my life.

Exercise

These two very different, yet similar, essays about grandmothers illustrate the point that there is no one (good) way to write. Have your small group draw up a chart listing similarities and differences between the two essays and the two grandmothers.

1. Compare the two introductions. Note that neither essay starts out with a general thesis statement about the role of the grandmother in the writer's life.
2. List and compare the various writing strategies, such as narrative and describing used in the two pieces. Does using a variety of strategies contribute to the effectiveness of each essay?
3. Does the use of dialogue add to each essay's impact? Why?
4. Look for effective details and images and strong verbs.
5. Compare the writing styles of these two authors.
6. Note that both essays lead up to similar conclusions, or theses, which are explicitly stated in the final paragraph of each. Comment on those conclusions.

Keep the above criteria for analysis in mind while reading and comparing the two essays about effective teachers that follow.

Susan Krenn's use of dialogue, strong verbs, and vivid descriptive images bring this portrait of a dedicated and demanding teacher to life. Note that most of the quotations are the writer's own thoughts, phrased in the form of direct speech, and not words that were actually spoken. Find words and images that you find especially striking.

A Special Nun
Susan Krenn

Being a new student can be a terrifying experience, especially in an accelerated class. But, thanks to a very special nun, I learned about determination.

It was in September of 1974, when, at the age of 16, I first entered an all-girls school called Divine Savior. Strange faces floated past me, all in pairs or groups. I felt very up-rooted and lost. "My parents have done me in," I thought. But the worst was yet to come!

At 11:00 A.M. I entered the accelerated algebra class. Standing in front of the fifty or so desks near the big blackboard stood a nun, tapping a ruler in her hand. My first thought was, "Does she use that thing?" Standing a very erect 4'8", weighing in at 85 pounds in her crisp black dress and funny hat, she reminded me of the Wicked Witch of the West from the *Wizard of Oz*. Her dried out apple face, full of lines and wrinkles, with a long narrow nose holding up granny glasses, looked gruesome. She cackled out where I was to sit and then as I listened to her lecture I realized I was in the advanced algebra class. "Trouble! How do I get out of this?" I wondered. Later, after class, more confused than ever, I explained I wished to drop her class. Cutting me off, she gruffly told me to meet her promptly after school at 3:15.

Well, the last thing I wanted to do was meet with this crabby old nun whose penetrating raisin eyes unnerved you. The time unfortunately arrived, however, so I quickly walked in, hoping to get it over with. She acknowledged me with a nod and proceeded to ignore me. After a few hour-like minutes she called me to her desk. She opened the conversation by informing me that I would not drop her class and that I was to meet her every day after school. In the same breath she said, "Open your book, we'll start today!"

I was so intimidated, I never thought to argue. We worked together til May. She was the most dedicated teacher I've ever had the fortune to meet. She explained everything in a way that made math easy to digest. In these sessions she never let up, pushing me to the breaking point. I never dared miss the tutoring sessions for fear of those snappy blue-black eyes looking disapprovingly at me till I just wanted to melt away under the linoleum. June's report card arrived; I received an "A" in algebra. Her faith in me, which incidentally was greater than what I felt in myself, taught me an important lesson not only in algebra but in life. Always work harder and never give up was my pattern from thereon.

Find this paper's thesis. Does the paper illustrate that thesis?

Flo Seefeldt was a returning student when she wrote this fine tribute to her warm but demanding teacher in a segregated, two-room school house in Mississippi that had limited books, supplies, and equipment. An employee of the University of Wisconsin—Milwaukee for more than twenty-five years, Flo began as a custodian, moved on to clerical work, and then into various administrative and advising positions. She eventually wore several hats in the Department of Enrollment Services, where among other things she created a program to motivate pre-high-school students to prepare for college. As Flo sees it, a major purpose of the program is to "give our children a sense of consciousness for self-discipline" to help them succeed. That sounds like a message Flo may have learned from her teacher at Davis Hill #2 School.

My Best Teacher
Flo Seefeldt

Mary Alice Wilkinson was the best teacher I ever had. She taught grades six through eight at Davis Hill #2 school in Clinton, Mississippi.

Mrs. Wilkinson was a very thin black woman—you could even call her skinny. She had big legs and they were unusually bowed. She was about five feet three inches tall with a large pair of feet. I remember how men used to talk about her legs and how good they looked. Then they would add, "Boy does she have big feet. They look like boat paddles." She was about twenty-four years old when I had her as a teacher. She was a smart dresser—she looked like a model every day. She had the nicest personality of any teacher I have ever had. Mrs. Wilkinson had a soft, pleasant voice and always had a big smile when she talked with you. When I started at Davis Hill School I was in the fourth grade. Mrs. Wilkinson was my teacher from the sixth through the eighth grades.

Mrs. Wilkinson stressed learning. She said, "Learning is what you come here for. Don't waste your time coming to school if you are not interested in learning. To learn you must listen and ask questions. If you don't ask questions I can't help you because I don't know what you are not understanding. I can talk all day, but if you don't understand what I am saying, it is not helping you, and I am here to help you."

She was a good teacher and made you conscious of yourself and others. I remember many things she taught me. Once she spent two days teaching me a lesson about stealing. It was during Christmas time. We brought our new things to school that "Santa Claus" had given us for Christmas. Christmas was a time when we got fruit, and every day afterwards for awhile children brought an apple or orange for lunch. I came from a big family, which means our fruit did not last as long as that of some small families. One day I stole an apple. When asked about it I lied and said it was mine. All I can say is the teacher knew all the time I was not telling the truth, but she never let me know until later—two days later, to be exact.

The very day I took the apple, the new cap I got for Christmas disappeared. Every child in school denied even seeing the cap, but it was gone. I felt so hurt I was sick, having to go home without my new cap. Two days later I was still feeling just as badly. When time came to go home, Mrs. Wilkinson asked me to stay after school. She wanted to talk with me. She knew I needed to learn a lesson about stealing. She had taken my new cap and hidden it for two days. I was feeling at my worst about someone stealing my cap, my new cap. I stayed after school and this is how she put it, "Do you remember taking Joe's apple and not being honest about it?" I started to cry. She said, "Don't cry, I want you to learn something from this. No matter how badly I feel for you, I can never feel as badly for you as you feel for yourself, and you can never feel as badly for anyone as they may feel for themselves. Do you understand what I mean?" Then she continued to explain that the day I took the apple and lied, Joe too had cried, because he was hurt over someone taking his lunch and had felt just as badly as I had. She said, "When you take something that belongs to another person without asking, you hurt them, just as you are hurting now. So remember this feeling." She gave me my cap, kissed me on my tear-wet cheek, and said, "Let this be a learning experience for you." This was a good learning experience for me, and I will never forget the precious time she took to teach me, "Thou shalt not steal."

Mrs. Wilkinson spent many hours after school tutoring children and encouraging them to read, and to help others learn to read. She wanted students to teach others what they knew. She called it "keeping the learning going." If a student was a slow learner, she would stay after school to help him/her. She was interested in the way we could read, write, talk, and count—also in what she would call "social conduct and appearance." She believed a whole person was one who did the best he/she could with everything. The way she put it, "The way you treat each other should be your best!"

She took our class on trips to visit the capitol building when we were studying history, and took us to different cities and their zoos when we were studying geography. She helped us to write about these trips, and sometimes we got silver dollars for the best story. Many of the community people used to have fund-raising events to repay Mrs. Wilkinson for monies she spent taking us on educational trips, buying us books, and also sometimes buying clothes for children whose parents couldn't afford to buy them. Most of us kids thought she was rich, but our parents knew better. They said she spent all the money she earned teaching us kids on us kids and was working for free.

Mrs. Wilkinson is still teaching. I hear about her through friends and relatives who still live in Mississippi.

Observe that Flo used both descriptive and narrative strategies, as well as a nice sprinkling of dialogue, to draw her portrait of Mrs. Wilkinson. Flo's paper again demonstrates that writers often combine strategies in their works.

Exercise

In your journal, write your responses to the following questions.

1. What are the writing strategies used by each author to show, rather than tell, the reader what each teacher was like?
2. Make a chart listing the similarities and differences between these two teachers. (For models and suggestions on drawing up charts comparing two people, see Chapter 11.)
3. Make a list of adjectives, or modifiers (descriptive words like *demanding*) that apply to both of these teachers.
4. Think about good teachers that you have had. Does your list suggest certain qualities that would characterize most good teachers?

Like the authors of the previous essays, Scarlett Nelson uses both descriptive and narrative strategies in her striking piece. A returning student at the university, Nelson faced a sudden change in her financial situation in the middle of the semester. Rather than give up her dream of becoming a journalist, Nelson reluctantly opted for a new occupation, a choice vividly and movingly described in this essay. Note how the title arouses interest, one of several functions that a title can perform.

The Birth of Scarlett
Scarlett Nelson

In the early part of October last year, my fourteen year old son and I moved into a duplex. I also took in a friend as a roommate as I could not afford the rent by myself. A month later, my three year divorce battle was over. I had acquired the freedom that I had fought so hard to achieve, but at an astronomical price.

In January, I started U.W.M. bound and determined to get the education I had relinquished earlier for marriage and a family. A few weeks later, loss of a job forced my roommate to move out. Also, I found that my financial aid for school was cut in half because I was attending only half time. Meanwhile, the bills were coming in, the pressure was mounting, and the only income I had was county aid for me and my son which didn't even cover the rent. So out of desperation and motivation, I dusted off my high heel shoes, swallowed my pride (what I had left of it) and headed downtown.

I had seen several ads in the newspaper looking for exotic dancers. I had never done that kind of work before, though I could hold my own on a dance floor at a night club. Instinct led me to believe that the money one could earn would be fast and easy. So I entered one of the establishments to audition. It wasn't very crowded, but there were enough customers to unnerve me. After talking briefly with the owner, I went into the bathroom to change into my bikini swimsuit. I looked in the mirror as I peeled back the plastic from a bandaid that I would apply to my breasts for the moment when I would remove my top. A tear trickled down her face over a pained expression. I had come to love many things about this woman: her ability to smile in the face of adversity, and her determination to survive.

As I wobbled in my high heels towards the jukebox, many thoughts ran through my mind. Can I really pull this off? Will anyone recognize me? I stepped up onto the stage. The first song of my selection began to play and I started to dance. Before I knew it, I was smiling and spinning around as if I were in my living room. This was no big deal to anyone but me. I heard a customer say, "Nice legs." "Good!" I thought. "If they're only looking at my legs, maybe they won't notice the rest of me." As my second selection started, perspiration was beading on my forehead. The lights above the stage were hot and reflected brightly into the mirrors behind me. Colors of red, yellow and blue were often blinding as they pierced the corners of my eyes. "God help me through this," I whispered as I danced and spun across the stage to the other side. There sat a man holding out a single dollar bill. I quivered as I squatted down sideways with my hip facing him. As I gently pulled out the side of my bikini bottom, he slipped it in against my skin. I smiled and said, "Thank you" as if I had been doing this all of my life. Song number three came on. This was the moment I dreaded as it was time now for me to remove my top. Consumed with instant fear, I scanned the audience for the owner's face. As my eyes met hers, I could feel that she knew my every thought. She smiled and nodded as if to say, "Go ahead." I turned to look into the mirror, maybe for courage or to just get a last glimpse at the woman I used to know. My left arm swung around my back and pulled the tie that held my top in place. In the blink of an eye, it was over. I was now dancing topless in front of complete strangers. My principles were compromised, and any previous concerns about women being exploited were dismissed. I kept in the back of my mind the reality of my financial status. Desperation now had a home.

I was hired that evening. My new temporary occupation was that of an exotic dancer. Wouldn't this look terrific on a resume? When I was asked what I wanted my "stage" name to be, I thought about it briefly and replied, "Scarlett." It was a name which represented tenacity to me because it was taken from the movie, *Gone With The Wind*. The main character, Scarlett O'Hara, had to overcome many adversities in her life. She was constantly challenged but she always rose above it. It was my intention to do the same.

To date, I am still dancing. However, the money I earn is not as abundant as when I started. I believe that to be the case because of economic factors. Every now and then I get a five dollar tip from a customer because of my smile, my legs, or my quick wit. My pride though shaken is still intact. I check my principles at the door of the establishment where I am employed whenever I enter, but I remain "Scarlett."

In contrast to some of the other student essays recalling people, David Chapman's introduction contains an explicit statement of his thesis, a summary of his father's qualities that he intends to discuss. Illustrating those qualities with many concrete examples, David's essay is very clearly organized and easy to follow, in part because of his skillful use of transitions. David's outline for his very structured paper follows the essay.

Dad, I'd Like to Be Like You
David Chapman

Under the definition of father, Webster writes, "Any man deserving respect or reverence." This assertion precisely characterizes a wonderful person I would like you to know. He is man who beams love and compassion, moral courage and strength. For me, his sense of self-sacrifice transcends all limits of mankind. I'd like to introduce you to: My Father.

Upon first inspection, you probably won't notice anything special about my father. He's six feet tall, or so he says. Actually, he's only five feet-eleven and three quarters, and weighs in at two hundred and ten pounds. There was more than one occasion that my father's size impressed me, usually when my mouth was moving faster than the rest of my faculties. He is also very distinguished looking. He has salt and pepper hair combed back over his baldness, eyeglasses that give him the look of a vintage professor, and magnificent crow's feet radiating from the corners of his eyes—wrinkles he attributes to smiling. That smile is only a clue to the generous man it adorns.

When we were younger, my father made many sacrifices. In some ways, we left him no choice; there were four children, and the money he made was thinly spread. He often told me it was spent before he earned it, and we took priority. I never remember being hungry, nor ever feeling threatened by hunger. Also, my dad made sure we had new clothes at the start of school each year. Being well clothed and fed usually meant it took a combined family effort to persuade him to purchase something for himself. He refused to replace worn out clothing, and always brown-bagged his lunch. Once he was angry with my mother when she came home with a short-wave radio he had expressed an interest in, but said he couldn't afford.

The one thing my father sacrificed the most of was his time. No matter how exhausted he was from his labors, or how immersed he was in fixing the car, he always made time for his children. Every night, after dinner, he would lie on the living room floor and challenge us to roll him over. We rarely lost; we were confident the odds were in our favor. Our prize, of course, was our deep sense of accomplishment, coupled with a bed-time snack consisting of popcorn, occasionally ice cream, and, if we were lucky, pizza!

More than anything else I remember the principles he tried to instill in us. Honesty and sharing were the most painful of these lessons. One Christmas, when I was eleven or twelve, I shoplifted a very expensive men's cologne. Justifying this daring act was easy; it was a gift for my father. He opened his present that magical morning and exclaimed, "Oh, what a wonderful gift! I'm so proud of you, son. You must have saved all year to buy this for me. What kind of son would do such a thing?" Needless to say, I've never stolen since.

On an earlier Christmas, I was particularly obstinate. I refused to share my new electric train with my younger brother. My father was of the opinion that if I couldn't share it, I didn't deserve it. So he put away all my gifts supposedly until the next Christmas. My presents were returned to me in February on my birthday—on time bought back for "good behavior."

His tough discipline was a testimonial to his love and compassion. However if it became necessary to take corrective action, the pain of doing so could be seen in his eyes. Though this was obvious, he would remain steadfast in his decisions just the same. Once I committed a major breach of household policy, just three days before junior high school basketball play-offs. I was a starting guard, and this game meant as much to me as it did to him: he had been an All-City center in high school, and was very proud of his son. Thus, when it came time to reward me for my transgression, it was not easy for him. I was grounded for one week with no basketball. The punishment was severe, but I knew I deserved it. The morning of the game he asked me if I felt he was being too hard on me. I told him no, that I had it coming. "Besides," I said, "if you let me play now, the others will think they can break the rules, too." My father came home from work that night with a new basketball, and we spent the evening together running through plays for the next game.

Unfortunately, I didn't come to fully appreciate what type of man my father was until the day he called me in to tell me he was going to

> die. He discussed with me his special concerns about each of his children, and bestowed me, the eldest, with their charge in the event something should happen to my mother. He also went through the steps of what I should do when he left. He knew my mother well enough. She is not a very strong person, and she would be too upset with grief to help. He asked me to promise to be strong and firm, to call the necessary people, and to be an island of stability the family could cling to.
>
> For what seemed to be an eternity, we remained silent after his lecture, gazing into one another's eyes. Years of my life unfolded then, reliving all those memories I knew would last a lifetime. Many of the things we wanted to say, though they were unspoken, were not fully understood. I told him I respected him, and more than that, that I loved him, especially for all the times he made me feel I hated him. I told him about the time I caught him, slightly inebriated, having butt races down the stairs with my sister, and we began to cry. "Cry now, son," I remember him saying, "for in a few days you'll truly become a man."
>
> My father passed away two days later, and after I fulfilled my promise, I wept at the world's loss of a fine human being. I wept because I found what it meant to love, to be brave, to be strong. His principles direct my life to this day, and I'll be indebted to his sacrifice forever.

Most of the writing you will be doing in college and the workplace is called expository writing. As the name suggests, **expository writing** presents, or exposes, information in a clear, organized fashion so that readers can understand it. The purpose for presenting such information varies: Expository writers may seek to amuse, persuade, explain, or otherwise inform their audiences.

Like David Chapman, author of the previous theme, expository writers often include a **thesis statement,** which predicts the contents early in an essay, often, but not necessarily, in the first paragraph. Your instructors may require you to include a thesis statement in your introductory paragraph. This forecasting statement does not have to be a single sentence. (For more information on theses and introductions, see pages 30 to 39.) Be on the lookout for the thesis and pay special heed to each writer's organizational scheme as you analyze the remaining essays in this section.

By now you may be wondering whether the essays included as models were written mostly by A or B+ students. Actually, that is not the case. Most of these essays reflect many drafts and much revision, and several of them were written by students who did average work in the bulk of their writing. These pieces stood out from the rest of their essays because they found their voice and wrote on a topic that they cared enough about to put forth their best effort. The same can be said about the student essays on *special places* that follow.

Student Essays on Special Places

Exercise

Write a descriptive essay about a place you remember very well, a place rich in personal significance and remembered feelings. As you present this place on paper using lots of sensory description and vivid, concrete images, let your readers know how this place was, or is, significant in your life. The place could be a specific spot, such as a cabin on a lake or your grandmother's kitchen, or it could be a general kind of place, such as a soccer field or a dance floor.

What *sights*, *smells*, *sounds*, *tastes*, and *surfaces* will help your readers to grasp what you want to convey about that place? Call upon images that appeal to as many of the five senses as possible to paint a word picture of your special place.

When appropriate, add descriptions of motion: Are motorboats roaring past or birds flying overhead? What do those birds look like? Describe their motion in flight. Be sure that your description has a sense of unity and purpose and that it conveys a dominant impression. Let your readers understand how the place was (or is) significant in your life.

For topic ideas, read the following student essays about special places.

In the following essay, Jeffrey Schwigel recalls how bulldozers demolished the field he so lovingly recalls in this splendid descriptive essay about a childhood sanctuary. Below is the clustering he did before beginning to write.

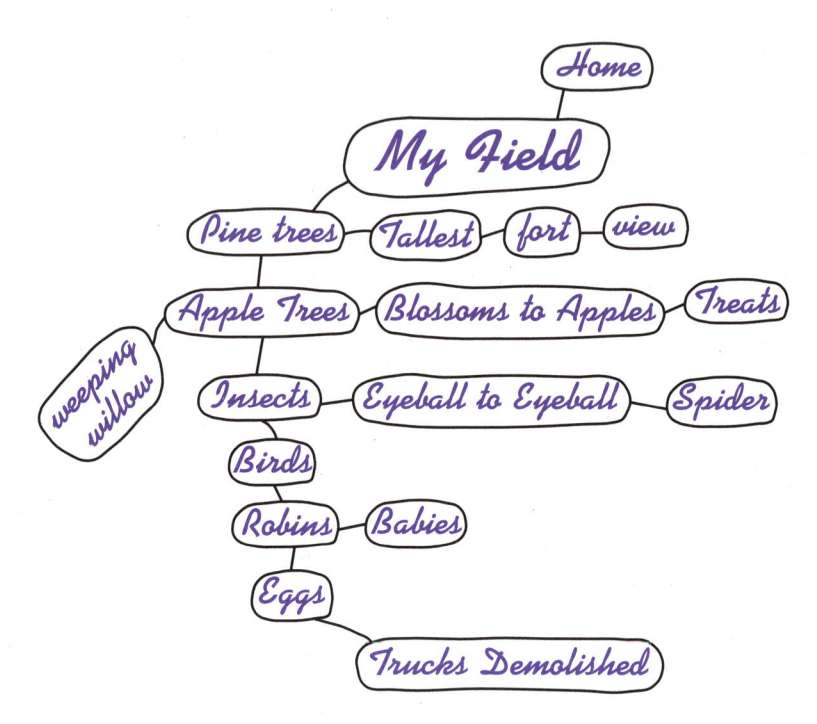

Clumpings for "In a World of My Own"

In a World of My Own
Jeffrey Schwigel

Now that I have started college, with its confusing lectures, demanding quizzes, and constantly increasing mounds of homework, my mind yearns for sanctuary. My thoughts drift back in time, wandering back to my childhood and the field behind the house where I grew up. This field was my favorite place: a world of wonder and imagination to me.

Spring was my favorite time in the field. As the snow and ice of winter faded away, the trees and wild flowers throbbed back to life, offering a beautiful display of colors, seemingly a full spectrum of blues, pinks, purples, and greens. The aroma of the wild flowers clung in the air, thick as the sap of the pine trees. As spring inched on, the cluster of apple trees started to blossom. They appeared as fluffy, pink clouds nestled on the branches of the trees, like cones of flavored whipped cream. I knew that the blossoms would vanish soon, and the trees would give way to young apples, which would grow and ripen, before getting picked and becoming the treats that we got each fall, like the sweetest of apple pies, lip smacking jellies, and my favorite, double dunked caramel apples.

On the side of the field farthest from my house, a group of pine trees lined up at attention. The scents from these trees hung in the air, as if a halo of odor encircled them. And in the middle of the thicket stood the tallest of the pine trees; this tree stretched skyward, making me dizzy if I dared to glance at its peak. When the wind whisked through the pine trees, they swayed from side-to-side as if they were chanting. I felt safest grasped in the branches of the tallest tree when the wind came drifting through, and because of the encompassing view offered by its height, it was in this tree I would place my fort.

Scrap wood made its floor, and the fort's walls were no more than fallen branches tied together with selected pieces of mom's clothesline *(though till this day she still doesn't know that I am the culprit responsible for stealing the rope)*. Although this tree top castle wasn't much, to me it was super, for this was my fortress in the midst of the forest—a home away from home, allowing imagination free range.

I would spend hours and hours up in my fort watching the monarch butterflies glide from place to place. They seemed to fly in slow motion with their over-sized wings. I wondered how they could land on the flimsiest flowers and never bend a petal.

The birds happily sang songs all day long, as they constantly worked on their nests. The robins here were abundant; they walked so proudly with their puffed out, banner bright chests. Four of them liked my fort so much that they built nests in it, one in one corner, one in the other. It never bothered me that they were there. However, their presence did take some getting used to, especially after some eggs appeared. My presence never bothered them, not even when the eggs hatched and all five babies were around. I enjoyed the company, even though I had to watch every move I made so I wouldn't step on the chicks. I named the mother robins, the biggest one Jay, and other Chirp. I would talk to them, as if they understood what I was saying. They would perch on the branches right next to me, never flinching when I moved. At times when all the babies would be singing out for food at the same time, I would close my eyes and just listen. They seemed to sing in harmony, in tones you could almost put words to. The birds fascinated me, and I spent many hours watching them. The field offered many things to challenge my six year old mind, and it was never boring.

One day while I was just browsing through the field, I tripped on a mound of dirt and fell face down into a pricker bush. I hated pricker bushes: they are so deceiving with their pretty purple flowers, and tingling smells, tempting you to grab a bunch to take home to mom, then sticking you with a handful of needles. After regaining my composure from the fall, and in a fit of anger, I decided that the mound I tripped over should be demolished. So with stick in hand I started knocking it down. To my amazement, this mound was home to a bunch of those yellow striped stinging critters called bees. Surprise, surprise, the run of my life was on. It wasn't too bad though. I got away after being stung only three times.

Needing something a little calmer than racing with bees, I decided to try critter hunting. Slithering through the chest high grass, pushing through the bushes on my stomach like a worm, eyes in search of some ground dwelling insects, I came eyeball to eyeball with the most hideous looking thing I had ever seen. Too scared to move, fearing I would be attacked, I lay there wondering: What is this horrid looking thing? It appeared to have fangs, and jaws like a catfish; its eyes were like marbles standing up off its head, blacker than night. As I squirmed away, the monster I had envisioned seemed to come into better focus; I had to laugh at myself when I realized that my imagination had scared me again, for my terrible foe was no more than a huge, ugly garden spider.

My favorite thing about my field was that it let me be me; there were no rules. Although I was never more than a shout from my house, it seemed a whole world away to me. I could be a pioneer, exploring new and vast terrain; or a jungle man in the trees, Tarzan lord of the jungle. I could be whoever my childish thoughts let me become, and go wherever my imagination allowed me to venture.

By the end of August the days started getting shorter, the apples were almost ripe, and the birds less active. I knew what was coming, and it came. A few short weeks later, the apple trees gave way to my shaking their branches, dropping their crop all over the ground. Some had already fallen on their own, but they were always soft, had plenty of worm holes, and always attracted those pesty yellow jackets. The leaves too were changing colors, adding beauty to the speeding changes of the season. Before long the leaves too were dropping to the ground like a blizzard of dry crumbled paper. The birds were rapidly disappearing now, and soon all that was left were a few small winter swallows.

As quietly as spring had led into summer, fall gave in to the snowy winter. As I looked out my bedroom window, I watched as a glistening white sheet covered up my dried out field. Impatiently I waited for spring to renew life to my field. I lay in bed wondering if my robin friends would return, and if we would spend another season together watching their babies grow up in my fort.

It has been many years since I have wandered through my field, which has long since been torn up. I remember watching as huge machines ripped down the trees and plow blades leveled the rolling hills. I can still recall the pain as I watched the men and their machines tear up my field, just to give rise to houses and driveways.

My sister Sue still lives in the house where my family grew up, and once in awhile when I stop to visit her and her family, I stroll through the backyard and look off into the distance at the huge pine trees that made up a part of my field. My big pine tree is still standing, though it is now in someone's backyard. One of the boards from my fort can still be seen nailed up high in its branches. Seeing that tree and board makes it somewhat easy to reflect back in time, yet I feel a ping deep within my stomach. It makes me think about the years gone by. Though it makes me sad to see that tree and the remainder of my fort, and not be able to climb it, I can always rejoice in the wonderful memories God has allowed me to store in my mind.

Gilbert Garcia's wonderfully warm and perceptive recollection of boyhood adventures in a strip of woodlands on the south side of Milwaukee won third prize in the University of Wisconsin—Milwaukee's freshman composition contest.

Adventures of the KK Trails
Gilbert Garcia

Located six blocks from my house is a stretch of trees no more than a mile long. To every busy-body drone of a person that's exactly what it is, but to me and the kids of my neighborhood that forest is a whole different world. There is more than just trees in there, our childhood is hidden amongst those branches, leaves, and grass. It is known by most adults as the KK Parkway, named for the street that runs right through the middle.

But more importantly to anyone born into the neighborhood after 1973 it has come to be known as the KK Trails, named for the hundreds of intricate maze-like trails that were created as a couple of friends and I tramped our way through the woods each and every day of our youthful summers. And at the end of each trail is its own pot of gold waiting to be discovered.

Hundreds of people probably drive through the parkway each day thinking of it as nothing more than a fast way home, a way of avoiding the hectic traffic of the "grown up" world, not even aware of the lifetime of pirate adventures, wars, and games of hide-n-seek that had gone on in these magical woods. At the time we thought we were never going to grow up, and quite frankly we didn't care.

What little did I know. Before I knew it, the trails were nothing but a memory. My days soon turned from frolicking in the grass to the malls, the movies, and a car. I had committed the biggest sin conceivable, the sin which we all swore never to commit: **growing up!**

I had turned my back on my own personal wonderland, the place where time didn't exist, except when the street lights came on, and we all knew we had better get home. This was the place where I had received my first kiss, the place I would go whenever my parents were fighting, the place where Steve Graham fell out of a tree and broke his leg, and Dan Nabroski carried him eight blocks all the way to his house. That's the kind of friends we were and the trails' magic just seemed to pull us together all the more.

I haven't stepped foot in the woods for almost six years now, not for any reason other than fear that I won't be allowed to enter, that some sort of invisible barrier will keep me from leaving all the worries of the "grown up" world and remembering how it feels not to have a care in the world, to be a kid. Is this my punishment for forgetting this mystical place? Or maybe I'm just kidding myself, maybe I'm just afraid that the magic itself will be gone, that it was nothing more than a bunch of trees, a place to keep us kids out of our parents' hair for awhile.

Yet no matter what is actually the case, I will always have the memories. Like when my friends and I would spend hours in a big oak tree that we call "BIG DADDY," just talking and talking. Or when we would race our bikes around a dirt track that we had created. Another wonderful memory I'll never forget is the day we set out to engrave our initials on every single tree, but about twenty minutes into it, we somehow ended up in a

> game of tag. That was the beauty of it: we were free to do whatever we wanted. To pick our noses, to scream, yell, play in the dirt—do anything, anything we wanted.
>
> I realized something the other day, that the magic isn't gone: you can't stop it, catch it, see it, or even destroy it. You can only let it have its way with you. I realized this when my little brother came up to me and asked me if I had ever heard of the KK Trails. Then I knew the magic isn't gone; it's only someone else's turn for the magic to have its way with them, to be taught about the wonders of childhood, in that stretch of trees six blocks from my house.

James Airoldi's essay catches the motion and essence of mogul skiing in a unique way. Perhaps you too can capture the motion and appeal of a sport or other activity that engages your whole being, and share it with your readers.

> ### Mt. Heaven
> ### James Airoldi
>
> By early afternoon the storm had moved east, leaving a deep blue sky and air so clean it was intoxicating. Those of us lucky enough to be on the mountain that day skied soft-packed powder until the lifts closed, timing it just right to get the last ride up. But even that wasn't enough. Without a word spoken, it was obvious that many of the same skiers would be there again the next morning to take the first chair up.
>
> The sun arrived on spears of light darting over distance ridges, while a thick blanket of cold air clung to the still-shadowed valley floor. I walked to the lifts, trailing plumes of vapor from my breath. Boots crunched noisily over the frozen snow, and skis newly waxed, rested comfortably on my well-insulated shoulder.
>
> Conversations with my friends were short and muffled. The clicks and chunks of bindings engaging ski boots coincided with the sounds of the lift straining to move after a night of frozen stillness. My eyes glanced high up the mountain toward steep slopes already gleaming in bright sun, the trees still white with yesterday's snow. The sense of anticipation was so tangible it seemed to hum in the air like high-voltage power lines.
>
> As the ski lift chair fought hard to cut its way through the cold wind, salty tears ran from my eyes past chapped lips into the dryness of my

mouth. Suddenly a smell that shouldn't have been there caught my attention. My friend had pulled out a wineskin filled with brandy, nectar of the gods. As he took a sip before passing it to me, I prepared myself for its invigorating effects. Tasting the sweetness of the liquor, I gazed across the wide expanse of the mountain and thought that if God lived on earth he would probably live here. With snow resting on the ground as well as on the out-stretched limbs of the evergreens, I couldn't, at the time, think of a more beautifully peaceful place in the world. To live here forever wouldn't be long enough.

I approached the start of my run slowly, carving gentle, long turns and feeling slightly anxious. I'd intended to stop and survey the mountain rather than just blindly plunging into it, but the snow was too perfect, and the moguls so round they looked like scoops of ice cream scattered down the mountain side. A line suddenly appeared before me through the maze of bumps, and my skis fell into it as if drawn by a magnet. The ski tips became blurs of motion. My legs and knees extended and contracted faster than I could think, yet my body floated motionlessly above them as if I were riding a roller coaster. My hands floated in front of me, tapping the snow with the ski poles, accompanying the rhythm dictated by the moguls.

Time seemed to have stopped, and I was alone in a pocket of exquisite motion. Voices and the sounds of the lift were muted, seemingly coming from miles away. There was only my concentration, the flashing skis, and the soft white trail I followed instinctively . . . .

To live here forever wouldn't be long enough.

Read through "Mt. Heaven" once more and find some of the most vivid descriptive images. How many of the five senses do those images appeal to? What simile aptly describes the moguls (bumps)? Can you find other similes or metaphors in the essay?

Tom Livesey brings to life the familiar scenes of another sport, this time from the viewpoint of a spectator rather than a participant.

Utopia
Tom Livesey

As my car door vacuumed shut, I inhaled deeply . . . and exhaled. Ah, this is what summer is all about. The fresh air, warm sun, family and friends, the sizzle of the family meal cooking on the grill. The crackled voice of an announcer, and a concession worker marketing his pennants and caps at the top of his lungs. Yes, this is what summer is all about . . . BASEBALL.

The long walk on searing asphalt to gate forty-two began. I felt like a child playing "hooky" from school; my stomach was tense, but a good tense. The thought of work and calling in sick frequented my thoughts to remind me that I was not really sick, and then disappeared.

The thrill of a professional baseball game brings euphoria to me; I feel like a twenty-four year old going on twelve. With the home team's cap on my head and a huge sack of salted peanuts under my arm, I seem to forget how far I have to walk as I maneuver through armies of cars that look like troops in formation. I cannot help but enjoy the wonderful odors. Almost every automobile's owner has a group around it, cooking delicacies on a small grill; laughter and music fill the air. Walking briskly and trying to look at everything around me that day I accidentally bumped into a young woman, making her spill her beer. The young woman and I both looked down as the full cup of liquid spilled from the cup onto the hot asphalt. As the steam rose from the hot surface, the young woman began to laugh, apologized to me, then walked away. I looked away from the woman in disbelief, knowing the accident was my fault. Then I saw it: gate forty-two, the ticket sales window.

It just so happened I was the only one in line. I walked up to the scratched Plexiglas window and peered through the circular opening. An older man asked, "Can I help you?"

"Yes sir, I would like one ticket, lower box, first base line."

"That will be $18.00, please."

I reached into the pocket of my faded blue-jean shorts to pull out a wrinkled, but crisp twenty dollar bill, and handed it to the man cheerfully. "I'll be back with your change in just a minute." As I waited for the man, I could feel a cool breeze coming from the old air conditioning unit in his office. The air conditioner was leaking and made a large puddle next to where I was standing. The cool breeze felt good. I folded my arms and rested against the stainless steel counter of the ticket office. The counter was cold, but refreshing. The long walk had fatigued me.

"Here's your change, son, enjoy the game."

I was startled when the man spoke; I had almost dozed off. As I turned around I saw that a group had formed behind me. I could not help but think again how lucky I was to have bought my ticket when I did.

I looked at my watch and noticed it was only fifteen minutes until game time so I decided to go in and try and find my seat. What a crowd! People were everywhere. People talking and concession workers yelling made the inside of the stadium echo. "Programs here! Get your programs here!" The familiar hub-bub caught my attention. I walked over and handed a tall, lanky man dressed in red, white and blue a five dollar bill. He gave me my program, saying: "Thank you," in a deep voice, which was nothing like his sales voice.

I walked away ready for a long "trek" to find my seat, but it just so happened I was actually in the right section. I could not believe it; it was like I was dreaming; everything seemed to be going so well. I walked up the long cement runway into the stadium. When I reached the opening I felt the adrenaline in my body surge. I looked at the beautiful field—the colors were so true. The clay on the playing field looked as smooth as silk and undisturbed. I walked towards the home team's dugout to find my seat with no problem. I pushed the newly red painted seat down and wiped away some water from rain that had fallen earlier that day. I sat down and absorbed everything around me, the people, the sounds, colors, everything. I felt like I was the luckiest man on earth.

Then a voice engulfed the entire stadium asking everyone to rise for the singing of the national anthem. I stood up, removing my cap, and watched Ole' Glory shimmering in the summer breeze while I, and everyone around me, sang. The announcer began calling the names of the players and their positions. As the players took their positions, I sipped my soda pop. The cold drink soothed my dry throat. As the game went on, the day turned into twilight and then turned into night. The night was perfect: stars dotted the sky and there was a soft, cool southerly breeze that gave my sun burned arms "goose bumps." My seat was so close to the playing field that I could hear the "smack" of a fastball hitting the catcher's mitt. I could hear players rooting each other on, much like I did when I was a kid.

Sitting this close to the playing field helps me realize this game is still the same one that I have played for so many years as a boy, teenager, and now as a young man. As a boy and teenager, to me playing ball meant long, but enjoyable, spring and summer days, chewing bubble gum and batting like my favorite player. It brings back the friends I once had, riding our bikes in large groups, baseball gloves dangling from

> handle bars, a bat balanced in one hand. Staring at a player who is only two years older than me, I stop to wonder, "Does he have the same memories as I do? Does he long for the warm summer days of playing ball until you just can't see the ball anymore, or has the business side taken over the memories?" But then my mind and thoughts come back to the game.
>
> This truly is "Utopia," at least for me. All the wonders of life come alive at a baseball game. It truly is the perfect creation.

Which of the techniques of effective description does Tom Livesey use to bring this familiar experience to life? Which of the five senses does he appeal to in his essay?

Exploring and Developing a Topic: The Early Stages

To find ideas for a topic, review the essays in this chapter that recall places and people. Pay special attention to the cluster diagram, or clumping, that Jeffrey Schwigel used for his essay (page 314).

On the other hand, these student essays may have suggested the perfect topic choice for you. If so, write that topic in a circle on a blank page of your journal and make a cluster diagram around it. You may prefer to jot down points in a kind of informal listing, or outline. That is another good way to get started: simply write the topic, such as "My Aunt Sal," at the top of a page.

If you are still undecided about a topic, write and circle the word *places* on one blank page of your journal and the word *persons* on another. Then jot down all of the special places or persons that seem promising for a descriptive essay. Narrow down your choice to one or two, and do some clumping about those topics. Select the one that seems the most interesting for some additional prewriting.

In any case, always write down as many points as you can to help make that place or person come to life on paper. Points that do not add to the essay's effectiveness can always be discarded later. Remember, your audience is made up of readers who do not know that person or place in the same way you do.

Exercise

Form small groups. Have half of your group members make a list detailing everything they observe in this photo. Have the other group members make a cluster design about the photo. Put the words *old-fashioned room* in the center of the clumping. When finished, compare the points listed by the two subgroups.

Making an Informal Listing

Suppose that you decide to describe your aunt's house in a small town in Georgia. Close your eyes and imagine the house, then make a list of what you recall from your visits there. The list might begin something like this:

   sidewalk
   front yard
   driveway
   porch
   the house itself
   inside the house—my favorite spot?
   attic

Next, fill in descriptive details for the items on the list.

sidewalk—grass growing between bricks; toy bikes and wagons strewn about
front yard—trees (what kind? how many?)
   —tire swing in the maple tree

As you fill in the details, you may decide that you have far too many for a focused description. Try to remember what made that house important to you. What pieces of furniture or other items were special? What did you like to do in that house? Suppose it suddenly occurs to you that the really special adventures occurred when you and your cousin (name? age? etc.) went up into the attic. Maybe the attic would be a good topic. Make a list of *everything* you recall about the attic. The listing might look something like this:

attic—entered by a ladder pulled out of the hall ceiling
   —looking around to see if we would get caught going up there
box of old toys—give details
a small chest of letters—give details

You can always discard points while revising your essay, so it is best to include everything at first. And, of course, many additional ideas should occur to you throughout the writing process.

Using your cluster diagram or informal listing as a guide, freewrite on your topic in your journal. Without worrying about organization, syntax, or grammar, write down everything you can recall about that person or place. You can use your cluster diagram and freewriting as mines for a more organized first draft of a theme about the topic. Make another rough outline of the subtopics you might want to include in the draft, such as "my Aunt Sal's dramatic wardrobe and hairstyle," to help you organize the essay.

You may be one of those writers who needs to write an exploratory draft as the initial stage of the prewriting process. That's another good way to begin as long as you regard all forms of prewriting as material to be revised, shared with other writers, and revised again.

As you develop and revise your essay, refer often to the student essays and the guidelines preceding them in this chapter.

Should your prewriting lead you to the conclusion that your topic choice is not a good one, repeat the above process to find another one. Another option would be to confer with a tutor, instructor, or fellow student about your prewriting, asking for ideas about ways you might approach and better develop your topic. Often a topic is an excellent one; it only requires an outside eye asking the right questions to help a writer develop it effectively.

Shaping the Contents: Focusing on a Dominant Impression

Whether you decide to describe a person or a place, the techniques for writing the description are similar. In either case, the subtopics and details being recorded in your freewriting should eventually point you toward an overall focus, toward a dominant impression that will give unity and purpose to your descriptive essay.

Do you want your readers to visualize a terrifying place, a comfortable room, a unique campground, a nurturing relative, a dictatorial coach, or an unfair boss? Note that all these overall impressions still lack specificity and are likely to raise many questions in a reader's mind. What did your boss at the frozen custard stand *do* that was so unfair? Show, rather than tell. The reader needs several clear anecdotes or illustrations ("for instances") of your boss' unfair actions to believe the claim. Show the reader what you mean with concrete examples. Exactly how did the boss play favorites? Did certain employees always get special breaks such as the desirable hours? How did the boss talk to some, but not all, of the employees: rudely, loudly, sarcastically?

Did your boss bellow, snarl, or swear at you and the other employees in front of customers? Use strong verbs and dialogue to convey exactly what was said during one of those humiliating encounters. Add to your portrayal with a description of the boss' appearance during one of those ranting sessions. In such a situation, appearance and actions often complement each other. What about movement? Did he stomp around or wave his hands in the air? Paint a portrait with words.

The phrase "a comfortable room" is equally vague. The reader instantly wonders what makes it comfortable. Name the room—my grandmother's kitchen—and locate it—"in a log farmhouse on a muddy little creek in southern Mississippi." Add details so that your readers can depict her kitchen in their minds. What sensory impressions—smells, surfaces, tastes, sights, sounds—best convey the dominant atmosphere in that homey room? What time of day or season of the year was your favorite in that kitchen? Why? Describe some of the movement that was so much a part of that special room.

I have a friend whose two cats regularly amble around on the kitchen counter, stopping occasionally to lick out a bowl or sample the gravy, while Helen is cutting up garlic and stuffing a chicken. Cats are okay with me (I am not a true cat lover), but as the cliché has it, "only in their place" which for me is *not* the kitchen counter. Why am I writing all of this? Because cats and the Gerhardstein kitchen go together, and a description of that kitchen without the cats would be more drab and less telling. Come to think of it, I *might* even miss the cats if the counter were declared off-limits to them.

On the other hand, the routine that goes on in any kitchen is so marvelously depicted by Truman Capote in *A Christmas Memory* that it is no longer mundane.

The black stove, stoked with coal and firewood, glows like a lighted pumpkin. Eggbeaters whirl, spoons spin round in bowls of butter and sugar, vanilla sweetens the air, ginger spices it; melting, nose-tingling odors saturate the kitchen, suffuse the house, drift out to the world on puffs of chimney smoke. In four days our work is done. Thirty-one cakes, dampened with whiskey, bask on window sills and shelves.

Capote's brilliant literary images also transform an equally mundane activity, counting money, into a gem of descriptive writing.

Silently, wallowing in the pleasures of conspiracy, we take the bead purse from its secret place and spill its contents on the scrap quilt. Dollar bills, tightly rolled and green as May buds. Somber fifty-cent pieces, heavy enough to weight a dead man's eyes. Lovely dimes, the liveliest coin, the one that really jingles. Nickels and quarters, worn smooth as creek pebbles. But mostly a hateful heap of bitter-odored pennies. Last summer others in the house contracted to pay us a penny for every twenty-five flies we killed. Oh, the carnage of August: the flies that flew to heaven! Yet it was not work in which we took pride. And, as we sit counting pennies, it is as though we were back tabulating dead flies.

Exercise

In your journal, describe an activity that you perform routinely, using strong verbs and literary images. Very likely you will soon discover that an overall chronological organization best suits this description, as you are writing about a routine. Within that overall chronology, however, spatial organization may work best for certain parts of the piece.

Organizing a Description

Your descriptive essay will undoubtedly rely on more than one type of organization. Spatial organization will probably work well for more or less purely descriptive sections. If some of your illustrations are narratives, chronological organization would be more appropriate.

Look at the organizational schemes of some of the student essays in this chapter for ideas. Also look at the suggestions in Chapter 11 for picking subtopics and planning the organization of a paper. As your descriptive essay evolves, regularly consult the student descriptions of people and places for additional ideas on making your description more effective. In addition, keep the following cautions in mind.

Avoiding Potential Pitfalls

Travel brochures have a generic quality: The same blurb could be attached to any number of similar settings all over the globe. Vacation spots frequently have tall swaying palm trees, multicolored beach umbrellas, cozy intimate cafés, deep, dark forests, or awesome snow-covered mountains. Undoubtedly you could add several items to this list. So could most of your readers, which is why they were hoping for something more interesting and original from you. They were looking for your voice, for your special insight. That is why you should be wary of simply writing a generic description of everyone's tropical island or mountain resort.

A similar trap awaits writers who describe the familiar highlights of a trip to Northern Wisconsin, Portugal, Las Vegas, or Washington, D.C. If your readers have not been to Washington, D.C., themselves, by now they have seen numerous photos of the Lincoln and Jefferson Memorials, the cherry blossoms, and the Capitol Dome. They have probably stayed at highrise hotels or motels with flower-lined driveways and have shopped in huge, crowded malls and tourist boutiques. They know that Las Vegas is in the middle of a desert and has many gambling casinos.

Another potential pitfall is writing a brief description of so many of the places visited on a trip that the reader is not left with a vivid picture of any of them.

> *The first morning we headed for Grandiose Mall where I picked up some souvenirs for . . . . Next it was lunch at a tiny Italian restaurant with comfy black leather booths and candles on every table. That evening we . . . . Then it was up at the crack of dawn the next morning for a fifty-five minute bus ride to the zoo.*

Speaking of bus or plane rides, it is almost always advisable to leave the trip to your destination out of a description. Bus trips tend to be longer than anticipated, noisy if the passengers are under twenty-five, and monotonous. If *you* think the trip was monotonous, why bore your readers by recounting it?

Instead, get right to the place you want to describe. Focus on your special place, be it a corner of your backyard, a favorite park, the top of a mountain, or a cabin in the northwoods. As you plan a description of your place, you may find it necessary to narrow your focus further. Reread Anne Moody's wonderfully graphic description of her childhood home for some ideas (page 137).

There is another "tender" trap of which you should be aware, "the Valentine essay." This writing product usually results when students are given an assignment to remember a person. Who is easier or more pleasant to recall, who is more often in one's thoughts than a boyfriend or girlfriend? As visions of the loved one's face swim in front of our eyes, all sorts of dreamy, generic descriptions seep onto the page: "She has legs that *just won't quit*." "He has the broadest shoulders I've *ever seen*." "His dimples make his face *so cute*." I may be cynical, but these ooey-gooey phrases always remind me of the old joke: "Her teeth are like *stars* . . . they come out at night." Cupid's darts have a tendency to make us all a little weak at the knees; just don't let them make you weak in the head as well.

Remember, there is a fine line between sentiment, or true feelings, and sentimentality, or exaggerated and overstated feelings. Be aware that while your audience is happy to learn that your beloved is attractive, you invite your readers' skepticism when you claim that he or she is the god or goddess of beauty incarnate. Love is notoriously poorsighted: Who hasn't been introduced to the "perfect date" of some smitten friend and found the object of that affection to be more of a shipwreck than a dreamboat? To be an effective writer, it is your job to find a satisfactory answer to the age-old, mystifying question: "What does she see in *him*?" Take two steps back and tell your reader what it is that makes your loved one so special and dear to you. Describe the cover of the book—the person's looks—if you must, but concentrate largely on describing the content of the book—the person's character.

Be *specific* about that character; airy phrases, or clichés, like "He is always there for me" are not nearly as convincing to your audience as concrete examples: "I'll never forget the time he drove out to Walgreen's in a snowstorm at 3 A.M. to buy me Tylenol and cough drops. I told him not to, but he went anyway." That type of devotion *is* something a reader can appreciate and admire; you might convince your readers that love is not so blind after all.

Chapter Eleven

Comparing and Contrasting

Do any of the examples below suggest a comparison or contrast topic that you might like to explore?

Loquacious Aunt Miranda and taciturn Uncle Ross
Classical guitar versus jazz guitar
My old neighborhood then and now
Two stereos or cars or diseases or dogs
Jogging versus swimming
My old and my new neighborhoods
Cross-country or downhill skiing
Me ten years ago and today

As you consider possible topics for a comparison essay, you will probably realize that including lots of description and analysis in your paper will help you make your points clear to your audience. Likewise, if you decide to compare two friends, relatives, or teachers, you would want to incorporate well-selected short narratives, or anecdotes, to show your readers how these people act. Should you choose to demonstrate that one item being compared was preferable to, or less desirable than, the other, argumentative strategies would be essential. While effective comparisons utilize various other writing strategies discussed in this text, they also have several characteristics of their own.

To *compare* means to compare and contrast. Writers use comparisons to analyze two or more places, objects, events, ideas, or people, mainly—but not solely—to point out their differences. To have a sound basis for comparison, considerable similarity should exist between whatever subjects are being compared. Contrary to common wisdom, however, you could compare apples and oranges, although it would be difficult to write an essay comparing oranges and orangutans, or apes and apples.

Besides being a useful writing strategy, comparison is a frequently used and important way of learning and thinking. Everyone regularly makes comparisons in their daily decision-making, mentally comparing shoes or cans of soup or weighing various employment or entertainment options. Often we discuss these choices with friends or family members before making a decision.

Comparisons are found in all types of writing as well, so it helps to pay attention to the ways other writers use them. Observe how comparisons add flavor and specificity to descriptive writing, just as you probably use apt and colorful comparisons in daily conversation. "I met this cool guy last night. He reminded me of _____." "My dad bought a new hat shaped like _____."

Comparisons can be incorporated into many kinds of essays to add interest, to strengthen an argument, or to clarify and inform. Journalists and sports writers regularly rely on comparisons. While technical and scientific writing is full of them, professional writers sometimes use extended comparisons that make up a whole essay. Composition teachers may also assign whole themes using comparison.

There are many uses for comparisons outside of composition courses. Making mental comparisons and drawing analogies is a useful study and learning technique. Because comparing requires students to think and write critically (to draw analogies and so on), essay examinations in a wide range of courses may include comparison questions: Compare the regimes of Hitler and Stalin in the years before World War II. What are some of the similarities and differences between an Impressionist and an Expressionist painting? Compare the use of suspense in a Stephen King and an Alfred Hitchcock film. Learning some of the techniques of writing an effective comparison can help you to better answer comparison questions on essay exams.

Writing an Extended Comparison

Open with an introduction that states *exactly* what is being compared. Your introduction might also list the criteria, or qualities, being used to draw the comparison, or your thesis. The introduction to the essay question on Hitler and Stalin might sound something like the following.

> Although there were similarities in the methods of rule of Stalin and Hitler, their aims and policies before World War II were also different in many ways.

The criteria selected for that response are:

—methods of rule (discuss similarities)
—aims before WW II (discuss mainly differences)
—policies before WW II (discuss mainly differences)

There are two major ways to organize the body of a comparison essay: whole by whole or point by point. A **whole-by-whole comparison** examines one subject entirely before turning to the other one; a **point-by-point comparison** looks at each point of similarity or difference and applies it to each subject. Suppose that you are responding to the question about Impressionism vs. Expressionism for an art exam. In the body of a whole-by-whole comparison, your entire analysis of an Impressionist painting would come first, followed by your analysis of an Expressionist painting. In a point-by-point comparison, alternate between Impressionism and Expressionism, discussing selected criteria—subject matter, composition, use of color, line, and texture—about each one in turn.

If this seems confusing, a careful look at the following student comparison of two famous jazz trumpeters may help to clarify your questions about writing and organizing a comparison essay. Observe the important role transitions play in this comparison. The first transition is annotated with a "T."

Two Jazz Trumpet Players

Dizzy Gillespie and Miles Davis are two of the most prominent and innovative jazz trumpet players alive. These two jazz giants have enjoyed increased popularity among musicians and jazz enthusiasts alike. Possessed of both talent and charisma, Dizzy and Miles have used the same vehicle—jazz—to express their imagination and creativity. There are many similarities as well as differences between these two jazz musicians.

John Birks Gillespie (Dizzy is his professional nickname) came from a poor southern black family where he was the youngest of nine children. Dizzy spent his teens playing for the school band, studying music theory at home and working in local dance bands. After high school Dizzy stayed around his hometown for several years before landing his first professional job with Cab Calloway's big band. Cab's big band was traveling to New York. The trip brought Dizzy to the city where there was an abundance of young musicians, one of whom was a kid from the mid-west named Miles Davis. (T)

Miles Dewey Davis III was brought up in a middle-class family. An only child, he started playing the trumpet at an early age. The son of a successful dentist, Miles was fortunate enough to escape poverty and was able to attend New York's famed Julliard music school after high school. Once in New York, Miles found studies at Julliard too restrictive and dropped out after one semester to seek work playing jazz in the many nightclubs around the city.

As there are contrasts between Dizzy's and Miles' backgrounds, so are there contrasts in their appearances. Miles is a small, slim, graceful man with a quiet manner and a soft voice. When playing, Miles assumes a relaxed stance with his shoulders raised, head bent, trumpet pointed towards the floor, and his back occasionally turned towards his audience. Miles rarely plays more than thirty minutes at a time and is never seen mingling with the crowd. Conserving his energy, Miles seems to put little effort in entertaining his audience which is quite the opposite of the way Dizzy plays.

Dizzy is an energetic performer. Wearing horn-rimmed glasses, goatee and comical smile, Dizzy gyrates his stout frame around the stage, joking casually with his audience. The most striking feature of Dizzy's appearance is his face. When playing the trumpet, Dizzy's cheeks expand well past the point of normalcy, causing a distorted facial look like that of a frightened pufferfish. When soloing, Dizzy leans back, closes his eyes, puffs out his cheeks, and fills the horn with the music he loves.

Dizzy's style of jazz comes from the be-bop jazz revolution of the 1940s. Be-bop jazz is characterized by fast, intricate melodies played at breakneck tempos, where articulation and mastery of the instrument are essential. Dizzy, who is considered one of the elder statesmen of the be-bop style, still plays much the same way he did in the forties. Although still popular, be-bop has evolved into cool and modern jazz, both of which characterize the style of jazz which Miles Davis plays.

Miles developed his sound largely from the cool movement during the early fifties. Cool jazz came to the southern California jazz clubs; it uses soft, flowing sounds against Afro-Cuban rhythm to add tonal color and rhythmic flavor to the new jazz. Miles' trumpet playing is light, tender and relies on understatement to get his music to the listener.

Both Dizzy Gillespie and Miles Davis are extremely talented trumpet players who influence a good number of younger jazz musicians and share their music with an appreciative jazz audience. As long as they are alive, and well afterwards, these two great jazz trumpet players will bring their music and enjoyment to many fans of jazz.

Exercise

1. Did this writer use a whole-by-whole or a point-by-point organization?
2. List the three criteria or topics, about the musicians that were used for the comparison.
3. Observe that the author chose a topic that he knew well, one that interested him. He then used a comparison to convey considerable information about these two musicians.
4. Reread the essay, finding all of the writer's transitional cues. Observe that these transitions both refer to previous topics and predict a switch to a new topic.
5. What simile, or analogy, did the author use?

Prewriting for a Comparison and Contrast Paper

The prewriting for the essay comparing the two jazz trumpeters may have followed the stages shown on the next page.

Exploring for a Topic

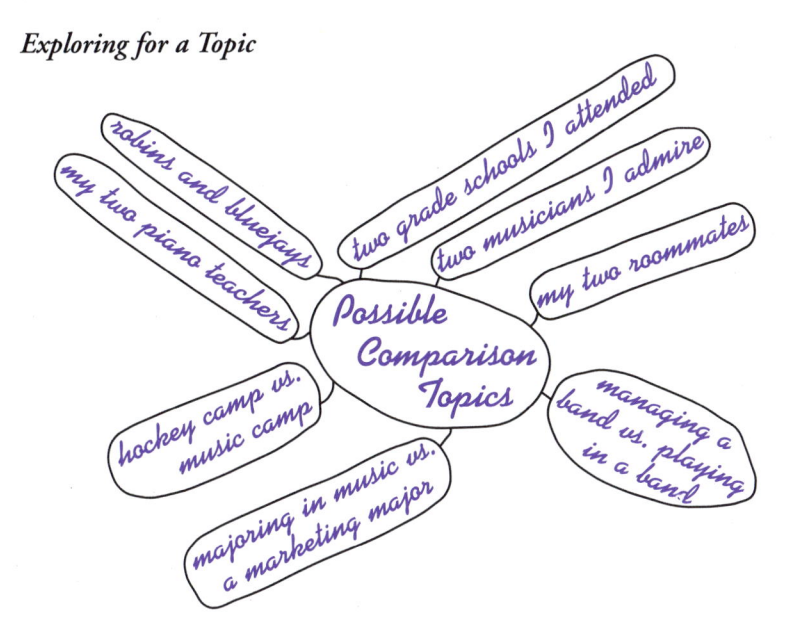

Possible Comparison Topics:
- robins and bluejays
- my two piano teachers
- two grade schools I attended
- two musicians I admire
- my two roommates
- managing a band vs. playing in a band
- majoring in music vs. a marketing major
- hockey camp vs. music camp

Narrowing the Topic Choice

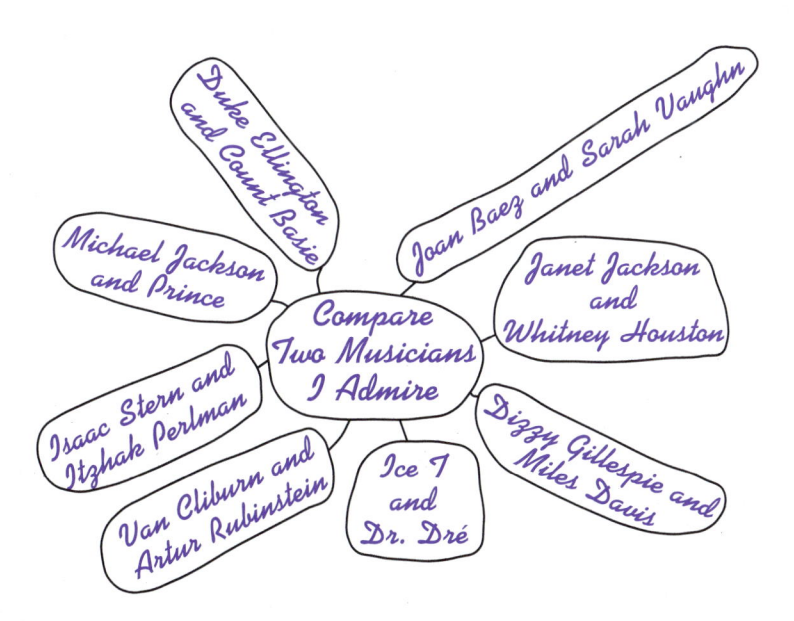

Compare Two Musicians I Admire:
- Duke Ellington and Count Basie
- Michael Jackson and Prince
- Joan Baez and Sarah Vaughn
- Janet Jackson and Whitney Houston
- Isaac Stern and Itzhak Perlman
- Van Cliburn and Artur Rubinstein
- Ice T and Dr. Dré
- Dizzy Gillespie and Miles Davis

(Chose the trumpeters—I know the most about them.)

Comparing the Two Trumpeters

Dizzy Gillespie	**Miles Davis**
poor southern black family—9 kids	middle class—father dentist
energetic performer (describe)—jokes with audience	relaxed stance—never mingles with crowd
first professional job with Cab Calloway	attended famous Julliard
	dropped out after one semester
in school and local bands	cool movement of '50s (explain)
studied music theory at home	New York jazz scene
be-bop jazz of '40s (give details)	played trumpet at young age
came to New York	conserves energy on stage

Deciding on Criteria and an Organizational Scheme

A table like the one above might provide a stimulus for some freewriting about each of the two trumpeters that would bring out more descriptive details and examples. Viewed together, the chart and the freewriting would then suggest subtopics, or criteria, for an organizational scheme for a preliminary draft of the comparison.

Listing the Criteria

— their backgrounds
— how they appear when performing
— their jazz styles

Organizational Scheme

The next step would probably be to decide whether to use point-by-point or whole-by-whole organization, or a combination of the two. Remember that a writer can always switch to the other method in a later draft. The important thing is to get started.

Informal Outline. Preparing a more detailed, informal outline could be useful at this point. Here is how one might have looked for the essay about the jazz trumpeters:

Introduction
   Name the two talented, charismatic trumpeters and note they have similarities and differences.

Body of the Essay

   Backgrounds

      John Birks (Dizzy) Gillespie
         —*youngest of 9 children in poor southern black family*
         —*played trumpet in school and local bands; studied music theory at home*
         —*got job with Cab Calloway and went to New York*

      Miles Dewey Davis III
         —*only son of dentist; middle class family*
         —*attended famed Julliard one semester*
         —*began playing in New York jazz scene*

   Appearance when performing

      Miles Davis
         —*slim and graceful; quiet manner and voice*
         —*relaxed stance (describe); plays 30 min.; saves energy and doesn't mingle with crowd*

      Dizzy Gillespie
         —*energetic (describe); gyrates and jokes with crowd*
         —*cheeks, etc.—like frightened pufferfish*

   Jazz styles

      Dizzy
         —*be-bop of '40s; breakneck tempo; intricate melodies; articulation crucial*
         —*style still much like was in the '40s*

      Miles
         —*cool jazz movement that came to southern California in '50s*
         —*soft, flowing sounds; Afro-Cuban rhythms*
         —*light, tender, understated*

Conclusion
   Sum up: two extremely talented trumpeters who will continue to be heard by many long after their deaths

Considering Invention Strategies for a Comparison Essay

Making a chart of similarities and differences can be especially helpful in deciding what criteria to use in a comparison essay.

Exercise

Comparing two supervisors or bosses

1. On top of each column, fill in the names of two supervisors you have worked under and the places they worked. (If you have not had two bosses, substitute coaches or some other authority figure.) Then fill in similarities and differences between these two people.

First Supervisor   **Second Supervisor**

Similarities

Differences

2. Look over your listings to see whether they suggest three or more criteria—qualities such as "willing to work around class schedules"—that could be used in a theme comparing these two supervisors. List those criteria.

Exploring Possible Topics for a Comparison Essay

In your journal, list approximately six topics that you might be interested in developing into an extended comparison. Then do some freewriting on one or more of those potential comparison topics in your journal. Select the topic that seems to hold the most promise, and make a chart listing the similarities and differences of the items. Next, list the tentative criteria that you would develop in an extended comparison essay.

Choosing a Topic for a Comparison

Make sure to choose a topic that interests you. If you are interested in your topic, your readers will catch your enthusiasm. Be sure to write so that your essay has a distinctive voice.

Beware of the "so-what factor." Undoubtedly your readers know that baseball is played on a diamond that has four bases, or that Oprah Winfrey and Phil Donahue are both talk show hosts. In other words, do not rehash what's familiar about the familiar. Let your readers know that you are informed on your topic, either from your own or others' experiences (that are familiar to you), or from your research. Cite outside authorities clearly and exactly; show your readers exactly how you are personally familiar with any topic.

As a member of University of Wisconsin—Milwaukee's track team for two years . . . .

In an interview on May 6, 1993, Officer Khadijah Cooper of the Milwaukee Police Department explained to me how any neighborhood can set up a Block Watch program. Officer Cooper also pointed out several advantages of the program.

Organizing a Comparison

There are two major ways to organize a comparison: whole by whole or point by point. A combination of these two methods may also be used. The writer must choose an organizational framework, because clarity is so important in a comparison.

Suppose you opt to compare two coaches or two singers. With the whole-by-whole method, you would first write everything you want to say about one person, then you would write about the second person. Generally speaking, it is helpful to the reader if the various points are brought up in the same order in each half of the paper.

With the point-by-point method, you would discuss the various criteria, alternating between the two persons being compared as each point is brought up.

> Insert **transitional comments** to avoid too sharp a turn in the discussion.

Transitions, such as "on the other hand" or "in contrast," are very important as you move from one topic to another in a comparison essay. **Transitions** are cues, or signals, provided along the way to let your readers know what to expect next. Reading an essay without clear transitions is like driving down a road without traffic signs. If the signs are there they are almost taken for granted and traffic flows normally, but if they are missing it is immediately obvious.

Transitions can be words, phrases, sentences, or whole paragraphs. They may refer to the topic just discussed or predict the next topic. For additional information on transitions see pages 45 to 50.

Exercise

1. Compare two places that are important to you or have had a big impact on your life: two neighborhoods you have lived in; your grandparents' home and your own home; your neighborhood today and a few years ago; or two of your favorite retreats or vacation spots. (Remember, no generic vacation spots; see page 328–29.) Remember that your audience is *not* familiar with these places. Use vivid descriptions to help your readers to see these places in their minds.
2. Compare yourself now and a few years ago.
3. Compare two products you know well; two courses you have taken; two recreational activities you recommend; two musicians that you are very familiar with; or military life and civilian life from your own experience. (Let the reader know early along that you were in the military or involved in the sport or whatever you are discussing.)

Chapter Twelve

Informing and Explaining: The Purpose and Nature of Informative Writing

Paris and sidewalk cafés: The two are almost synonymous. What visitor to Paris in decent weather does not hope to spend at least a few hours in one of these famous institutions? At a time when coffee houses, where one can spend hours conversing with friends, reading, or even composing on a laptop computer, are on a rapid increase in the United States, it is somewhat surprising to learn that they are on the decline in France.

The following article on French cafés, written by William J. Kole for the Associated Press, is an example of informative writing. Millions of such articles appear daily in a wide range of publications in today's "information age."

Trouble Brewing for French Cafés
William J. Kole

Paris—The French café, the soul of the sidewalk for more than three centuries, is fighting for survival in a society no longer willing to sit and watch the world go by.

Several hundred café owners demonstrated beneath the Eiffel Tower on Monday to protest high taxes that they say are driving them out of business.

But that's just part of the problem. Industry insiders say 4,000 bistros a year are going bust because more French are eating fast food, shunning cigarettes and booze and simply staying home, American couch potato-style.

Desperate café owners trying to put a friendly face on sometimes gruff service have even taken the extraordinary step of sending waiters to smile school.

Yet, cafés keep disappearing from the French landscape almost as quickly as the steaming espresso they serve in thimble-size cups.

"When the last café closes, it's the soul of the village that dies," said Christian Couderc, owner of a suburban Paris café.

Intellectuals and workers alike have long gathered around small bistro tables to socialize with neighbors or exchange news and ideas, making cafés the quintessential symbol of French society and culture. Before World War I, cafés numbered more than a half-million.

By 1980, there were just 80,000. Today there are fewer than 50,000, including 10,000 in Paris. In 1994, more than 1,500 cafés closed in Paris alone.

The wave of terrorist bombings that has killed seven people and wounded 160 since mid-summer has not helped: Nearly 70% of the cafés say business is down since the bombings began.

President Jacques Chirac made things worse, critics contend, when he raised sales taxes across the board last summer to 20.6%, from an already stiff 18.6%. Food and drink prices were driven up even higher. In some Paris cafés, a beer can cost up to $8.

"You think we want to charge these prices?" asked Bruno Mangel, a Paris café owner among those demonstrating Monday. "The tourists come here and can't believe it."

French cafés trace their beginnings to 1672, when the Procope—still doing a lively business—opened on a small side street on the Left Bank in Paris.

In the first half of this century, Ernest Hemingway, Jean-Paul Sartre and other luminaries romanticized the café as a social center, a debating club and a haven from the pressures of modern life.

The cafés that remain are far from empty. Ten million French say they visit one at least once a week, and plenty of foreign tourists seek them out for coffee and a croissant or a simple meal.

Yet nearly one in two French people never sets foot in a café, according to a 1994 survey commissioned by the Perrier mineral water company.

"I can't stand them. Who wants to sit around and breathe all that smoke?" said Veronique Levert, a Parisian who says she would rather work out than hang out.

Exercise

Check the title (headline) of William J. Kole's article for what it may predict about the contents. Read through the article quickly, then reread it more critically with the following questions in mind. Have your group take notes on those questions as you discuss them.

1. Where was the author when he sent this article to the Associated Press? Is that of any importance?
2. What is Kole's *thesis?*

3. What *purposes* might Kole have had in mind when he wrote this article?
4. List several categories of people Kole may have viewed as his potential readers, or audience.
5. What kinds of evidence, such as quotations from primary sources, or people directly involved, does Kole use to back up his thesis?
6. Kole's sources suggested several reasons that may explain why the French café, "the soul of the sidewalk for more than three centuries," is fighting to survive. List those reasons.

(*Note:* The quoted phrase in the above is an example of incorporating words from an outside source into one's own sentence. Kole summed up the traditional role of the French café better than we could. Because these are his exact words, they belong between quotation marks.)

Using Outside Sources: Primary and Secondary Sources

"Trouble Brewing for French Cafés" contains several quotations from primary sources, in this case café owners and café patrons. (Can the reader tell whether Kole got these quotes from interviews he conducted or from written sources?) Because he chose widely, these quotations add flavor and credibility to Kole's article—after all, these are the people directly involved in the situation.

In addition to direct quotations, Kole's article contains other information, such as statistics on the decline in the number of French cafés, that should be cited when used in a research paper. However, such information should be paraphrased, or put in your words, rather than quoted verbatim. In general it is best to quote sparingly, and almost never from secondary sources such as Kole's story. Because Kole does not write as a direct witness to the events he is reporting, and because he has included background information that he obtained from outside sources, "Trouble Brewing for French Cafés" is basically a secondary source, not a primary source. For instance, Kole is not an official spokesperson for the French government or one of the several hundred protesting café owners. Direct statements from those people, as direct participants in the events being described, would be primary sources.

Suppose that the following material from Kole's article was quoted verbatim in a research paper about opposition to the government of French President Jacques Chirac during his first few months in office.

> *Several hundred café owners demonstrated beneath the Eiffel Tower on Monday to protest high taxes that they say are driving them out of business.... President Jacques Chirac made things worse, critics contend, when*

> he raised sales taxes across the board last summer to 20.6%, from an already stiff 18.6%. Food and drink prices were driven up even higher.

Are Kole's exact words important here? Would they add flavor to a research paper or an article in a scholarly journal? Does using a blocked quote serve any real purpose in this instance?

Suppose that the same data were paraphrased something like the following.

> *Angered by President Jacques Chirac's across-the-board increase in sales tax from 18.6% to 20.6%, a rise they claimed was driving them out of business, several hundred French café owners demonstrated against the high taxes beneath the Eiffel Tower on October 23, 1995.*

Is anything of substance lost in this paraphrase?

However, because the paraphrase contains statistical data and other information that is not common knowledge, Kole's article should be cited as the source of that data. Material need not be quoted directly to require documentation.

William J. Kole probably had a fairly general audience in mind when he wrote his story about the decline of the French café. Often, however, an author writes for a more specific audience. The nature of the intended audience has a major effect on what and how the material is presented.

For example, if a doctor were writing an article about the care of AIDS patients, the contents would vary for each possible audience: other physicians; medical students; nurses; nurses' aides; families of AIDS patients; or youth in a sex education class. A biologist would not submit the same article about the AIDS virus to a journal read primarily by fellow biologists, as she would for the more general audience of the *New York Times*.

People regularly refer to informative articles for many purposes: to find out what is going on in their community and the world; to get information about what stereo to purchase; to determine the effectiveness of the latest medicine for arthritis. Newspapers, company newsletters, magazines, scholarly journals, textbooks, instructions from the boss of the previous shift, comments on papers from instructors: Informative writing makes up the bulk of the contents of such writing. Much of the writing that you will do in the university or workplace, such as research papers, laboratory reports, business letters, and memos, will be informative writing.

At the university and in most careers you will also be expected to read a great deal of informative writing. Become a critical reader of that material, looking for models of how you want to write—and how you *don't* want to write.

The purpose of informative writing is to convey information and provide explanations in clear, precise language, an aim not always attained, as readers of "clear, easy-to-follow directions," legal documents, or tax and insurance forms know all too well.

> Please wait until the Depository has been enabled.
> TYME machine

Technical writers label this kind of writing "C.O.I.K.," which stands for "clear only if known." One might well ask: If something is known then do I need the explanation? If I need an explanation, don't I need it in words that are understandable?

How can you, as an informative writer, avoid the same C.O.I.K. trap that so many authors of instructions fall into? The best way is to keep your audience in mind and try to anticipate which explanations and definitions of terms will be needed. If you are leaving directions for the person who regularly takes over your cash register, you can assume a lot of knowledge about the workplace routine on the part of your reader. However, if your boss asks you to write up directions for shutting down the register for a new employee who will be alone on duty for the first time, you will need to give more detailed directions. You should always automatically keep that new employee in mind as you write the instructions.

In the case of a known audience, the task of deciding what information to include is easier than when writing for an unknown audience whose knowledge of a topic can only be surmised. Generally speaking, it is better to err on the side of being too clear, rather than not clear enough. To judge how successful you have been, ask several readers to go over drafts of your informative essays, pointing out COIKERS, or places unclear to a general audience.

One student who failed to get outside opinions was a soccer player who was attempting to explain some of the problems faced by college athletes on athletic scholarships. Tony was fully aware that many other students—and even faculty—think that college athletes often have an easy free ride to the university, and he wanted to explain where they were wrong. Tony's essay, however, failed in its mission because of C.O.I.K. problems. It was not the unclear terms that confused his readers, however, but his unconscious assumption that most readers know much more about a college athlete's schedule and demands than they actually do. Tony failed to explain the restrictions and time commitments frequently placed on athletes: for instance, many teams practice several hours a day most of the year, not only during soccer season; coaches demand a certain amount of fitness training all year; and many athletes on scholarships often cannot hold other jobs during the school year, which can make it difficult financially for those without outside sources of spending money, as most athletic scholarships cover only basic expenses. The result was an essay that failed to achieve its purpose because he failed to keep his audience in mind: only another university athlete would have known all of the details about an athletic scholarship and the requirements for team membership needed to follow Tony's paper.

We found out much of the above information when we handed Tony back his essay. Had he included it earlier, he would have done a much better job of persuading his readers. Showing a draft to students who were not on a university team probably would have helped him clear up most of the C.O.I.K. problems in his essay.

Tony's paper is but one example of the kind of assumptions on the part of the writer that make much informative writing hard to follow. If you write about being in the Army, on a championship skating team, or on the police force, the same cautions apply. Are most of your potential readers likely to be former police officers or skaters or enlisted personnel? Try to imagine the questions readers who have not shared those experiences might ask. If you are writing on a technical topic, such as how to change a tire or use a photocopy machine, try to anticipate what terms may need clarification for any nontechnical readers.

Always figure that your audience is somewhat uninformed about the topic and is seeking to know more about it. If you do not know considerably more about a topic than your readers, should you be writing about it? Informative writing provides the opportunity for writers to share expertise with those seeking information on a topic. Be as clear as possible, and keep your audience in mind at all times. Doing so is always important in writing, perhaps even more so in informative writing where clarity is so crucial.

It is also important to make certain your readers know where you are headed at all times. State your thesis early in an informative essay. Then be sure to demonstrate clearly how all of the material you include fits into that thesis.

Tony the soccer player might have written the following thesis, not necessarily in the first paragraph, but early along in the essay.

> There are several prevalent misconceptions about the easy life of the student on an athletic scholarship.

He should also have established himself as an authority, which is often a good tactic for the writer of an informative essay, by stating that he was attending the University of Wisconsin–Milwaukee on a soccer scholarship. Then he could have used some or all of the following techniques to inform his readers about the demands put on the student athlete.

As in all writing, support generalizations with specific details and illustrations, or examples, that clarify them. In the case of the college athlete, an illustration could be a typical weekly schedule, tallying the exact number of hours of required practice, fitness training, and so on. An explanation might detail how many months that schedule holds, what is demanded during off-season months, and so on. If you are explaining the steps in a process, for example, how to change a tire, you might also include the reasons for each step, as well as pointing out things to avoid when appropriate.

Another way to be more concrete is to include descriptions and analogies, or comparisons, to clarify terms and explanations. Analogies allow writers to bring the reader from the familiar to the less familiar or unknown: A widget is a kind of _____ that operates like a _____.

In this visual age, do not discount the value of visual materials. Draw or photocopy diagrams, charts, or maps. Photocopied materials can provide excellent supplements in a paper, as long as they are carefully labeled as to the exact source. Note how charts and photos are labeled in various textbooks for models of how this is done.

For a student model of informative writing based on both personal experience and outside authorities, see Mary Mangan's essay on contact lenses on page 357. Note that Mangan relies partly on factual description to inform her readers.

Understanding Informative Descriptive Writing

> **Joe Hardy Named MBDA Coordinator for American Indian Programs**
> **Ivette M. Rodriguez**
>
> Joseph R. "Joe" Hardy, an enrolled member of the Navajo Tribe, Fort Defiance, Ariz., has been selected to head the Minority Business Development Agency's (MBDA) American Indian business development programs, MBDA Director Joe Lira announced recently.
>
> Prior to joining MBDA, Hardy was a management consultant in Arizona. In addition, he owned and managed his own retail business in New Mexico. Hardy's previous experience with minority business development included the management and operation of the MBDA-funded Indian Business Development Center serving the Navajo Nation in Fort Defiance, Ariz. . . .
>
> At MBDA, Hardy will be working on a number of initiatives to promote entrepreneurship and develop business opportunities for Native Americans.

Informative descriptive writing, such as the above biographical sketch, can be useful by itself, as well as in many kinds of writing. This excerpt simply highlights some of Joseph R. Hardy's achievements in a factual manner. It does not attempt to persuade the reader that Hardy is the best man for his new position, nor does it attempt to catch something of Hardy's character on paper.

Unlike literary description, informative description explains and clarifies, rather than evoking the emotions or appealing to the literary tastes of its readers. Informative description is widely used in scientific, technical, and business writing. At times it is used to sell products, using factual rather than subjective, emotional appeals. Compare the following statements.

> *EDS (the world leader in applying information technology) created the Geographic Information System (GIS) to assist engineers in the design and drafting of new roadways. It's the first system of its kind to combine detailed topographic data and computer graphics all on one screen. Engineers using the system can view every road, bridge and waterway in Indiana with the push of a button. They can also analyze the viability of proposed new roads in seconds. This enables the engineers to pinpoint the most effective routes for new roads.*

Now look at this almost purely subjective appeal, containing almost no hard data.

> *Sounds a lot like a muscle car doesn't it? Yet the Lexus Coupe is far from being muscle bound . . . . Once you drive what* Motor Trend *named the 1992 Import Car of the Year, you must be prepared to answer a lot of questions. Autographs, mind you, are optional.*

Like all informative writing, informative description must be clearly and logically presented to be effective. While informative writing tends to be more dry and boring than other types of writing, that need not be the case. Dullness is not a requirement for *any* writing, and writers should staunchly resist being boring.

By now you may well be thinking, "Now wait a minute here. If *clarity* is so important, why are many of the articles and textbooks that I have to read so difficult to understand?"

Anyone who has read much academic prose ought to concede that you have a point, but few have thrust the rapier at the perpetrators of such verbiage as aptly as Patricia Nelson Limerick in her review of four books on Hawaii in the February 1992 *American Historical Review.* For Limerick, an "unspoken assumption" rules the writers of many scholarly books: "any charm or grace in prose will erode the seriousness of the study, while dense, difficult phrasing certifies the content as substantial and sophisticated." Limerick challenges quantitative historians to "ensure that difficult technical prose will not rob" them of their audience. She is puzzled about why one author wrote up the "results of considerable labor" using the "standard social-scientese mechanisms for fending off readers—polysyllables, passive voice and jargon" (126).

If you are lucky, you are still not far enough into an academic discipline to know exactly whereof Limerick is speaking. To translate, *polysyllables* means ponderous big words *(confluence* for *junction).* The passive voice makes writing less vital: all the examples of unclear jargon (the specialized language of a profession) were deleted (passive voice) by the annoyed editor. The active voice is generally preferable. The annoyed editor deleted all of the examples of unclear jargon.

Teachers of composition courses are mercifully spared most pedantic jargonese. You will know it when you see it; do not emulate it. Develop a crisp, clear writing style now, and stick to it when writing papers for upper-level courses, for postgraduate courses, and in the workplace. While the most important thing is to be clear, do not hesitate to liven up informative writing and all types of writings with well-told anecdotes, apt descriptions, and humor, as did many of the student writers whose works are included in this textbook.

The following account of an experiment conducted by five German university students appeared in *The Week in Germany,* a publication of the German Information Center in New York. It provides evidence that writing can indeed be lively and humorous, as well as informative.

How Obedient Are Germans?

Germans take no end of ribbing for the allegedly excessive number of rules and regulations in everyday life. When a U.S.-American journalist recently joked that "order über alles" was the watchword of the entire country, five students at the University of Trier (Rhineland-Palatinate) decided to test his theory.

They described their term project as one in which they would conclusively determine whether "mature citizens would obey absurd rules." The students had official-looking signs made, one that declared "women only" and the other "men only," and installed them on the doors of the telephone booths in the lobby of the Trier main post office. Then they settled down to watch.

Of the sixty-nine telephone users observed, nearly all of the women and three-fourths of the men followed the signs and used the booth to which they were "assigned." Almost all of the telephone users crabbed about the "ridiculousness" of the restriction, yet only one woman and nine men dared to use the phone designated for the opposite sex. One young mother was heard to explain to her young child, presumably unable to read as yet, that "we can't use the empty booth, it's only for men." Even as they dismissed the signs as "baloney," two male teenagers passed the "women's" booth up to use the one for men. A more daring elderly woman entered the "men's" booth with her male escort, but not before she checked to be sure no one was looking.

Ulla Weiß, one of the experimenters, said that the students were surprised by the results. Given the women's movement and antiauthoritarian child-rearing practices, she said, they expected that women and young people "wouldn't fall for such nonsense." Her colleague Medine Demir avowed that "I wouldn't have obeyed these silly signs—at least I hope so." And what about the one woman who dared to disobey? It turned out that she was French. When taken to task for using the "wrong" telephone, she did leave the booth, but not without remarking that "only the Germans would come up with this sort of idea."

Can you guess from the context, as well as from the words themselves, what *order über alles* means? Examine your own penchant, or lack thereof, for following rules and societal conventions. Would you have used a phone booth designated for the opposite sex?

The next informative article, from the same publication, demonstrates that Germany in the mid-1990s, like the United States, one of the richest industrial nations in the world, also has many homeless people living in its cities. An account of how the initiative of a few determined women has resulted in at least a small amelioration of the problem challenges a common assumption that things have become too complex and intractable for anyone to make a difference.

Initiative Reaps Berlin's Riches to Feed the Poor and Hungry

"It can't hurt to ask," as three determined women in Berlin have discovered. The facts of the situation were quite simple. An estimated 20,000 homeless people live in the capital city, a quarter of them children. Every day, it is believed, fully 20 percent of all food in the city is thrown away. Why not use that food—day-old baked goods, restaurant surplus, fruits and vegetables—to feed the homeless, as do groups like "City Harvest" in New York? That was the question Reina Mehert, Ursula Kretzer, and Sabine Werth asked themselves, and that is how *Berliner Tafel* ("Berlin Table") was born.

Mehert, Kretzer, and Werth began modestly in early 1993 by asking Berlin produce wholesalers for unsold fruits and vegetables destined for the dumpster. Using their own cars they then distributed the food to local homeless shelters and soup kitchens. Then they turned to bakeries and hotel restaurants. Along the way, they enlisted prominent Berliners and local media outlets for free publicity, and asked local business to help out with donations of goods or services. One thing led to another, and *Berliner Tafel* now collects DM 200,000 worth of foodstuffs monthly and feeds 2,000 needy people every day.

The success of *Berliner Tafel*, as the *Frankfurter Rundschau* reports, is likely to make changes in the group's organization and operations necessary. Steadily rising donations of old clothing, kitchen utensils, and household appliances—not to mention food—threaten to overwhelm *Berliner Tafel*'s decidedly casual approach to collection and distribution. The group, the *Frankfurter Rundschau* speculates, might end up adopting

> the administrative ways of more established charitable organizations or possibly even affiliating itself with one.
>
> Come what may of *Berliner Tafel,* its founders take pride not only in what they have achieved, but also in the example they have provided to others. A group in Hamburg has just embarked upon a similar program, and inquiries have come from Kiel (Schleswig-Holstein), Frankfurt, Essen (North Rhine-Westphalia), and Munich.

Exercise

Perhaps you too know someone who has "made a difference." Write about that person, or persons, and what they accomplished in your journal. Then consider revising that journal entry into a developed essay. Additional research, such as conducting interviews or finding written sources, may be needed to strengthen your paper. You might want to relate your essay to the above article, perhaps by quoting from it as the source of inspiration for your essay or by drawing parallels between the *Berliner Tafel* and the incidents you are depicting.

In addition to conveying information, informative writing can have a wide variety of effects on readers. They may agree or disagree with the writer, have their minds opened up or changed about a topic, or be inspired to read more about it. Some may even be moved to act based on the material presented, whether that is the writer's explicitly stated intent or not.

Luke Jefferson establishes himself as an authority on his topic early in this essay. He then demonstrates the validity of his claim by including lots of pertinent factual information and concrete examples that attest to his expertise with videocassette recorders.

Buy a Hi.Fi. V.C.R. and Not a Mono
Luke Jefferson

> Like many people, I find myself considering the purchase of a new v.c.r. for my personal use, but unlike many people I have owned one before and I'm sure of what I want. My last v.c.r. was a Mitsubishi, their top line hi.fi. (stereo) model with high resolution quality. My reasons for picking this particular model had a lot to do with where I worked, which was AMERICAN T.V. & APPLIANCE of Brown Deer, Wisconsin.
>
> After a year of working with some of the best video equipment made, I started narrowing my selection of a v.c.r. The first decision was whether to

buy hi.fi., which is stereo, or a good mono deck. When I first started working at American, my questions, like so many other peoples' were: Will I notice a difference in sound? Will the picture look better? What if I only want to tape one or two shows a week, and that's all? For a few people the latter may be strictly true; these people will only tape a few shows a week so sound and picture quality are really not a high priority for them. But the majority of people whom I've spoken to and who have purchased a stereo v.c.r. from me soon find new shows to watch and tape. Because they have stereo, their favorite movies also take on a new dimension. The statement I most often hear is: "It's like being in a theater; the voices and music don't sound monotone or muted anymore."

The best description I can give of the difference between hi.fi. and mono is the way my friend in the t.v. department explained it to customers and me. He closed his hands together tightly over his mouth and said with a slow monotone whispery voice "This is mono." Then, while the customer was straining to hear him, he would open his hands into the form of a megaphone and say with a startlingly clear voice, "This is stereo!!" The customer was obviously impressed. Finally, he would describe "surround sound" by opening his hands wide like he was going to shout, and turn round and round, saying "This is surround sound; can you hear the difference?" By this time the customer was entranced by my friend's graphic description and was willing to listen to his pitch on a particular product. After this presentation, most customers were interested in hearing the difference between mono and stereo. Since all new videotapes are recorded in hi.fi. (stereo) or Dolby Surround, the full audio range of sound that's heard in a theater can also be heard in your home. All you need is a stereo t.v. or a home stereo system, and most people have one or both of these.

With old tapes such as *Gone With The Wind* or *Casablanca* being remastered, most listeners will want to hear the new improved edition of these films. Re-mastering is a process that separates all the different sounds and voices and literally combs out the popping and hissing that most people associate with old movies; re-mastering also enhances the picture quality, resulting in essentially a new version of a classic movie. What the video industry has done in the last few years for picture quality has been nominal, but the change in sound quality has been phenomenal. With television shows like *Star Trek: The Next Generation* and most shows on The Fox Network broadcasting in Dolby Surround, a person can now record the full range of sound on the show. Dolby Surround and Dolby Pro-Logic can only be played and recorded on a hi.fi. deck; what this gives you is left and right channels plus a rear and center channel.

The video industry knows that hi.fi. (stereo) is the future of audio equipment so they're giving the consumer an increasingly limited choice in excellent mono video equipment. Today a great mono deck can be purchased for around $299.99 to $400.99, the same price as a great hi.fi. deck; hopefully, they've made the choice easy for you. Even the way t.v.s are advertised today emphasizes the sound performance rather than the picture. When the RCA commercial talks about their 35" t.v., the commercial's focus is on the sound quality, and the new audio/video industry phrase Home Theater. Home Theater is a 27" to 60" t.v. with a stereo v.c.r. This is the future of v.c.r.s. Plus, with so many different cultures in the U.S. today, the English language is not predominant in some communities. Now one of the added benefits of stereo is s.a.p., or second audio programming. This is a second language being broadcast on top of the regular channel. With the press of a button, the picture remains the same but a different language is now being broadcast. For instance, by the American-Canadian border French might be heard on this channel; and by Mexican-American borders Spanish can be heard on the second audio channel. Also the state and local weather is broadcast on these alternate channels throughout the day.

One new feature the manufacturers are working on is descriptive programming for the visually impaired. All these features, plus the better picture quality, are why I will choose another hi.fi. v.c.r. and I believe you should, too.

Note that the author establishes himself as an authority early in the essay, then gives lots of graphic examples and reasons to develop his argument. How would you improve this essay? Are there terms in it that need more explanation? Are his explanations clear?

Writing to Inform: Citing Outside Authorities

Informative writing lets writers call on their own and others' expertise. Notice how Mary Mangan establishes herself as an authority on contact lenses at the start, so that her readers are much more likely to believe what she says. In addition to writing from her own experience, Mary incorporates information gained from an interview and from written sources into her essay, carefully identifying these sources as she introduces them to establish their credibility. The authors' names and the page numbers in parentheses refer the reader to the "Works Cited" (bibliography) list following the essay. Readers can check the "Works Cited" list to locate the complete source and better judge the validity of the information being presented.

Mary Mangan's essay is a good model to follow if you decide to incorporate information from outside authorities into your writing.

Extended Wear Contact Lenses
Mary Mangan

Extended wear contact lenses: How safe are they? Can they be worn for seven days straight without repercussions? Working as an ophthalmic assistant for the past five years, I have seen everything from the slightest red eye to the worst corneal ulcer sit in my exam chair, and they were mostly due to the misuse of contact lenses.

The name "Extended Wear" is actually deceiving to a lot of people so they tend to misuse these lenses. Extended wear contact lenses are made with a higher water content in order to allow patients to keep them in for a longer period of time without discomfort, as opposed to the daily wear lenses that must be removed daily, cleaned and stored overnight. Despite their reputation as lenses that can be safely worn for seven days without removal, extended wear lenses can cause problems. In a recent interview, local optometrist Dr. Kurt Haefs explained to me that many eye care practitioners therefore prefer to prescribe the soft contact lenses designed for extended daily wear, but not overnight use. With the higher water content they are generally more comfortable than harder daily wear lenses, even when worn for 12–15 hours a day, and they also provide a margin of safety for the patient who occasionally naps or inadvertently leaves them in overnight.

Remember, however, overuse of any contact lens can cause problems. From protein in tears, along with pollens, dusts and dirt in the air, contact lenses tend to build up deposits on them. Some of these deposits can be removed with daily cleaning, but not all, and eventually the build up ruins the lens, causing irritation and blurred vision for the patient. At this point the lens must be replaced. These deposits are also a breeding ground for bacterial growth where infection can start. If lenses are not cleaned regularly the chance for infection increases; and if the lenses are kept in the eye for an extended period of time the protein deposit build up becomes more abundant, thus increasing the chance for infection even more. According to Dr. Haefs, during sleep the eye tends to dry and swell, causing the contact lens to tighten on the eye. When the contact lens tightens, less oxygen is allowed to the surface of the eye, causing more swelling and dryness. Removing contact lenses before sleep affords the eye as much oxygen as possible during the night when fewer tears are being produced, and also prevents debris from being trapped under the lens for long periods of time.

In the March 1992 issue of *Contact Lens Spectrum,* Dr. Penny Asbell reported that patients who wear contact lenses on an extended wear basis are at 10–15 times greater risk of a corneal ulcer (an ulcer on the surface of the eye) than those who wear them on a daily wear basis. Dr. Asbell states, "Incidence of ulcerative keratitis with cosmetic soft lens use was 4/10,000 users per year for the daily wear lenses and 21/10,000 users per year for the extended wear lenses" (25). Dr. Asbell not only endorses daily wear use of contact lenses, she also suggests using a disposable lens program as well. She believes that disposing of the lens after one or two weeks of use and replacing it with a fresh lens eliminates problems before they can occur. "With a disposable contact lens system, where the lens is discarded on a weekly basis, the maximum hours of wearing time on one lens is approximately 150 hours," she explains. "For regular daily wear lenses after six months, the time in use approaches 2500 hours and for extended wear lenses it is over 4000 hours of wear." Like most optometrists, Dr. Asbell recommends getting rid of a lens before it degrades as a definite help in "maintaining a healthy eye, greater comfort and the best vision possible" (25).

The most recent innovation in contact lens wear is the disposable contact lenses used on a daily wear basis. According to Harold A. Smith, M.D., Professor of Ophthalmology at the University of Toronto, these lenses are designed as an extended wear lens, but recommended by many eye car practitioners for a two week daily schedule, after which the lenses are disposed of and replaced by a fresh pair (37). The patient only needs to remove the lenses at night and store them in a disinfectant solution and then reinsert them in the morning. This routine eliminates the rigorous cleaning needed for regular daily wear and extended wear contact lenses, and also disposes of the lenses before build up can cause problems. Moreover, these lenses are comparable in price with the regular daily wear and extended wear lenses because the purchasing of cleaning solution is reduced substantially.

Although these above statistics are alarming, the risk factors for all types of contact lenses are small provided they are worn and cared for correctly. Contact lenses can be a wonderful alternative to eyeglasses when worn properly. By careful patient education and attention to regular follow up care and emergency care when needed, the risks are reduced even more. Your eyes are one of your most precious assets—treat them as such.

> **Works Cited**
>
> Asbell, P.A. "Understanding the Risk of Corneal Ulcer." *Contact Lens Spectrum,* March 1992: 25–27.
>
> Haefs, Kurt. Personal Interview. 19 April 1992.
>
> Smith. H.A. "Daily Wear Disposable Lenses." *Contact Lens Spectrum,* July 1991: 37–38.

Exercise

1. How does Mangan establish herself as an authority?
2. What three outside sources does she use?
3. Are the sources adequately introduced into the text to make them believable?
4. What is the thesis of Mangan's essay?

Note that Luke's and Mary's essays are both informative and persuasive. Both writers have shared their knowledge about a product (contact lenses or VCRs) to help their readers make an informed choice should they decide to purchase either of these items in the future. Informative material may turn out to be convincing on the strength of facts and examples alone. However, informative writing is frequently not intended to be persuasive, and is therefore less likely to provoke skepticism or disagreement. Compare these two statements, or theses.

Informative: There are three major types of contact lenses: regular wear lenses; extended wear lenses; and disposable lenses. Each of the three types has advantages and disadvantages.

Argumentative: Switch to disposable contact lenses and you will never be sorry.

Unlike the first statement, the second one invites a challenge: According to who? On what authority? Convince me: My boyfriend tried disposable contact lenses and had terrible problems with them.

Chapter Thirteen

Arguing and Persuading

Arguing is a natural human activity; it is even a form of entertainment for some people. Most of you probably get into occasional arguments during conversations, and, as college students, you should now get in the habit of regularly arguing, or persuading, on paper. Use your journal as a place to react strongly to at least one item you read every week: Agree or disagree with the article in question, and ask questions. Have some fun and experiment: That is the purpose of your journal. Imagine what questions you would pose to the author if he or she walked up to you while you were reading a particular piece. Always take a definite position, and write freely and often. This will give you lots of practice at argumentative, or persuasive, writing, one of the most useful kinds of writing in everyday life. Letters of application, editorials in the campus newspaper, and a note to a professor asking for an extension on a research paper: These are practical examples of persuasive writing. Persuasive writing is also widely used in many careers, such as journalism, business, and advertising, to name but a few.

Persuasive writers—like all effective writers—employ a variety of strategies in their arguments. The first student essay in this chapter, David Merriman's "Jake's Hang Gliding," clearly demonstrates the use of at least four writing strategies. In part, David's essay is a narrative about a group of friends' first hang-gliding jump. It opens with their spur-of-the-moment decision to drive out to Jake's establishment and ends with a few comments on the writer's overall reaction to the jump. Lively, well-selected descriptions make David's experience come to life and give the reader a real feel for the adventure. We are able to share David's initial trepidation, his relief upon discovering that he was not the only one tempted to "chicken out," and finally his "ecstasy" at noticing a "bird flying below to my left" and at his becoming "one with the air." While not the author's major thrust, the essay is somewhat informative in that it gives the reader some data about the sport of hang gliding.

"Jake's Hang Gliding" is also an effective argument; the writer attempts to persuade "anyone who feels the need to cleanse themselves of all negativity" to try hang gliding, "the ultimate tension remover." We found him quite persuasive. We have not yet paid Jake our fifty dollars for "the experience of a lifetime," but we are thinking seriously about it.

Jake's Hang Gliding
David Merriman

In today's society there is a great deal of pressure and stress placed upon young people. Young people need to find ways to vent their frustration in a legal and positive manner. I believe I have found the ultimate tension releaser.

Last weekend a few of my friends and I were trying to think of something to do. We were all bored on a Saturday afternoon and all of us were feeling some type of stress. My good friend Steve was paging through a *Shepherd Express* and found an advertisement for a place in Kettle Moraine that offers hang-gliding lessons. Steve suggested that we try it. His suggestion was received and shrugged off unanimously. Approximately five minutes later, on the Discovery Channel, footage of a man hang gliding in the Grand Canyon was being shown. It must have been fate because after seeing the program the four of us were in the car on our way to brave flight.

The drive to Kettle Moraine did not take long; in fact it seemed painfully short. The seriousness of what we were doing didn't hit me until I saw a billboard that read "Hang Gliding . . . Five Minutes Ahead." I started to feel anxious, and at the same time, nauseous. I wondered if the others were as terrified as I was; I feared being branded a coward by my friends. I secretly began hoping for a flat tire or any kind of car trouble, anything to avoid confronting this challenge. It was no use. We made it to "Jake's Hang Gliding" after all.

As soon as we arrived a large bearded man with a megaphone voice said, "Hi there, guys. Are you ready for the experience of a lifetime?" I was not feeling too ready for the experience of a lifetime but I wasn't going to be the only one to chicken out. Each of my friends paid the man the fifty dollar fee. Reluctantly, I did the same. Jake immediately began teaching us the basics of hang gliding. After about two hours of lessons we were ready to become one with the air. All we needed was a volunteer to go first. We all decided that since it was Steve's idea, he should be the "lucky" one. Steve had no objections, so he began strapping himself to the hang glider. He put his helmet and gloves on, Jake checked him over and gave Steve the okay to jump. Steve stood there for a minute or two looking over the cliff's edge; then before he jumped he turned to me and looked at me. His face was ashen white with sheer terror. It was then that I knew I was not the only one who was totally afraid. Steve jumped and immediately began to sail forward two hundred feet in the air. He didn't look quite as graceful as an eagle, but he was close. When he came back from his run he was one big smile and he nodded to me. I knew it was my turn next.

I put on all the equipment and strapped myself in the harness. Jake looked me over and gave me the thumbs-up. It was my turn to jump. At this moment I became transfixed by the horizon and the skyline. I could barely hear my friends around me; all I could hear was the wind. Then I did it! I jumped, and my heart flopped around in my chest like a bird's wings. I let out a scream of complete ecstasy. This was it man! This is what it is all about. The energy, intensity, and beauty of what I was doing was incredible. After the initial shock of the jump I calmed down and my body and mind were at peace in flight. I noticed a bird flying below to my left. I thought to myself, "I wish I could do this every day!"

The ride lasted about five minutes, but I didn't want it to end. I landed several hundred yards from where I started. After I got back to the cliff, Steve and I talked together and waited for the others to jump. Steve and I have always been close friends, but today we shared something intimate. We

> were definitely bonded in a whole new fashion. We overcame our fears and our biological limitations. We flew!
>
> Since the jump, flying has woven into the fibers of my being. It has become a part of my past, my present, and my future. I know I will jump again soon. I strongly recommend hang gliding to anyone who feels the need to cleanse themselves of all negativity. Who knows what is next? . . . Parachuting?

As you may have observed, "Jake's Hang Gliding" contains four of the five writing strategies covered in this section: narrating, describing, informing, and arguing. The only strategy David did not use is comparing. However, as David almost always arrived in class carrying a motorcycle helmet, he probably could have gone on to write an equally interesting essay comparing two forms of adventurous travel, hang gliding and motorcycling.

David Merriman and Dan Bartz, author of the lively essay about a flight into space (page 276), both remarked separately that they "really got into these essays" and found them easier to write than previous papers. Undoubtedly that happened because they both picked topics that captured their interest and thus were more enjoyable to write about.

As "Jake's Hang Gliding" again demonstrates, writing strategies are not mutually exclusive: To inform or explain, the writer must often describe. One method of describing or characterizing a person is to narrate, to tell short stories, or anecdotes, about something that person did, or does regularly. Narratives can be greatly enhanced by descriptions of people and places. To heighten reader interest, a short, appropriate narrative is often an effective opener for an informative or persuasive essay.

Understanding What Makes an Effective Argument

> Persuasive writing needs a clear, exact claim.

The **claim,** or thesis, of an argument essay should be reasonable, clearly stated, and precise. The writer's purpose is to persuade his or her readers to accept that claim and possibly to follow a certain course of action. The claim must always be *debatable,* one that readers need some persuading to accept. There is no point in arguing about easily verifiable facts or about commonly accepted opinions.

Easily Verifiable Fact: Tea and coffee contain caffeine.

Common Knowledge: Many people drink coffee for breakfast.

People must eat to survive. Who would argue with that claim? Rephrase it to read, "To be healthy, people should eat only two meals a day," and you have an argument on your hands.

Avoid unbalanced or sweeping claims that your readers are unlikely to take seriously. Consider the following claims.

Every couple should rent a stretch limo on their wedding day.

High school graduates would all benefit from deferring entry to college for at least a year after graduation.

Readers of these blanket assertions can instantly think of many exceptions or counterarguments. For example, some students finish high school with a clear idea of what they want to study in college; many students are mature enough to profit from immediate entry to college.

This statement would thus be more persuasive if **qualifiers**—words like *probably, usually,* or *often*—were added to tone down the claim.

With some exceptions, high school graduates would probably benefit from deferring entry to college for at least a year after graduation.

A claim must be balanced.

Identify the qualifiers in the last sentence, and note how they soften the claim.

A Claim Must Be Backed Up with Solid Reasons

Persuasive writers make claims, then give solid, clearly phrased reasons to back up those claims. As might be expected, advertising copywriters are particularly skilled at providing detailed information that makes products seem attractive.

Consider automobile advertising. The reasons used in an argument may be based on factual data, such as a car's anti-lock brakes or child-proof rear door locks, that appeal to the readers' logic, or reason. The reasons may be phrased so as to appeal largely to the readers' emotions.

> *Your children are your most valued treasures. Avoid a preventable tragedy for your family. Ensure your child's safety with Mercury Sable's child-proof rear door locks.*

Advertisers, politicians, preachers—people whose job is to persuade and move people—know very well that appeals to people's emotions are often more effective than appeals to reason.

Analyze the next two statements, noting whether they appeal to emotions or to logic.

> Eat Dannon's low-fat yogurt because it is a healthy, low-calorie food.

> Eat Dannon's low-fat yogurt to have a more appealing, beautiful body and feel better about yourself.

Exercise

1. List five reasons why high school students might benefit from deferring entry to college for at least a year. One reason is already listed for you.
   a. working full-time first—maturing experience

2. If a claim is debatable, a good case can also be made for the opposing viewpoint. List five reasons for the following claim: "Some high school students would benefit from entering college right after graduation."

Purely Personal Opinions Are Not Convincing

The claims in an argument should be backed up by solid, objective reasons, not just personal preferences or opinions.

Personal Preference: Drink tea because it tastes better than coffee.

Personal Opinion: Because they are a waste of time, college students should not take art classes.

Would personal preferences like these two examples sway many readers to share these views?

To be persuasive, claims must be more than an assertion of the writer's personal opinion. To be taken seriously by others, opinions or claims need to be backed up with reasons and evidence.

Frequently, that evidence needs to come from outside authorities. Go to your college library to research your topic, then use evidence from those outside sources to bolster your arguments. For ideas about how to incorporate information from outside sources into your essays, see the suggestions on documentation on pages 230 to 242, as well as the student paper on pages 244 to 252.

Exercise

Read through the following proposal, "Making It Safe," to get an overall view of the contents. Then reread it carefully, making annotations about each paragraph in the margins. Discuss the following questions with the members of your group, and take notes on the discussion in your writer's journal.

1. How does the writer begin, or introduce, her topic?
2. State the essay's thesis.
3. What purpose do the second and third paragraphs serve?
4. What two counterproposals, or counterarguments, are refuted?
5. Summarize the contents and purpose of the second-to-last paragraph of the essay.
6. What is the purpose of the last paragraph?
7. Does the writer use appeals to logic or to emotions or to a combination of both, in this proposal? Give examples.
8. What is the source of the contents of this essay?

Making It Safe

It was your ordinary evening at Best Buy Company; the store closed at 9:00 P.M., all the customers were gone by 9:15, and the employees were out by 9:30. The walk to the employee parking lot is very long. We are expected to park behind the store in a dark secluded lot. Approaching my car I noticed something odd. My attention was immediately drawn to the missing stereo equipment. A thief had struck again! My car wasn't the first to have been broken into and robbed in the employee parking lot, and unless some changes are made, it won't be the last.

One reason for all these robberies is the lack of lighting and security in the employee section of the parking area. The lot extends from the front of the store, around to the left side and back. The lighting in the front and side of the parking lot is adequate, but beyond the building the light supply is cut to half at best. And with no lights in the back of our parking lot it is easy for someone to hide in the shadows. Not only can they rob our cars, but they could also rob or assault the employees.

Another factor is the field directly behind the store. It is separated from the back parking lot by a small row of half dead trees and a large swamp-like ravine. Since the field and ravine are both pieces of land that are not serving any useful purpose at this time, the City of Wauwatosa is not taking any steps to secure them from vandals, who can easily take what they want from our parking lot and escape into these desolate areas.

One way of reducing vandalism in our cars would be to park them in the amply lighted side lot now designated as customer parking. The chances of our cars being broken into again would remain, though it would be less of a risk. Unfortunately, this arrangement might satisfy the employees' complaints, while generating more complaints from customers who would have to find available parking on the street or behind the store. Moreover, the risk of crimes being committed, this time to customers' cars, would be there still and the problems would not have been solved.

A second idea is to put a large security fence around the parking lot. Then nobody would be able to get into the lot unless they drove in, or walked in from the front. The chances of cars getting vandalized would decrease since vandals wouldn't be able to enter from the field. Since the fence could be very tall and have a barbed wire top, climbing over would be difficult. In order to build the fence the store needs to get permission from the City of Wauwatosa. Assuming the city does approve the construction, the fence would cost the store several hundred dollars to build and keep up, and it would only alleviate, not solve the problem.

The most reasonable approach to the problem is to install brighter, larger flood lights throughout the parking lot. Putting up security cameras is also very important. Six cameras could be strategically placed around the building, one on each corner, one in the middle of the back wall, and one in the middle of the left side wall. All areas of the parking lot would then be lit as well as on video tape, so employees need not be afraid to walk to their cars at night. Vandals would be less likely to break into someone's car, simply because they could not hide in the shadows any longer. All they would have to do is look up and see the video cameras; knowing they're on video tape, they'd be more likely to walk away.

Putting up lights and cameras would cost a fair sum at first, but in the long run it would be considerably cheaper than continuing to hire security people to walk through the lot every few hours. This solution would help prevent any further robberies as well as create a happier and safer work environment.

Exploring Ways to Support a Claim

Persuasive writers use several kinds of evidence to make a good case for their claims. These types of evidence can come from their own experiences or observations, from outside authorities, or from experts on the topic.

Facts

Facts that bear directly on a topic greatly strengthen an argument. For instance, a car advertisement might state that a certain car has child-proof rear door locks, a verifiable fact that any potential buyer could check on.

Statistics

Persuasive writers frequently use statistics to support their arguments. Try to determine the validity of statistics before using them in an essay. Do they come from a qualified, unbiased source?

It is important to be skeptical about statistics, especially those used in television commercials and printed advertisements. In a particular advertisement, the manufacturer might make a strong claim about the product's efficiency. It may be difficult to tell whether the authority quoted is qualified. A wary person would decide to check further before buying this product.

Only use statistics from qualified authorities in your arguments, and inform the reader exactly who or what your source is to add credence to your evidence. A convincing endorsement for a dictaphone might read something like the following.

> *"We have cut our staff from eight to six employees thanks to Dictaphone," Roberta Flemming, Director of Medical Records at Riverview Manor, informed this writer in a recent interview. "Not only has Dictaphone saved us many staff hours, but our records are more up to date than before."*

Because statistics change regularly, they must be dated exactly when introduced. For example,

> *In the United States, government spending on the elderly rose (in then current dollars) from $3,860 per person in 1965 to $11,350 per person in 1990, according to the May 30, 1992, issue of the* Economist.

Comparisons

Comparisons can add to the persuasiveness of an argument. You might support an argument in favor of a system of government-provided universal health care with the following comparison.

> *Funded by tax revenue, Great Britain's national health care system eliminates the fear of losing health care benefits that prevents many Americans from leaving jobs they dislike.*

If you were opposing universal free health care, the following comparison could support your position.

> *Americans with adequate health insurance usually have fairly quick access to all types of surgery. On the other hand, persons needing nonemergency surgery often have to wait a long time in Great Britain.*

Anecdotes and Scenarios

In addition to factual data, statistics, and comparisons, persuasive writers may use anecdotes and scenarios to support their arguments. Anecdotes are brief stories or narratives that provide concrete, true-to-life evidence for an argument. The following anecdote could be used for a car advertisement.

Two-year-old Eva Lopez was alone in the back seat of the car. While rounding a sharp turn at a fairly high speed, her mother happened to catch a glimpse in the rearview mirror of Eva determinedly trying to open the door lock. Mrs. Lopez screamed, but that did not deter her daughter. Juanita Lopez is certain that Mercury Sable's child-proof rear door locks saved Eva's life that afternoon.

Anecdotes, or case studies, presenting illustrations of various points can be scattered throughout an argument. Another technique, employed by many public speakers, is to open a persuasive essay with an appropriate anecdote to catch the reader's attention from the start. Recall that "Making It Safe," the second argument essay in this chapter, begins with an anecdote about the writer's missing car stereo.

Anecdotes describe instances of what actually happened, while **scenarios** are narratives that depict what could happen. Writers frequently use scenarios to predict problems likely to ensue if, for example, people do not heed current warnings about environmental issues or population growth.

A lead story about the 1992 Earth Summit in Rio de Janeiro in the May 30, 1992, *Economist* took the form of a grim scenario. It opened with a prediction that world population growth would "almost certainly have doubled" by the middle of the twenty-first century, and "may have quadrupled" before eventually leveling off. "Most of these extra people will be crowded into the third world, mainly in the countries that already find it hardest to provide food, water, jobs and health care for their people." By 2050 Bangladesh may have 245 million people, a population density of 1,700 people per square kilometer. By 1990, only a "handful of countries," such as Holland or South Korea, had more than 400 people per square kilometer. Apart from a few city-states like Hong Kong, no society has ever "managed people as tightly packed" as the population figures projected for the next century.

Be sure to accurately document and identify the source of a "borrowed" scenario. Observe that the clearly identified scenario above is largely a paraphrase—a summary in the writer's words—from a 1992 article in the *Economist*.

You may also create your own scenarios. For example, you might predict what would happen to your younger brother if he does not finish high school or write a scenario of what could result if the office equipment in your workplace is not adequately maintained and regularly updated. Then back up your predictions with concrete evidence.

Remember that even the best combination of all of these types of supporting evidence is unlikely to be effective without a good topic. In turn, a good topic can be strengthened by quotations and paraphrased evidence from outside authorities that back up the writer's claims.

Finding a Good, Lively Topic

When choosing a topic for an argument or persuasive essay, pick something that you care about so that your essay will have a strong voice. Freewriting or clustering on one or all of the following promptings in your journal may be a good way to focus on a topic.

It's about time someone . . .

It makes me furious that . . .

Try taking a class in . . .

Something that really concerns me is . . .

When choosing a topic, it is best to avoid complex, often-discussed topics, such as gun control or the problems of the welfare system, unless you have already done considerable research on the topic or have special, personal experiences or knowledge that would bear on the matter. Otherwise your argument may become a dull, rather stiff rehash of what has already been said by many other people. You might also fall into the trap of making broad generalizations about the topic that are not adequately backed up and therefore not convincing to your skeptical readers.

Too often, student arguments can be boring because they repeat the familiar. Their authors leave out their best weapon, their own experiences, when in many cases those very experiences prompted them to write about the topic in the first place! The best persuasive essays give students an opportunity to share personal insights with readers who have not had the same experiences or have not looked at a topic in the same way as they have. These writers wisely avoid broad, unwieldy topics like the national debt or nuclear fallout.

Try reading editorials and letters to the editors in a variety of publications to see how other writers argue effectively. In addition to improving your persuasive writing skills, critical reading of a wide range of persuasive essays can make you a more skeptical analyst of the claims of others.

"No matter how objective a publication is, it always has a slant." This warning from her high school English teacher strongly influenced Alice Pfeifer, author of the regular "Media Watch" column in the *Milwaukee Advocate*. Because Pfeifer has opted for a career of reading—and writing—for justice, the *Advocate* featured the young Milwaukean as its "People Who Make a Difference" choice for the May/June 1992 issue. Like Pfeifer, work at becoming "an avid, yet suspicious" reader of the popular press.

Reading critically and widely also exposes readers to the many techniques experienced writers use to liven up their prose. Pay attention to these techniques and use them to make your arguments more convincing and interesting.

Exercise

Analyze former Democratic Congressman Jim Moody's argument (below) about the health-care crisis in the United States, one of the major issues in the 1992 elections and an issue of ongoing concern to many Americans. Read through the entire essay for an overall view of his argument. Then reread it carefully, keeping the following questions in mind as you prepare for a small group discussion of Moody's arguments. Annotate the text and take notes in your journal, both on the questions below and on the points covered in your group's discussion of Congressman Moody's proposal.

1. What claim does Moody make in this position paper?
2. What is the purpose of the first four paragraphs of his essay?
3. What is Moody defending in the second half of the essay?
4. Which of the arguing strategies discussed in this chapter does Moody use to defend his position?
5. Does Moody adequately document the sources of his data? Would you like more information?
6. What counterarguments does Moody bring up?
7. Which of his assertions raise questions in your mind?
8. What is the purpose of the article's concluding paragraph?

Exercise

Do your experiences and observations support Moody's position that there is a "health-care access crisis" in the United States today? Write your reactions to Jim Moody's article in your journal, supporting your positions with specific examples. Have you, your friends, or family members been unable to obtain adequate health care? Why?

Universal Health Care Act Would Solve National Insurance Crisis
Jim Moody

We've all seen it. All of the major networks have devoted significant segments of prime-time air time to the coverage of the issue of health insurance reform. The access crisis in America's health care system has become an issue for national debate.

Working America is underinsured. The following figures speak for themselves:

- Thirty-four million Americans (14% of our population) have no formal health-insurance coverage.
- Over 300,000 working Wisconsinites have no health insurance (about 1/2 million, overall).
- Twelve million American children have no access to health care because they are not covered by health insurance.

Today, the United States spends 14% of its Gross National Product (GNP), one out of every seven dollars, on health care. At the current rate of increase, the United States will be spending 40% of the GNP (or 4 of every 10 dollars) on health care by the close of the century.

The costs of administrating the American health care delivery system are way out of line—it's that simple. Administrative costs account for 24% of total health care expenditures. The American health care provision system is shackled by paperwork chains which prevent the cost-effective delivery of medical services.

In response to this national crisis, I have introduced into the Congress a bill, the Universal Health Care Act of 1991, which would address the four issues central to meaningful reform of the health insurance system:

1) Universal Access;
2) Choice of Health Care Provider;
3) Comprehensive Coverage; and
4) Cost Controls.

My bill, if passed, would provide access to health care for every American. Among the many advantages of a Universal-Access system are: protection of working families with automatic health insurance coverage of the unemployed and improving American competitiveness by lifting the burden of health insurance provision from the shoulders of American businesses.

The single payer envisioned by the Act would make payments to any facility or individual authorized by the state to provide health care services. Thus my proposal retains complete patient choice of doctor, hospital, and/or other health care provider.

The Act would completely cover, without the need for deductibles or co-payments, such diverse services as long-term care for seniors, unlimited coverage of catastrophic care, preventative (including prenatal) care,

> home health care services, nursing facility services, dental care, inpatient and outpatient care, and prescription drugs.
>
> The General Accounting Office estimates that a single-payer system such as the one envisioned by the Act would save $67 billion in the first year alone. That amount would be enough to completely cover the expansion of coverage to include everyone. The biggest reduction in health care expenses would be realized as a result of an elimination of the administrative waste that exists under the current system.
>
> Advantages with a single-payer system include: 95% of Americans paying less for health care than they do today; a family of four with an annual income of $40,000 saving $1,590, compared to the present system, and, on average, employers' outlays for health insurance cut in half.
>
> I am confident that a program such as mine, providing for Universal-Access and employing a single payer, is the best way to end our health care access crisis. I encourage you to call my District Office at 555-1331, and make your voice heard!

Exercise

Expository writing, such as argumentative or persuasive essays, need not be dull and can even be funny. Spice up arguments with anecdotes, illustrations, or interesting descriptive sections. Like the writers of the student essays included below, you will get the best results by choosing a topic you care about. In a short essay it is best to avoid large, complex topics like the proper disposal of nuclear waste. Likely topics are specific problems in a facility you frequent or in your home, dormitory, or workplace, or your experiences as a member of a club or team.

Option 1: Making a Proposal

Write an essay that proposes a solution to a problem. Address your essay to someone in a position to help solve the problem. Your essay should:

- define and describe the problem, and, if relevant, discuss the causes;
- propose a solution;
- discuss benefits from that solution; and
- demonstrate why your solution is better than alternate proposals.

Prewriting: Exploring the Topic

As you consider the proposal option, ask yourself the following questions: What problems do I regularly encounter in my residence or workplace or on campus? Can I propose a reasonable solution to one of those problems, one that others might consider adopting? Remember that a big task like reforming your college's registration system would involve many variables and expenses about which you do not have expert knowledge. You might, however, propose that faculty members be in their offices at prescribed times to advise registering students, explaining the advantages of such a system.

Do some freewriting, and make a cluster diagram or scratch outline about your proposal topic. Discuss your idea with friends, other members of your English class, and a tutor or your instructor. Review "Making It Safe" for ideas on developing and organizing a proposal.

Option 2: Taking a Position
Write a position paper on a controversial issue. Examine the issue critically, take a position on it, and develop a reasoned argument to support your position. You may well want to buttress your argument with information from outside authorities.

When choosing your topic, avoid broad, often-discussed topics like racism or alcohol abuse unless you bring pertinent personal experiences to the topic. Everyone knows that you should not drink and drive. However, if one of your brothers is dead and two of your friends are in wheelchairs because of an automobile accident in which you were the driver—and the only person who was not seriously hurt—then you *do* have something to say about that much-discussed topic. Pick a topic that is of a manageable size and that you feel *strongly* about. Some possible topics are:

1. Foreign language study should or should not be required for a college degree.
2. College students should or should not be required to perform a prescribed number of hours of voluntary service to graduate.
3. It should be legal or illegal for cosmetic companies to perform experiments on animals.

Prewriting: Exploring the Topic
Do some freewriting, jotting, or clumping about your strong convictions and important experiences. Perhaps, like guitarist Chris Gebhard whose essay follows later in this section, you want to encourage others to discover a particular skill or hobby that you enjoy. Maybe you have done volunteer work, taken a course, or had a job that has been an important influence in your life, possibly leading to a career decision. Perhaps you are, or have been, a member of an organization that has benefited you enormously; if the organization has been a bad experience, write an essay warning readers against joining the group. Or write to the group's leaders with constructive suggestions for strengthening it.

Browse through the student essays later in this chapter for possible topics, as well as for models for developing an argument. If no idea strikes you, make a cluster diagram around this heading:

(*Topics I feel strongly about*)—(*unequal funding for women's athletics*)

Pick the most promising of the topics engendered by the clumping, then freewrite about it in your journal. Talk over the position topic with friends, class members, and your instructors, and ask for their suggestions for developing the paper.

While you are deciding upon a topic, consider the following exercise.

Exercise

Option 1: Write a letter to the person you think is responsible for the problem or has authority to fix the problem. This someone could be your boss, your alderman or alderwoman, a hospital administrator, a school official, and so on. Use details to support your case, and propose the action required to "solve" the problem. In other words, what do you want the person to do?

At the top of your paper, describe in a short paragraph the person you are writing to, as well as the strategies you are employing to persuade this person to your point of view.

Option 2: Write an essay or editorial on a controversial topic for publication by the magazine or newspaper of your choice. You will probably want to choose a local publication, perhaps a college newspaper. The essay must bring about awareness and understanding of the problem and may include a recommended solution. Include a title that will both be informative and grab the attention of your readers.

At the top of your paper, describe in a short paragraph the type of publication you have chosen and the audience you are writing for. Note what your goal is and, if applicable, what action you expect your readers to take.

The following student essays may help you make a final choice about both the format and topic for your persuasion paper, as well as to select strategies for developing an argument. Several of the essays demonstrate how a good writer can take a rather familiar topic and make it interesting by using many details and taking a somewhat different slant. All of these essays demonstrate the importance of using personal experiences as a major weapon in an argument; some show how outside authorities can be used to corroborate and supplement those personal experiences.

Reading these student essays may suggest a topic on the media for you to pursue. How do specific television programs or commercials stereotype the elderly? What role does television play in shaping our values? Because the purpose of commercial television is to provide a vehicle for advertisers to sell their products, from childhood on American viewers are manipulated by television producers and the sponsors who pay for their programs. The pervasive role of the media, especially television, is a much-discussed topic in American life. Nonetheless, the next two student writers have commented on that familiar topic in an interesting and lively fashion.

Most of us have seen hundreds, even thousands, of television commercials directed at children, yet Sean Veternick's essay makes us pay more careful attention to the effects of such commercials on their intended audience. Analyze Sean's essay and decide exactly what makes it effective. Use marginal notes and underlining or highlighting to mark effective places. Also denote places where the argument could be improved. Write your overall reactions to his essay in your journal. Then consider the following points.

1. Note that Sean's catchy title comes from a line in his essay.
2. What is Sean's thesis? Where is that thesis first stated, and is it repeated?
3. Do the anecdotes and illustrations in Sean's essay support his thesis well?
4. What organizing techniques are used in those anecdotes?
5. Make a scratch outline of "Take It from an Ex-Kid" in your journal.

Take It from an Ex-Kid
Sean Veternick

T.V. commercials which are broadcast during children's shows often take advantage of the gullibility of their audience. The advertisers use various techniques to capture a child's attention. Unfortunately for parents, the children frequently do develop an interest in an item. This interest often turns into a desire for the product or the activity. And what rational way do children go about trying to get something? They beg their parents, of course. Now the burden of possession has been placed on the parents, which I feel is not right.

Some of the most persuasive commercials shown during such shows are children's cereal advertisements. One method used in selling these items is to use fictional characters that are related to the product. These animations help kids associate the product with one of their interests, cartoons. For example, Trix cereal uses an animated rabbit to sell their product. Kids see the Trix rabbit and the first thing that pops into their minds is Trix cereal. The most well known form of selling children's cereals is to include a free toy inside the box—ask any parent. I can remember when I was a kid; I would beg my mother to get a certain cereal that had a free toy in it. The bad thing was that the cereal often sat untouched in the pantry for months and the paper or plastic toy usually fell apart within the first couple days. Another method of advertising "kiddy cereals" is to make them appeal to the parents. Kix cereal used a catchy slogan, "Kids like Kix for what Kix has got; Moms like Kix for what Kix has not." An ad depicted a parent and a child singing this melody, while the child merrily chowed down the product. A commercial like this is passing a frequently used message: if kids like it and it's good for them, why not buy it?

Toy commercials during children's shows definitely take advantage of their audience. They illustrate children playing with their product to show how much fun it is. But take it from me, an ex-kid, the toy usually isn't as fun as they show. Super action figures, miniature plastic dolls of action cartoon characters on television, use this concept. They also usually run their commercials during their T.V. shows. Both of these principles were used by the advertisements for Silver Hawk action figures. Most of their advertisements were run during the *Silver Hawk Show*—Monday through Friday at 2:00 P.M. on Milwaukee's channel 24. All of their commercials began with an action clip from the T.V. series and then showed children playing with the actual dolls. The idea such advertisers are trying to send to their audience is "create your own adventure." However, I don't know how hard I tried when I was a kid, but it just wasn't the same as the cartoon strip.

Advertisements for kids' entertainment places use mainly visual illustrations to persuade their young audience. All they need to show to grab a young person's interest is a child having a great time at their entertainment place. For instance, a commercial for Chuck E. Cheese's pizza place depicts a child playing on various toys and games and eating pizza. What the child sees is a great amount of fun and of course he or she will want to go there. However, what the commercial fails to show is how busy the place usually is, the number of kids crying and screaming and how expensive these places seem to be. I know all this from a personal experience when I took my niece to Chuck E. Cheese's. I really don't know if she had fun or not, since most of the time she couldn't play on any toys because there were too many kids on them. After we ate a bad pizza and she played with a couple more games, I decided it was time to go home. As we left I asked her if she had a fun time and she replied, "I don't know." Then she asked me if I had a fun time and I looked in my empty wallet and realized I spent nearly twenty dollars and I also replied, "I don't know." This made me wonder if we went to the same Chuck E. Cheese's that was advertised on T.V. Another way these types of businesses advertise is to show that they provide another way to form family togetherness. Personally, I think if you take your children to the park, you'll have a better time and spend a lot less.

As you can see, these commercials do in fact take advantage of the gullibility of children. Most cereals aren't as good and nutritious as they say, the toys aren't as fun as they illustrate, and many kids' entertainment places seem to lack a sufficient amount of entertainment.

Think about your own opinions on the influence of television programs and commercials on children. How do children you know respond to television commercials? Analyze some commercials aimed at children. Do your findings support, or challenge, the arguments in "Take It from an Ex-Kid"?

You may decide that the pervasive influence of the media is a topic you too wish to explore in an essay. Do some freewriting on the topic. Why do you watch television? Do you ever find yourself watching a program that does not interest you? How much television do you watch? In your journal, keep a record of your television viewing for a few days. Does anything surprise you about that record? Analyze several commercials and write about them. Do they contain stereotyping? What kids of appeals—to logic or to emotions—do they use to promote their products?

Now read the following two student papers on weight loss and the so-called perfect body. Amy Brinkman, who has an extensive background in dance and theater, both as a performer and a teacher, works in a profession that puts an especially high priority on appearance. She bases her essay on her own experiences, but also relies on clearly introduced outside authorities to support her arguments.

Observe that Amy employs facts, statistics, and anecdotes drawn from her own experiences and observations, as well as from outside authorities. Instead of listing the sources of these authorities in a "Works Cited" list at the end of her essay, Amy identifies them in her text: "An article by Gwenda Blair in the April 1992 issue of *Self*" is the first such in-text citation.

Whether citing outside authorities or recounting her own and others' experiences, Amy never loses track of her overall thesis and purpose. For instance, she makes it clear that an anecdote about a young anorexic friend typifies the problems experienced by many teenagers, especially girls, thus putting her friend Anna's story into a wider context. Summarize Amy's claim, or thesis, in your journal.

To Be or Not to Be . . . Thin
Amy Brinkman

If only it were different—somehow better—then life would also be better. I can't count how many times I have heard people (including myself) say that is how they felt about their body. Exactly how it would be better is unimportant; it just would be, that's all.

When I take a trip down memory lane and come across photos of myself in a swim suit, the most vivid memories are those of feeling awkward. There aren't enough curves here and too many there; my waist is too high and too large; my eyes are too small and of course I would like to take off some weight. I'm not fat but I'm never the size I want to be.

Sound familiar? It should. Primarily because of magazines, television, advertisements and certainly the movie industry, more women are striving for the overall perfect body—maybe at the risk of their own health.

The pressure that American women of all ages feel to meet an ideal body shape, which is unattainable for most of them, is so pervasive it almost becomes invisible. Social pressures may be invisible, but their results are very real. According to surveys done by the Kingsely Institution American women have more negative feelings about their bodies than women in any culture.

An article by Gwenda Blair in the April 1992 issue of *SELF* summarizes some 5,000 women's responses to a readers' poll on body image. Only 7% of the respondents said they are happy with the way their bodies look. It's not hard to see why: 94% think about their weight constantly and frequently draw negative conclusions; of that 94%, 84% consider themselves overweight. What do they want? According to that same readers' poll: flatter stomachs, thinner thighs, less body fat, slimmer hips, stronger arms, no cellulite, better proportions; in some cases smaller breasts and in others larger ones. When asked whom do they see as having the ideal female bodies, the results of the poll were somewhat predictable, Madonna, Cher, Raquel Welch, Jane Fonda and Linda Hamilton.

Notice anything that these women might have in common? That's right, they're all celebrities. How can so many women be eating their hearts out because they don't look like Madonna or Cher? Most celebrities have had major body makeovers, not to mention face work. They probably have personal trainers and quite literally, it's their job to look good!

So why are American women so obsessed with the idea of the perfect image? Because all day, every day, movies, television, magazines and billboards show us beautiful skin, perfect smiles and long, long legs. The wonderful world of advertising would like us to feel safe in knowing that if we weren't born with natural beauty, we can invest in endless amounts of products that will result in "the look." But I say all the beauty products in the world aren't going to make your legs longer or change the shape of your face from square to pear shaped. My point is—what's wrong with the way most of us look now? Don't get me wrong; I'd be the first one in line for free give-aways of Cher's body, but that's not going to happen. So instead I work with what God has given me, or closer to home, what my parents have given me. I know staying in shape and eating right is part of being healthy, but sometimes being in shape is confused with having a so-called perfect body.

According to one study published in the March 1992 issue of *McCALL's,* the average American sees between 400 and 1,400 advertising images each day, most of which are endorsed by thin, gorgeous women. The be-thin message is repeated so often we become blind to it. We don't even realize how much we are influenced by it.

The problem with the "ideal" body image that society has embedded into our subconscious is not just its effects on adults but the message it sends to our teenage girls who are most vulnerable. Serious problems may occur in the process of achieving a certain body type including eating disorders such as bulimia and anorexia nervosa. Recently Anna, a young girl I've known for some time, was hospitalized for anorexia and severe depression. I guess I wasn't surprised since any time anyone would give Anna a compliment she would respond with at least four reasons why she wasn't even worthy of a few kind words. She is an attractive girl with long brown hair, warm brown eyes and a cute figure, yet along with thousands of girls her age, seventeen, she thinks of herself as anything but attractive. Anna told her doctor that all she wanted was to fit in and be popular. She also felt that she had lost total control of her life and that losing weight and striving for the perfect body would change all of that.

Even though we all know it's not true, many women believe that if they could just look right, they would be right. Because this constant fretting about how we look is something that is learned, not innate, part of the solution may be in changing the way so many children are raised to feel about themselves and to try decreasing the amount of emphasis that is placed on looks. It would be impossible to shelter children from the media and even more impossible to monitor what they are thinking. But we can reassure them that they are who they are because God creates everyone as individuals, not from the same mold. We can help them understand that to be themselves and accept who they are is to be happy. Young people have so many pressures to deal with that they need to be made aware that this illusion of beauty is fabricated by the media, and that no matter how many hours a day they work out and how thin they become, most people never achieve the same look as Cher.

> Although we may never see a slightly overweight, plain looking but happy model on the cover of VANITY FAIR, we can accept doing whatever we can to look and feel healthy, and put the remainder of our energy into improving the rest of our lives and forgetting about letting others decide what is beautiful and what is right for each of us.

The American obsession with appearance, especially with being slim, is likewise the topic of Sherry Klawitter's essay. Unlike Amy Brinkman's essay, which goes beyond her own experiences and cites outside authorities, Sherry writes entirely about her own painful experiences, supporting her thesis that being somewhat overweight is a burden made worse by the actions of others.

What specific illustrations does Sherry give to demonstrate how others sometimes treat her—and by implication other overweight people in our society? Make a rough outline of Sherry's essay in your journal. Write your reaction to her conclusion. Is it convincing? Why or why not? Is it the most effective way she might have ended her essay?

Happiness?? Fat Chance!
Sherry Klawitter

Though some people may not think that being overweight is a physical limitation, others, mainly overweight people themselves, consider it a physical and psychological burden. Though I may not be severely obese, I still consider my weight a physical limitation that affects me in almost everything I do.

The tasks of everyday life have become a challenge to me. Walking from class to class and feeling fatigued as a result makes me realize that my weight is indeed a physical limitation. I also suffer from many backaches caused by my being overweight. Even walking to the mailbox puts me out of breath. My occupation as a waitress has also brought on new challenges as well. At the end of a shift my body, especially my legs and feet, feels the effects of even the slowest of nights. I am also unable to work long shifts because my energy level seems to diminish before my shift is over.

On campus, I feel that I am singled out. When I pass by a group of my peers, they often hurl insults at me, like "cow" and even "fat pig." People stare boldly and whisper as I walk by. It seems as if they tease me with their eyes. Even my best friend has gotten into the act on occasion by calling me "porky," "blimp" and even "fatso." I feel like an outcast, and often sit alone hidden away in the union, where no one will see me. Why do people make it their obligation to make me aware of my weight?

School is not the only place where I feel this rejection. My family also seems to disapprove of my weight. They often comment on my weight, even when others are present, never concerning themselves with my feelings. It seems that my father considers me a family disgrace because I do not fit his image of a daughter. I learned this one night after he told me he could not stand his daughter being "as big as a house." My mother seems to think making me feel guilty about my weight will somehow get me to shed my extra pounds. More often than not they have brought me to tears with their constant cruelty.

Facing this constant torment from so many directions is frustrating and confusing. I feel frustrated because I do not know how to handle my feelings and confused because I'm not sure of all the emotions I feel, but anger is certainly the most dominant of all my emotions. I clench my fists and usually try to hide my anger, so I will not strike back at my tormentors. I am also afraid at times. I fear rejection from my boyfriend and my peers, a fear that forces me to hide away at home many nights. In a way, I am ashamed because I've always been slightly overweight, and it's always been beyond my control. I feel left out, because in modern society an overweight female is often the target of ridicule and almost always viewed as sexually unattractive.

As a result, I hide away in my room night after night reading and escaping from this hateful world. I find myself dreaming of being someone else, someone who has the slim beauty I have always longed for. Out in society I cover myself in baggy clothes, but hiding my weight is only half the battle; I still have to deal with my emotions. I usually choose to ignore my feelings, but in cases of extreme depression I try to talk my feelings out with a friend. If I let the feelings bottle up, I end up exploding and crying for hours. Sitting down with someone I trust helps me let down my defenses and bring my feelings out into the open.

Some people make it their obligation to make me aware of my obesity because in American society obese people are considered sight pollution. Since I am not picture perfect, the sight of me sometimes provokes disgust. Today our society is so bent on fitness and being slim that others regularly disregard the feelings of obese people. Maybe someday I will be in a position to change my weight, but right now doing so is not foremost in my mind. Despite the fact that society places a stigma on the overweight, things could be worse. I consider myself lucky when I realize the serious handicaps of others.

Exercise

Explore the topic of the American obsession with weight and appearance in your journal. Are your own experiences and observations similar to those of Amy and Sherry?

One or another of the student persuasive essays in our collection may suggest a good topic for your argument essay. Perhaps you or someone you know well has also had problems with racism or other forms of prejudice like the authors of the next essays.

The type of indignities African Americans still suffer every day is the subject of the next two essays. Yet Charity Turner, author of the first piece, was able to remain amazingly restrained and unemotional about the outrageous incidents she describes, thus adding to the impact of her essay.

A Time for Change
Charity Turner

For eighteen years I had never experienced prejudiced behavior until I started working in the retail business. One day after I began working at a Sears Department Store, my mother and brother came into the store to shop. I stopped my mother and started to talk to her while my brother walked into the men's department. As we stood chatting, we noticed two undercover security guards behind us. Their conversation went like this: "You see that black guy in the men's department? Let's watch him; he looks like a born thief." Then they started to laugh. My mother was very upset. She told them that was her son they were discussing and she didn't appreciate what they had said about him. One's reply was, "He still looks like a thief to me." It was a struggle trying to hold my mother back from fighting. Her anger scared me because I'd never seen my mother get so upset; she usually stayed calm in situations but this wasn't any ordinary situation. I thought my mother was going to get arrested for trying to fight them. That was the first time I had ever experienced prejudice. I never realized how much it could hurt or how angry I could become; I actually felt blood rushing to my head.

After that incident I began to notice how I would be watched when shopping in other stores. It got to the point where I almost stopped shopping completely. I also became very discouraged working at Sears. I quit, but then a year later, when I was working in a retail store again, I soon had another bad encounter. I started working at Marshall Field's and noticed a man who would come into my department every day and literally stare at me. I felt like he was undressing me with his eyes. I dreaded leaving work because I thought I would see him when I'd catch the bus. I also hated coming to work because I knew he would be there watching me. How did he know when I was going to be at work? What did he want from me? I decided I didn't want to find out the answers to these questions. So I called store security and told them that a man had been watching me. I was shocked when I found out he was security! I was so upset that I was being watched that I quit and started working jobs that I hate most—office work. Ever since my experiences with store security, I haven't tried to work in a store. I just don't want to go through that again.

Now when I go in stores and know that security is watching me, I let them know that I don't appreciate their attention. The response I get is, "I'm just doing my job, lady." Which is understandable, but I know they are watching me for one reason—the color of my skin. Am I being too sensitive? I DON'T THINK SO! I also have friends who have had the same problems I have. One friend told me that her boyfriend went into Marshall Field's to get her a thousand dollar engagement ring that she wanted and security literally surrounded him. Her boyfriend was so disgusted that he wasn't going to buy the ring, but he did anyway because he knew how much she wanted it. He said that security looked surprised and stupid when he pulled out his credit card.

I could go on and on about bad experiences with security, but it hurts to remember those bad times. It is time that store security personnel make a change in their behavior and attitudes toward black shoppers. I'm not saying that all store security is bad because I'm sure there are some good security guards. But the ones who have a set opinion of what a shoplifter looks like should change their ways. I think that security guards should go through a sensitivity training course because if they don't start being sensitive to the needs of black shoppers, the stores they work for are going to lose a lot of money. Blacks aren't going to shop at those types of establishments anymore. I think that once security personnel realize that black doesn't mean thief, things will change for the better.

Jackie—It Wasn't Fair
Jennifer Schaefer

It all happened when I was in sixth grade and believe me it was a time I will never forget. I was riding the plain yellow school bus to school, which seemed pretty routine except for one minor detail. As I was sitting next to my best friend Jim like I did everyday, he looked up at the front of the bus and said to me, "Who is that?" I could not see who he was talking about so I just answered, "I don't know!"

As we proceeded to pick up more people, I noticed that every time someone got on the bus, they stared at the person Jim was talking about. By this time, I was getting pretty curious, so I decided to stand up at the next stop. I saw a little girl with black curly hair wearing a blue shirt. I knew I had not seen her before, but that still did not answer my question about why everyone was staring at her.

We arrived at school and the people began to unload one by one, but of course I still could not see her face because she was in front of me.

Once I got into class, everybody was mumbling, but I still could not hear the whole story. All I could hear was: "What is she doing here?" and "Did you see her?" and one girl said, "Her name is Jackie." I was still trying to figure out what was wrong with this so-called Jackie person when our teacher walked in and announced, "Class, in a few minutes a new student will be coming in. Her name is Jackie, and please let's all be nice to her; you know it is her first day!"

The next few minutes seemed like hours, but then finally the door opened and in walked Jackie with brown curly hair, big brown eyes, a blue shirt, and black pants just like us. All eyes were fixed on her like flies stick to fly paper. Just then I heard everybody gasp; I tried to notice something else about her that might seem out of the ordinary, but nothing came to mind until I heard someone whisper, "She's black."

For me seeing Jackie as black was no different than seeing Jackie as white. Color doesn't matter; I had grown up with blacks since I was little. Some of my mom's friends were black; we would all go camping together, go to the lake, have sleep-overs. To me there was no difference other than the color of their skin.

Jackie was the first black student in our suburban school. She was an innocent victim in our class; the majority judged her for her color, not for who she was on the inside. In our school, all of the students were brought up with all white children around them. Virtually none of them had had contact with black people before, and that was mainly the parents' fault (choice). Some parents were even teaching their children not to talk to or go near black people because they were supposedly all bad. Jackie was tormented for weeks; the kids would taunt: "You nigger!" and, "Go home you fool!" and, "Why are you here?" At the same time the kids said to me, "You traitor, who do you think you are?" All because I wanted to be friends with her. The name calling and racist remarks never stopped and the parents became furious when they finally found out that it was true that Jackie was at our school. The parents had meetings to try and figure out a way to get Jackie out of "their" school.

I had been brought up with black people in my old neighborhood and I saw no difference in them, but when I tried to convince the other kids of that I was ridiculed and told to keep my mouth shut. I was also brought up thinking that everyone was created equal and that everyone had their own rights, and I could not understand why my belief did not hold true then.

Jackie put up with the racists' remarks for a year and a half until finally her father got a new job and the family moved to Illinois.

This was my first experience with the reality that many people do not give others the benefit of the doubt and that even in America people do not have all the freedoms we were granted in the Constitution. Unless everyone gives people of all races an equal chance, how will we ever become one?

When I finished writing this paper I called Jackie up at Northern Illinois University and read it to her. She laughed for a few minutes and then said, "My first day of Hell was the first day of our lasting friendship!" Jackie and I are still best friends who would do anything for each other!

As you reflect on these two essays, note that Charity used several incidents to illustrate her thesis, while Jennifer used one extended example. Compared to most of her classmates, Jennifer was certainly fortunate that her background let her see beyond the kind of racial and other stereotypes that lead to terrible discriminations against many minorities in our multicultural society. Perhaps you too have had an experience with discrimination that you want to share with your readers. Another idea is to read a children's book and analyze it for stereotypes.

As you read Chris Gebhard's essay, think of skills or hobbies that you enjoy and might encourage others to discover.

Music Participation Enhances Creativity
Chris Gebhard

There are things that people need to keep balance in their lives. Students need a break from their required courses, something that can keep school from becoming too monotonous. I feel that participation in music should be a part of everyone's college studies. Not only would music increase their academic performance, but it would enhance their lives overall. Most teachers agree that music and art increase creativity in other areas of study. I don't think that they should be required, but I know that music classes, no matter what level of a performer the person is, can be fun, educational, and rewarding. And students don't have to be performers to enjoy music.

Most people have played an instrument at some time in their lives. Some quit because they find other interests. Others might stop playing because they didn't think they were good enough. Some people are obviously better than others at playing an instrument, but that doesn't mean that everyone can't enjoy doing it. It's never too late to take an instrument up again or to start playing one. Much enjoyment can be gained even from playing a simple piece that is easy to learn. Most colleges offer great basic performance courses in guitar and piano. The student can learn the basics of music while also learning how to play simple, fun songs. For instance, the beginning guitar class here at UWM teaches such songs as "Eleanor Rigby" and "He's Got The Whole World In His Hands," as well as basic note reading and theory. This class would also be an excellent breather from a heavy schedule of academic courses.

I am a jazz guitar performance major, and as a requirement I occasionally teach segments of the intermediate guitar course. The students often tell me how much fun it is to get credits learning how to play music. They are taught everything from blues standards to fingerstyle and bluegrass songs. I often hear remarks about how good it feels to get a sense of accomplishment from learning their favorite songs. And each new song they play builds their enthusiasm. One student exclaimed, "I never thought music would be so easy and fun!" Another student told me that the class gives his mind a break before his two-hour economics course. There are, of course, basic requirements to all music classes that require some homework, but my point is that the creative benefits that come from music participation are worth a little extra studying.

The cost of an instrument might be a problem for some. But with a little looking around, a quality used instrument shouldn't be hard to find. A friend of mine bought a used acoustic guitar for $80 that plays just as well as many top of the line recent models. Even though that was a rare find, most music stores have reasonable prices on their instruments. You could ask a music teacher at school about the best local store, or listen to word of mouth. If the cost of an instrument is prohibitive, sign up for piano lessons. Most colleges have practice rooms for piano students. For instance, UWM has approximately fifteen piano equipped rooms in the Fine Arts Building. A fee of $2.50 gets you a key.

If a student didn't want to learn to play an instrument, there are other ways that a music class could still be taken. UWM has a two-credit course called *The Concert Experience.* The student attends and comments on concerts both off and on campus. I think many people would become inspired by seeing a great performer in concert. There are two other classes, *Chamber Music in Performance,* and *Elementary General Music Sampler,* that have no prerequisites, and students need not be performers to enroll. Any of these classes would be perfect for students that wanted to augment their schedule. In particular, education majors could get a great deal out of learning to teach with music as an enhancer: I have a friend, majoring in elementary education, who uses music in her practice teaching classes to keep the children interested and aware. A few times during every class she leads the children in a sing-along, accompanying them on guitar. She uses songs that she learned in the beginning guitar course here at UWM.

Music has always been a big part of my life. As a music major I can assure you how much fun and life-enhancing music classes can also be for you. The creativity that comes from experiencing and playing music can add to any student's college schedule.

Richard Serrano obviously had a good time writing this tongue-in-cheek proposal.

"Could I have some ketchup, please?"
A modest proposal from a condiment junkie
Richard Serrano

Ahh ketchup. How I do love it so. And for those of you out there who feel the same way, the following proposal should be of some interest. Alas, if you do not feel as I do about this condiment of the gods, I ask that you please bear with me as I map out a plan that could possibly restore a bit more order to the present chaos that is our world. You see, I am of the opinion that unless we enlarge the present size of ketchup packets, we may soon find ourselves facing mass hysteria and insanity.

This is a serious problem that has haunted me for most of my life. I don't treat ketchup as a simple condiment. No siree my dear friend. To me, ketchup is the main course, and the food merely serves as a host. My food does not get dipped into the ketchup. It's coated and drowned until it loses its original form and becomes a shiny, red mass. I've eaten ketchup with every dead animal that made it to my plate—not to mention quite a few vegetables. I've put it on beef (yes, even prime rib), pork, born and preborn poultry, all seafood, every form of potato, tomatoes, and ketchup has even made it onto my pizza.

Eating ketchup does not pose a problem when I'm in my own domestic empire. I buy the Heinz (only the best!) 64 ounce, super squeeze, giant size, mother load, ketchup jug, and I replace it every fortnight. Restaurants that utilize waiters do not present too much of a problem either. Whenever I empty their pint-sized ketchup bottles, the waiters grudgingly bring me full bottles. However, the places that have plagued me for most of my life have been the eating establishments that I not only frequent the most, but also hold the most dear to my heart: fast-food restaurants.

Most of you are aware of, and have experienced, this long-ignored problem. You've ordered your hamburger and fries and you ask for some ketchup. Through my years of experience I have found that this simple request will reward you with a puny packet of ketchup. Now I've worked in the fast-food industry in the past, and my superiors always instructed me to give the customers what they wanted. When a customer asked, "Could I have some ketchup, please?" I would fork over around 7–10 packets; if they wanted "extra" ketchup, then we're talking 20–30. Maybe that's just me, but I see those amounts as normal. When I get handed only two packets of ketchup, I start to get the feeling that these cashiers are from the planet Mars, where I hear that ketchup was never developed. What in the world can I do with two measly packets of ketchup? The person at the register may act as if you're asking for their own blood, and only hand out two more packets.

Now before we start clamoring for public lynching, let's try to keep a cool head. There are ways around this particular problem. If you ask for a specific number of packets they will have no choice but to oblige. Remember, you are the customer. You have the money and the power, so you'd better not waste either. Another way around the problem is to only go to places like Wendy's. Dave Thomas, founder and owner of Wendy's, is gracious enough to provide us with a spigot, so that we have total control over the ketchup. The ease of applying ketchup with a spigot brings to mind the other problem with those miniature ketchup packets.

For those of you who imbibe massive quantities of ketchup, and even the warped individuals who only partake in moderation, the act of transferring the glorious, red paste from packet to food not only wastes time and leaves a mess, but can also render the consumer extremely traumatized. Have you ever tried opening and squeezing 30 little packets of ketchup? If you do manage to tear on the dotted line without much difficulty, your food will surely be cold by the time you're ready to stuff your face. This again leads me to praise Wendy's, and others like it, for leading the industry in ketchup awareness.

Now just slow down people because I already know what you're thinking. You're about to tell me that ketchup spigots will save the earth and answer all of our problems. Well, I have one thing to say to that: takeout. Sure you can glob the ketchup onto your burger and then wrap it back up, but what about having an extra pile of ketchup for dunking your burger? I don't even have to mention french fries. I'm afraid that spigots, while noble in their attempt, are unable to provide the ultimate solution. Therefore I offer you my humble suggestion. Offer a variety of larger ketchup packets by doubling and tripling the present size.

This one sweeping change would solve all of the problems that I've mentioned here—from miserly fast-food workers to cold food. Who knows? Maybe with this one stroke we could set off a chain reaction that would bring about an end to our lesser problems such as war, famine, disease, and high tuition costs. The enlargement of ketchup packets just might wipe out the problems that have hounded people ever since the first human being uttered the all important words, "Could I have some ketchup, please?"

Drafting an Argument

Look over all of your exploratory prewriting, then, in your journal, make a cluster diagram about your final topic choice. Include every point and detail you can think of that might make your paper more persuasive or interesting. Superfluous material can always be discarded during the next stages in the writing process. Use your cluster diagram as the basis for a scratch outline or a listing of the reasons you intend to use to support your position or proposal. Decide on a tentative organizational scheme; perhaps you want to build up your argument gradually, leaving the strongest point until last.

Write an exploratory draft of the entire essay. State your claim, or thesis, and explain your topic clearly early in the essay. Before stating that thesis, however, you may wish to open with an introductory anecdote that arouses your readers' interest and leads into the topic. Some background material that describes and demonstrates the importance of the problem may also be essential at this point. Give the reasons for your position in the body of your essay. Add voice by including lots of information about your experiences with your topic. Remember that in an argument personal experience and caring about your topic are your best weapons. Conclude your essay by briefly restating your position or proposal and urging your readers to give it serious consideration.

Analyze your exploratory draft to discover whether you need to strengthen your argument with outside sources. If so, any research should be completed at this stage. You may wish to interview experts on the topic as well as using written materials.

Have someone read your exploratory draft to point out weak spots in your argument and places that need clarification or more development. Ask that person to be frank about suggesting ways to make your argument more convincing.

As you work on your argument essay, the following hints may also prove to be useful.

Some Pitfalls to Avoid in an Argument

1. Picking a topic that really arouses your interest and gives you a chance to use your own experiences as one major weapon.
2. Failing to make your thesis, or claim, clear to your readers, preferably by stating that thesis early in the essay.
3. Writing an argumentative paper "off the top of your head"; your lack of forethought and preparation usually shows. However, freewriting "off the top of your head" during the prewriting stage may well help you to discover topics you care enough about to develop for a persuasive essay.
4. Choosing a topic such as global warming that is too broad and complex to be adequately covered in a brief argumentative paper.
5. Choosing topics that are discussed all too frequently, such as the death penalty, unless you can bring special personal experiences, insights, or research to the topic. Remember that personal experience is your best weapon; it interests your reader and adds voice. Describe exactly what it is like to be on A.F.D.C. (Aid to Families

with Dependent Children) or an athletic scholarship; do not assume that everyone knows, because they do not. Use that evidence in support of your argument. Make your position clear and strongly defend it. Beware of the "so-what factor"; do not simply repeat dull material that has been said all too often or that almost everyone knows. Most people know perfectly well that smoking is bad for their health or that they will probably get better grades if they study harder. If you have no particular insights to share and the generally familiar is all you can come up with during your prewriting, drop that topic and begin working on another one.

6. Soaring off into the blue. Stay with your topic and avoid introducing extraneous material that does not advance your essay and may confuse your reader.

7. Losing sight of your audience. Remember that your purpose is to sell your readers on your ideas, or at least get them to pay serious attention to what you have to say. An argument should be more than a statement of your opinions. An effective argument contains a claim or a proposal for change, with solid, persuasive reasons to back it up. Include enough specific information and illustrations to make a strong case. Draw on your own experiences to support those reasons, and, where appropriate, use outside authorities to back them up.

8. Failing to respect your audience. We agree with Jack Rawlins, author of *The Writer's Way*, that it is beneficial to write for a specific audience to whom your topic matters and to treat that audience with respect. No one wants to be pressured into accepting another person's views. Do not write like you have the absolute truth on a subject and that no reasonable person could possibly hold another opinion about it; take a balanced view and use a reasonable tone. In other words, do not imply that "any fool knows" what you know (316–17).

9. Alienating some readers by using blanket generalizations ("All students think that . . .") or "loaded words." Do not refer to the President of the United States as "that idiot in the Oval Office" or use the term "baby murderers" to describe supporters of legalized abortion. Your readers are looking for a well-reasoned argument, not a harangue from a wobbly soapbox. Too much passion is *almost* as bad as none at all. (See #1.)

10. Preaching to the converted. Almost everyone would agree, for instance, that American high schools could use many improvements, and a large share of your readers could probably come up with a fairly standard list of suggestions on that topic. If you do not have something specific to say on a subject, choose another one. On the other hand, you *are* an expert on the high school you attended. Draw on your own experiences

for a concrete analysis—including good, specific illustrations—of what needs changing in that school. Write to an audience of people who are in a position to make some of those changes.

11. Exaggerating claims about a causal relationship. You may believe, for example, that the excessive and deplorable violence on television causes crime; many people may even agree with you. However, the direct causal relationship cannot be proved for any number of reasons. There was violent crime before television, and the causes of crime are complex. Should a specific criminal state that the idea for a specific crime came from a certain television program, this is not proof that the person would not have committed a similar crime without having seen that program.

12. Sounding as if there are simple solutions to complex problems; if there were, someone else would have tried them long ago. One of our students informed teachers, parents, and the police (her stated audience) that they should get kids back in school and off the streets during school hours. She talked in very general terms about the need for discipline, as though she had a simple solution and her audience had not had considerably more experience dealing with the problem than she did.

13. Forgetting to adequately "cue" your readers regularly during the course of an argument. Use transition words and sentences to signal your readers that you are moving from one part of your topic to another. Include necessary explanations during the course of your journey, and do not assume the reader knows all of the details, such as the requirements for acceptance into your college's education program. Otherwise your readers are like people standing on a platform watching their train leave without them because they did not hear the departure announced over the loudspeaker. Do not leave your readers standing: Announce where your argument is going and make sure they are all "on board."

14. Mentioning counterarguments to your thesis without refuting them adequately. Otherwise you run the risk of convincing your readers of the opposite viewpoint. Some counterarguments may have so much validity that it is better to leave them out, rather than introducing serious doubts into your readers' minds. You can also admit the truth of a counterargument and demonstrate that the benefits still outweigh it.

15. Failing to include and clearly cite the sources of statistics, debatable statements, or supportive information from outside authorities. Identify outside authorities clearly when they are introduced. When quoting from these authorities, remember to close quotes—to add the second quotation marks of a pair. Include enough information so that your readers understand why you are using an outside authority. Suppose that you were writing an essay encouraging more students to take advantage of the wide cultural diversity of the course offerings at your university. One expert might be introduced as follows: "Professor Tyrone Jackson, a member of the African-American Studies Department for over ten years, is very receptive to students who come to his office seeking information about his department's courses." Identify outside authorities in the text as you introduce them, and give credit through proper citations. Do not write: "Jack Rawlins wrote." Would most readers know who Rawlins was? Of course not, so why should they believe what he said? That is why we identified Rawlins as the editor of a textbook on writing in our discussion of plagiarism in Chapter 8. Another reason for citing outside authorities is to give credit where credit is due. Had we claimed Rawlins' ideas as our own, we would have been guilty of plagiarism. Using outside sources to strengthen your arguments is an excellent strategy, provided you acknowledge the sources clearly and accurately. Do not write:

> A psychologist proved . . .

> A Senate committee demonstrated . . .

Would that convince your readers? Do you believe television commercials that say "More beauticians use Hair Unsnarl than any other conditioner"? What beauticians, and who surveyed them? Include the full name and professional status of the psychologist you are citing. State exactly what Senate committee, and include the name and date of the document containing the information. For further information on how to use and document sources, see Chapters 7 and 8.

Exercise

Form small groups. Read each essay in this chapter quickly for an overall impression, then analyze it more carefully, keeping the following questions and comments in mind. Take notes on your responses to those questions for the author of the paper, as well as making annotations on the essay itself. Use those responses and annotations as your group discusses ways the writer might improve the paper. Concentrate on the contents of the argument, not the writing style.

1. What are the three strongest aspects of the essay?
2. Who seems to be the intended audience for this proposal or position paper?
3. Briefly summarize the writer's claim, or thesis.
4. Is the claim balanced, clearly stated, and well developed? Indicate places where additional explanations or background information would add to the clarity of the thesis.
5. Do enough solid, convincing reasons back up the author's claim? How might those reasons be developed more effectively?
6. What types of evidence or examples are marshaled to support those reasons? Where would you like to hear more?
7. Would additional evidence from outside sources strengthen the arguments of the essay?
8. Does the writer's voice come through? Are personal experiences a major weapon in this essay?
9. Do the arguments appeal to the reader's logic or emotions, or both?
10. Comment on the introduction and conclusion to the paper and suggest ways they might be improved.
11. Does the essay have an appropriate title that catches the readers' attention?

Chapter Fourteen

Letters of Application and Résumés: A Special Type of Persuasive Writing

Exploring Letters of Application

In **letters of application** you present yourself to your readers for one of any number of important purposes:

- a part-time job during the school year;
- a summer job (full-time or part-time);
- an internship in a field of study that you are considering or intend to pursue;
- a scholarship;
- admission to an academic program, such as a semester abroad or graduate school;
- a full-time professional position.

A letter of application is an argument, a claim that the applicant is uniquely qualified for a particular position. Like other argument essays, letters of application are organized topically. The letter is written for a specific audience—the potential employer—and the contents are selected and organized so as to best attract that person's attention from the start. The purpose of a letter of application is to obtain an interview. A professional looking **résumé,** which summarizes your qualifications in a clear, logical fashion, should accompany your letter. Letters of application must follow one of the standard formats for a business letter.

 Knowing how to write an effective business letter is a very useful skill. Employers insist that letters that go out under their logo be typed in one of several standard business letter forms and be free of errors. Business letters require careful proofreading to avoid their being instantly tossed into the wastebasket because of errors.

 Composing an effective letter of application will enable you to practice many of the composition skills needed in college. Like many of your essays for college courses, a letter of application is a type of persuasive writing. You, the applicant, are arguing that you are highly qualified for a position and, therefore, a better person to interview than most of the other applicants. Reasons supporting that claim, drawn from your education and experience, must be carefully marshaled, always keeping your audience—the potential employer—in mind. Try to put yourself in the potential employer's shoes.

 Remember that employers are naturally more interested in what *you* can do for them than what the job would do for you. If the job is related to your major, however, you can also mention that, as employers also like to hire people interested in a job or that particular field. Carefully consider what experiences in your background will most attract each potential employer, and stress them. If you apply for two kinds of jobs, one as an assistant soccer coach and the other as a night manager for Burger King, you would write two very different letters of application.

Keep in mind that a potential employer is much less likely to be impressed by your claims about your abilities than by the accomplishments themselves or by the testimonials of your previous employers. Be as specific as possible: Mention that you were salesperson of the month at Best Buy three times during 1990; include the full name and title of the supervisor who suggested that you should apply for the position as night manager at Calorie Counters' Non-Creamy Custard and urge the reader to contact that supervisor. Say something like: "Marcus Clay, my supervisor at Tony's Subs, suggested that a night manager position at Calorie Counters' would give me the opportunity to better utilize my management skills."

A letter of application must be organized topically, and the introductory paragraph should grab the potential employer's attention. State exactly what job you are applying for and briefly sketch why you are uniquely well qualified for that position. Then elaborate on some—but not all—of your qualifications in the body of the letter. Put your strongest suit first, keeping each potential employer's demands in mind. What would most qualify you to be an assistant soccer coach: Being on the university soccer team? Coaching at a soccer camp? Three months as a cook at Wendy's? A major in recreation? Decide which of your qualifications would most impress each employer and discuss them first. Both your organizational scheme and contents of your letter will vary from one potential employer to another.

A letter of application should not be too long. The concluding paragraph should state when you could begin a new position and mention times you would be available for an interview. Be sure to make it clear whether you must give at least two weeks notice to your present employer.

Tamara Bolden-Brown's letter helped her to get a fifteen-hour-a-week summer internship at radio station V100 between her freshman and sophomore years at University of Wisconsin–Milwaukee. At V100 she very much enjoyed her hands-on experience in two major aspects of the operation: broadcasting and promotion. Tamara participated in promotional activities for a number of local charitable causes and other events, broadcasting about them both from the station and on-site. She also worked on several commercials and assisted the station's disc jockeys during regular daily broadcasts.

4924 N. 10th Street
Milwaukee, WI 53000
April 25, 1996

Mrs. Bailey Coleman
Promotion Director
V100 Radio Station
2400 S. 102nd Street
Milwaukee, WI 53227

Dear Mrs. Coleman:

Please consider me for a broadcasting internship for the summer of 1996. As a frequent V100 listener, I am very impressed with the competence and lively broadcasting personalities of your employees. I find that V100 discusses a wide range of interesting topics, thus raising public awareness and helping to keep the public updated about events and issues. And your varied selection of music attracts listeners of all ages.

Ms. J. C. White, your morning talk show host, and I are both members of Pilgrim Rest Church, and she informed me about your challenging internship program. I believe my work experience qualifies me to be a successful intern at V100. I am presently studying at the University of Wisconsin—Milwaukee where my major is Broadcasting and Journalism. I hope this training will lead me to become a local radio personality.

My enclosed résumé lists my work experience. As you can see, I have had the pleasure of working several jobs with the public. When I was in third grade my teacher chose me to do our school announcements over the P. A. system. For the rest of my grade school years and throughout high school, I enjoyed doing P. A. announcements. My father is a local, well-known DJ who goes by the professional name of "Sweet Bob." He taught me much about music and being a disc jockey. At present, I write news releases about the activities at Pilgrim Rest Church for two community newspapers. I also narrated a video about a recent extension to our church building.

I am looking forward to hearing from you in the near future, so that we can arrange an interview at your convenience. I can be reached at home most afternoons at (414) 555-5268, or you may leave a message on my answering machine and I will respond promptly. Thank you in advance for taking the time to consider my letter of application and resume.

Sincerely,

Tamara Bolden-Brown

Tamara Bolden-Brown

Starting a Letter of Application

What is a good way to get started on a letter of application? Do some prewriting; try clumping, or brainstorming, on your topic. (See the next few pages for more prewriting suggestions.) Think about possible jobs you might apply for. Be sure to choose jobs you would be qualified for at this stage in your education, as you will have a much better idea about what a potential employer is seeking in an employee. Draw on your knowledge and previous experiences. You probably do not have enough experience yet to write an effective letter of application for a position requiring a bachelor's or a graduate degree, so leave that for later in your college career.

Try clumping about your educational background and other experiences. List every experience that you can think of that might interest a potential employer: a marketing club in high school; typing or computer courses; volunteer work at a hospital; coaching for Little League.

This prewriting will also be useful when you prepare your résumé, which should accompany your letter of application. In your letter, mention that additional information about your background is listed on an attached résumé. If you have never compiled a résumé, this is a good time to get started on one; otherwise update and improve the one you already have. Keep your résumé on file and add to it as you acquire additional qualifications.

Your campus may have a career center that provides useful materials on writing successful résumés and letters of application. Check those materials and the student résumés and letters of application in this text to guide you as you prepare your own.

Exercise

Do some clumping—make a cluster diagram—about your qualifications. Start by writing the word *qualifications* in the center of a page, then fill in all of your job-related skills. Next, list every experience—work, educational, volunteer, and so on—you can think of that would complete the following statement: "You should hire me because . . ." Include dates, places, and, if possible, names of supervisors who could recommend you.

Prewriting: The Next Step

Review your cluster diagram and your list of qualifications in order to decide on a specific position to apply for. Then do another cluster diagram or an informal outline tailored to that position. Consider the following questions.

1. Which of your skills would be most useful in that particular job?

2. Which experiences—education, work, volunteer—should you stress to best grab the attention of someone hiring for that position?
3. What would be the best order to present those qualifications in a letter? Review the student letters for some ideas about organization, attention-getting opening paragraphs, and so on.

Now do some prewriting about the potential employer.

Brainstorming about the Potential Employer

Writers should always keep their audience in mind, asking themselves, "Who will be reading this essay, this article, this letter?" In no case is this more important than when writing a letter of application to a prospective employer. The good—or bad—impression a letter of application makes on its reader—in this case a potential future boss—can be the make-it-or-break-it factor in being hired for a job. It is never fun to receive one of those dreadful form letters that begin: "Thank you for your recent application. We regret that at this time . . . ." While some rejections are inevitable, a well-thought-out letter of application will definitely be an advantage in your job search.

After you have done some brainstorming on your own qualifications, it is a good idea to turn your thoughts to the company, institution, or particular employer that you are applying to. Do a brainstorming session on what might appeal directly to them. What qualifications are they looking for in an applicant? What skills would you need for a job with that firm?

Next, ask yourself what you know about the place you are applying to: Have you ever used one of their products, for example, or shopped in their stores? Perhaps you have read a newspaper article about the company, or eaten dinner at the restaurant where you would like to work.

Mentioning something favorable about their workplaces will make your readers—your audience—feel good about themselves. This may be as simple as remarking that you have always shopped at Strong's Meat Market and found their meats to be far superior to any other product in town. When applying for a position at the Steak Pit, would the owner or manager mind hearing that the ambiance in the restaurant is always warm and friendly, the service invariably prompt and courteous? It is hard to overestimate the effectiveness of sincere flattery, sincerely meant. Certainly it is important to someone trying to run a successful business and please the public, as your prospective employer is no doubt trying to do.

On a more sophisticated level, you might mention to the owners of a small business that their want ad indicated they were looking for an aggressive, ambitious salesperson. Be sure to respond to their job description specifically, using their sought-after qualities, such as "hard-working," or "reliable," to describe yourself and your work habits. Make your audience aware that you know what they are looking for in an employee and that *you are it!* Always be sure to muster some enthusiasm for both the position and the institution you are applying to.

Remember that your letter of application is written to sell yourself, your skills, and your knowledge to a specific prospective employer. A well-thought-out letter will give you an advantage over other applicants who might have rushed off a hasty "To Whom It May Concern" note, without taking the time to do a bit of prewriting and prethinking, or brainstorming, about the job in question. The example below is of brainstorming on a prospective employer, in this case the manager of Barnstorm CDs and Tapes.

Clustering about the Potential Employer

Put the name of the institution to which you are applying in an oval in the center of the page. Then make a cluster diagram listing any information you have on the business or institution.

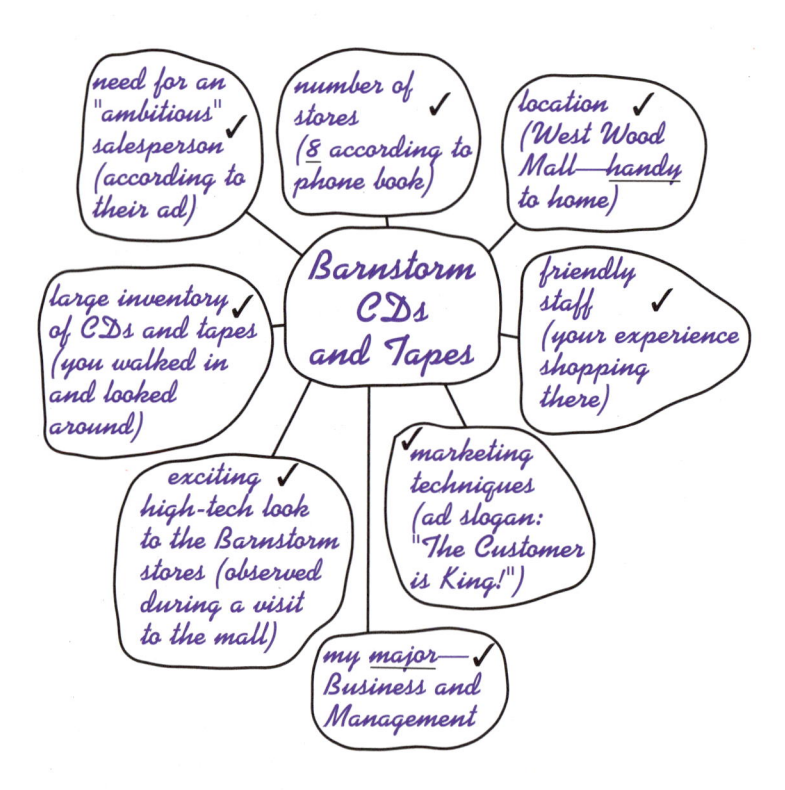

Barnstorm CDs and Tapes

- need for an "ambitious" salesperson ✓ (according to their ad)
- number of stores ✓ (8 according to phone book)
- location ✓ (West Wood Mall—handy to home)
- large inventory ✓ of CDs and tapes (you walked in and looked around)
- friendly staff ✓ (your experience shopping there)
- exciting ✓ high-tech look to the Barnstorm stores (observed during a visit to the mall)
- marketing ✓ techniques (ad slogan: "The Customer is King!")
- my major ✓ — Business and Management

A letter based on such brainstorming might sound something like Peter Piper's letter on page 403:

Mr. Howard Carter
Manager
Barnstorm CDs and Tapes
West Wood Mall
St. Louis, Missouri 52253

Dear Mr. Carter:

When I saw your advertisement in the St. Louis Blues, I had to apply quickly, since your company is seeking an ambitious CD/tape salesperson and I feel I would be well-suited for this job. As a serious music enthusiast, I am well acquainted with several of your Barnstorm stores, particularly the one in West Wood Mall. At Barnstorm, I have been impressed by your friendly, helpful salespeople, so the thought of working for Barnstorm myself is exciting.

On my enclosed résumé, you will notice that my experience working with the public goes back to my first job as a "soaper" at Bilbo's Carwash. My employer, Mr. Bilbo Baggins, will attest to the fact that I am an eager worker who enjoys meeting people and giving them good service. In 1991 and 1992 I was twice voted "soaper of the year" by my co-workers.

At the carwash, I learned the importance of putting the customer first. This principle was recently reinforced when I came into Barnstorm to make a purchase: one of your expert staff cheerfully called around to all of your seven branch stores to find the item for me, then had it sent to West Wood Mall, which was the most convenient place for me to pick it up. Your slogan: "At Barnstorm, the Customer Is Always King!" is no empty phrase, but truly reflects the corporate ideals of your company. I believe that my eagerness to please the public, along with my extensive knowledge of CDs and tapes of all types, make me an ideal candidate for the sales position at your store.

As a sophomore student majoring in Business and Management at the University of St. Louis, the evening and weekend hours you require at Barnstorm would be ideal for me. I am available for an interview at your convenience, and may be reached at home weekdays after 3:30 at (214) 555-3456. At any other time you may leave a message on my answering machine and I will return your call promptly. Thank you for taking the time to consider my résumé and letter; I look forward to meeting with you soon.

Sincerely,

Peter Piper

Peter Piper

Refer regularly to your prewriting, as well as to the suggestions and the letter form model that follows, as you draft and revise your letter.

Tips on a Letter of Application

1. If at all possible, address the individual who can interview and hire you, and not simply a firm such as "Gimbels." Remember, your possible employer is your audience.
2. Open your letter with an idea that attracts attention and stresses why *you* are qualified for the job in question. You want to convince the reader to read on. Make sure to note *exactly* what job you are applying for, and whether it is full-time or part-time.
3. In the body of your letter, include your work experience, education, volunteer work, and other experiences that would qualify you for that job. Select those qualifications with the job in mind. Include relevant dates, and note that more information is contained in your résumé.
4. Your closing paragraph should motivate the prospective employer to interview you. Also make it clear when you could begin work, when you can come for an interview, and exactly how you can be contacted. Make sure to allow at least two weeks notice for your present employer. Only list phone hours when you are likely to be available or when someone could take a message.
5. Avoid jargon and do not try to sound official. Do not write, "Attached herewith," "please find enclosed," or other overly formal phrases.

Check your letter carefully before handing it in. Imagine that you are the prospective employer reading that letter. Would that letter sell you? Why or why not? Check the total impact of your letter. Does the letter state or imply that you are looking for a *specific* job? Full-time or part-time? Does the letter interest the reader and develop strong selling points? Note the tone of your letter: Is it confident and firm, without touches of conceit, selfishness, or brashness? Is the tone modest, without faintheartedness?

Finally, look at the mechanics and grammar. If you have errors, correct them, and retype the letter if necessary. Verify the spelling of questionable words. Remember that many readers use spelling as an index to intelligence. Consider the punctuation: Have you used a comma where a period or semicolon is needed?

Form for a Letter of Application

Date

Your Street Address
City, State, Zip

Employer's Name
Company/Organization
Street Address
City, State, Zip

Dear _____:

Introductory paragraph includes:
- Why you are writing
- Position for which you are applying/inquiring—full-time or part-time
- Source of referral, if any

Body of the letter (usually one or two paragraphs) includes:
- Why you are interested
- How you are qualified
- What you can do for the employer—not what the employer can do for you
- Reference to enclosed résumé
- What you know about the company/organization/field

Closing paragraph includes:
- Request for meeting or interview
- A phone number and suggestions for appropriate times to reach you

Sincerely,

Your Name (with signature above it)

Revising Your Letter: Composing the Final Draft

Before composing the final draft, check to see whether you did the following:

1. Be enthusiastic about the kind of work you are seeking and about the place of work you are applying to.
2. Mention a previous supervisor who will rave about you to the potential employer or who recommended that you apply for this job.
3. Mention where you are in school and that the job fits your schedule.
4. If you already have a job that you will have to quit, give a plausible reason why you would change from your present job and mention that you must give at least two-weeks notice.
5. Draw attention to your résumé.
6. Don't forget to sign your name.

Polishing the Final Product

Appearance counts, so present yourself in the best possible fashion in a business letter.

1. Follow a standard business letter form.
2. The letter should look good on the page.
   a. Center it carefully.
   b. Have at least one-inch margins all around.
   c. Use spaces to aid readability, such as skipping one line between each paragraph.
3. Look up *everything* you are uncertain about, from the exact way a company writes its name to words you may have misspelled.
4. Proofread with extra care. A single error can direct your letter to the wastebasket.
5. Let your draft sit for at least an hour, then proofread it again—and again.
6. Never rely on your own proofreading.
   a. Find someone you know with good writing skills who realizes how important this letter is to you and will do a careful job of editing your letter.
   b. Ask a teacher or a professional who helps writers prepare résumés and letters to edit and proofread your draft.

Putting Together a Résumé

The résumé (also called a data sheet, or a vita sheet), accompanies a letter of application. Follow a standard form when creating your résumé. Type it accurately and space it properly. Regularly review the student models as you prepare your résumé. Remember to:

- Include factual material about you and your history that can be easily listed.
- Keep your audience in mind and imagine what a potential employer would want to know.
- Include dates of jobs, your educational history, volunteer activities or clubs, and so on.
- Be brief and clear.

If you are revising your résumé, seek input from people who can help you. Be sure to get *at least* one reader to proofread the final version.

The résumé on page 408 from Tamara Bolden-Brown shows the standard elements of résumés.

Considering Other Factors about Business Letters

Knowing how to write good business letters is very important. In the second edition to their handy guide *The Writer's Handbook,* Elizabeth McMahan and Susan Day remind readers that "letter writing is the most useful skill that people practice after finishing school" (335).

A letter of application is one of several kinds of business letters. Other common types are letters of request, thank-you letters, and letters of suggestion and complaint. Readers expect to receive business letters that are neat in appearance, typed correctly on decent stationery, and follow a prescribed format.

All of the lines of a business letter begin at the left margin of the page with the **full-block format.** The **modified-block format** has the heading—the writer's address and the date—and the closing on the right side of the page. Letters should be single-spaced and centered on the page, with margins of at least 1.25 inches on all sides.

The tone of a business letter should be polite, but not stuffy or overly formal. Avoid stilted expressions such as "Please find enclosed . . . ." Sound interested and enthusiastic as appropriate, but do not exaggerate. Letters of complaint should be firm, but never sarcastic. Because in most

Tamara R. Bolden-Brown
4924 North 10th Street
Milwaukee, WI 53005
(414) 555-5678

CAREER OBJECTIVE:	To work in television and radio.
WORKING EXPERIENCE:	
3/95 to present	Pilgrim Rest Church Duties: publicity work (currently working on a fifteen minute advertising segment to be aired over the radio.)
4/95 to present	University of Wisconsin—Milwaukee Financial Aid Office Duties: filing, typing, answering questions for students.
8/92 to 7/93	Froedtert Hospital: Surgical Technician Duties: Selected to participate in a six-week course for surgery assistant in August 1993. Prepared instruments for surgery; also responsible for sanitizing instruments.
3/91 to 7/92	Froedtert Hospital: Distribution Technician Duties: stocked bedside cabinets and kept inventory of medical supplies.
9/87 to 11/90	Kohls Food Store—Teutonia Avenue Duties: cashier, sales.
EDUCATION:	
8/94 to present	University of Wisconsin—Milwaukee Major: Broadcasting and Journalism June, 1998, expected date of graduation.
8/89 to 1/91	Milwaukee Area Technical College Major: Microcomputer courses.
9/84 to 6/88	Custer High School, Diploma
ACTIVITIES:	
1988, 1987	Two years on Custer High School varsity basketball team; Cocaptain senior year
REFERENCES:	References are available upon request.

business letters you will be asking a stranger to do something for you, use the kind of language and tone that are most likely to elicit the desired response. Imagine what tone and wording would be most appealing in a stranger's letter to you.

All of these cautions do not mean that you have to be dull or sound exactly like everyone else. Including something that is just a bit unusual—provided you feel comfortable doing so and are willing to take a chance—can set your letter off from the pack and pay dividends.

The most important thing is to be clear and concise. The opening paragraph should get the reader's attention by getting to the point quickly.

Begin something like this: "I am writing to notify you that the Center Street Art Center would be delighted to have you serve on its board of directors," then go back and cross out all the words from "I to that." With today's word processors, making such a change need not entail starting again on a new piece of stationery. Simply delete the wordy opener to read as follows: "The Center Street Art Center would be delighted to have you serve on its board of directors."

Because most recipients of business letters are busy people, the rest of your letter should be equally lean. A long, rambling letter will likely end up in the wastebasket. Plan what you need to include in advance, perhaps by making an informal outline. Put the most important information first; and include transitions so that your ideas flow logically. Conclude your letter politely, perhaps with a word of thanks.

Exercise

Write a letter of application for one of the two options given. Make sure that your letter follows one of the standard forms for a business letter, and include your résumé with your letter. The student models in this chapter may help give you some ideas.

Option 1: Make up a specific job opening and write a letter of application for that position. Invent the name of the potential employer, along with his or her title, address, and so on, or use an existing organization.

Option 2: Find a job listed in the classified ads for which you qualify. Get the essential information for answering the ad and write a letter applying for the position. Attach the ad to your paper.

Credits

Literary Credits

Cole, K.C. "Why There Are So Few Women in Science" by K.C. Cole, *The New York Times,* December 3, 1981. Copyright © 1981 by The New York Times Co. Reprinted by permission.

Collins, Glenn. "Campbell Soup Noodles Around" by Glenn Collins, *The New York Times,* November 17, 1995. Copyright © 1995 by The New York Times Co. Reprinted by permission.

Daie, Jaleh. "Choosing to Give Back" by Jaleh Daie, *On Wisconsin,* March/April 1995. Reprinted by permission from *On Wisconsin,* University of Wisconsin-Madison.

Darnton, Robert. From *The Kiss of Lamourette: Reflections in Cultural History* by Robert Darnton. Copyright © 1990 by Robert Darnton. Reprinted by permission of W.W. Norton & Company, Inc.

de Witt, Karen. "The Panel's Study Cites Job Bias for Minorities and Women" by Karen de Witt, *The New York Times,* November 23, 1995. Copyright © 1995 by The New York Times Co. Reprinted by permission.

Garson, Barbara. Reprinted with the permission of Simon & Schuster from *The Electronic Sweatshop* by Barbara Garson. Copyright © 1988 by Barbara Garson.

German Information Center. "How Obedient Are Germans?" from *The Week in Germany,* April 16, 1993, p. 7. Reprinted by permission.

German Information Center. "Initiative Reaps Berlin's Riches to Feed the Poor and Hungry" in *The Week in Germany,* December 16, 1994, p. 7. Reprinted by permission.

Kole, William J. "Trouble Brewing for French Cafés" by William J. Kole, as appeared in *Milwaukee Journal Sentinel,* October 24, 1995. Reprinted by permission of the Associated Press.

Lipner, Maxine. "Ben and Jerry's: Sweet Ethics Evince Social Awareness" by Maxine Lipner from *Compass Readings,* July 1991. Reprinted by permission of Skies America International Publishing & Communications, Beaverton, Oregon.

Moody, Jim. "Universal Health Care Act Would Solve National Insurance Crisis" by Congressman Jim Moody, *Milwaukee's East Side News,* June 1992. Reprinted by permission of the author.

Perrin, Noel. "The Androgynous Man" by Noel Perrin, *The New York Times,* February 4, 1984. Copyright © 1984 by The New York Times Co. Reprinted by permission.

Rodriguez, Ivette M. "Joe Hardy Named MBDA Coordinator for American Indian Programs" by Ivette M. Rodriguez in *Minority Business Today,* Winter 1992.

Women in Higher Education. "Only 4% More Graduate Women Study Science and Engineering Than in 1981" from *Women in Higher Education,* November 1995. Reprinted by permission of Women in Higher Education, 1934 Monroe St., Madison, WI 53711.

Illustration Credits

Chapter 1

3: *Masters of Caricature,* Ann Gould (ed.). London: Weidenfeld and Nicolson, 1981, p. 65; **10:** Alan Magayne-Roshak of University of Wisconsin-Milwaukee Photo Services; **18:** *Rotten Rejections,* André Bernard (ed.). Wainscott, NY: Pushcart Press, 1990, p. 23; **21:** *Books, Book, Books,* S. Gross and Jim Charlton (eds.). New York: Harper & Row Publishers, 1988; **27:** *Books, Book, Books,* S. Gross and Jim Charlton (eds.). New York: Harper & Row Publishers, 1988

Chapter 2

29: Courtesy of Ellen Lincoln; **31:** Alan Magayne-Roshak of University of Wisconsin-Milwaukee Photo Services; **39:** *Rotten Rejections,* André Bernard (ed.).Wainscott, NY: Pushcart Press, 1990, p. 15; **53:** The Far Side cartoon by Gary Larson is reprinted by permission of Chronicle Features, San Francisco, CA. All rights reserved.

Chapter 5

111: *Randolph Caldecott: A Personal Memoir,* Henry Blackburn. Detroit: Singing Tree Press, 1969; **119:** *Doré Gallery.* London: Academy Editions, 1978

Chapter 7

178: Greg Walz-Chojnacki of University of Wisconsin-Milwaukee

Chapter 8

240: *Books, Book, Books,* S. Gross and Jim Charlton (eds.). New York: Harper & Row Publishers, 1988; **241:** Historisches Museum der Stadt Wien

Chapter 9

258 top: *Rotten Rejections,* André Bernard (ed.). Wainscott, NY: Pushcart Press, 1990, p. 47; **258 bottom:** *Rotten Rejections,* André Bernard (ed.). Wainscott, NY: Pushcart Press, 1990, p. 87; **261:** Photo by Lott Simmerling, courtesy of Rita Simmerling Messerschmidt

Chapter 10

280: Alan Magayne-Roshak of University of Wisconsin-Milwaukee Photo Services; **282:** Alan Magayne-Roshak of University of Wisconsin-Milwaukee Photo Services; **290 left:** Alan Magayne-Roshak of University of Wisconsin-Milwaukee Photo Services; **290 right:** Alan Magayne-Roshak of University of Wisconsin-Milwaukee Photo Services; **305:** Alan Magayne-Roshak of University of Wisconsin-Milwaukee Photo Services; **313:** *Books, Book, Books,* S. Gross and Jim Charlton (eds.). New York: Harper & Row Publishers, 1988; **324:** Alan Magayne-Roshak of University of Wisconsin-Milwaukee Photo Services

Index

A

Abbreviations, 138
Action verbs, 69
Active voice, 72–73, 351
Adjectives, 282–83, 287–88. *See also* Modifiers
    participles as, 69
    possessive pronouns as, 57–58
Adverbs, 283, 287–88. *See also* Modifiers
Agreement
    pronoun-antecedent, 60–63
    subject-verb, 77–81, 84
Alliteration, 97, 291
Allusions in descriptive writing, 293–94
Ambiguous antecedents, 61
Analogies
    in descriptive writing, 293
    in informative writing, 349
Anecdotes
    in descriptive writing, 326
    in introduction, 279
    in narrative writing, 40
    in public speech, 38
    in supporting claims, 368–69
Annotations; in critical reading, 172, 174, 184, 185
Antecedents, 60–64
    agreement with pronouns, 60–63
    ambiguous, 61–62
    incorrect, 63
    unexpressed, 62

Apostrophes, 158–62
    in contractions, 58, 161–62
    in possessive nouns, 158–60
Application, letters of. *See* Letters of application
Appositives, 96
    for embedding ideas, 154–55
    using commas to set off, 153–55
Argumentative writing. *See* Persuasive writing
Audience. *See also* Readers
    effect of, on word choice and tone, 28–30

B

Bibliographic citations, 242, 394
    author/page, 238, 243, 356–58
    author/year/page, 244
    examples, 238, 252, 359
    in-text, 378
    quotation marks for, 236
Body of essay, 42–51
Brackets, 237
Brainstorming, 14, 45
Business letters, 408–9
    format for, 408–9
    letters of application as, 396–406

C

Capital letters, 168–70
    to begin quotations, 164, 167, 234
Capote, Truman, 327
Carroll, Lewis, 164, 165, 236

Causal transitions, 49
Chronological organization, 33, 254, 257
Claims, in persuasive writing, 363–65
    supporting, 367–69
    weighing, 209–29
Clauses
    dependent, 74, 111–12, 119
    independent, 74, 108–9, 111, 113, 114–15
    nonrestrictive, 152–53
    restrictive, 152
Clichés, 87–89, 96–97, 294–95
Clumping. *See* Cluster diagrams
Cluster diagrams, 13, 45, 257
    in comparative writing, 335
    in descriptive writing, 314, 323
    for letter of application, 400, 402
    in narrative writing, 271–72
    in persuasive writing, 374, 391
Coherence, 42–85
    grammar in developing, 52–85
    pronouns in aiding, 52–68
    verbs in, 69–85
C.O.I.K. (clear only if known), 347–48
Cole, K.C., 186, 196
Colons, 135
    in business letters, 145
    between independent clauses, 145
    to introduce lists, 126, 143–44
    to introduce quotations, 145
    in time expressions, 145
Comma faults, 116, 149
    editing, 116–17
    intentional, 117
Commands, 114, 139
Commas, 115, 135, 148–55
    with appositives, 153–55
    between clauses, 109, 149, 151, 152
    with coordinating conjunctions, 109, 150
    with interrupters, 155
    with quotations, 163–64
    in series, 152
    to set off appositives, 96
Comma splices, 116–17, 149
Comparisons, 291, 330–40
    extended, 332
    informal outline for, 336–37
    invention strategies in, 338
    organizing, 336–37

    point-by-point, 332, 340
    prewriting, 334
    in supporting claims, 368
    topics for, 339
    transitions in, 332, 340
    whole-by-whole, 332, 340
Complex sentences, 111–13, 113–14
Compound predicate, 107
Compound sentences, 107–9, 113
    recognizing subjects and verbs in, 110-11
Compound subject, 107
Compound words, hyphens in, 157
Computers. *See also* Word processing
    applications of in drafting, 18, 19–20
    in revising, 20
Conclusions, 18, 34, 39–41
    in narrative, 259–60
Conjunctions
    coordinating, 108, 109, 111, 113, 150
    subordinating, 111–14, 116
Connotations, 93–94
Contractions, apostrophes in, 58, 158, 161–62
Coordinating conjunctions, 108, 109, 111, 113, 150
Counterarguments, 393
Creative writing, experimenting with, 13
Critical reading, 172
    application of, in writing summary, 173–85
    in getting most from outside sources, 185–208
    in weighing claims of argument, 209–29
Criticism, accepting, 4

D

Dangling modifiers, 129–31
Dashes, 146–47
    versus colon, 145–46
    to introduce lists, 126
Declarative sentences, 137
Demonstrative adjectives, 64–65
Demonstrative pronouns, 64–65
Dependent clauses, 119
Description
    in informative writing, 349, 350–56
    objective, 281
Descriptive writing, 280–329
    allusions in, 293–94
    analogies in, 293

analysis of, 296–323
avoiding clichés in, 294
details in, 286–87, 326
examples of, 297–312
figurative language in, 290–92
focusing on dominant impression in, 326–27
imagery in, 290–92
informative, 350–56
modifiers in, 283–84, 287–88
motion in, 289–90
organizing, 327–28
pitfalls in, 328–29
prewriting in, 325
topic for, 323–35
verbs in, 289–90
Details, in descriptive writing, 286–87
Dialogue
effective, 272–74
quotation marks in, 231–32
Diction, 86–98
definition of, 86
Direct speech, 166
using quotation marks in, 231–32
Discovery drafts, 17
Documentation. *See also* Outside sources
incorporating outside sources into essays, 230–52
of statistics, 241, 346
Draft, 18–20
discovery, 17
first, 18–19
in persuasive writing, 390–94
using computers in, 19–20

E

Editing, 27. *See also* Revising
Ellipses, 165, 233–34
Emphasis, use of italics for, 236
End-stop punctuation. *See* Colons; Exclamation points; Periods; Question marks; Semicolons
Exclamation points, 135, 139
Exclamations, 114, 139
Explicit thesis, 31–32
Expository writing, 312

F

Facts, in supporting claims, 367
Feedback, in revising, 21

Figurative language, 290–92
First drafts, 16–17
Flashbacks, 254
Foreign words, use of italics for, 236
Formal speak, 89–90
Freewriting, 11–12, 256
Full-block format, 408–9
Full-stop punctuation. *See* Colons; Exclamation points; Periods; Question marks; Semicolons

G

Gender stereotyping, 131–33, 186, 201
Grammar, 52–85
adjectives, 282–83
pronouns, 52–68
subject/verb agreement, 77–81, 84
verbs, 69–85

H

Half-stop punctuation. *See* Apostrophes; Commas; Hyphens; Question marks
Homonyms, 20, 27, 161
Hyphens, 157

I

Implicit thesis, 31–32
Impromptus, 185
Indirect speech, 166, 232
Informal outlines
in comparison writing, 336
in critical reading, 174–76, 184
in narrative writing, 266–67
in prewriting, 15–17, 25, 174
Informative writing, 5, 342–59
analogies in, 349
C.O.I.K. (clear only if known), 347–48
descriptive, 350–56
generalizations in, 349
outside sources for, 345–46, 356–59
paraphrasing in, 346
persuasive, 359
purpose of, 346–47
Intensifiers, 93
Introductions, 18, 34–38
anecdote as, 38, 279
parallelism in, 127
thesis statement in, 35–36
Invention. *See* Prewriting

"I" point of view, 34
Italics
    for emphasis, 236
    for foreign words, 236
    for titles, 236, 238

K

King, Dr. Martin Luther, Jr., 128, 241
King, Stephen, 5, 235, 240

L

Language
    clichés in, 87–89, 96–97, 294–95
    colloquial, 87–88
    figurative, 290–92
    formal speak, 89–90
    pretentious, 89, 90–91
    sexist, 131–33, 186, 201
    slang, 87–88
    variety in, 92–98
Letters of applications, 396–406
    brainstorming in, 401–2
    cluster diagram for, 400, 402
    examples, 37, 398–99, 403
    form of, 405
    polishing, 406
    prewriting in, 400
    revising, 406
    starting, 399–400
    tips for, 404
Linking verbs, 76–77, 104–5
Lists
    colon in introducing, 126, 143–44
    parallelism in, 126–27
    semicolons in, 142
Logical transitions, 49

M

Margins, need for large, in drafting, 18
Metaphors, 292
Misplaced modifiers, 129–31
Modified-block format, 408–9
Modifiers, 102–3, 106–7. *See also* Adjectives; Adverbs
    appositives as, 96
    dangling, 129–31
    effective use of, 287–88
    eliminating weak intensifiers, 93
    misplaced, 129–31
    overused, 283
    using specific, 283
Moody, Anne, 135, 137

N

Narrative writing, 254–79
    analysis of, 264–78
    conclusions in, 259–60
    description in, 281
    effectiveness in, 262–78
    finding voice in, 261–62
    in illustrating general points, 279
    as introduction to speech, 279
    involving readers in, 258–59
    peer-group revising in, 264
    prewriting in, 256–58
    selection of topic for, 260–61
Nonrestrictive clauses, using commas to set off, 152–53
Noun phrase, 103
Nouns
    possessive, 158–60
    as subjects of sentences, 110

O

Objective description, 281
Object pronouns, 57
Organization
    for body of essay, 42–45
    chronological, 33, 254, 257
    in comparison writing, 336–37
    spatial, 33, 327
    topical, 33
Outlines. *See* Informal outlines
Outside sources
    citations for, 236–37, 356–57
    critical reading of, 185–208
    identification of, 234–35
    incorporating into writing, 185–208, 230–52
    paraphrasing, 346
    primary, 345–46
    quotations in, 231–35
    in research paper, 241-42
    secondary, 345–46
    statistics in, 241, 346

P

Paragraphs, 42–45
    analyzing, 42–43, 44
Parallelism, 125–28
    avoiding faulty, 125–26
    deliberate, 127–28, 291
    in lists, 126–27
Paraphrasing, 163, 166, 173, 237–39, 346
    versus quotations, 237–39
Parentheses, 147
Participles, 69
    as adjectives, 69
    past, 69
    present, 69
Passive voice, 72–73, 351
Past participle, 69
Peer review, 21
    for narrative writing, 263
Periods, 135
    after abbreviations, 138
    to end sentence, 108, 137, 149
Person. *See* Point of view
Personal pronouns, 54–55, 58
    classification of, by person, 55
Personification, 291
Persuasive writing, 5
    analyzing, 209
    anecdotes in, 368–69
    arguing effectively, 363–65
    claims in, 364–65, 367–69
    cluster diagram for, 374, 391
    comparisons in, 368
    examples of, 209–28
    informative, 359
    personal opinions in, 365–66
    pitfalls, 391–94
    qualifiers in, 364
    quotations in, 369
    reference sources, 394
    résumés and letters of application as, 396–408
    statistics in, 367–68
    thesis in, 363
    topic for, 363–69, 370–76
    transitions in, 393
Phrases, 102–3
    noun, 103

Plagiarism, 240–41, 394
Point-by-point comparisons, 332, 340
Point of view, 34
    avoiding unnecessary, 67–68
    and pronouns, 54–58, 67–68
Possessive adjectives, 57–58
Possessive pronoun adjectives, 54
Possessive pronouns, 57–58
Preciseness, 92
Predicate, 106, 110, 113–14
    linking verbs in, 76
Present participle, 69
Pretentious language, avoiding, 89, 90–91
Prewriting, 10–17, 325
    brainstorming in, 14, 45
    cluster diagrams in, 13–14, 45, 257, 271–72, 335, 374, 391, 402
    discovery draft in, 17
    freewriting in, 11–12, 256
    function of, 10–11
    informal outline in, 15–16
    writer's journal in, 13, 256, 323
Pronouns, 52–68
    antecedents for, 60–64
        agreement with, 60–61
    definition of, 52–53
    demonstrative, 64–65
    object, 55–56, 57, 59
    overuse of, 68
    personal, 54–55, 58
    point of view and, 54–58, 67–68
    possessive, 54, 57–58, 161–62
    relative, 112
    subject, 55, 57, 58–59
    types of, 54
    and word variety, 95
Proofreading, 27. *See also* Revising
Public speech
    anecdotes in, 38
    narrative as introduction to, 279
Punctuation, 134–70
    apostrophes, 158–62
    brackets, 237
    colons, 143–46
    commas, 115, 116–17, 148–55
    dashes, 146–47
    ellipses, 165, 233–34

end-stop (full-stop), 114–17, 135, 137–46
exclamation points, 139
half-stop, 135, 148–55
hyphens, 157
parentheses, 147
parenthetical elements, 146–47
periods, 108, 137–38
question marks, 139
quotation marks, 163–68, 231–32, 236, 238
semicolons, 109, 140–42

Q

Question marks, 135, 139
Questions, 114, 139
Quotation marks, 163–68, 238
    for bibliographical citations, 236
    in dialogue, 231–32
    titles in, 238
Quotations, 163–64
    and avoiding plagiarism, 240–41
    colon in introducing, 145
    direct, 166
    ellipses in, 165, 233–34
    identifying sources for, 234–36
    indirect, 166
    versus paraphrasing, 237–39
    use of brackets in, 237

R

Readers. *See also* Audience
    involving, in narrative writing, 258–59
Reading. *See also* Critical reading
    skimming in, 190
Reading critically, 172–229
Redundancy, 91–92
Reference sources. *See* Outside sources
Reflective writing, 174
Relative pronouns, 112
Repetition
    appositives in avoiding, 96
    redundancy in, 91
    as transition, 47
    varying wording in avoiding, 94
Reported speech, 166
Research papers
    example of, 242–52
    reference sources, 241–42, 243–44, 252

Restrictive clauses, using commas to set off, 152–53
Résumés, 407–8
Revising, 20–21
    editing in, 27
    getting feedback in, 21
    level of change in, 25–26
    peer-group, 22, 263
    proofreading in, 27
Run-on sentences, 114–15

S

Safire, William, 17
Scenarios, in supporting claims, 368–69
Scratch outlines. *See* Informal outlines
Semicolons, 135
    to join independent clauses, 109, 149
    in lists, 142
    as weak period, 140–41
Sentence fragments, 118–23
    avoiding, 121–23
    deliberate, 123
    -ing, 120
Sentences
    basic, 102
    changing length of, 101
    complex, 111–12, 113–14
    compound, 108–11, 113
    declarative, 137
    definition of, 107, 113
    fragments, 118–23
    imperative, 107
    kernel. See Sentences, basic
    parts of, 106–7, 110
    predicates of, 76, 77, 102, 106, 107, 110, 113–14
    run-on, 114–15
    simple, 113
    subjects of, 76, 77–78, 106, 107, 110, 113–14
    subject/verb agreement in, 77–81, 84
    types of, 101, 113–14
    varying word order in, 101
Sexist language, avoiding, 131–33, 186, 201
Shakespeare, William, 6, 292, 293
Similes, 291–92
Skimming, 190

Slang, 87–88
"So what" factor, 99
Spatial organization, 33, 327
Spatial transitions, 48–49
Spell-checkers, 19–20
Statements, 114
Statistics
    documenting, 241, 346, 394
    in supporting claims, 367–68
Steele, Danielle, 5
Stereotyping
    essays about racial, 383–86
    gender, 201
Style, definition of, 86
Subject pronouns, 57
Subjects, 106–7
    agreement with verb, 77–81, 84
    compound, 107
    in compound sentences, 110–11
    and predicates, 76, 77
Subordinating conjunctions, 111–14, 116
Summaries, applying critical reading skills in writing, 173–85
Synonyms, 94–95
    in achieving variety, 95
Syntax, 52, 100–5
    avoiding dangling and misplaced modifiers in, 129–30
    avoiding errors in end-stop punctuation in, 114–25
    avoiding faulty parallelism in, 125–29
    avoiding sexist language in, 131–33
    definition of, 86, 100
    experimenting with variety of sentence types in, 101–14

T

Thesis. *See also* Topic
    deciding on, 30–32
    explicit, 31–32
    implicit, 31–32
    statement in introduction, 35–36, 312
    versus topic, 31
Time transitions, 48
Titles, 41–42
    capitalization in, 170
    quotation marks for, 238
    use of italics for, 236
Tone, 28–29
Topic. *See also* Thesis
    choosing, 99
    in comparative writing, 339
    in descriptive writing, 323–25
    in narrative writing, 260–61
    narrowing, 7–8, 20
    in persuasive essay, 370–71
Topical organization, 33
Transitions, 38, 45–51
    addition, 49
    causal, 49
    in comparisons, 332, 340
    in cuing reader, 45–46
    in extended comparison, 332
    importance of clear, 44
    logical, 49
    in persuasive writing, 393
    repetition as, 47
    spatial, 48–49
    time, 48
    types of effective, 46–47
Trite writing, 88

U

Unity, 42–50

V

Verb phrase, 102–3
Verbs, 69–85, 104–5
    action, 76–77, 104
    agreement with subject, 77–81, 84
    compound, 107
    in compound sentences, 110–11
    helping, 74–76
    irregular, 71–73
    linking, 76–78, 104–5
    regular, 69–71
    state-of-being, 76–77
    tense of, 69, 74, 102–3
        future, 74
        past, 69, 74
        present, 69, 74, 102–3
        shifts in, 81–83
    using strong, 93–94, 272–74, 289

Voice
- active, 72–73, 351
- author's, 99, 261–62, 313, 339
- passive, 72–73, 351

W

Whole-by-whole comparisons, 332, 340
Wilde, Oscar, 5
Word choice
- connotations in, 93
- synonyms in, 94

Word processing. *See also* Computer
- applications of, in drafting, 19–20

Wordy expressions, avoiding, 98
Writer's block, 11, 14, 18
Writer's journal, 13, 256, 323
- clumping in, 13

Writing
- accepting criticism of, 4
- body of essay, 42–51
- coherence of, 42–85
- combining ideas, 98
- comparisons, 330–40. *See also* Comparisons
- conclusions, 34, 259–60
- descriptive, 280–329. *See also* Descriptive writing
- expository, 312
- informative, 342–59. *See also* Informative writing
- introductions, 34–38
- narrative, 254–79. *See also* Narrative writing
- organizational schemes for, 33–34, 42–50
- organization of, 33–34, 42–50
- persuasive, 360–94. *See also* Persuasive writing
- purpose of, 30
- reasons for, 4–6
- reflective, 174
- stages in process of, 8–27. *See also specific stage*
- style, 86–99
- summaries, 173–85
- therapeutic value of, 6
- titles in, 41–42
- transitional devices in, 45–51
- unity of, 42–50

Writing journal, 256
Writing style, 86–99
- colloquial, 87–88
- formal, 89–90
- pretentious, 89–91, 96

Instructor's Manual
Strategies for Writing

A Basic Approach

Ann E. Healy
University of Wisconsin–Milwaukee

Martha Walusayi
University of Wisconsin–Milwaukee

NTC Publishing Group
Lincolnwood, Illinois USA

Contents

Preface	IM-v
Part One Writing More Effective Prose	**IM-1**
Chapter One The Writing Process	IM-3
Chapter Two Shaping the Contents	IM-7
Chapter Three Using Correct Grammar and Usage to Aid Coherence	IM-11
Chapter Four Syntax, Diction, and Style	IM-17
Chapter Five Fractured and Nonfractured Syntax	IM-21
Chapter Six Demystifying Punctuation	IM-31
Part Two From Others' Writing to Your Writing: Reading Critically	**IM-43**
Chapter Seven Critical Reading and Your Writing	IM-45
Chapter Eight Documentation: Incorporating Outside Sources into Your Essays	IM-49
Part Three Writing Strategies	**IM-51**
Chapter Nine Narrating	IM-53
Chapter Ten Describing	IM-55
Chapter Eleven Comparing and Contrasting	IM-59
Chapter Twelve Informing and Explaining: The Purpose and Nature of Informative Writing	IM-61
Chapter Thirteen Arguing and Persuading	IM-63
Chapter Fourteen Letters of Application and Résumés: A Special Type of Persuasive Writing	IM-67

Preface

Strategies for Writing: A Basic Approach is based on several premises. Most important is the conviction that virtually all composition students have interesting things to say. Moreover, a surprising number of them are effective writers. We have thus included a wide variety of student writings in the text, ranging from figures of speech and short descriptive passages to model essays. We believe that student writing provides excellent models for composition courses, giving students suggestions for topic choices as well as examples of writing styles. Furthermore, seeing the work of their peers can be very encouraging to student writers. To put it in the vernacular: They can relate to it.

Strategies for Writing also reflects our conviction that, as with any skill, constant practice makes for better writing. The number and variety of writing assignments, from freewriting to complete essays, provide plenty of choices for you and your students to pick from. Students are also urged to keep a writer's journal. You may wish to check these journals occasionally to make sure they are being used effectively and regularly.

Practice by itself is not enough. Ask your classes how athletes, musicians, and artists improve their skills. Most students will agree that practice must be supplemented by tips from coaches or instructors and studying models, such as videos of sports events or the paintings of famous artists. In class, you might discuss how athletes frequently read articles containing hints on various methods to improve their game, just as budding and seasoned artists alike study books dissecting the drawing techniques of other artists. The text is designed so that students study model writing and discuss various kinds of essays as they prepare their own themes; encourage your students to apply these methods to improve their writing.

Strategies for Writing reflects our conviction that a composition text should be user-friendly and encouraging, and that it can be rigorous without being solemn or dull. The light, humorous tone is enhanced by the illustrations throughout the text. The illustrations, which relate directly to the matter under discussion, are included to add interest and to increase retention.

As a quick survey of the model essays shows, this textbook does not recommend teaching the five-paragraph theme with its somewhat formulaic structure: introduction (state thesis), body (develop thesis), and conclusion (restate thesis). Instead, by encouraging students to explore a range of essay types, they learn to let their topics determine the introduction, organization, word choice, tone, and so forth. In other words, students should write like real writers whose topic, purpose, and intended audience always govern what they say and how they present their material.

Our book also emphasizes the discursive, nonlinear nature of the writing process. Students are assured that there is no one correct way to write. And, as writing can be hard for everyone—no matter how experienced—they should not be surprised if they cannot simply sit down, outline what they intend to say, and then write it. Prewriting strategies, drafting, peer editing and other group activities, revision, and more revision are stressed throughout the text, along with frequent suggestions about how to proceed through and experiment with these stages of the writing process. Students are also encouraged improve their essays by getting suggestions from as many readers as possible during all of these stages.

Convinced of the crucial link between reading and effective writing, we have included a section on critical reading. Included are examples of marginal annotations, summary writing, and so on. Being able to summarize others' writings and make connections is an important skill, one that is essential for success in all subjects and beyond school. You may want to supplement this section by bringing in additional outside readings for students to discuss—both in small groups and in general class discussions—and write about.

Teaching grammar for grammar's sake does not result in good writing; however, instructors and employers do care about homonym errors and other wording and grammar slips, and they judge a writer's work accordingly. Nor are they alone in doing so: Ask students how they would respond to a letter urging them to subscribe to a magazine that was full of misspellings, incorrectly used or missing punctuation, and other grammar mistakes. Rather than separating the sections on grammar and usage as an independent handbook, we have incorporated them into the early chapters of the text. Correct word choice and punctuation are important aids to clarity and thus essential to effective writing.

Most instructors will probably opt to use the book's first two chapters, which focus on getting started, topic choice, the stages in the writing process, and methods for shaping the contents, early in the semester. The material in them applies to all of the writing being done by their students and can be returned to throughout the semester. The rest of the chapters are designed for you to use in the order you prefer.

Part One
Writing More Effective Prose

Chapter One

The Writing Process

This chapter is designed to get all students writing at the very beginning of the semester and to help hesitant students overcome writer's block. It opens with a discussion of the reasons why people write, assuring students that almost all writers find composing a difficult and time-consuming process. Tips on keeping a writer's journal and suggested topics for journal entries—which may turn into exploratory writing for future themes—are included in the chapter. Much of the chapter is devoted to the stages in the writing process, ranging from discussions and models of various prewriting strategies to suggestions about revising and proofreading. Students are assured that there is no one correct way to write and cautioned that pursuing a series of stages that works well for one piece of writing may not produce similar results for a different topic.

As any experienced writer knows, prewriting is crucial to achieving good results. You may want to demonstrate different prewriting strategies for each writing assignment, giving students an opportunity to experiment with them in class. Also encourage students to utilize prewriting strategies when they write essay exams in other courses, both to help them gather their thoughts and to organize their answers. To make sure that students really do use prewriting for all of their writing assignments, you might require them to hand in their prewriting along with their final drafts.

Encourage students to consult the models in the text as they go through the creation process. Assign selected essays for general and/or small-group analysis and discussion. If a model essay contains lively dialogue, ask a volunteer to read some of the lines of each of the speakers aloud and another volunteer to read the words of the narrator.

The importance of critiquing and revising is another major emphasis of this text. Students should learn to work with other students, having their essays critiqued by as many readers as possible, then revising with those comments in mind. Chapter One concludes with two model student essays, accompanied by directions for small-group revising exercises. Students can improve their own writing by becoming better critics of others' writing. Moreover, research demonstrates that small-group activities including peer editing are effective teaching tools. Dividing into small groups early in the semester also provides an opportunity for the members of a class to get acquainted and to get into the habit of working together.

Some students may be reluctant to subject their writing to the scrutiny of their peers. Begin the initial small-group revising assignment on neutral ground by having students use the model essays in the book rather than their own. Beginning each critique by pointing out the positive features of any piece of writing will also help students feel more comfortable with the peer-group critique. Having the entire class analyze the same student essays also provides an excellent opportunity for general class discussions of those essays in particular and of the revising process in general.

Answers to the Exercise on Page 7

Answers will vary.

Answers to the Exercise on Page 10

Answers will vary.

Answers to the Exercise on Page 12

1. Answers could include any or all of the following: Unfair grader; dullest, most dismal teacher; terrible speaker; no eye contact; always late for class and rushing around; drones in a monotone; looks at the ceiling; plays favorites; burned out; bored; late returning exams; directions for assignments are never clear; never allows enough time for assignments; humiliates students in public; scribbling; sprawling handwriting; not interested in either subject or students.
2. Answers will vary.

Answers to the Exercise on Page 14

Answers will vary.

Answers to the Exercise on Page 15

Answers will vary.

Answers to the Exercise on Page 16

Answers will vary.

Answers to the Exercise on Page 17

Answers will vary.

Answers to the Exercise on Page 22

Answers will vary.

Answers to the Exercise on Page 26

Answers will vary, but students could have underlined the following words or phrases.

Car Accident

<u>It</u> all started on a <u>sunny morning</u> while I was <u>on my way</u> to school about two years ago. I was driving along a <u>somewhat busy street</u> in <u>my newly purchased car</u>. <u>In the car with me</u> was <u>my four year old brother</u>. Suddenly I saw <u>this station wagon</u> <u>beginning to approach my car</u> and <u>not stopping</u>. The car <u>was headed</u> for the driver's side door; I immediately accelerated <u>to attempt to avoid hitting her from hitting my car</u>. I heard <u>a loud squeal</u> and then <u>felt</u> <u>this impact that I could not believe the force of</u>. The <u>loudness of the impact</u> by far overtook the squealing of the tires <u>attempting to stop</u>. My car <u>did</u> a 180° turn before the car <u>came to a stop</u>. I immediately <u>checked</u> my little brother to make sure that he was all right—thank God <u>he was</u>. After <u>the force of the impact</u> I began to grasp the concept that <u>the car had hit me</u>.

    I <u>got out</u> of my <u>car</u> and <u>approached</u> <u>the other driver</u> and the thing she <u>kept saying</u> was that she didn't have any insurance. When I heard this I was <u>really angry</u> because about a year and a half previous to this accident I had <u>another</u> and I knew that I could not claim the damages on my insurance unless I wanted my insurance <u>to go up</u>. After I <u>found this out</u> I <u>figured</u> that the best thing would be to call the police, so I

<u>called</u> 911 and it <u>seemed</u> like it took the officers <u>forever.</u> Every time I see an accident now I can <u>understand</u> how the people are <u>feeling</u> and <u>the emotions that are involved</u>. To this day I can still <u>recall</u> the <u>sound</u> and <u>force of the impact</u> and how it <u>made my car spin almost a complete turn</u>. In the back of my head I still have this <u>fear</u> of being involved in an accident that would be <u>of greater severity</u>. I just thank God that nobody was <u>hurt</u> in this one.

Chapter Two

Shaping the Contents

Chapter Two deals with many of the nuts and bolts of planning and developing an essay, ranging from having an audience in mind and deciding on a thesis to choosing an overall organizational scheme. Many student models demonstrate these crucial elements of effective writing.

About one-third of the chapter is devoted to the parts of a theme: title, introduction, body, conclusion. This section emphasizes that writing is not a linear process. Many writers are unable to begin a draft of any essay by composing the introduction. Rather than waiting for the perfect introduction to appear, students are encouraged to start on the body of the paper and to leave the introduction for a later stage in the writing process. Writers often find that the right introduction somehow appears later in something they have already written.

Particular attention is paid to writing effective introductions that set the scene and, most important, get the reader's attention. The exercise on the "slow-start introduction" (page 38 in the student text) is designed to help students write attention-getting introductions and can be done by students individually or in small groups. Their responses can then be used for a class discussion of effective introductions and two other important issues of wording: avoiding redundancies and cutting out unnecessary sentences that do not carry a narrative forward.

The section on conclusions stresses the importance of ending any piece of writing in an appropriate and effective manner. This section also contains student models that demonstrate some of the many ways writers may bring closure to a piece of writing, noting, as always, that the nature and purpose of the piece determine the contents of the conclusion.

The final third of the chapter discusses the elements of a well-composed paragraph and demonstrates how paragraphs and transitional cues are used to bind the parts of an essay together.

Following the well-organized, interesting paragraph on Katmandu (page 43) appears a much less interesting, poorly organized, and diffuse paragraph for students to critique (page 44). After students have analyzed it individually or in small groups, a class discussion of the rambling paragraph could touch on paragraph theses (explicit or implicit), sticking to a topic, effective organization of sentences in a paragraph, and the importance of transitions that provide logical connections between ideas.

Chapter Two concludes with a discussion of transitions and includes a list of the three major categories of transition words or phrases: time transitions, spatial transitions, and logical relationships. Numerous examples of effective transitions used in student essays are included. The transitions are highlighted in the first few examples, while students are asked to pick out the transitions in the later examples. After students have found these transitions, either individually or in small groups, the whole class could discuss the use of transitions in those paragraphs.

Assure your students that using adequate and effective transitions is one of the most difficult—yet most important—aspects of writing. Urge them to become more aware of transitions in other people's writing, and call attention to transitions during class discussions of various essays throughout the semester. When critiquing each others' essays, remind students to look out for places where transitional cues are missing. Return to this section on transitional cues as needed throughout the semester.

Answers to the Exercise on Page 32

Answers will vary.

Answers to the Exercise on Page 37

Amy Brinkman's thesis appears in the third paragraph. Answers summarizing her thesis may vary, but they should say that the media in particular are influencing more and more American women to strive for the so-called perfect body, even at the risk of their health.

Answers to the Exercise on Page 38

1. Answers will vary, but students should cross out sentences such as, "She was sitting in a chair near the reception desk," because they are clearly peripheral and add to the slow start.

2. Again, answers will vary, but examples of redundancies include the fourth and fifth sentences and the tenth and eleventh sentences.
3. Answers will vary, but the redundant sentences can easily be combined to read more smoothly.
4. Answers will vary.

Answers to the Exercise on Page 43

1. The topic of the paragraph is Katmandu, a city at the foot of the Himalayan Mountains.
2. The topic sentence is as follows: "The town doesn't seem real, but then it *is* real."
3. All of the sentences fit the topic.
4. The last sentence reiterates (in figurative language) the thesis that, while at first glance Katmandu may resemble a picture postcard, the underlying reality is very different.
5. The third sentence provides a transition.

Answers to the Exercise on Page 44

Answers will vary, but nearly every sentence is unrelated to the one before it and could benefit from a transition. The paragraph does not focus on one idea.

Answers to the Exercise on Page 50

Answers may vary, but students could have underlined the following spatial transitions in Evelyn Cornelius' description of "The Spider Room."

We then entered the place where all of our nightmares came from, a huge rectangular room <u>at the far end</u> of the basement. It was dimly lit by the bare, low wattage bulb that stuck out of the fixture <u>in the middle</u> of the ceiling. The paint had started peeling from the corners <u>near the ceiling</u>. Two good-sized windows covered with old, drab flower print curtains hung <u>high on the north and east walls</u>. There were drip-mark stains <u>on the walls near the windows</u>, evidence that water often leaked into the damp basement room. Matching the rest of the room, the floor was cold, bare, and concrete; we didn't dare go down <u>into the basement</u> without slippers. Boxes were stacked and staggered all about, leaving many places for an evil creature to hide. But the single thing that scared us more than anything were the countless long stringy floating cobwebs. They were everywhere. Spider webs covered the boxes, blanketed the curtains, and consumed the <u>corners of the room</u>. <u>In each one</u>, to our horror, lay a large child-eating spider. The inhabitant of each web was more gruesome and horrible than the one before it.

Answers may vary somewhat, but students will probably have underlined many of the following time transitions in Andy Blint's paragraph.

<u>Next</u>, as could be expected, <u>within a minute or so after</u> the <u>second</u> blast, the remainder of the 500–600 firework shells <u>still</u> in the building where the explosion had occurred <u>started</u> to go off. It sounded like a continuous drum roll of thunder. I hoped that the other manufacturing buildings, each of which contained large amounts of explosives, would not catch fire. <u>Meanwhile</u> the explosions intensified, and pieces of burning fireworks and fragments of building started to rain down on us. We ran to the employee parking lot, which was about 750 feet away from the danger. I turned to watch the remains of the building being thrown effortlessly every which way by the repeated blasts. Finally <u>after about two-and-a-half minutes</u> the blasts subsided. The once strong steel building, said to be state-of-the-art design safety-wise, was totally shredded and melted to the ground. A small but potentially dangerous fire remained. <u>Then</u> it hit me. Two girls had not made it out of the obliterated building.

Chapter Three

Using Correct Grammar and Usage to Aid Coherence

This chapter discusses some common grammatical and syntactical problems in student writing, focusing on pronoun and verb usage. The emphasis throughout the chapter is on good usage as an aid to coherence, rather than on correcting pronoun and verb slips as an aim in itself.

The first section of the chapter is devoted to pronouns, helping students become more aware of pronouns and pointing out the advantages of using them correctly. This section also covers common pronoun errors, such as having unclear or incorrect antecedents. The second section of the chapter covers verb usage.

Many of the exercises on pronoun antecedents and verb usage are self-explanatory, so that students who are having difficulty with pronoun use can refer to them. Depending on the needs of the class, you may decide to devote class time to some of the exercises on verb and pronoun usage. One idea is to have the class work together in pairs or small groups: divide selected exercises among the groups; then go over their results in general class discussions.

Answers to the Exercise on Page 54

Students should have underlined these personal and possessive pronouns in the following passage.

I sat with her for a long time and she seemed to be sleeping, but every so often she would open her eyes and look at me and ask, "Who are you?" I understood what was happening, but it was hard for me to accept. This person, a former ballet dancer, always full of energy and "on <u>her</u> toes," could not even recognize <u>her</u> own family. <u>I</u> thought of <u>her</u> many years as a heavy smoker and remembered that <u>I</u> had always tried to get <u>her</u> to quit. <u>She</u> would say something like, "<u>You</u> are right" or "<u>Who</u> cares?" and go right on smoking. <u>I</u> felt guilty because maybe <u>I</u> should have pressured <u>her</u> more.

Answers to the Exercise on Page 55

1. She, *third person* (person referred to)
2. I, *first person* (the speaker)
3. She, *third person* (person referred to)
4. You, *second person* (person spoken to)
5. We, *first person* (the speaker)
6. They, *third person* (person referred to)

Answers to the Exercise on Page 56

Students should have underlined the following object pronouns.

    Every so often Grandma spoke to <u>us</u>, but her questions indicated that she did not recognize <u>me</u>. As I looked at her, memories of our many good times together brought <u>her</u> even closer to <u>me</u>. Grandma's energy and love of life had been an inspiration to all of <u>us</u>. But now her lungs had been destroyed by the cigarettes Grandma had smoked so many years. I hated cigarettes that day and I still hate <u>them</u>.

Answers to the Exercise on Page 56

1. me, *first person* (Tim)
2. her, *third person* (Grandma)
3. us, *first person* (Tim and his family)
4. her, *third person* (Grandma)
5. them, *third person* (family members)
6. you, *second person* (Tim and his family members)

Answers to the Exercise on Page 59

1. He
2. she
3. She
4. I

5. I
6. she
7. she

Answers to the Exercise on Page 60

1. her
2. us
3. me
4. me
5. him
6. her

Answers to the Exercise on Page 61

1. players (they)
2. ice cream (it)
3. Lloyd (him)
4. speeding truck (it)
5. children's (them)
6. pronouns (they)

Answers to the Exercise on Page 63

Answers will vary. Below are some possible rewrites.

1. Brenda is an avid sports fan, but Ellen is not as interested in computers.
2. Brenda uses the computer efficiently, but she never took a course in computers.
3. Brenda told Ellen to read the directions again.
4. My aunt had a heart attack, but her heart was as good as ever after two weeks in the hospital.
5. His convertible hit a parked car, but his car was not damaged. (Or: his convertible hit a parked car but did not damage it.)
6. Dennis hurriedly plucked the feathers from the three chickens and popped the chickens into the oven.
7. Because the witness needed police protection, four police were assigned to her.
8. Nick got the keys from Justin before Justin left for school. (Or: Before he left for school, Nick got the keys from Justin.)
9. Victor is a wonderful actor who, like many other actors, cannot make a living acting.

10. When Monique told her mother about the broken lamp, her mother was upset.

Answers to the Exercise on Page 65

Answers will vary. Below are some possible rewrites.

1. That town in the midwest is known for thrifty habits.
2. Evan is working part-time in a computer lab at the university for the summer. Computer work may become his career.
3. Fighting over a will sometimes ruins family relationships. Such fighting should not happen.
4. Jealousy, unrestrained anger, and indifference to their wants can be very harmful to your children. You should try to get rid of such traits.
5. The worried father told his son to look for a better-paying job.
6. A group of biology students released two hundred rats in the girls' dormitory. The biology students were immediately arrested and jailed.
7. The lost pedestrian seemed to be approaching the police officer on the corner but then crossed the street.
8. At eighteen, I left home and hitchhiked to California. Hitchhiking is not satisfactory because it involves much standing on highways.
9. She broke her hand when she slammed it on the table.
10. Louise constantly complained to the neighbors about their destructive children; yet she let her own children run wild. She neither punished her son nor paid for the damages when he broke Mrs. Frank's window. Her inaction did not make her popular.

Answers to the Exercise on Page 66

Wording will vary, but the pronouns ought to be underlined as below.

   Hugh and Harry's conversation came to an uncomfortable pause after <u>he</u> made a crude remark against women athletes, then laughed as if <u>he</u> were embarrassed and tried to change the subject to <u>his</u> new motorcycle. <u>This</u> remark especially annoyed <u>his</u> friend, who had become a strong advocate of women's equality. <u>His</u> views on women's rights had changed considerably after <u>they</u> emphasized gender stereotypes in <u>his</u> sociology class. <u>He</u> kept urging <u>his</u> friend to take the class but had not yet persuaded <u>him</u> to sign up for it.

Answers to the Exercise on Page 68

1. lawyers, they
2. I, me

Instructor's Manual **IM-15**

3. we, we
4. I, I, I
5. you, you <u>or</u> one, one
6. writers, they, they

Answers to the Exercise on Page 68

Answers will vary. Possible rewrites are below.

1. Swimming is among the best exercises for getting into shape.
2. If you are a freshman in college, you should not be afraid to ask questions during the first week to avoid getting lost.
3. Her research paper was excellent; she had obviously worked hard on it.
4. He will conserve energy and save money by taking the bus to work every day.
5. Reading widely should improve your vocabulary rapidly.
6. You will find your writing style improving if you decide not to write so many pronouns.

Answers to the Exercise on Page 70

1. Joe used to be a poor loser.
2. Mary was embarrassed by the teacher's suggestion.
3. Dogs are supposed to be on a leash in the city.

Answers to the Exercise on Page 79

is, live, has, includes, swell, climb, ride, take, visit, dates, is, remain, have

Answers to the Exercise on Page 81

1. were (wolves)
2. are (groves)
3. runs (expressway)
4. was (porcupine)
5. were (places)

Answers to the Exercise on Page 81

1. makes (professor)
2. aid (diagrams)
3. improves (studying)
4. want (members)

5. has (price)
6. is (computer)
7. were (friends and dad)
8. appeal (visit)
9. gives (course)
10. take (Mary and Tom)

Answers to the Exercise on Page 83

spent, found, are, has, is, was, argue, agree, dates, seen, occupied, invaded, was, destroyed, is, were, damaged, are, are

Answers to the Exercise on Page 84

1. Jutiki, slams, runs
2. Jutiki and Mario, score
3. Tonya, makes
4. players, know
5. fans, cheer

Answers to the Exercise on Page 85

1. shrimp and guppies, swim
2. frogs, are
3. Fran and I, argue
4. Komika and Lavon, are
5. Cynthia, used; Mr. Lopez, passed
6. teachers, realize; giving, harms
7. I, have never
8. neighbors, phoned; they, called; they, moved
9. employers, are prejudiced
10. Mario and Gwenetta, were
11. meeting, was rescheduled

Chapter Four

Syntax, Diction, and Style

This chapter opens with explanations and examples designed to show the difference between style, diction, and syntax. Beginning writers need to learn to develop their own effective style, as well as to use appropriate tone, diction and style in every piece of writing. A discussion of things to avoid—ranging from clichés to "formal speak" to redundancies—follows. This section contains numerous concrete examples, practical suggestions, and exercises designed to help students turn wooden, ineffective writing into lively, precise prose.

The exercise on page 90 makes a good small-group activity. It can even be combined with the exercise designed to eliminate repetition on page 95. Ask several groups to reword the paragraphs about the basketball player and the old church, and the rest to reword the paragraph on page 90. Ask volunteers to read their groups' revised paragraphs aloud or to write them on the blackboard. Use these revised versions for a general class discussion on effective word choice, word variety, and other issues of effective diction.

The section on effective diction emphasizes using interesting, precise words (especially verbs) and striving for word variety. The next section explains the appositive and gives examples of how to use appositives to achieve word variety and improve writing style.

The section on the "so-what factor" can stimulate a lively class discussion about topic choice and idea development. Various other sections of this chapter, such as the exercise paragraph on childbirth (page 97), may be used for small-group activities as well as general class discussions. Students should refer to various sections of the chapter, as needed throughout the semester, in order to apply the suggestions to their own writing. Seeing examples of redundancies and doing exercises to eliminate them frequently works wonders on a student's writing. They probably have not thought much about diction, tone, or style, nor has it ever occurred to them that they do not *have* to write the stiff or redundant prose that they so frequently read and hear.

Answers to the Exercise on Page 90

Although the rewording of their paragraphs will vary, students probably will have noted and replaced most of the wordy and pretentious language. A possible rewording is shown below.

> Because I can end your employment, you would be well-advised to alter your work habits and attitude now. Otherwise, despite the fact that you have many skills that our firm needs, soon you will find yourself without a job. If you want to talk with me concerning this matter, please call my secretary about the most convenient time for an appointment.

Answers to the Exercise on Page 95

Answers will vary. A possible rewrite is shown below.

> Our family's favorite ski area is Arapahoe Basin in Summit County, Colorado. It has enough varied and challenging terrain to satisfy every skier from beginner to expert. Compared to many other Colorado ski spots, Arapahoe Basin is small and intimate, because it never draws huge crowds like the other three ski resorts in Summit County. Because Arapahoe is the highest ski area in North America, it has snow after it has melted in other ski areas. That's why so many diehard skiers flock there every spring after the other ski resorts have closed for the season.

Answers to the Exercise on Page 95

Answers will vary. Possible rewrites follow.

> Cosmos High School's Moses Moran won this year's award as the most valuable high school basketball player in Garden City. He was the city's highest scorer for every one of the four years he played first-string center. He also led all Garden City players in the percentage of successful free-throw attempts. Moran is also a good defensive player who grabbed more rebounds this year than any

other player on his team. Thus the Garden City sports writers also named him the best all-around high school athlete in Garden City in this decade.

The dilapidated, but beloved, red brick church that dominated the town's square was in terrible repair. The church had been the town's main attraction for over a century. Last year the county building commission reluctantly decided that the decaying structure had to be condemned. Because no one in the town wanted to see it torn down, the town council authorized a referendum to raise money to repair the old building. The church is already under renovation, since the citizens supported the referendum to save it by a sizeable majority.

Answers to the Exercise on Page 96

1. A very hard worker
2. Marc, Roberto, and Ramona
3. a city she had hoped to visit since her childhood

Answers to the Exercise on Page 97

Answers will vary.

Answers to the Exercise on Page 98

Answers will vary.

Chapter Five

Fractured and Nonfractured Syntax

This chapter discusses some of the most common problems students have with word order and includes many suggestions to help them improve their syntax. It surveys the many types of sentences available to writers and presents methods students can employ to determine whether what they have written is a sentence or not. Students are encouraged to experiment with a wide variety of sentence types, to vary sentence length, and even to take a chance on abandoning conventional syntax on occasion.

The section on modifiers and kernel sentences opens with an explanation of phrases and gives examples of the many ways phrases act as modifiers in sentences. The next section is designed to help students better identify subjects and predicates. Demonstrate to students how changing the tense of a sentence can help them find a verb phrase (predicate). Explain that when the tense of a sentence is changed, the word that changes form is the verb: Tom *eats* supper; Tom *ate* supper an hour ago; Tom *will eat* supper soon.

The distinction between action verbs and linking verbs is explained and demonstrated by examples in the next part of the chapter. Students are encouraged to use active verbs instead of linking verbs in most instances.

You may want your students to hand in the revised paragraphs that come out of the exercise on page 105 or to analyze their revisions in a general class discussion. Explain how the techniques used in revising this paragraph can help to eliminate many of those flat or repetitive phrases that appear in early drafts of almost anyone's writing.

The next section of this chapter discusses types of sentences, stressing the fact that most standard definitions of the sentence fail to take various exceptions into account (for example, imperative sentences that do not have a subject). Compound subjects and verbs are also introduced. The discussion of compound subjects and verbs leads quite naturally into a section on compound sentences and the seven coordinating conjunctions.

Going over the sentences in the exercise at the bottom of page 110 in class could provide an opportunity to review verb tense, along with action and linking verbs. Having students point out the coordinators in the sentences could lead to a brief discussion how to choose the appropriate coordinator.

The next topic in the chapter is the use of subordinators in complex sentences. Punctuating dependent clauses as if they were complete sentences is a frequent source of fragments in student writing. The wording of the sentences in the exercise on page 112 briefly addresses that problem. Because such fragments are a recurrent problem, this exercise can be useful for a broader discussion of fragments in general.

First, have the students work on the sentences in pairs. Urge them to cover up all of the words except the part that they suspect is a dependent clause; they should then try to determine whether the clause makes sense by itself. If it does not, it is probably a fragment. You may want to recommend using this method every time they suspect that they may have written a fragment in their own drafts.

After students have finished locating the dependent clauses in these sentences, go over the sentences with the entire class. Ask which word in each dependent clause makes that clause dependent on another clause to complete its meaning. List those words on the blackboard and explain that they are called *subordinators*. Point out that writers sometimes have the option of moving subordinate clauses that appear at the beginning of a sentence to the end of a sentence and vice versa. Ask whether reversing the order of dependent and independent clauses would be possible in any of the sentences they just analyzed.

The next section of the chapter is devoted to common errors in end-stop punctuation: run-ons, comma faults, and fragments. Stress the fact that length is not the issue in determining whether a sentence is a run-on. Because the students' answers to the exercise on page 115 will vary, the exercise should provide an excellent opportunity for a class discussion of the various ways to correct run-ons. Once again have the students work in pairs to eliminate these run-ons. It may be a good idea to have the entire class do the first two or three sentences together. During that general discussion, point out the several options for correcting each one. Once the class has finished the remainder of the sentences, ask for volunteers to write their sentences on the blackboard. Use these examples to discuss alternative ways to punctuate the sentences.

The exercise on comma faults on page 117 can be used like the one on run-ons. If you decide to cover both run-ons and comma faults during the same class period, you might have half of the class work on the run-ons and the other half on the comma faults. When they have finished, hold a general discussion that covers the various options for correcting both of those end-stop errors.

You might want to use the exercise on page 118 for a review of run-ons and comma faults. Have the class work in pairs or small groups to identify the errors and decide on ways to eliminate them. Then go over each of the sentences with the entire class, having students suggest various alternatives for correcting them.

Students whose essays continue to contain quite a few mistakes in end-stop punctuation should be urged to refer regularly to these sections of the text. Some of them may also require individual help with their drafts.

Closely related to end-stop errors is the matter of fragments. Some causes for fragments are discussed in the next section of the chapter. One or more of the fragment exercises in the chapter could be used for small-group activities, followed by a general discussion of ways individual groups converted the fragments into sentences. The discussion of fragments ends with a brief look at deliberate fragments.

The following sections of the chapter cover syntactical problems: parallel structure and misplaced and dangling modifiers. Particular attention is paid to the need for parallel structure in lists. Because problems of parallel structure appear so frequently, you might want to go over some of the related exercises in class after students have rewritten the sentences.

The chapter concludes with a discussion of the need to use gender-inclusive terms such as *first-year student* for *freshman*, *firefighter* for *fireman*, or *flight attendant* for *stewardess*. The discussion can be broadened to cover issues of gender roles and the effects of labels and labeling in general. It is important to emphasize that both men and women are harmed by gender stereotyping. The last exercise in the chapter (page 133) asks students to change the language in the sentences to gender-inclusive language.

Answers to the Exercise on Page 103

1. The words *five* and *frivolous* modify the subject *frogs*. The verb *flipped* is modified by *foolishly over the dam*. *Flip* is the present tense; *flipped* is the past tense; *will flip* is the future tense.
2. The words *three elongated* modify the subject. The verb is modified by *slowly away from the shore*. The verb is in the present tense.
3. The words *seven slippery* modify the subject. The verb is modified by *soon* and *through the meadow*. The verb is in the future tense.

Answers to the Exercise on Page 104

1. Aunt Sue <u>is</u>
2. She <u>seems</u>
3. Sue <u>stayed</u>
4. Sue <u>remained</u>
5. Aunt Sue <u>become</u>
6. she <u>be</u>

Answers to the Exercise on Page 105

Answers will vary.

Answers to the Exercise on Page 107

1. He and his father <u>fished and hunted</u>
2. Tricia and Bruce <u>gathered and placed</u>
3. boys and girls <u>clambered</u>
4. chickens <u>scratched and pecked</u>
5. She and I <u>whispered and giggled</u>

Answers to the Exercise on Page 110

1. ideas, but
2. meaning, so
3. place, or

Answers to the Exercise on Page 110

1. principal <u>mumbled</u>, he <u>slouched</u>
2. vocalist <u>strode</u>, she <u>tripped</u>
3. surface <u>was</u>, singer <u>tripped and fell</u>
4. pianist <u>rushed</u>, vocalist <u>smiled</u>
5. pianist <u>returned</u>, singer <u>stood</u>
6. audience <u>expected</u>, singer <u>remained</u>
7. She <u>remembered</u>, pianist <u>was</u>
8. concert <u>was</u>, everyone <u>clapped</u>

Answers to the Exercise on Page 112

1. [If a clause does not make sense by itself,] it is probably a dependent clause.

2. [When you punctuate a dependent clause as if it were a sentence,] you have written a fragment.
3. A fragment is a phrase or clause [that does not make sense by itself.]
4. Often the fragment only needs to be connected to words before or after it [that complete the fragment's meaning.]
5. [Although you may try to avoid them,] fragments tend to creep into early drafts of essays.
6. Do your best to eliminate fragments [because they may confuse your readers.]
7. [Because there are so many kinds of sentences,] it is not always easy to spot fragments or end-stop punctuation errors.

Answers to the Exercise on Page 115

Answers will vary. Here are some possibilities.

1. Two frogs were sunning on a log; suddenly, one frog hopped into the pond and disappeared beneath the bridge.
2. A tall chap was dozing on the veranda of a summer cottage. His friend sat reading in a nearby rocking chair.
3. The phone rang, and Keysha answered it.
4. No one responded, so she hung up in disgust.
5. A few people put cutesy messages on their answering machines, but I sometimes hang up without leaving a response if the messages are too cutesy.
6. Do you have an answering machine? My friends regularly complain because I do not have one.
7. My dad has an answering machine, but he always forgets to turn it on.

Answers to the Exercise on Page 117

Answers will vary. Here are some possibilities.

1. Traditionally, the masculine gender pronouns *he* and *his* were used to refer to people in groups containing both sexes; today, many women are actively trying to change that tradition.
2. Each pupil should bring his own lunch to the school picnic. Such usage implies that all of the pupils in the class are boys.
3. Every doctor should know her patients well. This usage insinuates that all doctors are female.
4. Certain masculine gender words such as *policeman* are no longer appropriate; today's police forces include many female officers.

5. Gender-neutral terms like *police officer* or *mail carrier* are more appropriate, and they accurately reflect the changes in today's workforce.
6. Yet many popular publications are resisting this trend to get rid of sexist language; unfortunately, these publications still use masculine pronouns to refer to people of both genders.

Answers to the Exercise on Page 118

Rewrites will vary, but here are some possibilities.

1. CF—My mother's car stalled on the freeway; fortunately, no one smashed into it before the police arrived.
2. RO—Did you detect the terror in his eyes as he opened the door into the cellar? Maybe he had been watching too many Stephen King movies lately.
3. CF—Do not forget to lock the door when you leave; this neighborhood has seen too many burglaries in the past month to take any unnecessary chances.
4. CF—One guest was late, but the others came right on time.
5. RO—The teacher stomped out of the room. The students were stunned at his reaction.
6. RO—My friend's uncle never has a kind word for anyone. Why does her family put up with his insults every holiday?
7. CF—"You were late. Did you get in trouble?" mother probed.
8. RO—Many are called, but few are chosen.
9. CF—The train pulled away from the platform five minutes early, and a few angry passengers were left behind.
10. RO—One expects a train to be late; one does not expect a train to be early.

Answers to the Exercise on Page 119

1. [Although]—Anita is a very good photographer.
2. [Because]—Jon and Anita are friends as well as roommates.
3. [Until]—Jon finished writing that last computer manual.
4. [While]—Jon and Anita were unpacking books in their new apartment.

Answers to the Exercise on Page 121

Answers will vary.

Answers to the Exercise on Page 121

1. [Having proofread what she viewed as a masterpiece on a major turning in her life.] <u>The proud student turned in her theme on Friday morning</u>. [Convinced that even Mr. Nitpicker could not find a single error in it.]
2. [A genius at spotting every mistake no matter how minor.] <u>Mr. Nitpicker was notorious for the many red marks he put on every student's paper</u>. [Plus requests that the paper be resubmitted in two days with all of the mistakes corrected.]
3. [Once the deadline passed.] <u>Mr. Nitpicker threw all revised papers that were handed in into the wastebasket</u>. [Unnecessarily humiliating the poor student who was late.][Right in front of the entire class.]

Answers to the Exercise on Page 122

Answers will vary. Here are some possible responses.

1. She was convinced that nothing but good could result from her efforts.
2. Jerry had a large music collection, including compact discs, albums, tapes, and sheet music.
3. Having packed all of her supplies for the journey, Heather left for the airport.
4. Because that principal did not attempt to understand the students' viewpoint, she wrongly expelled the two innocent sophomores.
5. I decided to join the marching band, as I knew that I could not make the football team because of a back injury.

Answers to the Exercise on Page 122

Answers will vary, but here are some possible rewrites.

1. During the last year of my high school athletic career, I suffered a knee injury that still hurts today and will probably bother me for the rest of my life.
2. While Peter was on the third floor of the library looking for Hermione, she was on the lower floor looking for Peter.
3. Learning to eat low-calorie, balanced meals and saying "no" to rich deserts is about the only sure way for many people to lose weight and not gain it all back again.

4. It was fear of being caught that caused the thief to lie completely still on the floor of his car for half an hour, hardly daring to breathe until the police left the alley.
5. Running along the highway with a look of terror in its eyes, the eight-point buck suddenly paused and then sprang lightly into the dark forest nearby.

Answers to the Exercise on Page 124

Answers will vary, but here are some possibilities.

1. The snake could not climb the smooth steel wall.
2. The crocodile stirred suddenly and opened its long, narrow jaws.
3. My ex-husband, Horace, is a fine father; we just couldn't get along.
4. When you put the milk in the refrigerator, close the door quickly to save electricity.
5. We are taking our poodle, Snipper, to the vet today because she has worms and fleas.
6. My daughter Eleanor, who is usually a mediocre student, got an A on her European history exam.
7. Cigarette smoking is bad for your health; it causes lung cancer, emphysema, and heart disease.
8. Mr. Ramirez found a mildewed and dusty first edition of Darwin's *Origin of Species* in an antique shop in New York.
9. For our vacation in July, we camped in the Bayfield area near Lake Superior, which is one of the most beautiful spots in Wisconsin.
10. The professors and assistants at Prestige College went on a three-month strike for higher wages and fewer classes.
11. People scattered like frightened beetles as the wall of flame grew greater and greater as it advanced through town.

Answers to the Exercise on Page 125

Answers will vary, but here is a possible rewrite.

> Dridon slipped his supply bag over his shoulder as he started walking in the dry plain. The tiny reptilian life forms that scurried across his path were not like anything Dridon had seen on earth. The purple sun blazed through the thin, yellow, dust-filled atmosphere. The dust spread itself thinly over Dridon's body, choking him as it entered his mouth, nose, ears, and eyes. Dridon sensed the air for water, but he could feel none. The burnt and twisted ship, which had already been claimed by desert reptiles, lay behind him on the plain.

Answers to the Exercise on Page 126

Answers will vary, but here are some possible rewrites.

1. When Jose entered college he hated geography, history, and writing.
2. Once he learned how to edit and revise, his grades started to improve significantly.
3. Now Jose likes to read, write, and revise.

Answers to the Exercise on Page 128

Answers will vary, but here are some possibilities.

1. The discontented waitress complained about long hours, crabby customers, and low tips.
2. Writers whose sentences are not parallel make errors of syntax and confuse their readers.
3. Faulty parallel structure is ungrammatical and may puzzle your readers.
4. Her favorite summer recreational activities were swimming, jogging, boating, and camping.
5. That firm expects its employees to look intelligent, work efficiently, and dress fashionably.
6. I can recommend Francine Harris as a civic leader, a competent supervisor, a dedicated employee, and an enterprising person.
7. In spite of years of listening to his fussy mother's constant nagging, the bearded young man's appearance remained unkempt: a faded sweater with ripped elbows; run-down cowboy boots; and ragged jeans with large gaps in the knees.
8. Here is one formula for more success in a writing course: turn in interesting papers that are carefully typed; attend all classes, especially peer editing sessions; carefully make all reasonable designated corrections; and never be anything but prompt with assignments.
9. Finding an interesting topic, getting an early start, doing a thorough research job, and composing an outline are essential preliminary steps for a good term paper in any course.

Answers to the Exercise on Page 130

1. The frantic husband ran a red light while rushing his wife to the hospital to give birth to their first child.
2. The next thing the couple noticed was a police car with a flashing red light that was following their speeding vehicle.

3. The police officer sympathized with the man and his nervous wife, who was crying in the backseat.
4. The couple's car followed the police vehicle, lights flashing and sirens blasting, the rest of the way to the hospital.
5. The emergency room provided a welcome relief to the frantic woman, who was too exhausted even to count her contractions any longer.
6. Within a few minutes a four-wheeled cart was moving her quickly toward the delivery room.

Answers to the Exercise on Page 133

Answers will vary, but here are some possibilities.

1. Our representatives' chief responsibility is to the voters who elected them.
2. A shrewd lawyer can get his or her clients off 80 percent of the time.
3. The police officer was accused of showing bias toward the defendant, who was homeless.
4. All children were told to bring their parents to the school meeting.
5. Humanity has progressed remarkably during the twentieth century; it has all but conquered infectious diseases!
6. When the mail carrier came to the door, she presented me with an envelope marked "Postage due—twenty cents"!

Chapter Six

Demystifying Punctuation

Punctuation may alarm student writers because it *can be* difficult and confusing. Assure your students that you realize that punctuation is complicated. Writers' choices of punctuation play a role in conveying their intended meaning. Point out variations of punctuation usage in the works of published authors, and encourage students to become more aware of punctuation in the works of writers whose style they admire.

In some cases, the "rules" of punctuation are not as rigid as students were previously taught. That may cause consternation because some students want to know the "right" way to punctuate and want to be told exactly when a comma is needed and so on.

This chapter points out how some punctuation marks help writers to convey meaning by indicating natural pauses and intonations in speech. The chapter also explains and illustrates how other punctuation, such as quotation marks, does not indicate pauses but conveys additional important information about a text. As one aid to using punctuation more effectively—but by no means the complete solution to punctuation problems—students are urged to read drafts of their writing aloud, listening for pauses that should be indicated by punctuation marks.

An unpunctuated excerpt from Anne Moody's *Coming of Age in Mississippi* is included early in the chapter (page 136) to dramatize the importance of punctuation. Punctuating this passage can be an effective and challenging small-group activity, or the class may work on it as a whole. After students have punctuated the excerpt and discussed their choices in a general class discussion, you may want to discuss the punctuation in Moody's original passage, which appears on page 137 of the student text.

A discussion of the several standard options for full-stop or end-stop punctuation opens the next section of the chapter. After students complete the exercises, discuss their choices to demonstrate that sometimes there is more than one right way to end a sentence; it is up to each writer to decide what end-stop punctuation mark best achieves his or her purpose.

Because students are less familiar with—and therefore sometimes avoid—the semicolon and the colon, the sections illustrating their usage are longer and more thorough. Special attention is devoted to punctuation in lists.

The next section discusses the use of the comma with appositives and illustrates the difference between essential (restrictive) and nonessential (nonrestrictive) appositives.

A brief section on the hyphen is followed by another general punctuation review, which is suitable for a small-group activity.

The section on the apostrophe is much longer because apostrophe errors are common in student essays. Many apostrophe errors are the result of careless writing and/or proofreading: for instance, forgetting the apostrophe in *don't* or *I'm*. Urging students who frequently forget apostrophes to proofread once just looking for places where they left out an apostrophe may clean up some of these omissions. On the other hand, from the frequency of apostrophe errors, it is obvious that they are more confusing to many students than most instructors think they ought to be.

Because apostrophe errors are such a common phenomenon in writing, we have included several explanations and exercises, each of which looks at the apostrophe in a somewhat different way. Unless many of your students make mistakes with apostrophes, you probably will not want to devote much class time to those exercises. Point them out to students who are having considerable difficulty with apostrophes, and go over their corrected exercises with them individually, trying to determine the source of their confusion.

The next section of the chapter is a discussion of the use of quotation marks. Because Lewis Carroll used such wonderful language, the quotations from his work lend themselves to being read aloud, and then punctuated, in class.

Students are likely to have questions about the differences between direct discourse and reported speech. After a class completes the exercise on page 165 individually or in small groups, go over the exercise in a general discussion. This exercise leads naturally into the topic of introducing quotations into one's own essays, an important skill that causes many students difficulty and is not easily mastered. Quoting is covered briefly here and in more detail in Chapter Eight.

The last section of the chapter is a brief review of capitalization.

Instructor's Manual IM-33

Answers to the Exercise on Page 137

Answers will vary.

Answers to the Exercise on Page 139

Answers will vary, but here are some possibilities.

1. A declarative sentence, like the one you are reading, usually ends in a period.
2. Do you ever leave out the necessary question marks in your essays?
3. Yes, and it makes me furious when I make these mistakes!
4. Maybe it would help to proofread once just looking for missing question marks.
5. It helps to be on the alert for question words, such as *who, have, when, why,* or *will,* at the beginning of sentences.
6. Have you ever tried that method?
7. Of course, but I still make mistakes.
8. The only punctuation mark that I always remember to use is the period.
9. Does that surprise you?
10. No, it makes me so mad I could spit!
11. Punctuation causes most students considerable frustration.
12. You said it!

Answers to the Exercise on Page 141

1. The semicolon can be a substitute for a period; it should not be used instead of a comma.
2. The subject of the first independent clause is *semicolon*. The verb is *shows*. The subject of the second independent clause is *period*. The verb is *be*. Corrected sentence: In the above example, a semicolon shows how closely the two clauses are related; a period between them would also be acceptable.
3. Commas can be used within sentences; semicolons can be used between independent clauses that contain ideas that are closely related.
4. Use a semicolon where a period would be appropriate; do not use it where you need a comma.
5. Anne Moody's family all slept in the same room; it was like three rooms in one.
6. Planning a trip is sometimes half the fun; the trip itself may even be a letdown.

7. For her interview Kanika selected a well-tailored gray suit; her small red scarf added just the right accent.
8. Semicolons may replace periods; they do not replace commas except in some lists.

Answers to the Exercise on Page 142

1. We had the usual lousy meal at Aunt Minnie's: greasy fish that was overcooked; soggy lettuce soaked in bland vinegar and oil dressing; boiled potatoes that were raw in the center.
2. Holiday gatherings at our house meant an amazing array of relatives: crotchety old Uncle Adrian in his maroon sweater; talkative Grandpa Burnett with his smelly pipe; jovial Aunt Flo with her yappy fox terrier, Henry.

Answers to the Exercise on Page 143

1. A complete Italian dinner often includes the following: a tasty antipasto for an appetizer; homemade pasta smothered in spaghetti sauce; plenty of garlic bread; red Chianti to aid the digestion; spumoni and after-dinner mints for dessert.
2. A complete Italian dinner often includes the following: antipasto, spaghetti, garlic bread, Chianti, spumoni, and after-dinner mints.

Answers to the Exercise on Page 147

Answers will vary, but here are some possibilities.

1. That campsite had every pest one could imagine: mosquitoes, flies, raccoons, ticks, and wasps.
2. Melanie was skilled in all aspects of the sport, such as passing, rebounding, shooting, and stealing.
3. Melanie was skilled in all aspects of the sport: passing, rebounding, shooting, and stealing.
4. For his birthday Franco did not receive the one gift he had hoped for—a motorcycle.
5. Franco was not really surprised that he had not received a motorcycle: his mother had often announced that she was violently opposed to his owning one.
6. The family had the usual Chinese restaurant meal: egg rolls filled with shrimp and chopped vegetables; sweet and sour pork that was a bit overcooked; crispy lemon chicken dipped in delicious sauce.

7. The meal had everything we could imagine, including shrimp, chicken, tossed salad, pasta, and anchovies.
8. Bryan came up with an appealing idea: close the family café for opening day at Brewer Stadium.
9. All the other employees—the cook, the dishwasher, and the busboy—supported Bryan's plan with enthusiasm.
10. Bryan's plan had the enthusiastic support of all the employees: the cook, the dishwasher, the waitresses, and the busboy.
11. Bryan's tightfisted father reluctantly went along with his son's proposal for one reason: improved employee morale.
12. His father was a sad employer on opening day—the game was called during the first inning due to heavy rain.

Answers to the Exercise on Page 149

Anne Moody's girlhood home was a poor two-room shack. Her parents made every effort to make it liveable.

Anne Moody's girlhood home was a poor two-room shack; her parents made every effort to make it liveable.

Answers to the Exercise on Page 150

Answers will vary, but here are some possibilities.

1. Anne Moody's parents put up wallpaper with great care, but it still bulged in some places.
2. The dull-colored wallpaper was tacked loosely to the wall with large thumbtacks, so it bulged in places.

Answers to the Exercise on Page 151

Answers will vary, but here are some possibilities.

1. Tomas went to a movie last night even though our descriptive themes were due today.
2. When Tomas got to class this morning, he observed his fellow students making last-minute corrections on some essays.
3. Although the due dates were listed in the syllabus and posted on the blackboard, Tomas still insisted he had not known about the deadline.
4. Because Tomas was usually so prompt and diligent about his assignments, his teacher extended the deadline for him.

5. Tomas' teacher gave him three more days to complete the theme as he had never missed a deadline before.

Answers to the Exercise on Page 153

1. the Democratic candidate for president; George Bush
2. Jesse Jackson

Answers to the Exercise on Page 154

1. The elderly man, a gnarled and humped-over figure, passed by the rowdy teenagers in silence.
2. A gnarled and humped-over figure, the elderly man passed by the rowdy teenagers in silence.
3. The two Wisconsin senators, Herb Kohl and Bob Kasten, both came to the groundbreaking ceremony for the new hospital wing.
4. Herb Kohl and Bob Kasten, Wisconsin's two senators, both came to the groundbreaking ceremony for the new hospital wing.

Answers to the Exercise on Page 155

1. No one in the Yasui family from Dayton, Ohio, would ever forget July 23, 1986.
2. That was the day when their relatives from Iowa arrived unannounced with four small children, two large, mangy dogs, and three scraggly gray cats.
3. Yelling, barking, and meowing, the whole tribe stumbled over each other as they scrambled up the porch steps.
4. The paperboy, a skinny redhead on a silver and black bicycle, gawked at all the confusion and almost forgot to toss the evening paper on the Yasuis' porch.
5. A stunned Mrs. Yasui, never one to hide her true feelings, greeted her husband's relatives with a wan smile.
6. Because his wife's lack of enthusiasm was so obvious, Mr. Yasui made an extra effort to be cordial.
7. Mr. Yasui, a portly, jovial man, made an extra effort to be cordial, because his wife was so curt with the new arrivals.
8. Cold and blunt as always, his wife was, of course, unaware that she was being unusually rude even for her.

9. However, the Iowa relatives did not seem to notice, or, if they did, they concealed their reactions amazingly well.
10. Everyone in the Yasui family heaved a sigh of relief when their guests left for Cedar Rapids, Iowa, on July 30, 1996.

Answers to the Exercise on Page 156

Answers will vary, but here are some possibilities.

1. The next day, Mae's long-time dream would finally come true—a trip to London.
2. During her sophomore year in high school, Mae had begun reading Sherlock Holmes' mysteries; those stories whetted a desire to visit the British capital that never diminished.
3. When she finished high school, Mae took a good-paying, dead-end job with one goal in mind: to save enough money for a plane ticket to the United Kingdom.
4. All of Mae's family—her mother, father, and two younger sisters—supported her dream.
5. Only one person was not enthusiastic about the plan: Mae's boyfriend, Horace.
6. Mae decided to ignore Horace, so early in April she went to a travel agent that a friend had recommended.
7. The agent informed her that several airlines, including Lufthansa, American, British Air, and United, flew regularly from Chicago to London.
8. Three airlines—United, Sabena, and British Air—even had exactly the same low midweek round-trip fare—$620.
9. After considerable cogitation, Mae finally made her choice: British Air.
10. Mae hardly slept a wink the night before her departure; all the necessary details of her preparations kept going through her mind.
11. She kept getting up and making a "final" check on the essential items: passport, air ticket, hotel voucher, London subway map, and a Sherlock Holmes mystery.
12. Outside the airport, Mae spotted a familiar figure: now white-haired Senator Ted Kennedy was getting out of a black airport limo.
13. Mae's plane, scheduled to depart at 6:00 P.M., took off right on schedule; warnings of frequent delayed departures and landings due to London fog had proved not true in this case.

14. Much to Mae's surprise, dinner on the plane was delicious: spinach and bacon salad with sweet-sour dressing; noodle-veal casserole flavored with sherry wine sauce; breadsticks, rye rolls, and Italian bread with garlic butter; and chocolate cake covered with whipped cream.
15. The Tower of London, Buckingham Palace, Piccadilly Circus, and Trafalgar Square—all of the sights of London—swirled in Mae's head.
16. The plane landed right on time. Mae's long-awaited two weeks in London had begun. She decided to check into her hotel and then head for the nearest Tube station.

Answers to the Exercise on Page 159

those boys—add '
the sun—add 's
Jane—add 's
James—add '
today—add 's
cereal—add 's

Answers to the Exercise on Page 160

boy' boy's
boys' ——
hour' hour's
women' women's
woman' woman's
boss' ——
Joneses' ——
family' family's
families' ——

Answers to the Exercise on Page 162

1. a boy's car; two boys' car; Two boys are running.
2. several teachers; the teacher's desk; two teachers' offices
3. one family's bills; three families' bills; Several families came.
4. children's dreams; three deers' eyes; mice's cheese
5. their houses; their hats; their nice houses
6. There is the picture.; There are the boys.; They're practicing.
7. Where is your car?; You're proud of it.; Its collar was lost.
8. Here's some candy.; its tail; They're calling you.

Answers to the Exercise on Page 162

Because of the apostrophe, *its* and *it's* have quite different meanings. Thus, *it's* obvious that *its* usefulness cannot be denied. Consequently, *you're* just going to have to face the fact that apostrophes will be around for some time. Unfortunately, *they're* likely to cause you some confusion, but take comfort that *you're* not alone. Teachers agree that many of *their* students find that *it's* a problem deciding when to use *it's* instead of *its,* or *there* instead of *their.*

Answers to the Exercise on Page 163

Held outside on their neighbors' huge lawn, the Rosenblatts' costume party was a tremendous success. The hostess' costume was a white satin wedding dress trimmed with ermines' tails. My daughter's black witch costume made a wonderful contrast to our friend's white gown. Her escort's elaborate devil costume won first prize by the guests' unanimous vote. The waitresses' crimson cocktail dresses, the bartenders' fuchsia tuxedoes, and the guests' brightly colored costumes turned the Venturas' lawn into a Renoir scene from another era. In fact, many of the artists at the party found their inspiration from women's dress during the nineteenth century.

Answers to the Exercise on Page 164

    The Caterpillar and Alice looked at each other for some time in silence; at last the Caterpillar took the hookah out of its mouth, and addressed her in a languid, sleepy voice.

    "Who are *You?*" said the Caterpillar.

    This was not an encouraging opening for a conversation. Alice replied, rather shyly, "I—I hardly know, Sir, just at present—at least I know who I *was* when I got up this morning, but I think I must have been changed several times since then."

    "What do you mean by that?" said the Caterpillar, sternly. "Explain yourself!"

    "I can't explain *myself,* I'm afraid, Sir," said Alice, "because I'm not myself, you see."

    "I don't see," said the Caterpillar.

    "I'm afraid I can't put it more clearly," Alice replied very politely, "for I can't understand it myself, to begin with; and being so many different sizes in a day is very confusing."

    "It isn't," said the Caterpillar.

Answers to the Exercise on Page 165

"In my youth," father William replied to his son,
   "I feared it might injure the brain;
But, now that I'm perfectly sure I have none,
   Why, I do it again and again...."

"You are old," said the youth, "and your jaws are too weak
   For anything tougher than suet;
Yet you finished the goose, with the bones and the beak—
   Pray, how did you manage to do it?"

Answers to the Exercise on Page 167

1. Patricia asked if Charles wrote long papers.
   Patricia asked, "Does Charles write long papers?"

2. Betty told John that as she had never skated before she would probably fall down.
   Betty told John, "I have never skated before. I'll probably fall down."

3. Emily whispered that she would not be able to attend the meeting because she was sick.
   "I won't be able to attend the meeting," whispered Emily, "because I'm sick."

4. Janet sobbed that she would never have made it through this crisis without him because her family could not help her.
   "Without you," sobbed Janet, "I would never have made it through this crisis. No one in my family could help me."

5. The history professor informed David that his grades were improving.
   "David," the professor beamed, "your grades are improving. Keep up the good work."

6. Ann asked her mother if she need any assistance from her.
   "Do you need any assistance?" Ann inquired. "If you do, call me at work. I can stop at your house on the way home from McDonald's."

Answers to the Exercise on Page 168

Answers will vary.

Instructor's Manual   IM-41

Answers to the Exercise on Page 170

3467 Main Street
Lake Mills, MN 01234
February 5, 1996

Professor Maxine Irwin
School of Architecture
421 Hoover Hall
Riverside University
Lake Mills, MN 01234

Dear Professor Irwin:

I have applied for a summer internship with Hagge Design Associates and would greatly appreciate your writing them a letter of recommendation for me.

    I was your student for two very stimulating courses during the academic year 1993–1994: Introduction to Architecture and Architecture Fundamentals I. In fact, it was your courses that confirmed my desire to become an architecture major. You gave me an A both semesters, as well as on my research paper, "Frank Lloyd Wright's First Usonian House." I still recall our class' field trip to see that house and meet its present owner, Professor James Dennis of the University of Wisconsin–Madison, as one of the high points of my college career.

    The form for the recommendation letter, which is due before April 1, 1996, is enclosed, along with my résumé and a transcript. As you can see, I will begin my junior year next August, and have accumulated a 3.6 average as of last semester. If you feel unable to recommend me, could you please return the form to me at the above address? A self-addressed, stamped envelope for that purpose is enclosed. Thank you very much for doing this favor for me.

                                                      Sincerely,

                                                      Marianne Doss

Part Two

From Others' Writing to Your Writing: Reading Critically

Chapter Seven

Critical Reading and Your Writing

The two chapters in Part Two are designed to help students develop several skills that are essential to success in school, as well as in many professions. Students may already be assigned book reviews, analytical essays, reports, or research papers in their other courses, and will benefit from becoming acquainted with these chapters early in the semester. The techniques discussed in these chapters should also help students improve their study skills and their ability to write effective essay exams. In addition, skills strengthened through these chapters will help to make your students better critics of other essays, both in this text and in other courses.

Chapter Seven opens with steps for writing a detailed summary: skimming and prereading; reading and annotating; preparing a scratch outline; writing the summary. The steps are applied to an annotated version of a student essay, "Making It Out" by Ricky Davis (page 174), so that students can follow the process from start to finish. Another student essay, Jerome Mason's "Stone City" (page 178), is followed by a series of questions designed to stimulate discussion and comparison of the two essays. These questions are suitable for a small-group activity, which could then be followed by a general class discussion. That discussion could lead to a scratch outline of "Stone City" on the blackboard.

Instead of asking students to hand in written summaries of "Stone City," you may prefer to have them summarize another essay in this text or another article of your choosing. Writing a detailed summary makes many students look at a text more carefully and analytically than they have ever done before. Many students comment that being able to write a good summary has benefited them in papers for other classes and when studying for exams.

Students who do not do a good job on their detailed summary assignment should be given careful guidelines for improving this first attempt as well as a chance to revise it. Assign at least one more detailed summary during the term. As students become more proficient, suggest that they might proceed directly from annotations to a summary without first making a scratch outline. Encourage students to make annotations and write summaries in their journals of some of the texts they read throughout the semester.

The first section of this chapter presents only one kind of summary, one that includes all the main points of the original text and follows the same order as that text. The next section of the chapter is designed to give students practice writing other types of summaries, summaries that allow them to use selected material from a text and incorporate it into their own analysis.

Two student models of such summaries follow science writer K. C. Cole's 1981 article, "Why There Are So Few Women in Science" (page 186). Cole's article and the two student summaries that accompany it are useful for many purposes. The summaries contain both direct quotations and paraphrases of material from Cole's article, thus providing good models for incorporating information from outside sources into one's own sentences.

The two student summaries of Cole's article are revised versions of impromptu essays written for our course. The class worked on the study questions that follow Cole's article during the week before the impromptu, then handed in their responses when they wrote their impromptu essay. Students were also encouraged to relate Cole's arguments to their own; Becky Manuell pursued this option but not Ken Shanovich, one of the major differences between the two essays.

Provided students know in advance what sources will be the topic of an impromptu, thus giving them adequate time to prepare, an impromptu based on outside reading is a useful assignment. It is probably better to not assign too much reading or writing on complex topics if you want good results. Word the impromptu question clearly and carefully so that it is doable in a limited amount of time.

Among other benefits, writing impromptus on outside readings helps students write better essay examinations in other courses. Also, if all students write essays based on the same sources, you will know the sources well enough to determine whether a student has missed a major part of the evidence, distorted facts, incorrectly interpreted or quoted a source's wording, and so on.

The small-group activity on page 195 asks students to analyze and compare the two student essays about K. C. Cole's article. The responses to that assignment could provide the stimulus for discussions on writing a comparison (see also Chapter Eleven), as well as on the broader topic of gender roles and gender stereotyping. Be sure to emphasize that gender stereotyping harms and hampers both sexes, a major theme of Noel Perrin's 1984 article, "The Androgynous Man" (page 201), which should be read along with K. C. Cole's work.

Cole's and Perrin's articles likewise provide opportunities for comparison, in particular for a discussion of the sources of their arguments. Perrin writes exclusively from his own experiences; Cole corroborates her experiences with those of others. After establishing herself as an authority early in her essay, Cole also inserts pertinent data from several outside authorities throughout her article. Her essay provides an opportunity to emphasize the need for authors to establish their credibility, something student writers often fail to do. Throughout the remainder of the semester, point out the various ways authors can, and do, establish their authority.

Discuss how some authors, like K. C. Cole, credit their sources right in the text, while others include a bibliography or a "Works Cited" list at the end of a paper. Refer students to the "Works Cited" list at the end of the model research paper in Chapter Eight.

Ask students to analyze the two essays on the workplace that make up the final section of the chapter, noting that both essays contain very biased, one-sided views of the workplaces they analyze. If any students have worked at McDonald's or similar fast-food restaurants, find out whether they share the views expressed in the first article. Encourage students to share their views with the class, to freewrite about those views, and possibly to write an essay on a topic related to their workplace.

In general class discussion, compare the methodology and sources used in the two articles. Does the use of dialogue adds to the articles' effectiveness? If so, how? Students should be as specific as possible, giving concrete examples to back up general statements. Point out places where quotations have been effectively incorporated into the writers' own sentences. You might divide the class into small groups to respond to the comments and questions at the end of each of these two essays, then have them share their responses in a general discussion.

Chapter Eight

Documentation: Incorporating Outside Sources into Your Essays

While some students may have had experience with documentation in previous courses, many have not. Even for those who have had some experience using and crediting outside sources, the documentation process may not be simple. Let students know they will probably master this skill gradually.

This chapter provides only an elementary introduction to documentation. Students should be warned, moreover, that there is no single acceptable documentation system. Caution your students to follow each instructor's guidelines to the letter and to ask questions when the directions are confusing. They may also want to invest in a writing or research paper handbook with a detailed documentation section.

The chapter opens with a brief commentary on the reasons for using quotations and other supporting data in one's writing and then giving proper credit for that information. Immediately following is an example of one writer's effective use of dialogue, coupled with an explanation of the rules that *New York Times* sportswriter Ira Berkow followed.

Dialogue is meant to be spoken. Have students read the dialogue aloud, asking one volunteer to be John Stockton; another, the woman he met in Barcelona; and a third, the narrator. Then have them punctuate the unpunctuated dialogue in the exercise on page 233, either with a partner or in small groups. After they have finished, ask for new volunteers to read this section aloud. Go over the punctuation conventions that the corrected versions should have followed and answer questions about any students find puzzling.

The next section contains additional information about the basics of using quoted material. Topics covered range from the use of the ellipsis to inserting brackets into quoted material.

When to paraphrase and when to quote is a problem for all writers, one that presents a special challenge to the less experienced. The examples in this section are designed to shed light on that dilemma. They also provide instances of interrupted quotes, in-text citations, and identifications of sources. Take advantage of them. Warn students to use longer, blocked quotes sparingly and ask them what they do when reading a text that contains quite a few of them. (They skip over them. So do we sometimes, unless we are very interested in the material.) Start with the basics, encourage students for their successes, and don't be surprised by their awkward attempts.

Chapter Eight concludes with Lisa Marinello's lively research paper about Euro Disney. In this global economy, the author's observations could be the starting point for a discussion of the need for considering local traditions when doing business or even simply traveling in other countries. Those students who may have worked or traveled abroad may have considerable personal experience to bring to such a discussion.

Lisa's documentation demonstrates the MLA system, while her paper contains examples of many of the characteristics of effective use of outside sources, such as using pungent, direct quotations. One idea would be to conduct a "scavenger hunt" through Lisa's paper: Have small groups search for a list of items such as a paraphrase, a direct quotation, a comparison, statistics, and so forth, and then discuss their findings with the whole class.

Part Three
Writing Strategies

Chapter Nine

Narrating

Five of the last six chapters are devoted to strategies writers use to organize and present their material: narrating; describing; comparing and contrasting; informing and explaining; and arguing. Again, most of the examples and models in these chapters, ranging from narrative or argumentative essays to similes, metaphors, and short descriptive passages, came from student papers. The last of the above strategies, arguing, is the subject of two chapters, Thirteen and Fourteen. Chapter Fourteen deals with a very practical kind of persuasive writing: the letter of application. Remember that the order in which these strategies are covered in the text does not constrain you to teach them in that order.

These five strategies are not mutually exclusive. Students should be regularly encouraged to observe how the authors of the model essays in the text, as well as writers in general, often interrupt a narrative with an apt descriptive passage, insert an appropriate narrative when explaining a concept or describing a person, and so on.

Each chapter contains numerous suggestions for both long and short writing assignments. You may also want to use your own assignments—which may or may not fit specifically into one of these chapters.

As the opening section of Chapter Nine suggests, narratives have long been a favorite method of human communication. That is one reason for assigning a narrative theme: many students like to write stories. Other reasons people write narratives are also explored in this chapter.

Encourage students to try a variety of the prewriting strategies discussed in the chapter (and earlier in the text) as they explore topics for a potential narrative. Point out Eric Williams' scratch outline on page 266 and Mary Nelson's cluster diagram on page 272. Some instructors may require students to hand in their prewriting, along with their drafts, with the final version of an essay.

The chapter discusses the importance of conclusions and introductions in a narrative. Emphasize the need to cut right to the interesting part of a narrative without getting bogged down in a rambling introduction that bores readers.

Reflecting our conviction that student writing provides the most effective models for their peers, Chapter Nine contains a number of student essays. Students may find inspiration for their own topic choice in one or another of these student narratives. Some of them demonstrate clearly that the topic need not be earthshaking, or even all that serious, to make an effective narrative.

Chapter Ten

Describing

Students can have a lot of fun exploring their abilities as descriptive writers. Many of them come up with remarkable descriptive passages, and even full-blown essays. The suggestions and examples in this chapter can be used in connection with a descriptive theme assignment or as an aid in writing many other types of essays. Emphasize that descriptive writing covers a wide range of subjects, from a scientist's detailed description of the inside of an artery to a novelist's depiction of a sunrise.

Describing is painting a picture with words: The similarity between painting and describing is a major theme of Chapter 9. The emphasis is on appeals to the five senses, on choosing precise, vivid words—especially verbs—and using fresh, figurative expressions. Numerous short writing exercises and writing opportunities are scattered throughout the chapter, which also contains an assignment for a more developed essay describing either a person or a place. Student descriptive pieces of various lengths are included as models.

Some of those student models, such as Laura Weiler's Wisconsin autumn scene (page 285) or Felicia Sutton's pineapple feast (page 285), show how vivid description can bring ordinary occurrences to life. Later in the chapter, two excerpts from Truman Capote's *A Christmas Memory*, one about baking and the other about counting money (page 327), show how a master of description can take such events to new heights.

The exercises on choosing the concrete instead of the general could be used for a general discussion after the class has completed them. One idea would be to have students put some of their responses to one or more of the exercises on the blackboard.

Use the student examples to discuss figurative language, as well as to explain and define simile and metaphor and other figures of speech. Excerpts from students' themes demonstrating the use of analogies and allusions are also included in this section of Chapter Ten. Encourage your students to identify examples of figurative language in the model student essays about people and places and to become more aware of such literary devices in everything they read. Throughout the term, find examples of effective images in your students' essays and urge them to share them with the class.

The chapter also discusses and gives examples of things to avoid, such as clichés, pat expressions, and oft-combined word pairs such as "babbling brook." We hope that the potential pitfall on page 328 spares you from having to read too many generic vacation essays. Ditto for the cautions against Valentine essays on page 329.

The assignment for an essay recalling a person, followed by student models, takes up the next part of the chapter, while the last section is devoted largely to writing essays about a place. Numerous suggestions for prewriting, along with more student models, are included. Whether they choose to write about a special person or a special place, students are urged to choose a dominant impression to give purpose and a sense of unity to their descriptive essays. Once they decide on that dominant impression, or once it emerges as they are exploring their topic on paper, they need to give specific illustrations to exemplify that impression. Susan Krenn's essay about a nun who was a strict but inspiring high school mathematics instructor provides an excellent example (page 304).

In a descriptive paper, illustrations of the dominant impression probably ought to include some, but not too much, physical description. Point out how the descriptive details in Krenn's essay add to the dominant impression. Ask the class what details from her essay stick in their minds and which of the five senses Krenn appeals to. Ask students how their dour uncle or flamboyant friend might dress or walk, what he or she might say, and in what tone of voice.

The best advice we have ever read about writing physical description comes from Richard Cohen's recent *Writer's Mind: Creating Fiction*: "The physical appearance of a character is often more a matter of tone, atmosphere, emotion than of sensory detail. . . . It's important for both reader and writer to form a clear mental image of the character" or place being described. However, the "image can be created with very few details." Instead of half a page cataloguing someone's facial features, select a few important, telling details: "one detail is better than two, if it's a detail that creates a vivid mental picture." (40-41)

You may want to emphasize that advice to your students. However, keep in mind that his cautions could cripple student writers who have not fully explored their potential for writing description. At any rate, as the student essays and excerpts in this chapter demonstrate, a surprising number of them seem to be applying that advice without having read it. Moreover, taking

Cohen's suggestions into consideration as you evaluate students' descriptive essays may enable you to be a more helpful critic.

The list of guidelines for small-group analysis of the model essays (page 297) should also help students to critique their own and their fellow students' description papers. First have the class apply those guidelines to the model person/place essays in the text. You may want to have each small group analyze one or two of the essays, and then discuss their critiques in a general class discussion that covers all of the student descriptive papers. Encourage each group to pick out examples of figures of speech and other figurative language to share with the entire class. It might be a good idea to have students list some of those images on the blackboard under the appropriate category.

Suggest that the groups pay particular attention to the effective use of dialogue in the essays they are critiquing. Reading the dialogue in Calvin Stewart's "Momma" (page 300) aloud is an excellent way to show how dialogue can help bring people to life. Ask for volunteers to read Momma's and Calvin's lines, and another to be the narrator who reads the material between the two.

Calvin Stewart's "Momma" is one of two sets of paired themes in Chapter Ten that can also be used for a discussion of comparison, possibly in connection with a comparison theme assignment. Comparing "Momma" and Laura Tetzlaff O'Mara's "My Gammy Grace" (page 298) should also add another, useful dimension to the small-group and general analysis of the two essays. The other pair is about instructors: Susan Krenn's "A Special Nun" (page 304) and Flo Seefeldt's "My Best Teacher" (page 305).

One key to organizing and writing a successful comparison is deciding on appropriate criteria. Ask the class to suggest criteria that they might consider when comparing two papers on a similar topic, then list those criteria on the blackboard. Undoubtedly they will come up with suggestions such as subject, use of dialogue, dominant impression, and so on. Supplement their list as needed.

Chapter Eleven

Comparing and Contrasting

You may have discussed comparisons throughout the semester. Comparing is a way of learning and thinking; a mental activity that people engage in constantly as they go about their daily living. Drawing analogies and comparisons and making connections is also an excellent study tool. Comparison is regularly used in the academic world: for instance, essay examinations in any number of disciplines include comparison questions. Writers frequently use comparisons, ranging from similes and metaphors to extended analogies, in order to clarify what they are saying or to enhance its effectiveness. Figurative language relies heavily on comparisons, as does much informative writing.

Chapter Eleven includes practical suggestions for writing an extended comparison theme. Organization and transitions are especially important in comparison essays, so those issues are stressed. Have your students analyze a student paper, "Two Jazz Trumpet Players," paying particular attention to its organization and transitions. The paper is followed by models for prewriting about a potential comparison topic.

After students have finished their small-group analysis of the model essay, review the essentials of comparison: deciding on appropriate criteria and choosing an organizational scheme. Make sure that everyone understands the two basic methods of organizing a comparison: whole-by-whole and point-by-point.

To give students practice at deciding on possible criteria and a scheme of organization, we bring in a collection of *New Yorker* covers and spread them out. (Other graphics, such as advertising photos, reprints of art works, or a collection of objects can be used for this exercise.) Students choose two covers they would like to compare, take notes on possible points for comparison, then decide on appropriate criteria for a comparison essay. They often discover that the two covers do not have as much in common as they thought and thus choose a more comparable pair. The *New Yorker* covers also provide an opportunity to note the connection between writing and drawing and emphasize the value of being a careful observer. This assignment turns out to be, in effect, prewriting for a comparison paper about the two *New Yorker* covers. However, we do not encourage students (aside from those with a strong interest in art) to develop their prewriting into a full-fledged theme paper.

The final section of Chapter Eleven focuses on suggestions for prewriting about a possible comparison theme topic suited to a student's own interests. Whether or not you assign a comparison essay, the material on comparison in general and on transitions and choosing criteria in particular should be useful to your students in writing many kinds of essays.

Chapter Twelve

Informing and Explaining: The Purpose and Nature of Informative Writing

Chapter Twelve opens with a short, informative newspaper article about French cafés that includes a bit of historical background, some rather surprising statistics, and a brief analysis of possible reasons for the declining number of cafés in France. You can use the essay to illustrate a number of things about writing, from the effective use of quoted material to the nature of primary and secondary sources.

The purpose of such writing is to convey information in clear, coherent fashion. To demonstrate its opposite, the chapter moves to a discussion, replete with models, of "C.O.I.K" (clear only if known) writing. You might ask students to bring in their own examples of C.O.I.K. writing. This section of Chapter Twelve also provides a good opportunity to discuss, once again, the importance of audience. The need, in many instances, for writers to establish themselves as authorities on their particular subject is also stressed.

Informative writing is an important part of many kinds of prose, such as persuasion and description. Although students are familiar with the kind of informative writing found in encyclopedias and other sources, many of them still tend to equate description with its more literary form. The chapter includes representative samples of both professional and student writing to demonstrate uses of informative description.

While informative writing can be dull, boring, and—even worse—difficult to understand—it does not have to be. The article "How Obedient Are Germans?" (page 352) is included to demonstrate that good writing can be lively as well as informative. Not all topics lend themselves to humorous accounts, but all informative writing ought to be interesting and clear.

Students who write dense, convoluted prose imitating a kind of pedantic academic language, or "officialese," that has become all too familiar. Moreover, some of them have been encouraged to write in that kind of language by former instructors. We have deliberately not included examples of such prose in this text.

One reason for composition students to read articles on a wide variety of issues is to stimulate them to make connections, while they are both reading and writing. Those connections frequently come out during class or small-group discussions of a reading. The article on the *Berliner Tafel* (page 353) provides such an opportunity: three determined women in Berlin had an idea about feeding the homeless that has expanded from a small-scale operation in their own cars to a program feeding 2,000 per day. The commentary following the article encourages students to do some prewriting on someone who has made a difference, prewriting that might evolve into a developed essay. If appropriate, students could incorporate quotes or other data from articles into their essays. This will give students practice at referencing other texts, which their instructors will expect in many courses.

The last section of Chapter Twelve contains two student models of informative writing. As always, the choices demonstrate our belief that students do much better when they write from their own experiences. Both writers establish themselves as authorities early in their essays. Luke Jefferson wrote purely from his own experience as a salesperson at an appliance store, while Mary Mangan supplemented what she had learned in five years as an ophthalmic assistant with information from outside authorities. The "Works Cited" listing at the end of Mangan's essay can also serve as a model for your students.

As the brief comment following Mary Mangan's essay states, both essays are informative and persuasive in that they both recommend choosing the product being described. The chapter ends by asking students to compare two hypothetical theses to distinguish between these two writing strategies, informing and arguing.

Chapter Thirteen

Arguing and Persuading

The last two chapters are devoted to persuasive writing. You may prefer to assign letters of application, the subject of Chapter Fourteen, before having students write a more general argumentative paper. Because the persuasive material in a letter of application comes almost entirely from the writer's own experience, these letters make a good transitional assignment from writing narratives and other expressive essays to expository writing.

The advantages of writing an effective argument should become more apparent to your students as they discover its practical applications. To encourage this, try a suggestion in the instructor's manual of Janet Marting's recent book on rhetoric and argument, *Commitment, Voice, and Clarity*: Ask students to bring in examples of viewpoint and argument papers from non-course-related sources. Looking for, then sharing, these examples makes students more aware of others' arguments. They will also discover that argumentative writing appears in a wide variety of publications, including many they are interested in. Furthermore, as Marting suggests, because instructors do not usually read the same publications as their students, they can "make us aware of fascinating examples of idea-based writing" by bringing in their discoveries.

Like Janet Marting, we believe that inexperienced writers in particular write better, livelier, and more interesting argument papers when they discover that their own experience is their best weapon. Conversely, we believe that having students write on broad, complex, and controversial topics, such as abortion or capital punishment—topics on which people's convictions are often based on moral values—usually leads to unconvincing argument papers. Papers on such topics tend to be a rehash of the obvious and/or full of passionate assertions unlikely to affect anyone else's equally passionate beliefs. How can students be expected to do more than skim the surface on such a broad subject?

On the other hand, as many of the sample persuasive essays in Chapter Thirteen demonstrate, students can come up with a wide variety of interesting topics based on their own experiences. The problem may be convincing *them* that they have something worth sharing with their readers. If a student has an athletic scholarship, has worked as a paramedic, or has spent a year studying abroad, he or she has experience that most readers do not share. Stress the importance of making that experience clear early in an essay in order to establish credibility. Encourage students to supplement their own experience with data and illustrations from outside authorities if it will strengthen their arguments. Some of the student models in the text, such as Amy Brinkman's "To Be or Not To Be . . . Thin" (page 378), provide examples of how to incorporate outside authorities into an argument based largely on personal experiences, those of the writer and her acquaintances.

David Merriman's "Jake's Hang-Gliding" (page 361) is included early in the chapter to demonstrate how persuasive writers may use a variety of the writing strategies discussed in this text to good purpose. Encourage students to observe how writers switch almost imperceptibly from one writing strategy to another as they lay out their arguments.

The section following David Merriman's paper demonstrates and explains some of the major characteristics of an effective argument: a balanced claim, clearly stated early in the essay; and solid reasons backing it. Reasonable people can be found on both sides of many claims, otherwise one would not have an argument. To demonstrate this, the exercise on page 365 asks students to list points supporting two opposing viewpoints on a topic.

The chapter also includes a discussion, with examples, of the various kinds of evidence that can be mustered in support of a claim. The small-group activity analyzing former Wisconsin Congressman Jim Moody's plan for a universal health care system (page 371) gives students a chance to evaluate one writer's use of evidence in an argument.

Because health care is an ongoing problem, Moody's essay may stimulate a lively discussion. Some of your students and their families may be among the millions of Americans without health insurance. Some may have stories about their encounters with the health care system that would affect the debate. Students should be cautioned, however, that this is a complex, broad topic that does not lend itself to a short essay proposing easy solutions. Point out that even the arguments of a person like Representative Moody, who is well versed in the subject, leaves many unanswered questions.

The small-group activity analyzing the essay "Making It Safe" (page 366) is particularly useful for introducing the topic of addressing, and in this case of discounting, potential counterarguments. Warn students that since reasonable people may have valid reasons for not agreeing with most claims on controversial topics, it is not always possible to discount counterarguments. Whether it strengthens an argument to openly acknowledge potential counterarguments varies with the situation. However, writers should be aware of potential counterarguments when planning and drafting an argument paper.

Discuss a broader consideration of using appeals to both logic and reason in an argument. Which of those appeals is addressed by the anecdote that opens the essay? Discuss the reasons writers often insert anecdotes and other illustrations into their writing. Encourage students to look for examples of effective anecdotes, as well as appeals to logic or to reason, in other essays in the text.

Chapter Thirteen also has many suggestions for exploring and prewriting about possible topics in order to make a good choice for the persuasion theme assignment on pages 373 to 374. The student models that follow, covering a wide range of subjects, should help students find a lively topic that interests them. To ensure that all students are familiar with a wide sampling of those essays, use the essays for a small-group activity, perhaps by first having the groups browse through the essays and choose one or two for a more in-depth analysis. Elicit guidelines for analyzing an argument theme from the class, and list those guidelines on the blackboard. Supplement the list as needed. Another option would be to use the revising guidelines sheet at the end of the chapter (pages 394 to 395).

After each group has finished its analysis, hold a general discussion about topic choice, formulating a clear, balanced claim, evidence used to support that claim, and so on. Ask the class to point out appeals to both emotions and reason in the student models. Discuss the effectiveness of each of the essays. Note that these student authors were obviously interested in their subjects and based much or all of their arguments on personal experience, their best weapon.

The last section of the chapter also includes a series of pitfalls for students to avoid as they draft their argument essays and prepare the final products.

Chapter Fourteen

Letters of Application and Résumés: A Special Type of Persuasive Writing

Letter writing is probably the most useful skill that your students will practice after leaving school. Letters are essential for obtaining a job, as well as for getting the kind of internships that may lead to that job. Giving your students practice at the essential skill of letter writing has practical, "real-life" applications.

We have included this chapter on letters for several other reasons. Writing letters of application makes a good transition from more personal, expressive writing to expository writing. Letters of application are also excellent for demonstrating the importance of audience—in this case, the need to tailor material to a specific potential employer. If time permits, asking students to write two different letters to two different potential employers in quite different fields would be a useful assignment. Another option would be to require students to hand in the prewriting for two different letters, but only write one letter.

Most students are already aware that employers are not likely to grant an interview to the sender of an error-ridden letter, so letters of application provide an opportunity to stress the importance of careful editing and proofreading.

In today's competitive job market, students are urged to have a series of internships, beginning as early as possible in their careers. Many writing students have never written a résumé or a letter of application, essentials for obtaining these internships. Assigning a letter of application in a composition course at least gives students a start on that time-consuming and demanding enterprise.

Stress that for any real job search, professional help is crucial. Draw attention to a career center or other resources in the community that students may consult before sending their cover letters and résumés. In this age of desktop publishing, the appearance and easy readability of a résumé in particular are crucial.

Even if you do not assign a letter of application, students can consult this chapter as an introduction to the practical and important skill of writing a business letter.

The chapter contains suggestions for prewriting strategies, including brainstorming about one's relevant experiences and about the likely wants and needs of a potential employer. A list of tips on a letter of application for students to review while composing their drafts and polishing up the final project can be found on page 404. Student models of letters of application as well as a résumé are included in the chapter. Urge students to consult these resources regularly as they revise their letters and résumés.

If you schedule individual conferences with students to go over their drafts, the letter of application and résumé are particularly well suited to those conferences. Students usually go away from such conferences with a number of practical ideas about strengthening their letters. Talking over their past experiences and career aspirations also provides an opportunity for you to get to know your students a little better.